D1521751

The Passionate Fictions of
Eliza Haywood

The
Passionate
Fictions
of
Eliza Haywood

Essays on Her Life and Work

Edited by
Kirsten T. Saxton
and
Rebecca P. Bocchicchio

THE UNIVERSITY PRESS OF KENTUCKY

Publication of this volume was made possible in part
by a grant from the National Endowment for the Humanities.

Editorial and Sales Offices: The University Press of Kentucky
663 South Limestone Street, Lexington, Kentucky 40508<n>4008

04 03 02 01 00   5 4 3 2 1

Library of Congress Cataloging-in-Publication Data

The passionate fictions of Eliza Haywood : essays on her life and work /
edited by Kirsten T. Saxton and Rebecca P. Bocchicchio.
        p.   cm.
    Includes bibliographical references (p.   ) and index.
    ISBN 0-8131-2161-2 (cloth: alk. paper)
    1. Haywood, Eliza Fowler, 1693?–1756. 2. Novelists, English—
18th century—Biography. 3. Women and literature—England—
History—18th century. I. Saxton, Kirsten T., 1965– II. Bocchicchio,
Rebecca P., 1967–
PR3506.H94 P37 2000
823'.5—dc21   00-028330
[B]

Contents

Illustrations

Acknowledgments

We dedicate this book to our parents, Ruth and Paul Saxton and Gloria Roland Pautz. Thanks for the love, support, and storytelling that helped to get us here.

This project was conceived at the University of California at Davis. We would like to offer special thanks to Joyce Wade, for her consistent help, humor, and faith in us. Her friendship, wit, and practical advice helped us through the rigors of this project.

The book would not exist without the wonderful essays by our contributors. We thank you each for your dedication, scholarly rigor, and good humor. We would like particularly to thank Toni Bowers—who participated in its early incarnation as an MLA special session—and Paula Backscheider—who has served as a mentor. Our thanks and appreciation also to everyone who read the manuscript at each stage; it is a far better book thanks to your combined efforts.

Rebecca would like to thank her husband Michael for his love and encouragement through it all . . . you make it possible for me to be my best.

Kirsten would like to thank the Williams Andrews Clark and Huntington libraries, where she wrote the introduction and her essay. Thanks also to my eighteenth-century novel class of fall 1999—thanks for their enthusiasm and for honing my readings of Haywood's texts, and to my research assistant Jennifer Campell, whose help was invaluable. Heartfelt thanks as well to my friends and family, who all make my life richer and more possible. Particular thanks to Ruth Saxton, my mother and best reader, for the splendid example she sets as professor, writer, and parent, and to my husband, Karl, for love and support.

Introduction

Kirsten T. Saxton

I first read Eliza Haywood on creaky microfilm machines when I became interested in learning more about Restoration and Augustan women prose writers. Spurred by a love of Aphra Behn, I was determined to track down references I had seen to this other, even more obscure author, Eliza Haywood, referred to as "the Great Arbitress of Passion," an epithet that tantalized me. I moved eventually from microfilm to rare book rooms, and to the few extant modern editions of her work I could find, eagerly poring over *Fantomina, Betsy Thoughtless,* and *The City Jilt.* Now we can read Haywood in any number of excellent modern editions; she has even made it into the *Norton,* albeit only the *Literature by Women* volume. This collection was spurred by my initial love of Haywood's works and my sense that she deserved further critical attention. An MLA special session garnered a host of wonderful papers on Haywood and the genesis of this volume was born.

Rebecca and I are delighted with the breadth and depth of the essays in the collection, and only wish it could have included twice as many. This book focuses largely, although not entirely, on Haywood's fiction, and we hope soon to see more Haywood studies focusing on her drama and journalism, as well as her fictional texts. We hope that this collection serves as a spur to other work, to a continuation of the exciting conversation that is Haywoodian studies, and to the proliferation of more of her works in scholarly editions and anthologies.

We hope also that the volume fills some of the gaps that we encountered when we began working on Haywood in the early 1990s, when we would never have guessed that she was one of the most celebrated novelists of her day.

The most prolific British woman writer of the eighteenth century, Eliza Haywood was a key player in the history of the British novel, and a leading figure in a brilliant and competitive London literary scene that included Jonathan Swift, Daniel Defoe, Alexander Pope, Henry Fielding, and Samuel Richardson. She came resoundingly to fame in 1719 with the publication of her first novel, *Love in Excess, or the fatal enquiry*, which, until the publication of Samuel Richardson's *Pamela* in 1740, was one of the three most popular works of eighteenth-century English fiction, an honor it shared with *Robinson Crusoe* (1719) and *Gulliver's Travels* (1726). After publication of *Love in Excess*, Haywood wrote a novel roughly every three months in the 1720s. She turned primarily to non-fiction work during the first half of the 1740s, returning to fiction in the latter half of the decade, and her 1751 novel *The History of Miss Betsy Thoughtless* was a stunning bestseller.

As well as being a prolific and acclaimed novelist, Haywood was a playwright, actress, writer of conduct books, translator, bookseller, publisher, and journalist, and from 1744–46 she was the editor of *The Female Spectator*, the first English periodical written by women for women. She, with her predecessors Aphra Behn and Delarivier Manley, was praised by contemporary poet/critic James Sterling as one of the "Fair Triumvirate of Wit": the three most popular, influential, and controversial women writers of the Restoration and Augustan eras. As was the case with Behn and Manley before her, Haywood's literary talent reaped her both rewards and reproach: she commanded a huge readership and earned financial success and independence, yet she also gained the disdain and malice of her male literary contemporaries, whose tendency to mock and deride her seems to have had less to do with her prose and more to do with her extraordinary sales and her critiques of the gendered status quo. After more than two hundred years of neglect, Haywood is finally receiving the attention she is due as the writer whose name was, in the eighteenth century, "more than any other native fiction writer . . . identified with the British novel" (Beasley, *Novels* 162).

In the early to mid-1970s, the rise of feminism within the academy led to a flurry of facsimile reprints of Haywood's work. By the 1980s, her masquerade novels (particularly *Fantomina*) had garnered feminist attention, most often influenced by contemporary psychoanalytic theories. Finally, in the 1990s, modern critical editions of her work were produced and her reprinted works are included in anthologies, ensuring that Haywood will now be read by scholars and students alike. This volume is the first critical book-length study on Haywood, and it reflects the range and depth of contemporary Haywood studies. Approaching Haywood's work from thematic, historical, and formal vantage points and from multiple theoretical positions, the essays speak to Haywood's centrality to eighteenth-century English literature and explore her texts' engagement with the critical social, aesthetic, and political discourses of her day.

Haywood may strike some as a slightly vexed feminist foremother both because of her politics and because of the nature of her writings. She was an ardent Tory who located in the monarchy a space for the female independence and freedom that she saw as an impossibility in the more morally strident Whig party. She believed in the concept of a natural elite, a ruling class whose innately higher moral and aesthetic values would lead England onward, away from what she saw as the money-grubbing tendencies of the Whigs. Her anti-Walpole writings of the 1730s and her 1740s periodical, *The Parrot,* explicitly support Tory causes, and she was jailed for some weeks in 1750 for her pamphlet-letter in praise of the Young Pretender.[1]

In addition to her royalist sympathies, Haywood was also famous for the scandalous nature of her early novels. Haywood inaugurated what exists today as an autonomous feminocentric sphere of romance fiction, fiction of seduction written explicitly by and for women (Ballaster 158). Known in her lifetime as "the Great Arbitress of Passion," Haywood wrote steamy prose fictions that shocked and titillated eighteenth-century audiences with legions of "unnumbered kisses . . . eager hands," "Shrieks and Tremblings, Cries, Curses, [and] Swoonings."[2] Reviled as "licentious and lewd" in her own day, Haywood then and now has often been dismissed solely as an extravagant exemplar of eighteenth-century female audacity.[3]

In fact, Haywood's well-plotted and carefully crafted novels may well have suffered from neglect because of their frankness about female sexuality and the complicated machinations of heterosexual romance, marriage contracts, and female economic independence. In her prefaces and narrative asides, Haywood explicitly defines her audience as female and presents her texts as a means by which women readers can negotiate the dangerous waters of heterosexual romance. Haywood's amatory novels of the 1720s and 30s subtly subvert and challenge reigning notions of gender, insist that woman's active desire is natural and inevitable, and attack the double standard by which women are denied active subjectivity. In *Love in Excess,* for example, the narrator declares: "[P]assion is not to be circumscribed . . . it would be mere madness, as well as ill-nature, to say a person was blame-worthy for what was unavoidable" (205).[4] Rather than assuming that women should have no sexual desires, Haywood creates a space for active, if dangerous, female appetite. It is not the desire per se that does in the Haywoodian heroine, but her lack of awareness of how to negotiate that desire within a heterosexual marketplace. Haywood's titles hint at her texts' focus on seduction and peril, a gendered battlefield of bed and hearth: *The Injur'd Husband* (1722); *The Unfortunate Mistress* (1723); *The Fatal Secret* (1724); *Fatal Fondness* (1725); *The Mercenary Lover* (1726). It is telling that the central work of her later, less erotically explicit stage, *Miss Betsy Thoughtless,* has been widely reprinted, while only a few of her more forthright fictions have become available, and these only in the 1990s.

In her own time, Haywood's "scandalous fictions" were tremendously popular with the reading public. However, the politics of representation were seriously attenuated in early eighteenth-century England; the nature and import of "truthful" representation was debated on multiple fronts, including that of literature. If a story could not claim to be historically true, based on fact, then it could not be taken seriously and could not engender any positive moral effects (McKeon, *Origins* 121). Since fiction as a project was seen to be largely characterized by irreverent mendacity, even when it was written by men, it is not surprising that fiction written by women would have engendered a particularly vitriolic response.

Haywood came onto the literary scene during the 1720s, a decade that heralded a regulatory moment in English history. The Waltham Black Act of 1723 created more than two hundred capital offenses and "signaled the onset of the flood-tide of eighteenth-century retributive justice" (Thompson 23). This regulatory spirit in the juridical arena was paralleled in the social one with the trend, which strengthened as the century progressed, of tighter divisional boundaries between gender roles and between the separation of the spheres of family and state. The role(s) of women became increasingly more circumscribed, ideologically if not practically, as social theories began to move toward the doctrine of separate spheres and the idea of domesticated and private femininity that would be firmly in place by the nineteenth century. The shift away from Restoration excess to a climate of more solid bourgeois values may have influenced Haywood's decision to limit herself to a purely "feminine" scope of romance, free from the overt political subtexts of Behn and Manley, and thus to position herself more solidly within the "feminine" genre of private affairs of the heart rather than approaching the "masculine" arena of public affairs of state into which Manley and Behn forayed. Paradoxically, rather than protecting her from vicious accusations of usurping a male authorial position, her fame as a female writer who wrote of love for an explicitly female audience resulted in her status as the most openly and viciously attacked member of the "Fair Triumvirate." The scornful critique Haywood's texts received anticipates contemporary critical associations of women's romance fiction with popular pabulum that deserves contempt and has no literary or social value.

After the first decades of the eighteenth century, fiction shifted toward the domestic novel, reaching its apotheosis in Richardson's *Pamela* (1740), and the plot of embattled feminine virtue increasingly worked to affirm gendered hierarchies rather than to critique gender inequities. In a milieu in which female subjectivity was increasingly configured in terms of privacy and domesticity and the passionate romance was increasingly viewed as suspect, Haywood's public role as woman writer, and the overt sexuality of her writings, made her an easy target for damning accusations of impropriety. In her own life and for long after, Haywood's body and the body of her work were regularly read as contiguous; for example, in the title of George Frisbie Whicher's 1915 study, *The Life and Romances of Mrs. Eliza Haywood,* it is unclear whether the "romances" on which the biography will focus are textual or sexual (Ballaster 159). Whicher's biography, long the standard source on Haywood, has recently been proven inaccurate, leaving Haywood the woman a tantalizing and perplexing mystery.[5] Virginia Woolf once complained that all that was known about Haywood was that "she married a clergyman and ran away." Today we know she did neither.

She was born Eliza Fowler in about 1693, probably the daughter of London hosier Robert Fowler. After leaving home, apparently against her parents' wishes, she appeared on the London stage as Eliza Haywood in 1715. It is unclear whom she actually did marry or how the marriage ended. Perhaps the contemporary story that her husband abandoned her was true, or perhaps he died or caused her to leave him. Two letters in which she seeks literary patronage have recently come to light and are of particular interest for their reflection on her marriage. The first, probably written around 1721, refers to her "unfortunate" marriage that resulted in "the melancholly necessity of depending on my Pen for the support of myself and two Children, the eldest of whom is no more than 7 years of age." The second, probably written around 1724, mentions "the Sudden Deaths of both a Father and a Husband, and at an age when I was little prepar'd to stem the tide of Ill fortune." Her two children were almost certainly both born outside of marriage: the first with a friend of Samuel Johnson, Augustan writer Richard Savage, who later attacked her viciously in print, and the second with her companion of over twenty years, bookseller William Hatchett, with whom she shared a stage career.

Haywood was not only an important novelist, she was also a vital player in the heady world of British theater. Her stage career began in 1715 in Dublin and continued uninterrupted until 1719–20, with the publication of *Love in Excess*. In 1723, she acted the lead in her own racy, successful comedy, *The Wife to be Lett,* a play cruelly satirized by Savage in *An Author to be Lett* (1729), whose title positions Haywood as a prostituted writer, both sell-out and slut. In the 1730s, she acted in six plays and was active in Henry Fielding's Little Theater at Haymarket. She and William Hatchett achieved great success with their adaptation of Fielding's *Tragedy of Tragedies*. Their opera *The Opera of Operas; or, Tom Thumb the Great* (1733) ran for eleven nights. Her earlier attempt to gain the patronage of the Prince of Wales with her historical tragedy, *Frederick, the Duke of Brunswick-Lunenburgh* (1729), failed, probably because she had publicized a liaison of George II in one of her few explicitly political works, the pro-Tory *Secret History of the Present Intrigues of the Court of Caramania* (1727). Her stage career came to an end in 1737 with a benefit held for her at the Little Theater the night before Walpole presented the Licensing Act to Commons and closed Haymarket.

An actress, dramatic adapter, and playwright, Haywood was also a theater critic and scholar. Her compendium, *The Companion to the Theater, or the Key to the Play*, originally titled *The Dramatic Historiographer, or the British Theater Delineated*, ran to at least seven editions between 1735–56. In it, she summarizes, glosses, and interprets (often radically) the "most celebrated dramatic pieces" of her age and critiques what she terms "the Whole Business of this Representation." Her summaries and interpretations became powerful rhetorical tools, particularly after the Licensing Act when the plays were no longer available to view.

Critics have essentially rebutted the once current argument that Haywood's hiatus from fiction stemmed from the biting satire that Pope directed at her in *The Dunciad*, his 1729 mocking send-up of Grub-Street "hacks."[6] However, until recently, she was perhaps most famous for her infamous appearance in the poem, in which she is imagined as a prize for which two publishers compete in a pissing contest: "See, in the circle next, Eliza place'd / . . . yon Juno of majestic size, / With cow-like udders, and ox-like eyes" (Sutherland, 1953 55–56). In his note to the lines, Pope condemns Haywood's "profligate licentiousness" and "scandalous books," defining her as one of those "shameless scribblers (for the most part of that sex which ought least to be capable of such malice or impudence)" (149n). Pope was not alone: Fielding satirizes Haywood as "Mrs. Novel" in *The Author's Farce* (1730), and Savage, who wrote a glowing prefatory poem on Haywood for *Love in Excess* and was the probable father of her child, defames her in his *The Authors of the Town* (1725) as a "cast-off Dame" who "Writes Scandal in Romance." Haywood herself participated in her era's penchant for scathing satire, subtly sending up Savage and his new mistress in her scandal novel, *Memoirs of a Certain Island Adjacent to the Kingdom of Utopia, Written by a Celebrated Author of that Country* (1725–26), and taking a swift jibe at Fielding with her mention of "F——g's scandal shop," in *Miss Betsy Thoughtless* (1751). While Fielding's and Richardson's "new species of writing" argued for each author's dramatically different, novelistic moral purpose, novelistic fiction in general was, to Haywood's Scriblerian literary contemporaries, a mercantile-driven anathema to the classical aesthetics and moral principles associated with true literary art, and it seems probable that, as David Brewer suggests in his essay in this volume, the voluminous attacks on Haywood were as much generic as specific, perhaps edged on by her sex and her tremendous success.

Eighteenth-century society associated female authorship with inappropriate public display, sexual transgression, and the production of inferior texts. Writing at a time when the only appropriate creation for women was sanctioned procreation, Haywood's critics read her authorship as aberrant. In her preface to *The Memoir of the Baron de Brosse* (1725), she poignantly describes the gendered inequities of power within the Augustan literary arena: "It would be impossible to recount the numerous Difficulties a Woman has to struggle through in her Approach to Fame: If her Writings are considerable enough to make any Figure on the World, Envy pursues her with unweary'd Diligence; and, if on the contrary, she only writes what is forgot as soon as read, Contempt is all the Reward, her Wish to please, excites; and the cold breath of Scorn chills the little Genius she has, and which, perhaps, cherished by some Encouragement, might in Time, grow to a Praiseworthy Height" (n.p.). Here, Haywood presents herself much like one of the heroines of her early fiction: she is damned if she does and damned if she doesn't. Yet, ironically, it is within the literal space of the proof positive of the successful commodity of women's writing—the pages of her book—that she defines the position of the woman writer as ultimately untenable.

Haywood's move from amatory to domestic fiction and conduct book literature was lauded for years as a moral conversion. By the mid-eighteenth century, Richardson had shifted and cornered the fictional market, offering an iconic vision of female passivity as a moral model, and Haywood altered her tone accordingly, producing a series of novels and periodical writings which, at least superficially, tended toward moral instruction, including, for example: *A Present for a Servant-Maid* (1743), *The Fortunate Foundlings* (1744), *The Female Spectator* (1744–46), *Life's Progress Through the Passions* (1748) *Epistles for the Ladies* (1749–50), *The History of Miss Betsy Thoughtless* (1751), and *The History of Jemmy and Jenny Jessamy* (1753).

Haywood's seeming "conversion" resulted in dividends for her literary reputation as well as her bank account. By the time of her death, Haywood's amatory fiction had become seen as an embarrassing sin of youth, atoned for by her later works, which were deemed, according to her obituary in the *Whitehall Evening Post,* "some of the best moral and entertaining Pieces that have been published for these many years" (Firmager 5). In *The Progress of Romance* (1785), critic Clara Reeve presents Haywood as the beleaguered victim of salacious literary mavens Behn and Manley who corrupted Haywood's innocence: "There is reason to believe that the example of the two ladies we have spoken of, seduced Mrs. Heywood [sic] into the same track; she certainly wrote some amorous novels in her youth . . . [but she] had the singular good fortune to recover a lost reputation and the yet greater honor to atone for her errors" (121–22).

More recently, critics have argued that her shift in topos was not morally but monetarily motivated, that Haywood deftly shifted her tone to make more money as it seemed the market for amatory fiction had bottomed out. However, it seems likely that neither extreme was simply the case: the claims that Haywood suddenly "saw the light" and threw out the politics that mattered to her for a quick buck do not adequately address the actual work she produced during these decades. In fact, in the 1740s and 50s, Haywood continued to explore the themes of gender, party politics, and power in formally innovative prose that responded to shifts in narrative style and structure afoot in the Augustan literary arena. For example, *The Fortunate Foundlings* (1744) anticipates Fielding's *Tom Jones* (1749), with which it shares many innovative narrative strategies; *The Parrot* (1746) consists of explicitly pro-Tory political propaganda; *Miss Betsy Thoughtless* (1751), as Paula Backscheider argues, shrewdly deconstructs women's delimited power within the marriage market, and, as Andrea Austin argues, it presents its revelation of women's poor lot within a sophisticated parody and formal pastiche.

It is useful to look for a moment at the ways in which Haywood herself comments on her role in the contested Augustan literary world. Other than a few letters, our only access to Haywood herself is through her self-presentations in prefaces, editorial comments, and dedications. Her comments reveal her consciousness of the paradoxes that bound her as a writing woman. For example, in her 1724 dedication to *The*

Fatal Secret, Haywood defends her amatory writing with the apologia that, as a woman, she was "depriv'd of those advantages of education which the other sex enjoy," and thus cannot "imagine it is in my power to soar to any subject higher than that which nature is not negligent to teach us." Here, she is simultaneously self-deprecating regarding female intelligence while slyly and aptly locating any fault of her, or any woman's, literary efforts, not in lack of capacity, but in the unjust fact that, as Restoration poet Ann Finch wrote, women are "education's, more than nature's fools" (101). Haywood's dedication to *The Female Captive* also masks trenchant critique with seemingly modest chagrin: "[M]any more Arguments than the little Philosophy I am Mistress of could furnish my wit, to enable me to stem that Tide of Raillery, which all of my Sex . . . must expect once they exchange the Needle for the Quill" (1721 edition).[7] In *The Female Spectator,* some twenty years later, she continues to critique the belabored role of the woman. In her opening address, Haywood defends her skill and her right to write: "With this Experience, added to a Genius tolerably extensive, and an Education more liberal than is ordinarily allowed to Persons of my Sex, I flatter'd myself that it might be in my Power to be in some measure both useful and entertaining to the Public" (1744–46 edition, 1:5). In *The Injur'd Husband,* Haywood mourns and rages on the fate of her own texts and her exclusion from the table of "significant" eighteenth-century literature: "Reputation is . . . so finely wrought, so liable to break . . . and down we sink in endless Infamy.—Consider . . . the Reasons why Women are debarr'd from reigning? Why, in all the Earth, excluded from publick Management? Us'd but as Toys? Little immaterial amusement, to trifle away an Hour of idle Time with?" (242). Haywood still has not broken into our established literary canon: almost no work has been done on her drama or journalism; her early works are grouped under the slightly suspect category of "amatory fiction," with its hints of lascivious, not quite top-drawer literary production, and her later novels are often dismissed as overly didactic, decent copies of male-authored work. I hope that this collection opens the door for continued conversations about Haywood as she, no longer "debarr'd from reigning," enters the canon. Haywood's experiments with form and theme, her engagement in current socio-political debates, and her breadth of literary accomplishment across the genres combine to make her a crucial figure in eighteenth-century letters.

Buried in an unmarked grave within sight of Poet's Corner at Westminster Abbey, where many of her contemporaries lie buried and lauded,[8] it seems fitting that Haywood herself should have the last word regarding the vagaries of reputation, women, and power. In her journal *The Female Spectator,* Haywood complains: "[Men say that] Learning puts the Sexes too much on an Equality, it would destroy that implicit Obedience which it is necessary the Women should pay to our Commands:—If once they [women] have the Capacity of arguing with us, where would be our Authority!" (1744–46 edition, 2:247). Haywood's retort succinctly and boldly critiques the sexist logic that denies female authority and aptly comments on her exclusion from literary history: "Now will I appeal to any impartial Reader . . . if this very Reason for keeping us in Subjection does not betray an Arrogance and Pride in themselves, yet less excusable than that which they seem so fearful of our assuming" (2:247).

In her essay, "The Story of Eliza Haywood's Novels: Caveats and Questions," Paula R. Backscheider questions the received "Story" of Haywood's career, particularly her mid-career "conversion" from amatory author to chaste, but mercenary, didactic. The essay interrogates the ways in which critical attention to Haywood has tended to view her texts as derivative and reactive and has neglected to connect her texts to one another in meaningful ways. Backscheider proposes a new story of Haywood's agency that is grounded in two features of early eighteenth-century novelistic activity: experimentation with form and establishment of the form's distinctive participation in hegemonic processes. She argues that this new story reveals Haywood as a major force in the development of the English novel.

Contrary to popular critical claims, Toni Bowers argues that Haywood did not dispense with party politics in favor of a "more general moralism," but continued, in *Love in Excess,* the tradition of Tory partisanship that had characterized the work of her predecessor Delarivier Manley, and indeed the tradition of amatory fiction, but in a different form, for different purposes, in a changed political climate. In "Collusive Resistance: Sexual Agency and Partisan Politics in *Love in Excess,*" Bowers argues that Haywood's first novel, like the works of amatory fiction that preceded it in Augustan England, functioned in its day both as a powerful work of Tory partisan polemic and as an allegory of female sexual agency.

Haywood uses and popularizes the myth of the persecuted maiden in her masquerade novel, *Fantomina*. Countering the claim that Haywood's fiction manipulates the myth as an "erotic-pathetic cliché" of female victimization, Margaret Case Croskery explores the ways in which Haywood uses it to focus on the power of erotic pleasure and the various possibilities open to sexually desiring females. In "Masquing Desire: The Primacy of Passion in Eliza Haywood's *Fantomina*," Croskery contends that, while *Fantomina* ostensibly begins as a typical tale of persecuted maidenhood, it only does so to introduce a paradigm it will radically rewrite, offering not only a playful alternative to eighteenth-century definitions of female virtue but also a serious alternative to contemporary psychoanalytic interpretations of the semiotic nature of sexual desire and the politics of seduction itself.

In her essay, "'Blushing, Trembling, and Incapable of Defense': The Hysterics of *The British Recluse*," Rebecca P. Bocchicchio establishes a historical context within which to understand Haywood's hysterical characters. Early eighteenth-century medical treatises construct both a woman who is polymorphously desiring—whose more sensitive nerves make her almost naturally hysteric—and a chaste modest femininity that refuses expression of that innate desire. Haywood's texts, the essay contends, argue against this naturalized figure of the female hysteric through an overproduction of hysteria itself: Haywoodian hysterics wear their hysteria like a mask that belies the construction of the "naturally" hysteric woman by revealing the characters' hysteria to be a result of social forces at work.

Haywood's novel, *The City Jilt*, revises the familiar plot of seduction and ruin to explore a plot of female vengeance and destruction. In my essay, "Telling Tales: Eliza Haywood and the Crimes of Seduction," I investigate the ways in which the novel not only serves as a corrective to the didactic masterplot that implies lost maidenhood translates to lost maiden, but also provides a complicated and subtle investigation into the function and nature of narration itself. I contend that *The City Jilt*, through its use of satire, plays on familiar tropes and genres to destabilize narrative cohesion. The novel, formally as well as thematically, attacks patriarchal fictions of law, heterosexual romance, and textual authority, revealing the telltale fictionality at the heart of those social and cultural institutions that attempt to confine women and their tales to the realm of fantastical romance.

Ros Ballaster, in her essay, "A Gender of Opposition: Eliza Haywood's Scandal Fiction," rethinks her earlier work on Haywood's scandal fiction to argue that Haywood, like Delarivier Manley before her, chose and manipulated aesthetics consciously and satirically for political effect. The essay makes a case for tracing in Haywood's scandal fiction both a shrewd critique of the gendered cultural and political poetics of the 1720s and 1730s and an attempt to configure a rival aesthetics more hospitable to the imagining of agency for women as writers and political "plotters." Through close examinations of Haywood's scandal fictions, the essay identifies Haywood's creation of a "mock-romance," a form that identifies a masculine force of "rigid" interpretation as restricting, perverting, and containing the uncomplicated libidinal affections of female romance.

Haywood's career-long resistance to domesticity is, according to Jennifer Thorn, an extension of the ambivalence about reproduction that characterizes Haywood's work. Thorn's essay, "A Race of Angels": Castration and Exoticism in Three Exotic Tales by Eliza Haywood," places Haywood's exotic tales in the context of her career-long interest in the imbalance of power between men and women: its alleged derivation in what Michael McKeon has called "the biological asymmetry of childbirth." The essay explores the meaning of castration in the tales' distinctive conjunction of reproduction, race, and romance and positions the texts within eighteenth-century England's tendency to entwine "the exotic" with "the erotic." While Thorn argues that these tales do not achieve the utopias to which they aspire, her essay reveals that they offer an important vision of decentered subjectivity that forces reexamination not only of gender roles but also of notions of nationalism and individualism.

Haywood contributed two texts to the Duncan Campbell stories: *A Spy upon the Conjuror* and *The Dumb Projector*. Based on a deaf-mute secular prophet who flourished from 1710–30, the Duncan

Campbell myth provides secular conversion stories that inspire awe as well as the irrational belief that there may be some connection between uncanny abilities and disability. Felicity A. Nussbaum's essay, "Speechless: Haywood's Deaf and Dumb Projector," places Haywood's Campbell stories in the context of anomalous beings of both sexes and women writers in particular. Nussbaum argues that Haywood implicitly makes use of this intertwining of imaginative power and physical defect to connect Campbell's predicament to that of early eighteenth-century women writers, perhaps responding to pervasive fears about the mercenary nature of the burgeoning group of writers of both sexes who sell the product of their imaginations.

"'Haywood,' Secret History, and the Politics of Attribution" takes off from Pope's odd attribution of *Memoirs of the Court of Lilliput* to Haywood, asking not if they are her work (most scholars think not), but why Pope claimed they were. What, David Brewer asks, does "Haywood" herself mean for Pope, who damned her in *The Dunciad,* and how does her meaning—loosely speaking, her reputation—shape the practice of attribution itself? This essay explores the ways in which "Haywood" was understood in her own time, analyzing her "meaning" to Scriblerians and non-Scriblerians, and argues that, for the former, "Haywood" functions as an exemplar of the generic category, a novelist, and that "Haywood," as used by Pope, can best be understood as something of a scapegoat, a figure pilloried in an attempt to distinguish the kind of writing "she" embodies from the Scriblerians' "higher" art.

In his essay, "Histories by Eliza Haywood and Henry Fielding: Imitation and Adaptation," John Richetti explores the ways in which Haywood's and Fielding's careers intersected on the stage and on the page. Focusing on three of Haywood's later novels—*The Fortunate Foundlings, Life's Progress Through the Passions, or the Adventures of Natura,* and *The History of Miss Betsy Thoughtless*—the essay traces Haywood's experiments with new forms of fiction and moral claims in order to examine their results. Reading Haywood's novels in terms of Fielding's notions of history, the essay contends that Haywood's use of realism derives precisely from a narrative perspective Fielding doubtless would have disdained as lacking true inventiveness; yet the essay argues that the virtues of her work in terms of its examination of female fate are inseparable from its limitations as a history in Fielding's sense.

Andrea Austin argues that, rather than being evidence of Haywood's moral reform or mercenary instinct, *The History of Miss Betsy Thoughtless* is Haywood's first formal attempt at parody. The essay, "Shooting Blanks: Potency, Parody, and Eliza Haywood's *The History of Miss Betsy Thoughtless*," explores the ways in which parody has, as a critical term, undergone a masculinization from the eighteenth century through to the postmodern period and contends that parodic works by women are often unrecognized or misread. The essay argues that reading *Betsy Thoughtless* as an attempt at parody is to see Haywood turning toward parody to promote a simple, central message not, in fact, very different from that of her earlier works: the inequity of woman's lot. In making this turn, Austin suggests, Haywood grapples with the considerable difficulties of writing women's parody and forges innovative techniques that become powerful tools of feminist criticism.

Eighteenth-century writers often explored their values through the trope of the pastoral garden. In his essay, "'Shady bowers! and purling streams!—Heavens, how insipid!': Eliza Haywood's Artful Pastoral," David Oakleaf contends that Haywood's use of the pastoral garden in her novels suggests her place within her own cultural-aesthetic landscape. Oakleaf argues that Haywood's texts demand attention to the pastoral artist's *craft*, not simply to the nymphs of the artist's seduction fictions. The essay focuses on *Betsy Thoughtless* to argue that careful reading of the novel reveals Haywood's self-conscious and artistic deconstruction of the language of seduction. Haywood opposes the hero's interested, but inartistic, imitation of the artful swain with the heroine's careful attention to style. Trueworth urges country life on the decidedly urban heroine, but she disparages "shady bowers" and "purling streams," refusing to play "Chloe" to his "Strephon" of the woods. Betsy refuses Haywood's own language of seduction because she prefers the role of the pastoral poet to that of the shepherd. Oakleaf suggests that we should read Haywood's self-identification with positions within a polarized aesthetic discourse less literally—notably her own denial of art in her dedication to *The Fatal Secret*—and instead focus on the ways in which her texts reveal her artistry at work.

Christine Blouch's essay, "'What Ann Lang Read': Eliza Haywood and her Readers," has as its impetus a nineteenth-century comment by critic Edmond Gosse that Haywood was read by "people like Ann Lang," whom Gosse collapses into a general reading category consisting of "servants in the kitchen . . . seamstresses . . . basket-women . . . and girls of this sort," i.e. generic, popular readers who read her generic, "strictly popular" novels. Blouch explores the ways in which "Ann Lang," an actual eighteenth-century reader of Haywood, has been reincarnated as a seamlessly constructed paradigm of reception still at play in today's criticism of Haywood. The essay traces the process of literary history and literary politics by which Ann Lang became so particularly problematic a relative in an already complicated reading genealogy, and explores the extent to which Ann Lang remains a legacy for today's reader of Eliza Haywood.

The essays in this volume do not approach Haywood from a single theoretical or topical position; rather, they reveal the ways in which Haywood's individual texts and *oeuvre* resist simplistic generalities. By recognizing the complexity and importance of Haywood's work, I hope that we may avoid characterizing her and her texts in terms that unwittingly resemble a set of stock characters: the literary tramp; the ruined maiden, seduced by Grub-Street; the heroic female martyr, victimized by cruel Scriblerian roués who destroy her good name and good works; the likable, but somewhat dizzy bawd; the eighteenth-century mother of the feminocentric popular romances, and so on. It is a bit myopic to approach Haywood's fictions solely as akin to, or different from, the eighteenth-century novel "proper." The history of the British novel and of Augustan literature in general is itself a novelistic project, with issues of parent and progeny, contract and inheritance, heir and prodigal. Haywood has, until recently, been largely absent from this highly fictionalized discussion, relegated, if mentioned at all, to the role of odd aunt or naughty kissing cousin. This collection arose out of the need for Haywood's texts to be examined on their own terms—as individual texts—as well as in connection with one another and with other works of fiction.

Varied, complex, and occasionally contestatory, the essays in this volume demonstrate that to successfully approach Haywood's writing we must recognize the formal and ideological complexities of her work. Her aristocratic Tory politics, exoticization of the East, *bricolage* of formal affect (a confluence of flowery language with a bluntness which approaches crudeness), overwhelming focus on heterosexual romance, self-presentations of female authorship within a frame of seduction, and forays into domestic fiction have troubled many twentieth-century critics. To situate Haywood's texts simply within existing genre or historical definitions—such as the novel or romance, a female tradition, or the Augustan era—is to ignore the ways in which Haywood's texts provocatively challenge such traditional schematization. The scope of Haywood's work—in drama, poetry, essays, scandal chronicles, and prose fiction—demands rereadings on multiple fronts, including the reassessment of the history of the British novel, the critical reconstruction of genre and period definitions currently underway in eighteenth-century studies, the instrumentation of party politics and nationalism, the development of eighteenth-century English drama, the role of the journal, the interrogation of the complicated constructions of the eighteenth-century female subject, and the notion of a female literary tradition.

Notes

1. In the 1740s, Haywood wrote, printed, and distributed texts, including anonymous political works such as the pamphlet entitled, "A Letter from H——G—g, Esq. . . . to a Particular Friend" (1749), which imagines the travels of Bonnie Prince Charles following the Jacobite Rebellion of 1745. She was arrested and held in custody for some weeks, but she denied authorship and was never prosecuted.

2. From *Adventures* . . . (1736 ed., 48) and *Idalia* . . . (17).

3. For example, in researching this volume at the Clark Library, I came upon a 1918 bookseller's mark (G. Smith) for a first edition of *The Opera of Operas* (1733), which, in addition to assigning authorship to Fielding, reads: "The work has also been ascribed to William Hatchett and the licentious Eliza Haywood."

4. All references in this essay are to David Oakleaf's 1994 edition of *Love in Excess*.

5. Christine Blouch is responsible for the updated biographical research on Haywood. See Blouch's important essay, "Eliza Haywood and the Romance of Obscurity," which serves as the most recent and authoritative biographical source on Haywood.

6. See in particular Ballaster's discussion of Haywood in *Seductive Forms*, 151–95.

7. Here, Haywood again recalls Finch's "The Introduction" (specifically the lines, "Alas! the woman that attempts the pen / Such an intruder on the rights of men" [100]).

8. I am indebted to Christine Blouch for her mention of this fact in her seminal essay, "Eliza Haywood and the Romance of Obscurity."

The Story of Eliza Haywood's Novels

Caveats and Questions

Paula R. Backscheider

At least since Clara Reeve's *Progress of Romance* (1785), The Story has been that, for purely commercial reasons, Eliza Haywood "reformed" and became a moral novelist. "Quite simply," Ros Ballaster writes, "by the mid-century, Haywood could no longer make money by selling her short romances of passion." Jane Spencer treats with ridicule Reeve's assignment of the change in Haywood's fiction to repentance, a "personal conversion," and says the change was "no doubt made in response to a change in the literary market." Cheryl Turner tells us that Haywood "caught the changing mood of her readership" in her "progress towards the moral high ground," and Janet Todd concludes, "In *Betsy Thoughtless* she clearly accepted the new mask of the woman writer and hung up her sign as teacher and chaste author."[1]

I respect these critics, true leaders in eighteenth-century feminist criticism and experts on Haywood. I've probably repeated The Story of Haywood's fiction, if not in print then in some classroom. Now I'm haunted by The Story. How do we know it's true? How accurate is it? How adequate an explanation is it? Given the surviving historical and biographical evidence about Haywood and what we know of the literary marketplace of her day, I am not satisfied that The Story can be validated *or* discredited.

Why does it matter? It seems to me that The Story is a barrier to

addressing—even recognizing—questions with which mature studies
of writers need to be concerned. And a collection of essays devoted to
her, a single author, signals a new phase in Haywood criticism.[2] I
want to explore two of these questions, both as a way of extending
our understanding of Haywood and of complicating, perhaps even
revising, The Story. (1) Why are we content with seeing Haywood's
texts as derivative and reactive rather than with studying her *agency*
in the history of the developing English novel? (2) How do we connect her texts, including those from the 1720s and from the 1750s, to
each other in meaningful ways? For me, these questions are inseparable, and to begin to address them I will suggest a story of her agency
grounded in two features of early eighteenth-century novelistic activity: experimentation with form and establishment of the form's distinctive participation in hegemonic processes.

Experimentation with Form. Histories of the English novel often neglect the decade before the publication of Daniel Defoe's *Robinson
Crusoe* and Haywood's *Love in Excess* in 1719, but a lot was happening. In fact, Haywood had a lively, fast-paced milieu in which to
work. Fiction and politics, the public and the private, and politics and
sex were being pulled closer together, entangled, and made inseparable. Not insignificantly, the decade began with the publication of
Delarivière Manley's sensational *New Atalantis* (1709). In the same
year Charles Gildon, a political and literary entrepreneur, published
*The Golden Spy: Or, a Political Journal of the British Nights Enter-
tainments of War and Peace and Love and Politics.* His subtitle calls
attention to the blending of topics and puns sarcastically on nights/
knights. *The Golden Spy,* like so many turn-of-the-century "novels,"
is made up of tales of love of the kinds that we now associate with
Aphra Behn and the early Haywood *and* of stories with fictionalized
discussions of the peace negotiations that were then under way.[3] Gildon
sprinkles his stories with names from the most famous French memoirs and romances (Grammont, Nemours), and the individual tales
are in turn reminiscent of the romance mode ("The History of Julio
and Sempronia"), the bawdy, scatological fabliau ("The Fair Extravagant"), the violent, salacious Southern European tale ("The Godly
Debochee" [*sic*]), and the fictionalized political dialogue ("The Trade

of the Camp," which is set in a coffeehouse)—all forms that Haywood would employ.

In that same decade, Joseph Addison and Defoe wrote memoirs, serial novellas, and fictions about Count Tariff, Lady Credit, and Sir Politick Falsehood,[4] and Jane Barker began *Love Intrigues* with allusions to England's recent wars and rebellions. It was the decade in which Defoe and others used the forms of memoirs, journals, and secret histories to fight the major political battles of the day. All of these forms had a long history, especially in France, of being vehicles for political commentary and argument, and all were well-developed forms.[5] These forms were what we call formula fiction; readers expected and got a certain kind of narrator, a set of characters in a predictable configuration, obligatory scenes, revelations, and confessions, and the "news behind the news"—in other words, "explanations" of the personalities, motives, and machinations behind news events.

Many of these forms used private conduct and conversations to reveal character and scheming. Their subjects were often power and privilege; politics, sex, economic gain, and cultural capital functioned in the narratives as signifiers, as subjects, and as metaphors for each other. In 1709, *The Diverting Works of the famous Miguel de Cervantes, Author of the History of Don Quixote . . . With an Introduction by the Author of the London Spy* appeared. It was one of many collections of novellas that were precursors to, or contemporaneous with, the type that Behn, Gildon, and many others wrote or collected and translated.[6] Lust, avarice, mercenary values, and "arousal literature" are all here. These Southern European–style tales can be traced backward at least as far as Boccaccio and, by the end of the seventeenth century, were likely to be violent, salacious, and morbid. Collections such as *Diverting Works* and those by Samuel Croxall and Aphra Behn brought together translations, adaptations, and original tales; little care was taken to attribute authorship.[7] Yet even the writer of the introduction to *Diverting Works,* Edward Ward, author of *The London Spy,* is notable, for Ward was one of the writers who helped make London a popular setting for fiction, a revolutionary step in the history of the English novel; the fourth edition of *London Spy,* the gritty tour of everything from the saltpeter house near Islington to Westminster Abbey, had just been published.

In 1719, the year of the publication of *Love in Excess,* Marie Catherine d'Aulnoy's *The Prince of Carency . . . Translated into English,* a 382–page French romance, appeared and was advertised for sale by W. Chetwood, one of the printer-booksellers for *Love in Excess.* These huge, multi-volume books not only contained sensational interpolated tales much like the Southern European novellas but were also recognized on the continent and in Renaissance England as having political purposes (Backscheider, *Spectacular Politics* 112–17). These romances are always about class, gender, power, and cultural capital. The language and the tone, of course, are very different, and the "work" done by salty, low, brutally honest comments—many ironic or funny—in Cervantes' writing and the later novellas is often done in romances by melodramatic lamentations. The cultural work is both moral lesson and social critique.[8]

The fictional forms that Haywood was using, adapting, and combining are obvious from this brief summary, and what she did with them text by text is important in itself, especially because, collectively, they demonstrate that of her generation she was the most active experimenter with fictional forms and introduced themes, plots, characters, settings, and topics into English fiction. Recognition of these experiments gives detail and concrete support to recent claims of Haywood's importance in the history of the English novel and of her texts' relationships to those by Richardson and Fielding.[9]

For example, *Love in Excess* differs from most of the French romances in ways that "advance" or point to major types of the English novel. The obstacles the lovers encounter in this text tend to come from their actions, personalities, and relationships rather than from accidents, coincidences, or national events, and, also unlike the romances, the hero, D'Elmont, is educated about women and love and genuinely changes. In most romances, the characters, especially the men, do not change—they are good or evil and remain so,[10] and the lovers are steadfast and faithful while being tested and overcoming the obstacles that drive the narrative. As early as this text, Haywood is using mistaken identities, masquerade, and intricate schemes, all more characteristic of the Southern European novella than of the romance and all devices that became signature strategies for her. The complicated scheme that Alouisa uses to banish Amena to a monastery is typical of the Southern European tales and the Spanish comedy of intrigue, which Haywood and her generation knew well. As *Love in Excess* swells to multiple volumes, Haywood uses conventional types of female characters as the means to explore women's sexuality, intelligence, and alleged "nature," but she also creates Melliora, a complex woman character who introduces complicated subjects for serious discussion. The poles that are Amena and Alovisa, and Melantha and Melliora give way in Part III to the rich variety of Ciamara, Camilla, Violetta, and more—characters like those Haywood and other novelists would continue to use and develop.

Haywood's experimental development is rapid. The problems, personalities, desires, and destinies are repeated, reconfigured, developed, and explored in the fictions that follow, among them *The Injur'd Husband, Idalia; or, the Unfortunate Mistress, The Rash Resolve, The Masqueraders, Cleomira, Fantomina, The Mercenary Lover, The City Jilt,* and *Philidore and Placentia. The British Recluse,* her second published fiction, juxtaposes the language and mode of romance with that of the novel. Its ending has been read both as a lonely, defeated retreat by ruined women and as a daring, triumphant ending in which the women discover they do not need men for happiness and which initiates a stream of utopian fictions by women, including the well-respected *Millenium Hall.* Sophisticated methodologies developed by theorists of popular culture, the avant garde, and the intersections of culture, reading, and taste allow us to see Haywood as a pioneer creator of the deliberately ambiguous, one of Umberto Eco's categories of art (143, 196). Eco and other theorists point out that writers attempting to express new ideas or revisionary accounts of experience rapidly adapt existing forms and introduce new ones. Many of these forms deviate from familiar forms and resist the kinds of satisfactory closure common to conservative texts.[11] For instance, Haywood refuses to punish "fallen" women in traditional ways and masterfully sends the reader back to her texts, their multiple meanings, and their possible interpretations. Thus, new possibilities for action, identity, and judgment are introduced into consciousness.

In text after text after *The British Recluse,* Haywood adds distinctively English elements to her fictions with the result that critics reading literary history "back" see *Miss Betsy Thoughtless* more as Richardson's "new species of novel" than as the amalgamation and development of characteristic features of Haywood's own fiction that it is. The basic plot of *Betsy Thoughtless* comes from *British Recluse,* and by the end of Haywood's life this rejection of an exemplary man for the excitement and flattery of fashionable flirtation, coquetry, and risk had become a staple of courtship and marriage novels. While Richardson may have been creating the novel of morality, Haywood was inventing the novel of fashion. The London setting, the pastimes of the characters, the immersion in economic and legal London, the language, even characters' shopping habits identify it as something new and something quite different from what Richardson was doing.

It is hard for us to realize what a revolutionary move the use of specific, contemporary London settings was when Haywood, Defoe, Ward, and a very few others did it, and even harder to understand why Defoe, not Defoe and Haywood, is credited with originating the realist novel. Associated with "low," "city" (also a pejorative) comedies, the use of identifiable London places and topical allusions to people, events, fashions, and pastimes was a deliberate political move.[12] She and Defoe not only capture the *habitus* but also the fact that their culture was now one of commodification, capital, credit, crime, and contracts. For example, the plots of *The Mercenary Lover* and *The City Jilt* (both 1724) turn on Clitander's and Glicera's manipulation of legal documents—as do major parts of *Betsy Thoughtless* (1751), Haywood's periodical exempla, and late tales such as that of Alinda in *The Invisible Spy* (1755). If Defoe's characters are always looking for bankers, Haywood's seek lawyers. The means of outwitting and even enslaving others often depend on legal documents, and her fictions from the 1720s on contain explanations of various documents, information on what makes them correctly executed and binding, and descriptions of how they may be used by unscrupulous people. *The City Jilt* explains executing valid mortgages in almost boring detail, and *Betsy Thoughtless* includes a range of technical legal maneuvers. For instance, Mr. Goodman understands when he does not have to pay his wife's debts, divorces her for criminal conversation (358ff.),[13] and is advised to complain "to the Court of Chancery of the imposition practised on" him and to "procure a *ne exeat regnum*" to keep his wife's lover in the country (234).

It is easier to find similarities than it is to find differences between the early and late fictions. For example, Clitander's careful selection of a Deed of Gift instead of a will in *The Mercenary Lover* is as central to the plot and to Haywood's explication of his character as is Le Bris's opportunistic trick to get Alinda to sign the contract in *The Invisible Spy*. Nor does Haywood eliminate sexual scenes in her "moral," "tamed" late fiction to the extent that some critics have claimed. For example, the way Le Bris fondles and takes advantage of his student Alinda is at least as explicit as anything Clitander does: "[H]e pull'd me to him, and making me sit upon his knee, —'You are very pretty, my dear miss, said he, and have no defect in your shape, but being a little too flat before;' —with these words he thrust one of his hands within my stays, telling me that handling my breasts would make them grow, and I should then be a perfect beauty." There is something strangely modern in this and the following scenes in this shocking reworking of the Eloisa and Abelard Story. Here, as in *Love in Excess,* Haywood explores complicated relationships between guardians and children. Alinda's later feelings are expansions of the instinctive disgust Haywood's character Louisa in *The Fortunate Foundlings* feels when Dorilaus forces kisses on her. In fact, Haywood's scenes of child molestation here and elsewhere are groundbreaking and deserve study both for themselves and as examples of her radical innovations in form and content.

Almost as important are her experimentations with levels of diction and narrative voices. By the middle of the century, something like a standard novelistic voice had been established, but early English prose fiction is notable for its varieties of discourses, and in Haywood's time the carefully wrought, artificial language of the romance is just as characteristic as the idiomatic, straightforward style of picaresque and criminal tales. It is important to remember that genres and discourses bear cultural capital and that class differences and conflicts and even world views are deployed when writers incorporate discernible traces of various kinds of language. For example, when Fielding uses and calls attention to the occurrences of older genres, such as the epic and the chivalric romance, he is often making status claims, doing such things as reminding his readers of his considerable classical learning and allying himself with such texts as Alexander Pope's urbane, masterful *Rape of the Lock*. Sterne's mastery of the novel form is also a display of superiority, of commanding wit.

Part of the necessary task of the novelists of the 1720s, the generation before Fielding, was the creation of a distinctively novelistic language, or, more accurately, a range within which the novelistic voice would come to be functional and respected. To some extent, the vilification and confusion that have surrounded Defoe's and Haywood's styles are results, first, of experimentations that struck their contemporaries as strange or even transgressive and, second, of their violations of the limits of what succeeding generations of novel readers and critics recognize as characteristic or even appropriate for the form. Richardson, in an introduction to Penelope Aubin's novels, and John Richetti, in our own time, isolate Haywood's 1720s writing from that of her contemporaries. Aubin "was a mistress of a polite and unaffected style, and aimed not at the unnatural flights, and hyperbolical flourishes, that . . . give [some of her sex's] performances too romantic an air for probability," Richardson wrote.[14] And Richetti expands, "The dashes, exclamations points, and ersatz cadences of the swelling prose are the real content of the scene and drive the reader along to the near-climax with which it ends. We are conscious not of logical progression but a . . . repetition of evocative words and phrases—burnings, blazings, mountings, burstings" (*Popular Fiction* , 1992 edition 201).

Rudimentary recognitions of a novelistic discourse that would become normative by the 1740s are not hard to find. For instance, Charles Gildon's attack on *Robinson Crusoe* is as much an attack on Defoe's language as upon his content ("An Epistle," 23, 38–9), and, as Richetti points out, Haywood uses an "erotic shorthand" that was rapidly going out of fashion. By the time he wrote *Roxana,* Defoe can refer to "knight errantry" and create a shorthand that sets his novel apart from improbable fictions with characters of impossible virtue and from the fading language held over from late Renaissance continental fiction.

In *Betsy Thoughtless,* Haywood distinguishes many of Betsy's suitors by their language, and each bears traces of distinctive fictional modes. Munden, the man she marries, writes, "I know very well, that it is the duty of every lover to submit, in all things to the pleasure of the beautiful object whose chains he wears. . . . Some business of great moment prevents my waiting on you this afternoon, but shall attend your commands to-morrow at the usual hour" (300). His use of the empty formulas of courtship novels ("chains he wears") and of transparent excuses reveals his priorities (business) and his reduction of human relationships to domination/subordination. The language code prepares the reader for his tyrannical, peevish conduct as a husband and his consumerism as an adulterous lover. Fineer, the fake fine gentleman writes, "Words cannot describe the ardency of my flame. . . . I lay myself, and all that I am worth, an humble offering at your feet" (301). Betsy, whose language is often incisively blunt and unladylike, remarks, "One would think he has been consulting all the ballads since fair Rosamond and the Children in the Wood." In this novel, the test of a character is the test of his or her discourse,[15] and the dialogue between Betsy and Trueworth at the end of the novel moves them both to a new plane. Haywood also codes class, age, and regional markers into her dialogue even as she uses changes in discourse to control tempo. For instance, when the servant girl returns to Betsy the cherished miniature of Trueworth that she believes she has lost, Betsy says, "I am glad thou hast found it . . . for it would have vexed me to the heart to have lost it" (573).

Just as Haywood's agency and innovation come from her blending, adaptation, and invention of form, so they also develop from her blending and inventing of discourses and narrative voices. Innovation of a form, however, carries considerable risks. When we dissect Haywood's novels in search of explanations for the harshest criticisms of her work, we highlight distinctive elements in her writing, most significantly the kinds of narrative voices she repeatedly creates. Her teasing opening to *The Invisible Spy,* in which she challenges readers to identify her sex and recites possible perceptions readers will have (that she is philosopher/fool, courtier/patriot) is in harmony with the long line of slippery, teasing narrators that she created in her fictions. They are often disguised observers, purported neutral observers, and shocked but uninvolved citizens. The Invisible Spy, who not only possesses a magic belt allowing invisibility but also a tablet that receives an exact impression of every word spoken, was but one of the spectators she created. Apparently neutral and uninvolved, her narrators can be stung to outrage or may have a sad, world-weary voice as does, for instance, the mother in *The Fruitless Inquiry,* who looks for a completely happy woman. Most often, they watch men, study their mores, and report on what seems to be a secret fraternity that condones forms of force and fraud.[16]

Characters whose perspective we are invited to share may be silent, "ruined," or abandoned women playing roles, sometimes in male disguise as is Amadea in *The Fair Captive*. These female narrators renounce female silence and passivity and suddenly and startlingly act, breaking or diverting what seems an inevitable chain of events leading to an all-too-predictable result. In contrast are a host of male characters who are largely self-centered, whose actions are almost entirely self-serving, and who take for granted the right to do anything, who believe, as Betsy Thoughtless's husband does, that a slight exertion will confirm his power. Haywood risks confusing or even alienating readers as she confronts them with these dislocations of passivity and agency, with sudden narrative movements from observation to active judgment, and with violations of expected gender possibilities.

Catherine Ingrassia has argued that the narrative voice and discursive experience identified with Haywood's early fiction are "idiosyncratic." I agree that they go beyond "individual" and are deserving this characterization and that, throughout Haywood's career, they remain distinctive and peculiar to her.[17] From her earliest publications, Haywood seems to have had an ironic self-consciousness about narrative voice that admits near-parody, metacommentary, deconstruction, and ironic double commentary into her texts.[18] Ingrassia is shrewd to note both narrative voice and discursive experience. Haywood used both to blend formulaic fantasy with social realism, thereby producing simultaneously a symbolic portrait of the power structure (class-gender systems), a London setting with rich, veridical details of the present, and a glimpse of a different society representing a new order.

What we are supposed to think, what literary conventions have constructed us to think, and something quite different are suddenly brought to our consciousness and jarringly juxtaposed.[19] Haywood is particularly good—and biting—when describing class and gender politics. Throughout her career, for example, she calls attention to how arbitrary assignment of gendered voices is and to how crucial gender is to modern perceptions of identity, and in *The Invisible Spy* she writes about these things quite explicitly.[20] Here and elsewhere her sophisticated understanding of reader response, literary conventions, and sexual politics places her with the great male writers of her time, including Richardson, Fielding, and Sterne, who were exploring author-reader relationships and fictional conventions.

Expansion of "Work." Simultaneously with the experimentation with form was the exploration of what influence prose fiction might have and what cultural work it might do. Both of these developments set the course for a distinctive English novel, and Haywood was, again, one of the most important of these innovators. Although her voice becomes stronger, clearer, and more specific about the power of publication and especially of novels, even *Love in Excess* shows that Haywood believed in the power of fiction and its multiple uses. Rather than a retrograde publication, that "romance" is the beginning of her active, lifelong participation in a generation's expansion and even institutionalization of the novel's participation in hegemonic processes.

At the most overt level, Haywood frequently discusses the influences of reading on characters, and her texts include sections similar to Defoe's and Fielding's that explain how to read and admonish readers about textual emphases.[21] In *Love in Excess,* the most admirable character, Melliora, reads Fontenelle's *Discourse concerning the Plurality of Worlds* "for improvement" (1994 edition 109). Later, when D'Elmont teases her for reading Ovid's *Epistles* or the *Heroides,*[22] she insists that she finds evidence of the "misfortunes" that attend passionate love and argues that right reading would have as its result, "the votaries of Cupid would be fewer, and the dominion of reason more extensive" (118). She explains what her reading has taught her: "[I]n a lovers mind illusions seem realities, and what at an other time would be looked on as impossible, appears easie then. They indulge, and feed their new-born folly with prospect of a hope . . . and in the vain pursuit of it, fly consideration" (119). D'Elmont immediately tests her learning with a sophistical argument and an embrace, which she repels with dignity, and he is forced to desist, to confess his true feelings, and, eventually, to reform.

The opinions about women and reading expressed in these discussions recur in her work and assume greater thematic importance. They are developed and discussed among a group of women in *The Tea-Table* (1724), and, significantly, suggest the direction her fiction will increasingly take. Not only is Haywood defending the "warm" scenes and "monstrous" villainy in her tales by asserting that they impress women with the need to guard against their gullibility and "softness," but she is also beginning to discuss fiction's part in reforming manners. What the women read and discuss at the tea table correlates exactly with the wisdom and commonsense they exercise in public, and a portrait of the ideal middle-class woman is as vivid in this text as in any "moral" novel of the 1750s—and reading is an important part of their lives and educations.

Haywood repeatedly weaves the power of the written word into her stories. For example, in *The Mercenary Lover*, Miranda finds three letters in her poisoned sister's pocketbook and uses them not only to strengthen her resolves but to control her husband, the murderous Clitander. She "keeps them by her, and daily reads them over, to preserve in Memory his Offences, and prevent his Artifices from the Success he aims at. The Knowledge [of] how much he is in the Power of one he has so highly injur'd, is a perpetual Rack upon his Spirits, and in infinitely more reasonable Apprehensions of Danger on her Account, than ever he had on that of *Althea*" (*Mercenary Lover, Selected Fiction*, 162). As do some of Haywood's other characters, Alinda, in *The Invisible Spy*, writes down her history and leaves it as powerful testimony of the wrong committed against her. Indeed, the narrator of this text becomes an avenging angel, snatching Alinda's story from the fire and publishing it.

Haywood continued to assert the power of literature and gradually expanded her dramatizations of the uses to which unscrupulous people can put it until she embraced the private and the public sphere. For example, she weaves fiction as arousal literature into her narratives, as when Melliora in *Love in Excess* warns against "softening amusements" (116) and when Clitander in *The Mercenary Lover* encourages Althea to read Ovid, Rochester, and books of "more modern Date" (contemporary fiction immediately comes to mind) that "insensibly melt down the Soul, and make it fit for amorous Impression." By the end of her career, Haywood wrote about the unscrupulous uses of periodicals and newspapers, as she does in explaining how the Elizabeth Canning case diverted the public from such serious election issues as the Jew Bill and the Clandestine Marriage Bill.[23] As early as *The Injured Husband* (1723), she wrote that "the press is set to work only to gratify a mercenary end" (preface) and expected her readers to be skeptical consumers aware of the self-consciousness with which writers used publication.

A major expansion of the "work" of the novel in the culture involved calls for social change. Were we to look at Haywood as engaged in the kinds of demands for reform (of marriage, of women's education, of women's values) and of critiques of social and personal spaces recognized in the work of dramatists and essayists,[24] we would find another revisionary Story. By the last quarter of the eighteenth century, the novel was widely recognized as a "well-worn channel of access to the public" and the chief propagator of morality.[25] Haywood has been denied her rightful place in this development, and resistance to seeing her with moral motives for publishing is almost as great today as in the past. It seems to me that this category of novelistic purpose comes to us from the late eighteenth–early nineteenth-century canon-making and discussions of the novel and also from the labels applied by John Richetti and the other 1960s and 1970s groundbreaking critics of women's novels. Rather than a marked break in Haywood's fiction, I find a remarkable consistency in her stated "morals" and the plots and themes that dramatize them (many summarized in Melliora's defense of reading), which position her with what came to be mainstream endeavors by women writers. When we examine her statements of purpose, her own claims for the usefulness of her fiction, its *work,* and place them in this tradition rather than in the category of "pious polemic" or "the erotic and pathetic,"[26] her statements strengthen the claims feminist critics have made for her establishment of sub-genres of novels,[27] and certainly they strengthen my claims about her importance in the history of the novel.

Haywood's work exhibits consistent attention to what would become novelistic treatments of appearance and reality themes, and she contributed to the novel's movement toward the psychological. For instance, her most frequent admonitions to both sexes are about illusions, warnings against having "no other Foundation for belief in what her Lover says . . . than the good Opinion . . . Passion has made [her or him] conceive" (*British Recluse,* 1996 edition 154). Cleomira, in *The British Recluse,* says succinctly what many other Haywood characters observe: "For ever lost to Peace by *Love,* and my own fond Belief" (160). A number of plots turn on this human propensity, as does *The City Jilt:* "She hesitated not if she should believe, because she wish'd it so, and had before set down in her own Heart for Truth, all that he now professed" (1724 edition, 5). Twenty years later, Haywood was writing the same thing: "The eagerness of their wishes to be addressed, gives charms to the address itself, which otherwise it would not have; and hence it follows, that when a young creature has suffered herself to fall a victim to the artifices of her pretended lovers, and her own giddy whim . . . she . . . detests the object of her former *imaginary* passion" (emphasis mine, *Female Spectator*, 1744–46 edition 1:10–11).

Haywood is particularly good at developing the poignancy of a young person who clothes a lover in idealistic dreams. After the death of her beloved father, Glicera turns to her fiancé, Melladore, for comfort: "[H]e scarce ever left her but in those Hours in which Decency obliged him to retire, he easily persuaded her to a Forgetfulness of *the Dead,* in the Comforts of *the Living;* and if Fate exacted the Life of one, she thought it yet a less terrible Misfortune to lose her *Father* than a *Lover* who was so dear to her, and by whom she believed herself so sincerely and tenderly belov'd, that she should know no want of any other Friend." Melladore seduces her and breaks their engagement, and Glicera becomes the City Jilt.

Haywood develops a range of tones to further her psychological themes. Betsy Thoughtless, although she never falls "victim to the artifices of her pretended lovers," is a wonderful example of a woman whose eagerness to be addressed, enjoyment of popularity, and "giddy whims" make her a victim. Here and in earlier fictions about coquettes, Haywood points out that there are worse things than lost virginity— miserable marriages and eternal regret over a good suitor foolishly lost. Men are almost as prone as women to overlay reality with what they wish to be true, to see what they desire rather than to use reason and allow themselves time to evaluate people and situations. Although the results for men are more likely to be comic, as in *Fantomina,* than tragic or pathetic, as in *Love in Excess,* this theme works to draw the sexes closer together and to contribute to the novel form's long-standing concern with psychology and themes of appearance and reality.

Although some of her characters have illusions about the wealth or virtue of others, fantasies about love are the most common, and Haywood was among the critics who revised and developed this topic in fiction. In *Love in Excess,* Haywood dramatizes various kinds of heterosexual love from raw lust to idealistic romance and narrates the steps in D'Elmont's and several women's educations in the meaning of true love, the dawning and understanding of ideal heterosexual love. The shorter fictions that follow always include one or both of these enterprises, and Haywood introduces new and thought-provoking reactions to mistakes and betrayals and, most significantly, new endings.[28]

Because Haywood's warnings in her early fictions of the power of love and the need to regulate the passions associated with it raise expectations in her readers of seductions, rapes, and "warm scenes," the seriousness with which she may have meant these statements and how they might have been read is obscured. Haywood attempts to correct the impression that the amorous scenes overbalance the larger themes. She begins to ask her readers, as she does in *Lasselia*, to "excuse the too great Warmth . . . , for without the Expression being invigorated in some measure proportionate to the Subject, t'wou'd be impossible for a Reader to be sensible. . . . [h]ow probable it is that he is falling into those inadvertencies which the Examples I relate wou'd caution him to avoid" (v-vi). This same apology can, of course, be found in the prefaces of novels by Defoe,[29] and it might be argued that Samuel Richardson's failure to include such a formulaic statement contributed to some readers' perceptions of prurience. Readers have probably never believed Defoe either,[30] but the degree of scepticism and the jeering comments on Haywood's "conversion" to modest, moral fiction are strikingly different. Her statements are still seen as dishonest camouflage for mercenary desires and a nymphomaniac personality, while Defoe is accused of creating a hypocritical or ironic narrator. She is seen as financially more needy and pandering to the corrupt and corruptible in order to sell books, while even the money-obsessed Defoe is consistently represented as having other, more important motives. Even the most unsympathetic tend to find him focused on crime prevention or the plight of the poor and dim-wittedly unaware of the salacious possibilities of his scenes. And few comment on Defoe's fraught depictions of sexuality and his writing of *Conjugal Lewdness* at age sixty-seven.[31]

In another act of expansion of the novel's uses, Haywood led in the movement of fiction away from portraits of courtship to critiques of marriage, and the implications of kinds of attachment assumed greater importance. Although her early writing had glimpses of married couples, new characters and relationships appear in her fiction, as they do in *The Rash Resolve* (1724) and *The Fruitless Inquiry* (1727).[32] Many of the characters are older, and a spectrum of older wives, such as those in *Betsy Thoughtless,* deepen Haywood's presentation of the situation of British womankind, model the realistic possibilities for action that women have, and create a dialogue with conduct-book fiction. The voices of the women who tell Betsy how to cope with her miserable marriage are both individual and horribly uniform ("endure," "be careful"), and the relationships between each husband and wife are carefully distinguished and yet undergirded and permeated by the sex-gender system of the time. *Betsy Thoughtless* is such an original novel because Betsy meets all of the hypocritical men of Haywood's earlier fiction, but, because she is Alexander Pope's "ev'ry woman is at heart a rake" with no desire to marry, their true nature and motives are usually exposed before she finishes flirting with them. Her marriage to Munden is the exception, and Haywood leaves open the possibility that Betsy's erratic behavior in courtship wore out his affection and his illusions about her. Some of the most intense scenes of marital fighting in eighteenth-century fiction depict Betsy attempting to preserve her legal right to her pin money, and the pacific advice given her by other women is in sharp contrast to the force of her rage.

As power shifted to the bourgeois, and marriage, not courtship, became the object of social discipline, Haywood, like most women writers, participated in the reform of marriage by drawing portraits of ideal, companionate marriages, but she was also the most relentless critic of bourgeois pretensions, self-righteous cruelties, and mindless hypocrisies. Betsy Thoughtless, like Burney's Evelina, is often misjudged and risks losing permanently the man she loves because she acts kindly toward a stigmatized, unfortunate person. She is told by a man who has tried to take her to a bagnio that "a young lady more endangered her reputation by an acquaintance of one woman of ill fame, than by receiving the visits of twenty men, though professed libertines" (211). Such moments are strikingly ironic[33] but also powerful critiques of society, its judgments, and its double standards. Moreover, they point to the evolution of the political dimension of the novel form.

From the beginning of her career, Haywood claims what will become a ubiquitous justification for the novel, and especially women's novels, throughout the century: that her novels offered experience and an education without the consequences of real-life missteps. Typical professions include: "My design in writing this little Novel (as well as those I have formerly publish'd) being only to remind the unthinking Part of the World, how dangerous it is to give way to Passion" (*Lasselia*, vi) and "If among all who shall read the following sheets, any one Person may . . . avoid the Misfortunes the subject of them fell into by his Inadvertency and giving a Loose to Passion; the Little Pains I have been at, will be infinitely recompens'd" (*The Fair Hebrew*, 1729, preface). Recognizing that their educations and their restricted lives left them dangerously naive, women like Haywood offered their novels as sources of information that would protect women from everything from social faux pas to fraud. The novel became a source of vicarious experience, especially for women. We watch the realization of this function in Haywood, and, perhaps, the dawning of novels addressed to women rather than to men and women.

What experience taught women above all was the need for self-control, and Haywood ties the two together expertly. In her earliest fictions, such as *Idalia* (1723), she writes, "If there were a Possibility that the Warmth and Vigour of Youth could be temper'd with a due Consideration, and the Power of Judging rightly; how easy were it to avoid the Ills which most of us endure?" (1). If there is a consistent message to women readers of novels in the eighteenth century, it is to exercise self-control, and the fact that novels with titles such as *Self-Control* (1811) and *Discipline* (1815) sold well reminds us of the exhortation's continued appeal. Statements and dramatizations of this theme are one of the career-long consistencies in Haywood's work. Charlotta and Louisa in *The Fortunate Foundlings* are admirable because they guard their responses to men as well as the expressions of their feelings carefully, and Charlotta is an especially attractive character because Haywood shows her struggling to do so.[34] She is, as Betsy Thoughtless will become, straightforward and sincere, and, as Haywood moves from critiquing courtship games to writing about marriages, she participates in creating a new kind of heroine who seems stronger and more adult than previous characters had seemed.

In the same decade, Haywood's allegedly moral and even pious fellow writers were making similar statements. "Since passions will ever have a place in the actions of men, and love a principal one, what cannot be removed or subdued ought at least be regulated," Mary Davys wrote in the preface to her *Works*. And these "pious" writers include "warm writing" about the power of love: "But neither Reason nor the nicest Sense of Honour, nor even Devotion could assist me; still you returned on my Imagination triumphant . . . ," Ethelinda writes in one of the letters in Elizabeth Singer Rowe's *Friendship in Death* (1728, 330). In urging women to be reflective and self-controlled, to regulate their responses and conduct, and to guard against the confusion of desire with reality, Haywood was not only consistent with all of her writings but also engaged in admonishing women to be independent and self-controlled, one of the most consistent enterprises of women writers of the entire century.

Were I to write a history of the novel, it would have four parts. The first would examine the novel's engagement with national politics (Behn's *Love Letters*, Defoe's and Gildon's novels, Manley's *New Atalantis*), and the second and third, in which Haywood would play central parts, would focus on the institutionalization of "the personal is the political" (Haywood's novels to 1740, Richardson's *Clarissa*, Fielding's *Tom Jones*) and on the dramatization of the consolidation of the interpenetration of the public and private (Fielding's *Amelia*, Haywood's *Betsy Thoughtless*, Scott's *Millenium Hall*).[35] Haywood is a major force in keeping the English novel political, expanding the meaning of political, and establishing the novel as the form in maximal contact with the present and most likely to be subversive. It is striking to see the extent to which she intuited that, in Catherine MacKinnon's words, gender is "a social system that divides power. It is therefore a political system" (160). A dweller in the Habermasian public sphere, she helped establish the novel as a "vehicle of public opinion [that] put the state in touch with the needs of society."[36]

Haywood created some strikingly original political fictions by adapting older forms, but, more significantly for the novel, she participated in elucidating the political dimensions of a range of topics hitherto relegated to the private sphere and of particular concern for women. An important part of Haywood's political activity was pioneering writing that made the novel "one of the few public discourses in which women were allowed to speak for themselves," to represent women rather than be the "imaginary representations" of men (Kaplan 867). After Rousseau, who insisted that "the thinker who wishes to separate politics from morals will never understand either" and linked the personal and political throughout his theories,[37] the number of women novelists who self-consciously engaged in such writing multiplied, and the novel was their most frequent choice of discourse.

Along with Aphra Behn and Delarivière Manley, Haywood expanded the understanding of how the personal is the political in scandalous memoirs. Her political writing has often been overlooked or misinterpreted because the strong roman à clef construction present in part 1 of Behn's *Love Letters* and Defoe's and Manley's work is absent. Haywood consistently attacks the privileged and draws the public and private together. Her experimentation and achievement are especially notable in *The Adventures of Eovaai*, which tells a sensational a story of virgin virtue threatened by a demoniacal villain in whom public and private characteristics and motives are more horrible for being inseparably identified. Her writing blends a strong defense of contract theory of government into a tale of magic, corruption, and romance come true that has come to be much admired.[38] She used many of the same techniques in *A Letter from H—— G——* (1749), which ties political essays and romance plots to the travels (both actual and unverified) of Bonnie Prince Charlie. In this text, explicit amorous scenes alternate with dialogues in which the Prince expounds the same political principles found in *Eovaai,* including condemnation of the influence of too-powerful ministers. The public and private are woven inseparably together here, too, and the Prince is praised in these terms: "How fit is he to govern others, who knows so well how to govern himself" (26). Haywood was arrested for publishing this text and, amusingly, her resistance to imprisonment is a creative blend of public and private information.[39] Both of these texts are excellent examples of a literary movement discernible in the period: commercializing political discourse and fictionalizing political argument.

Haywood is among the earliest of the fiction writers to make specific analogies between current political theories and domestic relations. Quite specifically, for example, she states that, once married, men are proponents of "passive obedience." What is an observation and a caution in fictions of the 1720s becomes a desperate struggle in

Betsy Thoughtless, and such allusions to microcosm/macrocosm and statements of the stakes for women are important preparations for the profound dialogic underpinnings of Richardson's *Clarissa* (1747–48). The English novel was born at the same time the struggle toward the "Revolution Settlement" was taking place—a struggle some might say did not end until the defeat of the last Jacobite rebellion in 1745. Fiction, therefore, was infused not only with the personalities and skirmishes of particular moments—Behn's discrediting of Monmouth's followers in *Love-Letters between a Nobleman and his Sister,* Defoe's of Lady Masham in the White Staff secret histories, and Manley's of Marlborough in *The New Atalantis*—but also with the larger cultural issues often abbreviated in terms such as court/country that signified balance of power, issues of taxation, and even the development and resistance to the Habermasian authentic public sphere. For instance, the Revolution Settlement and the proper checks and balances between monarch and people are very much the subjects of *The Adventures of Eovaai,* and in the last section of the book they are made specifically analogous to the roles of husband and wife. Government is for the good of the subject in both, and submission is a gift given to the deserving. *The Fortunate Foundlings* (1744), an almost entirely neglected text, pointedly begins in 1688, the year of the Glorious Revolution. Among other historical and political subjects, it surveys the career of Charles XII of Sweden, a saga already familiar to readers from books by Voltaire and Defoe, and offers interpretations of such key events as the treatment of Patkul.

Sensing that power is diffused throughout a society and can both censor and create realities, Haywood dramatized power relationships in order to describe the society she saw and the permeation of the class and sex/gender systems. In her hands, the novel continued to develop as the form most evaluative of society and of the class with hegemony over it. For example, with other writers, in her early career she condemned, stigmatized, and helped make extinct the rake and the assumption of privileges the culture had granted him. In *Betsy Thoughtless,* she caricatures this fallen aristocrat in the character of Sir Frederick Fineer. Throughout her publishing career, she sometimes drew the classes together,[40] as she does in seeing the common lot of women in texts such as *The Fruitless Inquiry,* and just as often she holds in the spotlight the differences between classes and how much class matters, as she does in *Fantomina* and *Anti-Pamela*. Sometimes she also ridicules the distinctions as false and even improbable, as in *Fantomina* and *The Fortunate Foundlings* and when she compares Glicera in *The City Jilt* to court beauties who accept gifts (29).

As Catherine Ingrassia has pointed out, Haywood's texts are more about public resistance than about the private sphere. Her heroines exist psychologically and physically in the public sphere, and, because their fathers or lovers are prominent men, the public judges and determines their character. Their judgments can, of course, disqualify characters from marriage or make them "universally admired" or "lamented." More important, their judgments expose how the public sphere and public opinion work. Judgments are often made on the slightest of contact, on the appearance of a single action or situation, and on "prejudices," applications of social rules in stereotypical, facile ways. Regardless of whether characters intend to prostitute themselves or relieve the suffering of a deserving person, their discovery in certain places or neighborhoods brands them, as is evident in *Betsy Thoughtless*.

Similarly political and groundbreaking was Haywood's creation of women characters who were, *above all else,* economic units. While most of the major eighteenth-century women writers—especially Frances Burney—dramatize the unfortunate consequences of having incompetent or evil guardians, Haywood initiates the theme and uses it to emphasize how inexorable the pressures are, in Jean Bethke Elshtain's words, to "privatize women" (214). They and whatever they have seem always on the verge of being real or cultural capital and available to men. Close reading of Haywood's works shows that she is able to depict how internalized such thinking is. Melliora, for instance, confused by her father's dying words, thinks he intends D'Elmont, her guardian, for a husband—she and whatever she possesses has been handed over to him. Haywood's texts show a growing insistence that women must do everything possible to secure their own property and never surrender control of it, and how that might be done is described pragmatically.[41] Women who have and surrender economic control come to hideous ends. Both faces of the lesson are emphasized in *The Mercenary Lover,* in which Althea signs away her

estate and dies a horrible death while Miranda saves her documents
and controls her murderous husband by controlling her property. This
text and others such as *The City Jilt, The Rash Resolve, The Force of
Nature,* and *The Fruitless Inquiry* open the possibility that capitalism
and the modern economic marketplace might allow women to be equal.
These portrayals, however, always show women acting at least in part
by surprise or stealth and in precarious positions; none have the easy
assurance and confident knowledge of her admirable male characters
such as Trueworth and Goodman in *Betsy Thoughtless.*

Elizabeth Bohls speculates, "The most painful, deeply repressed,
inarticulate and virtually inarticulable longings of eighteenth-century
British women were, I suspect, not sexual but finally political."[42] In a
different time and with an awareness of being excluded from access
to the people and places that would allow her to do what Behn and
Manley could, Haywood made the English novel political in a new
way, laying the foundation for the incisive revelations of social change
and class upheaval in Sarah Scott's *Millenium Hall,* Frances Burney's
Camellia and *The Wanderer,* and Jane Austen's *Emma* and *Persuasion.*

One of the most remarkable things about the English novel is
how self-reflexive and self-conscious it was from the very beginning.
As early as Fielding and Sterne, writers whom the twentieth century
has set up as founders of the novel parodied elements already identified as novelistic, called attention to them, and foregrounded their
artificiality. By the time Haywood wrote *Miss Betsy Thoughtless,* she
masterfully put literary and social discourses in dialogic relationship
to each other. Miss Flora in *Betsy Thoughtless* reacts to Trueworth's
engagement: "She tore her hair and garments, and scarce spared that
face she had taken so much pains to ornament. . . . But with the more
violence these tourbillions of the mind rage for a while, the sooner
they subside, and all is hushed again; as I remember to have somewhere read—'After a tempest, when the winds are laid,/The calm sea
wonders at the wreck it made'" (366). This is, of course, ridiculous;
however, the convention of hair and face tearing can be found in
Richardson's novels and countless more "moral" and "serious" novels, and it is as old as the Spanish and Portuguese novellas. Haywood
speeds up the sequence as satiric portraits do, parodies the opinion
that the more violent the outburst the sooner it is completely over,
and makes Flora, her scheming, and her trivial nature both an old-

fashioned story and a literary joke. Fineer's language is a parodic blend of genres. He describes his vision of their wedding night: "As Phoebus each night hurries himself into the Lap of Thetis, . . . so shall the next morning after our marriage behold us shine forth at once no less gorgeous than the bright ruler of the day, dazzling the eyes of the admiring world" (376).

As others have noted, the relationship of *Betsy Thoughtless* to Fielding and his novels is complex. For instance, the comments about him are both personal and part of the tone of *Betsy Thoughtless* as a fashionable novel of fashion. The authorial commentary at the head of each chapter works as Fielding's does in *Tom Jones* (to increase suspense, to sympathize or tease the reader, to make ironic comments, to direct attention and interpretation),[43] but there is also an element of parody both of Fielding's technique and his superior language. A common technique is lowering the level of diction: "Brings many things on the carpet, highly pleasing to Miss Betsy" (93). Many of the tags are deliberately superfluous, as is "Serves as a supplement to the former" (180). Some are familiar, frequent Haywoodian cautions: "Will prove . . . the extreme weakness of building our expectations upon mere conjecture" (432). Only a writer alert to good writing, pretentious writing, and, especially, novelistic discourses could put together such parodies.

Conclusion. It seems obvious that feminist theories have allowed us to interpret Haywood's work with increasing sophistication, and the application of the work of prose fiction theorists such as Mikhail Bakhtin has also provided new approaches. Today's emphasis on cultural studies, with its reconsideration of aesthetic standards and attention to material contexts, popular culture, and hegemonic processes, will contribute substantially to the elucidation of Haywood's texts and her career. Additional revisionary work will come as we continue to free ourselves from the fallacies of reading the history of the novel "back" and to comprehend more fully the implications of the fact that realism, any way we define it, was by no means accepted as the standard of novelistic practice and was certainly not the dominant mode for teaching. As I have argued elsewhere, the movement in the English novel throughout the century is toward the psychological, not the realistic, and Haywood's participation in associating the novel with the exploration of pathology, personality, and evil cannot be ignored.

It has been said that in great novels the characters come to know themselves better than any living individuals can ever understand themselves. Haywood seems ahead of Defoe, Aubin, and her other contemporaries in bringing her heroines to know themselves. Not only is there the kind of detailed movement from one emotion to the next, each of which the woman comes to understand and articulate, but many characters come to see themselves as separate from their hearer and from context (the world). This movement makes experiences, new possibilities for action, and other ways of experiencing visible and contributes to the subversiveness of many of her texts.

The number of topics, plot structures, and narrative voices that Haywood brought into literature is perhaps unmatched by any other eighteenth-century writer, and she is a major force in constituting the English novel as the form whose subjects are immediate reality, contemporary issues, and the politics of the personal. As Terry Eagleton reminds us, novels are "instruments which help to constitute social interests rather than lenses which reflect them" (*Rape* 4). While turning attention to her concerns, Haywood was insisting on the accuracy of her insights; of her characters, for instance, she once wrote, "no poetical Descriptions . . . if I have not made them speak just as they did, I have at least made them speak as Persons in their Circumstances would naturally do" (quoted in Ingrassia *Authorship,* 85). Out of her sometimes fantastic and often psychologically if not physically violent tales come dazzlingly "realistic" insights into the class and sex systems of her time. In "On the Origin and Progress of Novel-Writing" (1810), Letitia Barbauld wrote, "Let me make the novels of a country, and let who will make the systems." When a satisfactory new history of the novel is written, Haywood will have a place in this important theme.

How free writers ever are from genre conventions, their own horizons of expectation for the form in which they write, and the social forces that "construct" human beings can never be definitively known, but something of a unique person, a creative writer with agency, is always present. With the coming to maturity of Haywood studies will come increasing engagement with the questions and issues inherent in construction and agency and, inevitably, a drastic revision if not complete rewriting of The Story that has defined Eliza Haywood and her allegedly mercenary, bipolar career.

Notes

1. Respectively, Ros Ballaster, *Seductive Forms*, 197; Jane Spencer, *The Rise of the Woman Novelist*, 76–77; Cheryl Turner, *Living by the Pen*, 51–52; and Janet Todd, *The Sign of Angellica*, 147.

2. Other signs of this maturity are her near-ubiquitous appearance in recent anthologies and her presence in the center of new discussions of the story of the development of the English novel.

3. Great Britain presented conditions for peace in March 1709, and in May France accepted all of the articles except 37, which barred Louis XIV's grandson Philip from the throne of Spain. The Lords' 1707 resolution "no peace without Spain" resulted in a breakdown of the negotiations, but General Marlborough and Lord Treasurer Godolphin were blamed for extending the war.

4. See Joseph Addison, *The Late Tryal and Conviction of Count Tariff* (1713), and Daniel Defoe, *Memoirs of Count Tariff* (1713), his *Review* essays on Lady Credit, which begin on 1 August 1710, and his *Essay upon Publick Credit* (1710).

5. I discussed these forms in *Daniel Defoe: Ambition and Innovation;* see also Geoffrey Sill, *Defoe and the Idea of Fiction.*

6. See Charles C. Mish, *English Prose Fiction, 1600–1700,* and William McBurney, *A Check List of English Prose Fiction 1700–1739.* I have also searched the ESTC for the decade 1709–1719.

7. For instance, *Diverting Works* is a translation of *Para Todos* (1633), which was not by Cervantes but by Juan Perez de Montalban. It is six tales told by "the most Spritely Gentlemen" for the entertainment of a wedding party. Each night one will tell an "Amorous Adventure of his own," xi. I am grateful to my research assistant, Alice Kracke, for her work on this text.

8. I am using "work" as Fredric Jameson does; see especially "Metacommentary" and "Reification and Utopia in Mass Culture."

9. Among these are William Warner, "The Elevation of the Novel in England"; Ros Ballaster, *Seductive Forms,* 158; and Toni Bowers, "Sex, Lies, and Invisibility."

10. The women characters may become "sadder and wiser" or mature into an understanding of love, but their basic nature does not change. Male characters seldom experience change of any of these kinds.

11. I discuss the political implications of these strategies at some length in *Spectacular Politics,* 134–48.

12. Ingrassia points out the central importance of the fact that Haywood's "female subjects are frequently the daughters of bankers, merchants or aldermen: individuals of the middling classes consistently located in the socioeconomic and often geographical milieu of the City of London," *Authorship, Commerce, and Gender in Early Eighteenth-Century England: A Culture of Paper Credit,* 85. When page numbers for Ingrassia's works are not given, citations are to the manuscript, which she generously shared.

13. This essay refers to the Pandora edition of *The History of Miss Betsy Thoughtless,* the only one available before Christine Blouch's superior one.

14. It is instructive to compare the language and criticism, both contemporary and modern, of Penelope Aubin's seven novels published in the 1720s with that of Haywood's. The tone and diction of her novels is much more level and consistent and less idiomatic and ironic than Haywood's and Defoe's. See Samuel Richardson's characterization of Aubin's style in the preface to *A Collection of Entertaining Histories and Novels* (Aubin's seven novels), a collection published in 1739 by the prestigious group of, among others, Richardson, Arthur Bettesworth, Thomas Longman, and Charles Rivington; I am grateful to William Warner for calling my attention to this preface and the essay by Wolfgang Zach, which persuasively argues Richardson's authorship. Like Warner, I believe that Haywood is certainly the prime writer condemned in the quotation.

15. Bakhtin identifies this as one of the distinguishing features of the novel, *Dialogic Imagination,* 388.

16. Haywood occasionally uses the word "fraternity" to describe a male association that contrasts sharply to women's isolation or, in rare cases, small, supportive groups; cf., *Betsy Thoughtless,* and *Tea Table,* 20.

17. Ingrassia, *Authorship, Commerce, and Gender in Early Eighteenth-Century England.*

18. Defoe's "double" narrative voice has been the subject of much scrutiny and has often been criticized in the same terms as Haywood's; the most famous objections are, of course, Ian Watt's in *The Rise of the Novel,* and see Everett Zimmerman, *Defoe and the Novel,* 75–77, and Warner, *Licensing Entertainment,* 151.

19. Many critics have found this artless, confusing, or unpleasant. Dieter Schulz, for example, writes of an "ambiguous rhetoric, which seemingly adheres to ideological and stylistic patterns of romance, but actually undermines those patterns and supplants their idealism by lasciviousness," in "'Novel,' 'Romance,' and Popular Fiction in the First Half of the Eighteenth Century," 87.

20. See my "The Shadow of an Author: Eliza Haywood" and Warner, *Licensing Entertainment,* 216n. 18.

21. Martin Battestin has brought together an important collection of these; see *The Dictionary of Literary Biography,* 39, pt. 2: 557–658. William B. Warner's *Licensing Entertainment* gives a detailed account of the anti-novel discourse and the "symbiotic relationship" novelists like Haywood developed with this discourse in their own texts as both sides contested ways of reading. His discussion in chapters four and five of the debates over reading in Manley's *New Atalantis* and Haywood's and others' novels is especially illuminating. Most of my references are to his manuscript, and I am grateful to him for making it available before publication.

22. Here and elsewhere there seems to be a shadowy admiration for Aphra Behn; Behn contributed the Oenone to Paris from the *Heroides* to Dryden's *Ovid's Epistles, Translated by Several Hands* (1680) and translated two works by Fontenelle, *A Discovery of New Worlds* (1688) and *The History of Oracles* (1688). See Warner's important discussion of reading in *Love In Excess, Licensing Entertainment,* 111–21.

23. See my introduction to *Selected Plays and Fiction of Eliza Haywood.*

24. I am thinking of Mary Astell, Sophia, Mary Chudleigh, and numerous dramatists male and female. On the theatre's participation in discussion of these issues see my "'Endless Aversion Rooted in the Soul.'"

25. The phrase is J.M.S. Tompkins's and is quoted in Spacks, *Desire and Truth,* 175.

26. These are chapter headings in Richetti's *Popular Fiction before Richardson;* although I think we—and that includes Professor Richetti—have refined our knowledge of women novelists exponentially since the publication of his book in 1969, the way this book brought women writers to our attention and raised the level of criticism of them should not be forgotten.

27. See, for example, Margaret Doody, who says Haywood "established the seduction novel as a minor genre in English fiction," *A Natural Passion,* 149; Jane Spencer, who writes that Haywood is primarily responsible for the genesis of a sub-genre, one "begun by women and almost exclusive to them: the mistaken heroine who reforms," *Rise of the Woman Novelist,* 141, and Ros Ballaster, who argues that Haywood's amatory novels "mark the beginnings of an autonomous tradition in romantic fiction," *Seductive Forms,* 158.

28. Because others have explored Haywood's treatment of love plots and her use of gender and gendering in depth, including the merging of sex and economics, I shall largely omit this dimension of her work from my discussion. I should note, however, that I think many critics gender the readership and prioritize the sex of the writer earlier than historical evidence supports.

29. For example, Defoe writes in the Preface to *Roxana,* "If there are any Parts in her Story, which being oblig'd to relate a wicked Action, seem to

describe it too plainly . . . 'tis hoped you will find nothing to prompt a vicious Mind, but every-where much to discourage and expose it. Scenes of Crime can scarce be represented in such a Manner, but some may make a Criminal Use of them . . . and if the Reader makes a wrong Use of the Figures, the Wickedness is his own" (2).

30. See Joseph Bartolomeo, *A New Species of Criticism*, 19–20, 35–40; he begins chapter one, "Prefaces invite skepticism" (19). Perhaps the most derision has been visited on Defoe's preface to *Moll Flanders* with its comment that "as this work is chiefly recommended to those who know how to read it . . . it is hoped that such readers will be much more pleased with the moral, than the fable . . . ."

31. One exception is Carol H. Flynn; see "Consuming Desires: Defoe's Sexual Systems" in *The Body in Swift and Defoe*, 61–87.

32. Her original play, *A Wife to be Lett* (1724) deserves attention as a marriage critique.

33. The tectonic plates of language in Haywood's and other women's novels seem largely unexplored to me; an exception is Judith Kegan Gardiner's work in "The First English Novel," 212–13. Her remarks about Behn's *Love-Letters* here could productively be applied to many of Haywood's texts.

34. It could be argued that the acceptance of the "dilated" novel made it easier to do things that Haywood had tried to do in other ways.

35. The fourth would be on the novel's engagement with philosophy in the broadest definition of the term (political, economic, ethics, epistemology) with texts such as Godwin's *Caleb Williams*, Hays's *The Memoirs of Emma Courtney*, Charlotte Lennox's *Euphemia*, Holcroft's *The Adventures of Hugh Trevor*, Scott's *The Heart of Midlothian*, and Jane West's *A Tale of the Times*.

36. The quoted words are Habermas's, *The Structural Transformation of the Public Sphere*, 30–31; and see also Roger Chartier, *Cultural Origins of the French Revolution*, 34–7, and my introduction to *The Intersections of the Public and Private Spheres in Early Modern England*, 9–14.

37. Jean Bethke Elshtain, *Public Man, Private Woman*, xii.

38. In addition to the analyses of *The Adventures of Eovaai* in this collection, some important recent treatments are Jerry Beasley, "Portraits of a Monster: Robert Walpole and Early English Prose Fiction," Earla Wilputte, "The Textual Architecture of Eliza Haywood's *Adventures of Eovaai*," and my "The Shadow of an Author."

39. Thomas Lockwood, "Eliza Haywood in 1749," 475–76, and "William Hatchett, *A Rehearsal of Kings* (1737), and the Panton Street Puppet Show (1748)," 315–23, and for a detailed account of Haywood's prosecu-

tion see Catherine Ingrassia, "Additional Information on Eliza Haywood's 1749 Arrest for Seditious Libel," 202–4.

40. Haywood does the same thing with women. As Polly Fields says, Haywood shows "her central characters with other women collectively oppressed by the system, albeit acting autonomously" ("Manly Vigor and Woman's Wit," 259).

41. This is a topic explored in depth in Catherine Ingrassia's *Authorship, Commerce, and Gender in Early Eighteenth-Century England: A Culture of Paper Credit.*

42. Bohls, *Women Travel Writers and the Language of Aesthetics, 1716–1818,* 45. I argued in *Spectacular Politics* that women writers refused to be excluded from the public sphere and political debate; see chapters 3 and 4.

43. Examples such as these predominate and echo Fielding: "Contains nothing very extraordinary, yet such things as are highly proper to be known" (26); "Cannot fail of exciting compassion in some readers, though it may move others to laughter" (206); "very well deserving the attention of all those who are about to marry" (363); "Seems to demand, for more reasons than one, a greater share of attention than ordinary, in the perusal of it" (460).

Collusive Resistance

Sexual Agency and Partisan Politics in *Love in Excess*

Toni Bowers

Eliza Haywood's phenomenally popular first novel *Love in Excess* (1719–20), like the works of amatory fiction that preceded it in Augustan England, functioned in its day as a powerful work of Tory partisan polemic. But that polemic takes shape quite differently in *Love in Excess* than in the amatory fiction produced during Queen Anne's reign (1702–14). Dominated by the work of Delarivier Manley, amatory writing under Anne had featured obviously partisan allegorical plots. Few Augustan readers encountering *The New Atalantis* in 1709, for instance, would have had difficulty recognizing in the characterization of "Fortunatus" Manley's contempt for the first Duke of Marlborough, the age's most celebrated Whig, and for the political principles he represented. And for any who may have had such difficulty, a number of "keys" to the allegory's real targets speedily appeared. But when Haywood published *Love in Excess* at the start of the new decade, under a new dynasty and in the wake of the Jacobite Rebellion of 1715, she dispensed with Manley's allegorical style.

It has become something of a truism among critics that along with that style Haywood also dispensed with party politics *tout court*. In Haywood's work, according to recent consensus, amatory fiction's penchant for partisan involvement has been replaced with something else, though what that something might be remains a matter of some dispute—"a more general moralism," according to one critic, a readiness to "deliver nothing more than pleasure," according to another, "the articulation of passion itself," in the words of a third.[1] This essay argues, on the contrary, that *Love in Excess* continues the tradition of Tory partisanship that had characterized Manley's work, and indeed the tradition of amatory fiction, but in different form and for different purposes, in a changed political climate. Though it does not use allegory to make partisan arguments, Haywood's novel nevertheless serves Tory agendas. It does so most powerfully in its representations of female sexual agency, especially that of the novel's heroine, Melliora Frankville. By representing Melliora as a sexual agent at once rigorously virtuous *and* fully complicit in transgression, *Love in Excess* enacts and valorizes a model of virtue in which resistance and capitulation, though traditionally viewed as opposite sexual responses, paradoxically exist together and even enable each other, a model consistent with Tory strategies for constructing ideological integrity and partisan resistance at a difficult time.[2]

A central issue in *Love in Excess*—as in a host of influential works from the Augustan period[3]—is the problem of female sexual desire and expression, which together I call "sexual agency." Is it possible, Haywood's text repeatedly asks, for active sexual agency to exist alongside virtue in women? The question is dramatized in each of the novel's many overlapping plots, as characters act out hypotheses concerning the right and wrong ways for women to express heterosexual desire—which, it is taken for granted, all must feel. What defines female virtue in such a context is not the absence of desire, or even a refusal to express desire, but the *way* desire is expressed.

Every woman in the novel, for example, desires its irresistible hero Count D'Elmont, and virtually all, sooner or later, act on their desire. More than one takes sexual initiative with D'Elmont, transgressing to an extent that must have scandalized and titillated the novel's original readers. Haywood's desiring women scheme to encounter D'Elmont in secluded places, send him unsolicited love letters, and, when all else fails, even assault him physically, as in this scene between D'Elmont and the lustful Ciamara:

> Lost to all sense of honour, pride or shame, and wild to gratify her furious wishes, she spoke, without reserve, all they suggested to her, and lying on his breast, beheld, without concern, her robes fly open,

and all the beauties of her own exposed, and naked to his view. Mad
at his insensibility, at last she grew more bold, she kissed his eyes,—
his lips, a thousand times, then pressed him in her arms with strenuous embraces,—and snatching his hand and putting it to her heart,
which fiercely bounded at his touch, bid him to be witness of his
mighty influence there. (231)

Such temerity, however, goes unrewarded. Ciamara is the only aggressive woman who finds D'Elmont enough "moved by curiosity"
to give "his hands and eyes a full enjoyment of those charms," and
even here he is soon "restored to reason" (232). In all other such
encounters, D'Elmont responds to women's sexual overtures with cold
lack of interest, and makes it clear that women who take the initiative
in lovemaking become undesirable by virtue of their aggression. "Fie!"
the coquette Melantha exclaims as D'Elmont turns away her advances,
"is this an answer . . . to give a lady who makes a declaration . . . who
thinks it not too much to make the first advances?. . . . A woman,
where she says she loves, expects a thousand fine things in return"
(131). In response, D'Elmont reminds her that such a woman has
"more than a possibility . . . of . . . being disappointed," since "All
naturally fly, what does pursue,/'Tis fit men should be coy, when
women woe" (131).[4] Furthermore, the aggressively desiring women
in *Love in Excess* earn not only rejection but misery and death:
Melantha makes a hasty, loveless marriage, Alovisa is murdered, and
Ciamara commits suicide. Not just D'Elmont, but also Haywood, it
seems, delivers a strong disciplinary message to sexually "forward"
women.

   That message does not, however, extend to women's desire per se.
On the contrary, heterosexual desire is explicitly and repeatedly recognized in *Love in Excess* as an overwhelming, irresistible force for
women as for men. And since desire cannot be withstood, according
to a logic frequently repeated in the novel, those who fail to resist it
cannot be held accountable. For example, when the inexperienced
Amena capitulates to D'Elmont's sexual pressure, the narrator is entirely sympathetic: "What now could poor Amena do, surrounded
with so many powers, attacked by such a charming force without,
betrayed by tenderness within? Vertue and pride, the guardians of her
honour fled from her breast, and left her to her foe" (63). Later
D'Elmont himself claims to merit sympathy when, shortly after his

marriage to the scheming Alovisa,[5] he finds himself the helpless victim of "fierce, and raging" desire for his ward, Melliora. "Pity, even to criminals is allowed," he pleads, "and sure, where the offence is unvoluntary, like mine, 'tis due" (117). Most important, since desire is involuntary and all-powerful in *Love in Excess,* even when clearly transgressive it is not necessarily inconsistent with virtue, either for women or for men. "O! why" D'Elmont cries, "should what we can't avoid, be called a crime? Be witness for me Heaven! How much I have strugled with this rising passion, even to madness struggled!—But in vain, the mounting flame blazes the more, the more I would suppress it—My very soul's on fire—I cannot bear it—Oh Melliora!" (129). And indeed, D'Elmont's adulterous, near-incestuous desire for "the matchless Melliora" is *not* finally criminal in *Love in Excess,* but on the contrary, a force for good. It turns a heartless, merely ambitious libertine into a faithful lover and eventually into a virtuous, domesticated spouse, the soul of bourgeois respectability—as we learn in the novel's closing lines: "Those who in the Count's absence had taken a liberty of censuring and condemning his actions, awed by his presence, and in time won by his virtues, now swell his praises with an equal vehemence. Both he and Frankville [i.e., Melliora's brother], are still living, blest with a numerous and hopeful issue, and continue, with their fair wives, great and lovely examples of conjugal affection" (273). In *Love in Excess,* then, sexual desire is neither optional nor a punishable transgression; the question is not whether one will experience desire, but how one will express it. Not sexual *desire* but sexual *agency*—desire plus expression—is the problem.

The problem of sexual agency is thorniest, not surprisingly, in regard to the women in the novel. In *Love in Excess,* as in much of the fiction of Haywood's day, men's sexual behavior is a relatively straightforward matter—"self-interested," "short-lived and end-directed," as one critic has put it (Ballaster 175)—while women's sexual agency is potentially more problematic, more difficult to square with familiar measures of female virtue. Haywood's great achievement in *Love in Excess* is precisely the delineation of a strategy for reconciling the two. This strategy she works out in the characterization of the novel's heroine, Melliora Frankville, a sexual agent at once profoundly transgressive *and* exemplary of virtue. Furthermore, in the complicated construction of Melliora, Haywood implicitly mounts a Tory parti-

san argument, as we shall see. But first it is necessary briefly to sketch
the peculiar outlines of Toryism at the end of the 1710s.

In 1715, the year after Queen Anne died, two of her Tory
government's most powerful ministers, Robert Harley, Earl of Oxford, and Henry St. John, First Viscount Bolingbroke, were accused
of Jacobite collusion.[6] Oxford, whose guilt is still uncertain, was im-
prisoned for two years in the Tower. Bolingbroke escaped to France
where he confirmed all suspicions by signing on as James Edward
Stuart's Secretary of State and helping to engineer the Jacobite military invasion that took place later that year, one of several unsuccessful attempts during the Augustan period to regain the throne for the
Roman Catholic Stuarts in exile.[7] Though the Jacobite rebellion of
1715 failed to restore "the king across the water," it did accomplish
other, perhaps unintended, results. Most important, perhaps, the invasion reinforced nervousness in England about the Jacobite threat,
and the fact that Oxford and Bolingbroke seemed to have been implicated gave credence to the Whiggish insistence that all Tories were
merely Jacobites in masquerade. Indeed, the scandals of 1715 combined to undermine Tory credibility to an unprecedented extent—and
at a crucial juncture, too, when Britain was about to welcome a new
monarch, George I, and in his person a new dynasty, the foreign-born
Hanoverians. Only three years earlier, Tory ministers had won Queen
Anne's grudging trust after decades of Whig dominance, and at the
Queen's death Bolingbroke had overseen a systematic reduction of
Whigs from public office. Now Tories lost those long-sought victories
and entered a period of official proscription that would last for forty-
five years.[8]

For generations, historical interpretation of this period has been
dominated by the idea that proscription of such magnitude necessarily forced Tories either to capitulate at last to Whig ideologies or to
become Jacobites, either way erasing Tory identity and ideology from
the political scene. This argument drives a number of historical studies from Haywood's time until very recently, but perhaps its most
eloquent statement is found in W.A. Speck's *Stability and Strife,* a
distinguished work that has enjoyed considerable influence among
historians and literary critics, as well as in classrooms. According to
the argument for which Speck often serves as representative, the calamities and disgraces that beset the Tory party in the mid-1710s caused

a kind of partisan meltdown, the so-called "death of the Tory party," when Toryism disintegrated as an oppositional force.[9] Partisan struggle between Whigs and Tories, the central ideological and rhetorical conflict that had characterized political culture under Queen Anne, came to an abrupt halt after Anne's death, and was replaced by a degree of stability unimaginable during her reign.[10] Tories learned a form of compromise not far from abject capitulation, and that capacity for compromise helped to distinguish them from the ever-unequivocal Jacobites.[11]

In recent years, this interpretation has come under considerable attack among revisionist historians, and those espousing it have been reconceived not as impartial chroniclers but as part of a venerable but partisan tradition of Whig historiography. Reports of the death of the Tory party, the revisionists suggest, have been greatly exaggerated, and in fact a definitive—albeit beleaguered, complex, and collusive— Tory identity persisted throughout the period formerly supposed to have been characterized by Whiggish unanimity.[12] While "it would obviously be wrong to claim that the content of toryism remained stable from James II to George II," Linda Colley argues, "it would also be wrong to ignore the fundamental continuity in the tory stance on kingship, the Church, nonconformity and the organisation of the State. Even the mutations of toryism affirm this continuity" (*In Defiance* 117).[13] Colley refers to basic ideological tenets that had defined Toryism since the 1680s, when "Tory" came to stand for allegiance to Crown and Church and for non-resistance to royal authority.[14] According to revisionist interpretation, these were consistently understood to be Tory doctrines well into the eighteenth century—indeed, at least until the accession of George III—and they were ideals vastly more popular and sympathetic among "large sections" of the population than the perceived tenets of either Whigs or Jacobites.[15] In the minds of many in Britain, perhaps a majority, Tories seem to have been perceived as true Englishmen in contrast to both papist Jacobites and self-interested Whig politicos. It is true that internal conflict within the Tory party often derailed concerted action and that Tories were poorly organized in comparison to the highly efficient Whigs;[16] nevertheless, Tory resistance was far from extinct or irrelevant. The reduction of official situations for Tories meant *not* that all Tories disappeared or were transformed into Whigs or Jacobites, but that many continued to be active indirectly, underground, outside parliament and official channels; Tories became, as Colley puts it, "spokesmen for extra-parliamentary discontent" (*In Defiance* 174).

This thesis has been carefully demonstrated and by now carries considerable power. Indeed, it has become customary for historians to talk about two "ages of party": a first period of overt struggle[17] lasting roughly until the 1722 elections (a resounding defeat for Tories), and a second period of more underground party strife lasting until the reign of George III.[18] Despite traditional historical representations of full-scale Tory disintegration, it now appears more accurate to understand Toryism as a multiple, organic phenomenon in Augustan society, perhaps *especially* so after Queen Anne's death in 1714 and the failed rebellion of 1715. In short, although the tradition represented by *Stability and Strife* has influenced virtually all historians of Augustan England, it now seems indisputable that Speck's arguments form part of an unselfconsciously partisan narrative, a narrative implicated in a Whiggish dream of Tory evaporation that goes back to the partisan animosities of the Augustan period itself.

With all this in mind, it is illuminating to note the importance of the Whig version of Augustan history to the work of critics who deny partisan functions to Haywood's *Love in Excess*. In a discussion of "The Decline in Scandal Fiction," for instance, Ros Ballaster has argued that *Love in Excess* marks a "shift" in the very "nature of amatory fiction," a move away from partisan political concerns; while "the over-arching structure of a Tory ideology remains in place" in Haywood's work, that work is not, finally, "politically motivated," as Manley's had been a decade before (Ballaster 153, 156).[19] Not surprisingly, this argument is founded on a view of Toryism—and indeed, of what counts as political motivation and partisan work—that relies entirely on Speck's *Stability and Strife*.[20] In light of more recent historical work, however, the suggestion that Haywood's amatory fiction is without partisan function because it is not explicitly political becomes inadequate. It no longer seems necessary that amatory fiction be overtly partisan in order to perform important partisan functions.

Indeed, under the weight of proscription after 1715, Tory literary resistance might have been unimaginable *except* as the residue of apparently apolitical stories—stories like *Love in Excess*. When she constructs the heroine Melliora, a woman whose virtue can encompass even the most transgressive forms of heterosexual desire, Haywood implicitly mounts a defense of Tory practice and offers a rubric for the recuperation of partisan identity and integrity in the wake of thirty years of collusion—since the compromises of 1689—with principles many Tories could not subscribe to, yet dared not oppose.

Melliora first enters the novel in part 1, where, at her father's deathbed, she is introduced to her new guardian, D'Elmont. Despite D'Elmont's cynical marriage to Alovisa, he falls instantly in love with Melliora and begins a program of seduction familiar to readers of amatory fiction: D'Elmont engages Melliora in debates on love, encourages her to read Ovid, gazes on her while she is sighing by melodious streams, sneaks up on her while she sleeps, and so on. But Melliora is not simply the *object* of D'Elmont's desire: she is also an actively desiring sexual *subject*. She falls for D'Elmont at the same moment he falls for her—with better excuse, since initially she takes him for the suitor intended for her by her dying father—and her desire is every bit as strong as his. "Their admiration of each other's perfections was mutual," we are assured, "and tho' he had got the start in love, as being touched with that almighty dart, before her affliction had given her leave to regard him, yet the softness of her soul, made up for that little loss of time, and it was hard to say whose passion was the strongest" (90–91).

By making the attraction between Melliora and D'Elmont fully mutual, *Love in Excess* rejects cultural codes that assign primary sexual desire and initiation to men, making women mere respondents in a drama of gendered pursuit and resistance. As if in answer to the novel's sexually aggressive women, as well as to the victimized maidens who fill Augustan seduction stories,[21] Melliora's desire is carefully constructed to avoid both impertinence and passivity. Her virtue is not a matter of keeping apart from physical desire, of resisting desire as a foreign element appropriate only to men, or of failing to acknowledge whatever desire she may secretly harbor. Such models are manifestly at work in seduction stories contemporary with *Love in Excess*.[22] But for Haywood, female sexual virtue consists not of the absence or denial of desire, but in acting on desire in particular ways. Melliora's virtue is exercised *within*, not just *in response to*, transgressive sexual desire.

But at the same time, paradoxically, the desire that Melliora and

D'Elmont share *is* hierarchical as well. That Melliora feels originary sexual desire means, much of the time, little more than that she has twice as much resisting to do: she resists D'Elmont's raging male desire, like any number of besieged maidens in amatory fiction, *and* she resists her own desire for him. There is small likelihood that D'Elmont will share the work of resistance, though Melliora repeatedly begs him to do so. "What," he responds incredulously, "when I have thee thus! thus, naked in my arms, trembling, defenceless, yielding, panting with equal wishes, thy love confest, and every thought, desire?" (122). D'Elmont plots Melliora's seduction along resoundingly conventional lines, resolving, for instance, to rape her if necessary: only too easily "perswaded to follow his inclinations," he agrees with the rakish Baron D'Espernay that "on the first opportunity, Melliora should fall a sacrifice to love" (119). Even when D'Elmont momentarily falters in this resolution ("O her father's memory! My obligations to him! Her youth and innocence . . .!" [119]), he continues to see himself as the primary, indeed the only, sexual agent in the affair. Whether Melliora "falls a sacrifice," he assumes, will be entirely up to himself. "Love . . . has sent me here," he intones melodramatically after sneaking into her bedroom, "to charm thee, sweet resister, into yielding. . . . I will this night be master of my wishes!" (122).

In response, Melliora speaks what amounts to a different sexual language. Recognizing that it is "vain for her to resist" her lover physically—even "if she had had the power over her inclinations" (129)—she appeals instead to D'Elmont himself, asking him to refrain *because she desires him so much.* "I confess," Melliora replies, "I feel for you, a passion far beyond all, that yet, ever bore the name of love, that I no longer can withstand the too powerful magick of your eyes, nor deny any thing that charming tongue can ask" (129). Surprisingly enough, this confession does not herald Melliora's capitulation, as readers of amatory fiction before *Love in Excess* might have learned to expect. Typically, amatory fiction's women resist male advances only *until* they are overcome by answering desire: virtue, signaled by resistance, is opposed to desire, which always leads to capitulation. But Melliora describes her passion in breathless detail in order better to *resist* D'Elmont, to deflate his stagey pretences ("could'st thou . . . consent to see me pale and dead, stretched at thy feet, consumed with inner burnings?") with a desire all the more authentic for being realistic: "'[T]is better to die in innocence, than to live in guilt" (129).

By way of response D'Elmont attempts another well-worn line: the suggestion that as a woman Melliora cannot know "the thousandth part, of what this moment I endure" because her heart is "steeled . . . and frosted round with virtue." Melliora, though, will have none of it. "Unkind and cruel!" she cries, "do I not . . . bear, at least, an equal share in all your agonies? —Hast thou no charms—Or have I not a heart?" (129–30): I *do* have a virtuous heart, but it is *not* steeled and frosty; I want you just as much as you want me. Melliora's outburst goes far to explain the enormous popularity of *Love in Excess* in its day: not often did Augustan readers encounter such a forthright statement of lust in the mouth of a paragon of female virtue! Strangely enough, though, Melliora's passionate sexual agency functions here the way reductive female "virtue" functions in more traditional seduction stories, as the incentive and enabler of sexual self-restraint. Resistance is fully complicit with desire just as desire is a constitutive part of virtue. Melliora emerges as a surprising kind of female protagonist: a woman who declares sexual desire for a married man (her guardian, no less) and yet remains a paragon of virtue. Female virtue and sexual agency, even of the most transgressive kind, are not mutually exclusive options.

What makes this possible? Partly, I think, the fact that Melliora is also careful to subordinate her agency to D'Elmont's. Insisting on her "most susceptible, and tender heart," she begs the would-be seducer to save her from her own desire, thus apparently abdicating the agency she had so decisively assumed: "Now's the time to prove your self the heroe," she urges, "subdue your self, as you have conquered me, be satisfied with vanquishing my soul, fix there your throne, but leave my honour free!" (129) In fact, of course, Melliora never fully relinquishes control to D'Elmont, despite her supplicating language and even despite a series of encounters in which her resistance weakens steadily, until, by the end of part 2, only a bedtrick gone awry preserves her from a final, successful assault. Always she continues to lust for D'Elmont, to tell him about it, and, significantly, to renounce him against his passionate entreaties, even after his wife is dead and the two are technically free to marry. To this negative extent, at least,

Melliora retains sexual agency in their affair. But her declaration of
abdication is important because it signals the duplicitous form that
agency will take. To preserve her complicated status as virtuous, desirable, *and* desiring, Melliora's sexual agency henceforth will be mani-
fested indirectly, and through D'Elmont's. Her resistance will take the
form of asking D'Elmont to resist *her*—not primarily because of her
virtue or her vulnerability, as is usually the case in amatory writing,
but because of her desire.

Thus Haywood imagines a heroine whose active, transgressive
sexual desire operates in concert with her virtue by means of a paradox that we might call "collusive resistance," a kind of submission
that is itself ultimately a form of agency. Unlike amatory heroines
before her, Melliora feels and expresses transgressive lust, and does so
without losing her status as virtuous heroine. At the same time, paradoxically enough, Melliora's difference—her capacity for sexual agency
with virtue—is both complicated and enabled by conformity to that
familiar token of feminine allure, submission to men.

Perhaps this is why Melliora's and D'Elmont's subsequent encounters tend to devolve into more conventional exercises of male agency
and female passivity, leaving behind, to some extent, the early, more
complex encounters between equivalent sexual agencies. After a brief,
intriguingly mutual out-of-body orgasm, a moment when neither of
the lovers needs to pursue or resist—"She sunk wholly into his arms
unable to speak more. Nor was he less dissolved in rapture, both their
souls seemed to take wing together, and left their bodies motionless,
as unworthy to bear a part in their more elevated bliss" (130)—traditional gendered roles reassert themselves with something of a vengeance, as D'Elmont prepares "to take from the resistless Melliora,
the last, and only remaining proof that she was all his own" (130).
That D'Elmont is prevented by one of many carefully timed interruptions does little to alleviate our certainty that Melliora will ultimately
be "taken." "Oh! fear me not," D'Elmont is soon assuring the Baron,
"I will not be denied, each faculty of my soul is bent upon enjoyment" (145). Meanwhile, the formerly assertive Melliora feels "ready
to die with shame" over her confession of desire (134) and falls into
"dispair" when D'Elmont does not immediately attempt again to steal
into her room at night (143). Eventually regarding herself "as the
most guilty person upon earth" because of her desire for D'Elmont,

Melliora even contemplates "laying violent hands on her own life," though she settles at the end of part 2 for inflicting self-punishment in standard fashion, by entering a monastery (165, 168). The familiar pattern, in short, has by no means been superceded: the man still burns and plots, the woman, as usual, is plotted against, blames herself, and receives punishment. To a significant degree he functions as sexual agent, she as respondent. At the same time, however, Melliora's agency remains, though in somewhat attenuated form: she does in fact manage to resist D'Elmont until the end of part 2, at which point she acts decisively by becoming a novice and abjuring desire (as she thinks) forever. More fundamentally, there always remains in her person the unexpected juxtaposition of unlawful desire and unmitigated virtue.

As it draws to a close, Haywood's novel works increasingly hard to contain the radical possibilities Melliora represents. This project of containment becomes disturbingly clear in a scene late in the novel, where roles D'Elmont and Melliora had played early on are reversed— now *he* is asleep, and *she* is sneaking up on him. Melliora has been abducted from the monastery by the Marquess De Saguillier, a rake who openly states his creed: "[A]ll women may be won by force or strategem" (266). D'Elmont knows only that Melliora has disappeared, and is searching for her. In a coincidence characteristic of romance, he happens to pause in his quest to enjoy the hospitality of a friend, the same Marquess who is secretly holding Melliora prisoner. One night while D'Elmont is sleeping, Melliora creeps into his room and offers herself to him sexually, though without revealing her identity.[23] D'Elmont, as usual, makes it clear that female sexual initiative will not be tolerated: "I can esteem the love of a woman, only when 'tis *granted*," he informs his anonymous visitor, "and think it little worth acceptance, *proffered*" (256). But Melliora's forwardness, it turns out, is a special case, inflected by the earlier submission that granted sexual authority to D'Elmont. "'Tis but one look I ask," she implores at his bedside, "and if you think me unworthy of another, I will for ever shun your eyes" (256–57). One look is, of course, enough, and D'Elmont promptly springs into action: "[H]e flew out of the bed, catched her in his arms, and almost stifled her with kisses"—which she "return[ed] with *pretty near* an equal eagerness" (257, my emphasis). When at last D'Elmont "released her from that strict embrace he had held her in," Melliora is found "blushing, with down cast eyes" (257). His expression of desire is direct and aggressive, while she exercises the half-hearted resistance that is a hallmark of seduced maidens in amatory fiction: "He gave a loose to all the furious transports of his ungoverned passion. . . . Strongly he pressed, and faintly she repulsed. Dissolved in love, and melting in his arms, at last she found no words to form denials, while he, all fire, improved the lucky moment" (265). In a final, almost laughable, echo of the earlier bedroom scene, the lovers are interrupted by a knock on the door just when D'Elmont (but, significantly, not Melliora) is on the point of being "possest of all" (265). This time, however, the interruption does not herald another female admirer eager to throw herself on D'Elmont, but the staging of Melliora's ultimate submission—her formal abdication of all agency to D'Elmont (still her putative guardian) and her brother Frankville, who has accompanied D'Elmont in search of her. "This day shall give me to him who best deserves me," she declares; "[B]ut who that is, my brother and Count D'Elmont must determine; since heaven has restored them to me, all power of disposing of my self must cease; 'tis they must, henceforth, rule the will of Melliora" (267).

Final "disposal" of Melliora must wait, however, until her subjugation has been underlined by the quite literal prostration of her two final female foils, Charlotta (the fiancée of the Marquess De Saguillier until she was ruthlessly abandoned by him in favor of Melliora and who now serves in his household, disguised as a maid) and Violetta (who has traveled with D'Elmont and Frankville disguised as a boy page, merely in order to be near D'Elmont, whom she secretly adores). The prolonged abjection of these two comparatively minor female characters at the very end of the novel has seemed to some readers an unfortunate lapse on Haywood's part, a piling up of unnecessary story lines that merely delays and sours the happy ending to come. In the context of our discussion so far, however, we can recognize the odd intrusions of Charlotta's and Violetta's stories as necessary to an understanding of the costs involved in Melliora's final union with D'Elmont, a union that requires that she at once achieve and disown sexual agency.

The jilted Charlotta would certainly be within her rights to blame and distrust the unfaithful marquess. Instead, however, she grovels before him, winning him back by a combination of self-abasement and flattery so outrageous as to constitute a satire on masculine vanity.[24] Charlotta is not content merely to forgive this scoundrel; rather, she implores him to "banish from your mind all thoughts that you have injured me," actually "falling on her knees" and declaring that such a "humble posture . . . best becomes my prostrate soul" (269). Her entire self-denigration before the man who has not only disgraced and discarded her, but who is still at this moment seeking the hand of another woman, could hardly be more complete.

Except, perhaps, in the even more appalling abjection of Violetta who, in love with D'Elmont and aware that he has found Melliora at last, "dies for him, and asks no other recompence, than a last farewell" (270). "I would not deprive him of a moments happiness," Violetta gasps out in a death agony apparently brought on by little more than a generous wish to be out of the way. On the point of expiring, she is at last rewarded by the attentions of D'Elmont, who, forgetting "even the complaisance he owed to Melliora," rushes into Violetta's bedroom "like a man distracted" and "throwing himself on the bed by her" carries on in his usual inflated and near-comic style—not about her impending death but about her earlier decision to forgo "gay dresses" and don "a mean disguise" for someone so "unworthy" as himself (271). Not to be outdone, Melliora magnanimously commands Violetta to "Live, . . . and enjoy the friendship of my lord" (272). But Violetta insists that she must die, not only because of her hopeless love for D'Elmont but because she has now *revealed* it: "[L]ife after this shameful declaration," she insists, "would be the worst of punishments" (272). In keeping with the ethic of female desire at work throughout the novel, Violetta insists even at the point of death that her passion for D'Elmont is not *in itself* blameworthy ("nor do I yet believe my love a crime, tho' the consequence is so" [271]).[25] Indeed, she makes a great point of the virtuous character of that passion: ". . . I loved, 'tis true, but if one unchast wish, or an impure desire, er'e stained my soul, then, may the purging fire to which I am going, miss its effect, my spots remain, and not one saint vouchsafe to own me" (271). Desire itself—even desire that makes one "unable to support" the absence of the beloved, makes one leave home, break a father's heart, "wish . . . to know no other paradise" than the beloved, and prize him "more than life" (271–72)—is emphatically not inconsistent with virtue. What *is* criminal is Violetta's *declaration* of desire.

How can this be? In Melliora, as we have observed, Haywood imagines a woman who exercises active and transgressive sexual desire, who declares her desire forthrightly, and who does so without losing her status as virtuous heroine. In Violetta, while sexual *desire* is still irresistible and consistent with virtue, the new possibility of virtuous sexual *agency* for women seems to be withdrawn: expressing sexual desire, acting on it, is a crime deserving of death. What the contradiction reveals, I think, is considerable ambivalence about the feat achieved in Melliora—the representation of female sexual agency that is both collusive and resistant, both assertive and submissive. This ambivalence is apparent in the fact that while Melliora's active desire does emerge as part of her virtue, that virtue is still signaled by feminine submission; and by the end of the novel, submission has been elevated as the one indispensable mark of virtue in all three women—Melliora, Charlotta, and Violetta. In this way, while Melliora continues to constitute a remarkably unorthodox model of female sexual agency and is rewarded for it (she is, after all, the one who finally wins the prize, D'Elmont), the model she offers is disciplined so as to remain consistent with—not too threatening to—traditional patriarchal notions of feminine virtue and availability. Those notions are reinforced to the point of parody in Charlotta and Violetta; their tales, by interrupting and elaborating the final resolution of the main plot, place emphasis on the submissive aspects of Melliora's paradoxical submissive-and-resistant characterization. In this way, the really new aspect of female sexual agency that Melliora represents—the possibility of mutually constitutive resistance and complicity— is cast at the novel's end as an eccentricity, an exception that functions primarily to prove the rule.

The representation of Melliora in *Love in Excess* is important for what it can teach us about imaginable relations between female virtue and sexual agency in Haywood's day. But the assumptions on which Haywood bases her depiction of Melliora as a virtuous-while-complicit subject are political in a much broader sense. For the postulate that enables Melliora's story—the idea that virtue is not necessarily compromised by unavoidable complicity with transgressions against divine and social order—was in 1719 a statement with distinct partisan insinuations.

In partisan terms, Haywood's representation of Melliora's complicit-yet-virtuous sexual agency, her enactment and valorization of an indirect opposition I am calling "collusive resistance," is a means of authorizing a form of political agency structurally like that which had come to characterize Toryism since the 1680s. In Melliora's sexual agency, Haywood offers a model for reimagining collusion itself, the issue that bedeviled Tory credibility, and a chance to conceive of Toryism as more than a sellout. Unavoidable complicity even in wrong-doing, Haywood suggests in Melliora, need not, under certain conditions, be inconsistent with virtuous resistance. Concession, collusion, even capitulation can all be aspects of autonomous agency. By 1719, when *Love in Excess* first appeared, this was a message that Tories desperately needed to hear, a thesis capable of acknowledging decades of capitulation yet still providing reassurance of ideological integrity and viability.

Furthermore, in the characterization of Melliora Haywood argues, in effect, not merely for the acceptability but actually for the *supreme virtue* of resistance-within-complicity. There is resistance and there is complicity, but a model that fuses the two is *melior,* better. Thus Haywood does not merely redefine collusion as a means of resistance; she defines the habit of collusive resistance as preferable to that which is merely compromising and collaborative, on one hand, or merely negative and oppositional on the other. In this suggestion, I believe, Tories could find a means of distinguishing themselves from both Whig corruption and Jacobite abdication. *Love in Excess,* in short, models new ways of interpreting concession and capitulation, and teaches readers to imagine certain kinds of complicity as co-existent with autonomous integrity. By offering a heroine who is at once virtuously resistant to her lover's illicit desire *and* at every point complicit with it, Haywood offers readers a way to understand the beleaguered Tory position as a position of complex and collusive integrity—even difficult, heroic virtue—a place of ideological purity *within* unavoidable complicity.

My point is not that *Love in Excess* should be read as an organized allegory of Tory ideological crisis. There is no stable allegorical system of reference here and, as has often been observed, this fact starkly distinguishes Haywood's work from Manley's. But that divergence is not satisfactorily explained by saying that Haywood's work dwindles into "general moralism" (Ballaster 156) after the expiration of the Tory party, or that it is engaged in "the effacement of the public realm and the restriction of amatory narrative to private, personal, and secret transations" (Richetti *English Novel* 48). That Haywood "betrays no interest in *direct* political intervention" does not necessarily mean that her work is non-partisan or apolitical, that "the 'secret history' is *now* one of sexual intrigue"—as if that had never been the case before (Ballaster 154, my emphases). Recent historical interpretation allows us to understand, on the contrary, that Haywood's lack of "direct" partisanship may mean only that the partisan functions of *Love in Excess* are *in*direct, in keeping with Tory modes of resistance after 1715. *Love in Excess* offers a powerful instance of Tory thinking, an indirect primer in Tory interpretation and enablement.

Haywood's novel, in short, offers not a retreat from partisan politics but a shift in the paradigms available for the representation *of* partisan politics—a representation that is more of an evocation, a resonant gesture, than a straightforward depiction. In the creation of a heroine who acts on her desire, *Love in Excess* invites readers not only to interpret partisan struggle in new ways, but to imagine a new kind of partisanship altogether, even a new kind of politics, where possibilities exist outside the restrictive binaries that make "resistance" and "complicity"—like "loyalty" and "opposition"—seem exclusive alternatives necessitating an impossible choice.

Notes

1. Ballaster, 153; Warner, "Formulating" 284–85, 290; and Richetti, *English* 38.

2. This is not to say, of course, that Haywood never employed *Atalantis*-style writing. She manifestly did so in works such as *Memoirs of a Certain Island* (1724–25) and *Secret History* (1726). My concern here, however, is to understand Haywood's partisan narrative strategies in *Love in Excess*. The complicated connections between Haywood's work and that of her predecessors is a subject I take on in some detail in a book I am now writing, tentatively titled, *"Force or Fraud": Gendered Agency and Party Politics in*

British Seduction Stories, 1680–1750. There I argue that in terms of method, *Love in Excess* owes less to Manley's *Atalantis* than to earlier works of amatory fiction, notably Aphra Behn's *Love-Letters Between a Nobleman and His Sister* (1684–87). In *Love in Excess*, as in Behn's *Love-Letters*, Tory partisan agendas are supported by means of subtly revisionary representations of female sexual agency. For how this works in Behn's *Love-Letters*, see Bowers, "Seduction Narratives."

3. Besides the early amatory fictions of Behn, Manley, and Haywood, in which female sexual agency is always crucial, we might think, for example, of Pope's *Rape of the Lock*, Lillo's *London Merchant*, and Richardson's novels, to name only a few of the most prominent examples.

4. Cf. 256. "Woe" is pronounced "woo" (Oakleaf 131n. 2).

5. Haywood also calls her "Alovysa" and, sometimes, "Aloisa" (e.g. *Love in Excess* 104, 42). Significantly, the name is, as Oakleaf notes, "a version of Eloisa or Eloise, English forms of Heloise, the name of the medieval woman famous for her tragic love," whose story Pope had retold just two years before (1717) in *Eloisa to Abelard* (Oakleaf, *Love in Excess* 42n. 1).

6. That is, of treasonous plotting on behalf of the Roman Catholic descendants of James II, who lost the throne at the Glorious Revolution of 1688–89. James died in exile in 1701. Thereafter, Jacobite hopes centered on his son James Edward, (known to the Jacobites as James III (of England and Scotland), to his enemies as the Pretender and (after the birth of his own son) the Old Pretender. Later, Jacobites struggled to restore James Edward's son, Charles Edward (Bonnie Prince Charlie or Charles III for Jacobites; for those with Hanoverian sympathies, the Young Pretender). For accounts of the falls of Oxford and Bolingbroke, cf. Cruickshanks, "Religion and Royal Succession" 35–36; Bennett 173–95; Colley, *In Defiance* 57–58; Brian Hill, *Growth* 154–56; and Szechi 160–95.

7. Jacobite invasions of Britain were undertaken in 1708, 1715, 1718, and 1745; the most considerable of these were the "'15" and the "'45." There were also a number of invasion plots and scares — in 1720–21, 1743–44, and even as late as 1759.

8. For Anne's late willingness to permit Bolingbroke "to purge the government and armed forces of remaining Whigs," see Brian Hill, *Growth* 143–44. Cruickshanks gives specifics about the subsequent "purge" of Tories under George I: "Tory army officers lost their commissions, sometimes without compensation. . . . Tory lawyers could no longer become judges or K.C.s. The lower clergy, who were overwhelmingly Tory, could not become bishops. . . . Tory merchants could no longer get government contracts, or directorships in . . . great public companies. Moreover, many Tories, from old

parliamentary families, could no longer afford to stand for Parliament" (*Political Untouchables* 3–4). For more on proscription, cf. Bennett 175–204; Colley, *In Defiance* 21–23, 55; Cruickshanks, "Religion" esp. 34; and Jones esp. 87–88.

9. I borrow the phrase "the death of the Tory party" from Holmes's essay "Harley, St. John and the Death of the Tory Party" in *Britain*. Cf. Speck *Stability* 128–29. Cf. Plumb, *Growth of Political Stability* 172: "[B]y 1725, Tories were outcasts . . . by 1733 . . . Toryism as far as party politics at the centre was concerned had become quite irrelevant." Cf. Bennett 185–87, 192–95; Clark, *Samuel Johnson* 6; Brian Hill, *Growth* 146–68; Szechi 54, 194.

10. For influential works enforcing the idea of late-Augustan stability, even unanimity, see Plumb, *Growth of Political Stability*; Holmes, *British Politics*. What ideological division did persist took shape, according to this argument, not on partisan lines but along a new power binary, "Court vs. Country." For one rebuttal to this view, see Cruickshanks, *Political Untouchables* 2. For a fairly nuanced contrast between the aggressively partisan 1710s and the more quiescent (though not necessarily homogenous or non-partisan) 1720s, cf. Downie, *Development of the Political Press* 119–26; Jones 87–88.

11. Szechi 53. For an attempt to undermine the stereotype of Jacobites as untouched by doubt and incapable of compromise, see Bowers, "Tories and Jacobites."

12. See J.V. Beckett's excellent and fair-minded summary of the debate and recent points of consensus (1–18). The revisionary thesis is variously argued in the work of Cruickshanks, Clark, Fritz, and Colley, to mention only a few of the most influential names. For representative formulations, see Cruickshanks, "Religion" 39–41; Brian Hill, *Early Parties* 57. Clark (*English Society* 1–41) offers a spirited attack on "Whig historiography," a tradition that he traces back to Burnet's *History* (pub. 1724–34), taking in the work of MacCaulay (pub. 1848–61) and Trevelyan (pub. 1931–34) as well as their more recent heirs (e.g., Plumb, Speck, and Holmes).

There is, of course, considerable variety of opinion among the revisionists. Colley (*In Defiance*), e.g., pointedly disagrees with the majority's interpretation of Augustan Tories as fundamentally "careerist" (25), and Clark is virtually alone in his contention that a majority of Tories remained consistently loyal to the exiled Stuarts.

13. Cf. Szechi, who in the course of a consideration of Jacobite elements within the Tory party offers a subtle reading of the various factions within Toryism; despite Toryism's many internal divisions, Szechi too finds ideological coherence between 1689 and 1750. Cf. Clark's *Samuel Johnson*, which, in the process of attempting to define Johnson's ideological allegiances, illu-

minates the changing positions of Tories during the reigns of the first three Hanoverian kings.

14. Cf. Cruickshanks, *Political Untouchables* 1. And cf. Feiling, who traces Tory beginnings to the sixteenth century (13–96).

15. Colley, *In Defiance* 89, 125. Cf. Holmes, *British Politics* 248, 284. Colley demonstrates (119ff, 173–74) that even after 1715, "electoral oligarchy . . . did not always favour the Whigs," tracing the "tenacity" of the Tory party through mid-century (119). "If one considers . . . post-1714 whig advantages . . . ," she observes, "then the problem to be investigated is not why the tory position in the constituencies deteriorated in this period, but rather how the party was able to survive at all" (124).

16. Bennett 173–79, 195–97; Colley, *In Defiance* 53; Holmes, *British Politics* 38, 286–93, 300–307, 329–35.

17. "Overt" need not, of course, mean "sincere." Whether the famously furious partisan activity under Anne was really ideologically driven or to some extent merely ritualistic or serving other interests is a point for the historians to decide. For the former opinion, see Cruickshanks, *Political Untouchables*; for the latter, see Colley, *In Defiance*.

18. Dickinson and even Speck now subscribe to a distinction between the *parliamentary* and the *political* relevance of Tories (and of partisan activity more broadly), a distinction first constructed in the work of revisionist historians (e.g., Cruickshanks, "Religion" 41).

19. Cf. Oakleaf's introduction to *Love in Excess*, where he argues that Haywood seeks to replace ideologically derived "social judgment" with the "private" (i.e., individual and subjective) "authority of desire" (13–14).

20. The only historical study besides *Stability and Strife* cited in Ballaster's chapter on Haywood is Bertrand A. Goldgar's *Walpole and the Wits* (1976), mentioned briefly in support of her dismissal of the possibility of "literary-political opposition" on the part of "such Scriblerians as Pope, Gay, Swift, and Arbuthnot" on the grounds that these writers' resistance was "by no means an organized campaign" and only took place in imaginative writing, rather than in what we would now call journalism. Colley's argument that Tory resistance was necessarily indirect but nevertheless potent exposes weaknesses in such reasoning, particularly in the assumption that instances of resistance in imaginative writing do not count as "political opposition."

21. Stereotypical female victims abound in Augustan amatory fictions. The title character in Haywood's *Lasselia* (1723) perfectly illustrates the type: beautiful, young, inexperienced, and ultimately ruined. In *Love in Excess*, the role is played by Amena, who epitomizes all that is naïve, presuming, responsive, passive, and victimized. Significantly, Haywood dispenses early with that familiar tale (and with Amena herself) in favor of female charac-

ters who act against type, testing varieties of female sexual agency. Alovisa, Melantha, and Ciamara represent one version of a more overt female sexual agency, Charlotta and Violetta (discussed below) represent another; all are, to some extent, perversions of the ideal set forth in Melliora.

22. For example, recall that it is secret desire ("an Earthly Lover lurking at her Heart") that makes Pope's Belinda a legitimate target for rape (*Rape of the Lock,* 1714 ed., 3.144). The same assumptions are much in force more than twenty years later in Richardson's *Pamela* (1740), when the virtuous title character resolutely denies being physically attracted to the sexually insistent "master"—until he proposes marriage.

23. Later we learn that this is in fact Melliora's *second* visit to the guestroom. The night before, as Melliora soon confesses, she had found D'Elmont sleeping and decided not to wake him, since he slept "so fast, that even fancy was unactive, and no kind dream, alarmed you with one thought of Melliora!" (265). D'Elmont's dreamless sleep is important, because it recalls the parallel scene in part 1 where Melliora declared her love unconsciously, while dreaming. This narrative expedient preserved the heroine's claim to virtue while revealing her desire, and tempered her later waking declarations. In the later scene, notably, there is no need for the indirection of sleep-talking: D'Elmont is allowed to speak his desire directly.

24. Charlotta's flattery of the marquess is also obligingly cast as a manifestation of competition between women. "Come, my lord," she cajoles, "you must at last take pity on my sufferings; my rival, charming as she is, wants a just sencibility of your deserts, and is by that less worthy even than I; Oh, then remember, if not to me, what 'tis you owe your self your own exalted merits, and you will soon determine in my favour" (269).

25. The "crime" Violetta refers to most immediately is the death of her father, a result of her sudden disappearance from home. "By my shameful flight," she says, "I was the murderer of my father" (271). Less directly, she refers to the "crime" of declaring her love for D'Elmont, as is made clear later in the same paragraph.

Masquing Desire

The Politics of Passion in Eliza Haywood's *Fantomina*

Margaret Case Croskery

The heroine of Eliza Haywood's *Fantomina; or Love in a Maze* (1725) indulges her sexual desires with remarkable freedom, creativity, and sensual enjoyment. Instead of insisting (as many eighteenth-century novels were wont to do) that "virtuous" women should repress their sexual desires, Haywood grants the heroine of *Fantomina* the same urgency of sexual desire that Restoration drama grants its rakes. Although many critics find Haywood's characterization of the passionate woman problematic, *Fantomina* actually offers an alternative paradigm for understanding Haywood's use of passion to explore the politics of seduction.

Haywood's popular fictions of the 1720s are often considered important primarily as examples of the "fable of persecuted innocence" that Richardson would later perfect in *Pamela* and *Clarissa*.[1] This "fable" typically featured a heroine who was seduced and then pathetically abandoned. It was popularized in the seventeenth century by the enormously successful *Les Lettres Portugaises* (1669), which was followed by numerous translations, imitations, and adaptations over the next half century.[2] Describing Haywood as a "magnificent technician" of the persecuted maiden trope, John J. Richetti regrets her continued production after *Love in Excess* of fable after "fable of persecuted innocence, exploiting over and over again the same erotic-pathetic clichés and the same rhetoric of love's power and the tragic and compulsive dramatic universe it implies" (*Popular* 208). To be sure, Haywood's novels, dramas, and periodicals certainly include many vignettes of women seduced by men who eventually betray them. But her plots are almost all driven by the tangible, amoral, directive, conflicting, incarnate experience of female desire, as opposed to the simple threat of male sexual predation. More often than not, persecuted maidens such as Amena (*Love in Excess*, 1719–20) serve as cautionary backdrops in Haywood's tales, rather than as controlling fictions.[3] The distinction is an important one. Without it, Haywood is too easily characterized as a hack-writer simply exploiting popular fantasies of female victimization for mass consumption, or as a proto-feminist unfortunately capitulating to the patriarchal oppression she simultaneously indicts. *Fantomina* escapes both criticisms. It champions the primacy of passion as an essentially amoral, motivational force capable of redefining female virtue. It thus poses not only a playful alternative to the Restoration paradigm of male and female sexuality, but it also provides a serious alternative to our own modern psychoanalytic interpretations of the semiotic nature of sexual desire. In fact, a careful reading of *Fantomina* allows a developed appreciation for both her sophisticated understanding of the politics of seduction and the shared contingencies of social and narrative fictions.

Praised by her contemporaries as "The Great Arbitress of Passion," Haywood was famous for the manner in which she portrayed the powerful experience of male and female sexual desire.[4] In *Love in Excess* (1719–1720), Haywood's narrator comments authoritatively that "passion is not to be circumscribed; and being not only, not subservient, but absolutely *controller* of the *will*, it would be mere madness, as well as ill nature, to say a person was blame-worthy for what was unavoidable" (1994 ed., 205). Using this argument to excuse both male and female sexual desire, the love-smitten heroine of Haywood's *The Force of Nature* (1725) dodges the claims of an unwanted suitor by reminding him that "Passions are involuntary, and perhaps 'tis as impossible for you to shake off yours, as it would [be] for me to forget mine" (13). Haywood's heroines are rarely punished simply for experiencing sexual desire, nor are they always punished simply for acting upon it. Thus, for example, despite Melliora's obviously strong sexual desire in *Love in Excess,* she embodies the novel's ideal of a virtuous heroine and she ultimately achieves conjugal felicity.[5] In another example from the same novel, Melantha beds the man she desires, despite the fact that instead of pursuing her he actively tries to avoid her. Indeed, even after discovering she is pregnant, she suffers no ill consequences for her aggressive sexual behavior. In *The Fruitless Enquiry,* Haywood's narrator expostulates that "It is a fault . . . to wish with too much ardency, which Heaven sometimes punishes with the utmost severity" (49), but Haywood's earthly plots rarely treat that fault harshly. Although some of Haywood's novels insist on the distinction between passion as "a chaste and holy Flame" (*Persecuted Virtue*) and the strictly sensual experience of lust, the "vilest passion" (*Fruitless Enquiry* 28), Haywood is less interested in maintaining the distinction between lust and love than she is in portraying love as "an Heroick Passion" that "ought never to be repented or ashamed of" (*History of Jenny and Jemmy Jessamy* 3:134). Indeed, the virtuous heroine of *The Fruitless Enquiry* ultimately achieves what she wishes for with "too much ardency."

However, as many critics have noticed, there are problems with this emphasis on the overwhelming power of passion.[6] Haywood's emphasis on the involuntary female response to her own desires seems to imply a lack of female agency even as it champions the power of female desire. Jane Spencer comments that Haywood's "frequent narrative pronouncements, in *Love in Excess,* about the inescapable power of love, especially over weak women, debar her from the cogent analysis of the politics of seduction, which is Manley's strength as a feminist" (117). So too, Ros Ballaster argues that Haywood's heroines accomplish at best an ambiguous form of mastery, one based only on a deferred closure of the heterosexual romance. In *Fantomina,* Ballaster argues, the heroine's desire allows her merely to "re-enact" the seduction scene, not to control it (181–92). Thus, the Haywoodian heroine cannot quite successfully assert herself as an agent in the heterosexual romance, since she is ultimately at the mercy of her own passion and/ or the patriarchal social structures rendering that passion neurotic.

However, Haywood's greatest hallmark—her firm, rather Humean decision not to ignore the role of passion as "*controller* of the *will*"— complicates without compromising her standing in the canon as an effective feminist voice. When a Haywoodian heroine suffers, it is usually because her innocence has made her incapable of recognizing or achieving her own desires. In *Love in Excess,* for example, Amena's story of (almost) seduced maidenhood reminds the reader "how miserable is that womans condition, who by her mismanagement is reduced to so poor a comfort as the pity of her lover" (73). In this manner, Haywood's amoral portrayal of the experience of female desire (in which "mismanagement" rather than the fact of desire forms the basis for judgement) seems remarkably aligned with David Hume's claims about the basis for judging passion: "Where a passion is neither founded on false suppositions, nor chuses means insufficient for the end, the understanding can neither justify nor condemn it" (416). Haywood's amatory fictions of the 1720s do not, of course, develop the philosophical implications of a passion-based account of virtue Hume considers later in his famous *Treatise* (1739–40). Haywood never claims, as Hume would do, that "Reason is, and ought only to be the slave of the passions" (415), but she certainly represents this subordinate relationship in her fictional portrayal of the amoral, controlling force of passion, whether or not she is conscious of its full philosophical implications. Thus, it is simply worth noting that Haywood's emphasis on the primacy of passion as a motivating force does not necessitate, any more than Hume's later claims would do, a loss of moral or political agency.

This insistence upon the compatibility of female agency and female passion exists in all of Haywood's fictions, but it is perhaps easiest to see in *Fantomina.* An ostensible tale of seduced innocence, this story radically rewrites the tale of the persecuted maiden. Its heroine is introduced as "A young lady of distinguished Birth, Beauty, Wit, and Spirit," fresh from the country, visiting London chaperoned only by her aunt. The narrator prepares the reader for her inevitable ruin by stressing her inexperience and lack of supervision: "She was young, a Stranger to the World, and consequently to the Dangers of it; and having no Body in Town, at that Time, to whom she was oblig'd to be accountable for her Actions, did in every Thing as her Inclinations or Humours render'd most agreeable to her" (258).

Naturally, trouble ensues. One evening at the theater, *Fantomina's* heroine observes the conversations between some prostitutes and gentlemen. Wondering "in what Manner these [prostitutes] were address'd" and why men of taste "threw away their Time in such a

Manner" (257–58), she decides to satisfy her curiosity by disguising herself as a prostitute. Subsequently, she is so charmed with the attentions of the rakish Beauplaisir that she arranges to meet him privately, still maintaining her disguise as prostitute. Although the heroine intends not to run "any Risque, either of her Virtue or Reputation" (261), she is compromised by both her disguise and her inexperience. By depending "on the Strength of her Virtue, to bear her safe thro' Tryals more dangerous than she apprehended this to be" (260), she commits the first fatal error of most persecuted maidens. Although she fears the consequences of continuing to meet Beauplaisir, she thinks she can protect her own virtue, despite the fact that her desires for him have become "wild and incoherent" (261). It is thus no surprise when this heroine finds herself in the conventional trap of the persecuted maiden: "Shock'd . . . at the Apprehension of really losing her Honour, she struggled all she could. . . . In fine, she was undone; and [Beauplaisir] gain'd a Victory, so highly rapturous, that had he known over whom, scarce could he have triumphed more" (262–63).

This scene is powerfully disturbing in no small part because Beauplaisir cannot distinguish between the heroine's pain and his own "Victory." Indeed, the heroine's own confusion about the social ramifications of disguising her identity (a confusion analogous with her conflicting desires to resist and encourage a sexualized atmosphere) raises the deepest questions surrounding the definition of consensual sex. Persecuted maiden stories often stress just these questions; however, when a heroine's innocence has led her into a seduction she has resisted, the persecuted maiden genre typically resorts to the pure pathos inherent in the heroine's swan-song of despair. (Clarissa, for example, temporarily goes insane.) However, the pathos of female victimization rarely dominates the Haywoodian story. Here, the heroine flirts with despair only briefly. Beauplaisir's offer of money in response to her tears made her "quite forget the Part she had assum'd" and she demands of Beauplaisir, "Is this a Reward . . . for Condescentions, such as I have yeilded to? —Can all the wealth you are possess'd of, make a Reparation for my Loss of Honour? —Oh! no, I am undone beyond the Power of Heaven itself to help me!" (263). This fustian language is typical of the persecuted maiden genre but not typical of this heroine's normal speech patterns, nor, obviously, does it belong to those of the prostitute she impersonates.

After almost confusing the role she is playing with that of the traditional persecuted maiden, this heroine chooses another role entirely—one in which she maintains her integrity by continuing to act upon her own desires. Beauplaisir is confused when the heroine hurls aside his money in an attitude of high disdain completely out of character with the profit-motivated, street-wise prostitute he believes her to be. This incongruity is analogous with the heroine's own decision to privilege her personal character over the public identity she has assumed, without losing the benefit of her diguise, and it introduces a subtle cognitive dissonance into what should (according to the persecuted maiden formula) be a moment of undiluted pathos. Shifting the reader's attention from the heroine's misery to her seducer's point of view, Haywood further emphasizes Beauplaisir's concern, rather than the heroine's despair. Beauplaisir "omitted nothing that he thought might make her easy," and all the while Haywood reminds us how puzzled he is: "[T]he Destraction she appeared in . . . heighten'd his Wonder, so it abated his Satisfaction: —He could not imagine for what Reason a Woman, who, if she intended not to be a *Mistress,* had counterfeited the Part of one, and . . . lament[ed] a Consequence which she could not but expect" (263). His concern is real, and he has some reason to be confused about the role he has played in forcing her will.

Through Beauplaisir's confusion and concern, Haywood shifts the reader's attention from pathos to strategic issues of self-representation. The "mirror" of Beauplaisir's initial confusion after the rape forces the heroine to see her disguise as prostitute from his point of view. Simultaneously perceiving herself as persecuted heroine and willing prostitute, the heroine experiences an internal dislocation of self. This moment is analogous to that described by Jacques Lacan of an infant's first traumatic gaze into a mirror, when "self" becomes "other" (Lacan, *Écrits* 1–7).

Haywood, however, is no Lacanian. She allows her heroine to understand the concept of self-as-sexual-object only in order to assume greater control over an alternative relationship to self. Her new perspective allows her to recognize the inadequacy of the role of the prostitute/persecuted maiden and to create an alternative public/private persona. Soon, her "Eyes resumed their softning Glances," as she guesses at Beauplaisir's confusion and appreciates his concern. She decides to create a fictional analogue for her "true Name and identity" to avoid "the Danger of being expos'd, and the whole Affair made a Theme for publick Ridicule." She resolves that if "he boasted of this Affair, he should not have it in his Power to touch her Character: She therefore said she was the Daughter of a Country Gentleman, who was come to Town to buy Cloaths, and that she was call'd *Fantomina*" (264).

Her name is not "Fantomina." That is simply her second disguise, and it represents a more sophisticated public fiction than her earlier disguise as prostitute. Behind it, she remains remarkably safe from the loss of honor, financial ruin, and emotional harm which traditionally plague the maiden raped by a man who does not intend to marry her. When Beauplaisir asks why she has feigned her identity as a prostitute, the heroine understands that without this knowledge, he cannot "touch her Character." This moment marks the heroine's embryonic realization that her control over her own desire depends upon a presentation of self that capitalizes upon an ostensible, not an actual, loss of agency.

The couplet by Edmund Waller on the title page of *Fantomina* first signals this text's playful relationship to paradigmatic power dynamics within representations of sexual agency: *"In Love the Victors from the Vanquish'd fly. / They fly that wound, and they pursue that dye."* This couplet rhymes itself into a paradox that Haywood's *Fantomina* will explode. Waller's pun on the word "dye," equates the "little death" of sexual orgasm with death itself to complicate an ostensibly simple comparison between love and war (that is, both love and war involve "Victors" and "Vanquish'd," but in love the victors fly from the vanquished). The deceptively simple dis-analogy and the balance within the rhyming iambic pentameters hide the internal paradox produced by the final pun. (In love, it seems, both wounded and wounder "dye.")

As the victor/vanquished trope played itself out in Restoration drama, the "Victor" was often the rake who managed to "wound" and then "fly" his mistress with the most creative zeal. For example, George Etherege's Dorimant recites this very couplet after casting off one mistress to begin pursuit of the next in *The Man of Mode* (IV.iii.52–53). Significantly, Dorimant's status as rakish "victor" wanes precisely when he begins pursuit of the woman he will ultimately marry. That union, like most restoration marriages, is not part of the play, because (as Aphra Behn's sequel to *The Rover* and Lord Rochester's biography both demonstrate), marriage is incompatible with the fundamental sexual energy of the Restoration rake. Since "They pursue that dye," Dorimant's decision to chase Harriet signals his ultimate vanquishment as a sexually victorious rake.

Fantomina explodes the victor/vanquish'd paradigm by playfully exposing its operation within both Restoration comedies and stories of persecuted maidens. As the emotional "negative" of Restoration comedy, persecuted maiden stories typically exchange the comedic lens for the sentimental, focusing not on the joy and wit involved in the chase, but on the misery produced as predators catch and abandon their prey. The paradox of the rake's victory thus becomes the double-bind of the persecuted maiden, forced to chose between the task of repressing her irrepressible desires or facing sexual betrayal, familial ostracization, and/or social ruin. By incorporating elements of disguise, wit, and sexual freedom found in Restoration comedy into a narrative which initially evokes the same "horizon of expectation" as stories of persecuted maidens, Haywood draws attention to the fact that both genres share the same victor/vanquish'd paradigm. This conflation highlights the inadequacies of the paradigm in both genres.

Recent approaches to *Fantomina* have used the lens of Lacanian psychoanalysis in order to understand better the manner in which this story calls these gendered dichotomies (subject and object, victor and vanquished) into question.[7] I am suggesting, however, that Haywood's psychoanalytic understanding of desire preempts Lacanian-style analysis. In Lacanian theory, desire for the physical pleasure of bodily union, *jouissance,* is only a by-product of a zero-sum game in which the unconscious (formed by the language that structures it) is doomed to pursue a need (a lack) that does not involve the body. Instead it "results from a logical exigency in speech" (Lacan, *On Feminine Sexuality* 10). These logical exigencies of language subordinate the body and its sexual drives to the "law of the signifier" and explain the behavior of the Restoration rake. Using Lacanian semiotics, then, one may ground Waller's paradox in a modern understanding of subjectivity. Because a subject "fades" before the object of desire, he never actually satisfies his desire by possessing it. The persecuting rake must seduce and run in order to satisfy the never-ending (because unachievable) desire of the subject to occupy its position as subject. For Lacan, too, sexual victory implies vanquishment.

However, *Fantomina* overturns fundamental assumptions about the semiotic structure of the unconscious crucial to Lacanian psychoanalysis. And while this novel could hardly be described as "domestic," it is vitally involved in the process of destabilizing what Nancy Armstrong describes as the "reigning metaphysics of sexuality" (25). From the moment the heroine sees herself in the "mirror" of Beauplaisir's initial confusion, the fact of her own desire reveals possibilities within "otherness" that Lacan's traumatized infant might not at first imagine. Once she recognizes these possibilities, she bridges the ostensibly unbridgeable gap between subject and object. *Jouissance* becomes the goal rather than the by-product of a sexual consummation she refuses to define in terms of the politics of subject and object, or victor and vanquished. Although Haywood carefully orchestrates *Fantomina* so that part of the pleasure of reading derives from guessing which role the heroine will finally occupy ("victor" or "vanquish'd") the heroine never fully inhabits either role, because her deliberate and successful manipulation of her role as "other" demonstrates the manner in which those social norms that identify a sexually active female as morally compromised victim are themselves social fictions. In fact, the power of female sexual desire to create alternative social fictions is precisely what *Fantomina* celebrates.

Fantomina undercuts the Lacanian ideology implicit in the victor/vanquish'd scenario of persecuted maiden stories in which the loss of sexual virginity is tantamount to the loss of virtue itself. Richardson will explore a similar idea in *Clarissa*, but he does so by separating the physical fact of sexual violation from the supreme virtue of chastity. Lovelace's virtues are those of the Restoration rake, while Clarissa's virtues are those recommended by contemporary conduct books. Lovelace is charming, handsome, witty, and sexually potent. Clarissa (like many a persecuted maiden) is innocent, trusting, gentle, tender, and, most important, capable of great suffering. Which is to say, she is ripe for exploitation. Like Waller and Haywood, Richardson complicates the simple binary opposition between victor and victim by placing a hero from Restoration comedy in a novel of domestic fiction. When Lovelace reflects ruefully that Clarissa "can look me into confusion, without being conscious of so much as a *thought* which she need to be ashamed of" (Richardson 943), the thoughts of which she need not be ashamed are, of course, sexual ones. Lovelace rapes Clarissa and the physical victory is his, but his "conquest" is bereft of victory because she does not in the least enjoy it. Instead, the sexual shame she experiences at the loss of her physical integrity devolves upon Lovelace as well. Soon after the rape, Lovelace becomes the supplicant, unable to obtain permission even to visit the woman he had hitherto held captive.

Although Richardson went to great lengths to create a female victim whose sexual desires are trumped by her virtues, the disturbing implication of his otherwise laudable attempt to separate the fact of rape from the loss of female virtue is that his story portrays female sexual desire as compromising moral integrity.[8] Such was the plight of most persecuted maidens in the amatory fictions which preceded and followed *Clarissa*. Haywood's novels should be sharply distinguished from this familiar tradition, however. Her use of the myth of the persecuted maiden in *Fantomina* is as sophisticated as the use Richardson makes of the myth in both *Pamela* and *Clarissa*. However, Haywood's use of female victimization, and her association of female passion with female virtue, is so different from Richardson's that it might even be misleading to speak of her as a precursive writer of persecuted maiden stories.[9] Lovelace fits the Lacanian paradigm—the ostensible satisfaction of his desires only reveals the impossibility of ever attaining them. Haywood invokes that paradigm only to undermine it.

Consistently, Haywood grants her heroines the right to sexual desire, and refuses to define female sexual virtue in terms of chastity or a victimized sexual objecthood. Enthusiastically projecting a self that can be perceived as "other," *Fantomina*'s heroine remains outside the paradigm of victorious subject and victimized object that play such a central role in both Restoration drama and fictionalized accounts of persecuted maidens. Instead, she defines virtuous love in terms of sincerity and constancy, without ever questioning her own right to sexual curiosity or desire. When she asks Beauplaisir for his vows of constancy after the rape, she tells him that his "Love alone can compensate for the Shame you have involved me in; be you sincere and constant, and I hereafter shall, perhaps, be satisfy'd with my Fate, and forgive myself the Folly that betray'd me to you" (264).

Instead of castigating herself for acting on her own desires, this decid-edly Humean heroine seeks to "forgive" herself only the "Folly" of being betrayed. From this point on, she refuses to equate sexual desire with moral culpability. Constancy, not chastity, becomes the primary signifier for virtue (female *and* male). Indeed, the narrator remarks to the reader that "with her Sex's Modesty, she had not also thrown off another Virtue equally valuable, tho' generally unfortunate, *Constancy*. She loved *Beauplaisir;* it was only he whose Solicitations could give her Pleasure; and had she seen the whole Species despairing, dying for her sake, it might, perhaps, have been a Satisfaction to her Pride, but none to her more tender Inclination" (268). This remark defines con-stancy as a virtue that, far from being polluted by sexual desire, actu-ally seems contingent upon it. The radical redefinition of constancy as a positive, moral expression of sexual desire suggests that a tradi-tional female virtue (constancy) can be predicated upon female pas-sion. It is because passion is *"controller* of the *will"* that the heroine's constancy remains steadfast. In true Humean fashion, Haywood's definition of both female virtue and agency are motivated and de-fined by passion.

Furthermore, this heroine's fantasies of sexual desire include both parties "languishing" and both "compelling." She wants "to hear him sigh, to see him languish, to feel the strenuous Pressures of his eager Arms, to be compelled, to be sweetly forc'd to what she wished with equal Ardour" (268). By thus eliding traditional gendered sexual roles, *Fantomina* introduces the possibility that in the fluid realm of sexual desire, gendered subject-object distinctions (and thus the roles of victor and vanquished) are more in flux than they are in semiotic structure.

But the heroine is not allowed unalloyed enjoyment for long. De-spite his vows of eternal constancy, Beauplaisir eventually plans a lengthy visit to Bath in order to pursue new sexual conquests. "Fantomina's" reaction to this potentially devastating state of affairs reminds the reader just how far she is from being rendered helpless by passion: "From her first finding out that he design'd to leave her be-hind, she plainly saw it was for no other Reason, than that being tir'd of her Conversation, he was willing to be at liberty to pursue new Conquests; and wisely considering that Complaints, Tears, Swoonings, and all the Extravagancies which Women make use of in such Cases, have little Prevailance over a Heart inclin'd to rove, and only serve to render those who practise them more contemptible, by robbing them of that Beauty which alone can bring back the fugitive Lover, she resolved to take another Course" (267–68). As Richetti reminds us, "Complaints, Tears, Swoonings" are the primary emotional capital (the pathetic half of the "erotic-pathetic cliches") within the typical persecuted maiden story. However, almost as if to debunk the emotionally charged affect of those stories that depend upon the near-hysterical misery of their heroines to exploit the emotions of their readers, Haywood emphasizes this heroine's calm decision to forgo such hysterical laments. "Fantomina" has better roles to play than that of the persecuted maiden. This attitude toward the hysterical "extravagancies" of the distressed maiden is evident throughout Haywood's works, even in those which allow more tragedy into the plight of the persecuted maiden.[10]

By refusing to exploit the potential misery of the abandoned sexual victim, Haywood again subtly transforms the traditional moral codes (which punished active expression of female sexual desire) into her own hierarchy of virtues derived from an insistence on the directive force of passion. The "Beauty which alone can bring back the fugitive Lover" was standard eighteenth-century conduct book parlance for the moral beauties of patience, submission, and clemency (or, at least, silence). These were the common prescriptions for the virtuous wife seeking to reclaim an adulterous husband.[11] Here, however, Haywood humorously appropriates the standard conduct-book rhetoric for her own use, matter-of-factly interpreting "that Beauty" as erotic control. And the heroine plans her next step accordingly.

She secretly follows Beauplaisir to Bath and transforms herself into a country lass (whose name, "Celia," hints at the innocent relationship to sexual pleasure of the pastoral shepherdess). Like Pamela, this heroine also dons the country-attire of a "round-ear'd Cap." Unlike Pamela, she delights in the very artifice of the transformation: "The Dress she was in, was a round-ear'd Cap, a short Red Petticoat, and a little Jacket of Grey Stuff; all the rest of her Accoutrements were answerable to these, and join'd with a broad Country Dialect, a rude unpolish'd Air, which she, having been bred in these Parts, knew very well how to imitate, with her Hair and Eye-brows black'd, made it impossible for her to be known, or taken for any other than what she seem'd" (268). So disguised, she takes a job as chambermaid in

Beauplaisir's new lodgings. When Beauplaisir attempts to seduce "Celia," she feigns a virgin innocence (but succumbs to his amorous embraces with lusty alacrity).

These successive disguises (from "prostitute," to "Fantomina," to "Celia the country lass") steadily introduce comedy into this story's initially tragic "horizon of expectation." Instead of the certainty that this heroine will fall victim to the traditional misery of the persecuted maiden, it now seems that she will use disguise to her sexual advantage, much like the heroine of a Restoration comedy. However, as I have discussed above, Haywood eludes the victor/vanquish'd paradigm in both genres by refusing to claim the victory her sexual masquerade allows.

As Terry Castle reminds us, masquerades were inherently a public activity "equated with the sexual act itself; the metonymic relation between masquerades and sex becomes a metaphoric one" (43). Haywood's own warning about this metonymic relationship demonstrates her acute awareness of it (43). But by creating a "private masquerade" (an activity as oxymoronic as a "private carnival"), the heroine of *Fantomina* literalizes the metaphor, utilizing the powerful masquerade trope against itself in order to explore the role masks play in *creating* desire in both the spectator and the masked agent.

Here it might be objected that despite this discovery, female victory still eludes this Haywoodian heroine (Schofield *Masking*, 47–48), or that "In the melancholy reiteration of female defeat at the hands of the fictionalizing male libertine," *Fantomina* provides only a temporary respite from the ultimate persecution necessarily awaiting the seduced maiden (Ballaster 192). However, *Fantomina* refuses to equate sexual victory with either sexual pleasure or the pleasure inherent in possessing the epistemological upper-hand. Her fantasies, like her masquerade disguises, thus escape complicity in what Luce Irigaray describes as the male economy of sexual desires, where a woman "can 'appear' and circulate only when enveloped in the needs/desires/fantasies of others, namely, men" (Irigaray, 133–34).[12] Haywood illustrates instead, the power of desire to subordinate the categories of subject and object to the fictions that create those dichotomies.

Certainly Haywood does not ignore the fact that private desires cannot exist outside of the social ideologies that structure them, but she ultimately refuses to privilege the political over the personal any more than she privileges reason over passion. The danger of indulging female desire within the constrictive forces of a patriarchal ideology is one she takes pleasure in exposing and avoiding. *Fantomina*'s heroine embraces the psychical and physical pleasures involved in eliding realms of sexual object and subject, and she recognizes the capacity of both male and female desire to write fictions of seduction for each other. If the heroine does not begin her adventures with an awareness of the danger inherent in disguising one's self as a sexual-object, she quickly learns it by gaining a better understanding of the manner in which disguise can function both to obscure and to amplify sexual agency. At first, the heroine mistakenly delights in the ostensible power the attractive female object exercises over her male admirers. She "was not a little diverted in her Mind at the Disappointment she shou'd give to so many, each of which thought himself secure of gaining her" (258). This is a serious mistake. By donning a private mask outside the public masquerade arena where such a disguise announces its own ambivalence, the heroine forgets that she has abandoned the protection of her own social identity with its attendant status and power. She mistakes her power as an object for that of a subject and discovers too late that she has no control over Beauplaisir's actions. Although, as we have seen, Haywood quickly mitigates both Beauplaisir's "triumph" and the heroine's misery, this first "seduction" scene is actually a rape, and it marks the moment at which the heroine learns she cannot simply follow personal desires without regard to the patriarchal social structures that largely define the public arena in which those desires exist. However, as soon as the heroine realizes that "the personal is political," she also realizes that both the personal and the political are fictions as capable of being defined by desire as they are of defining it.

Male sexual mastery is also linked to the fragility of such social constructions. If the heroine's first shift from "prostitute" to "Fantomina" mildly suggests that Beauplaisir's sexual "victory" is possible only because of the heroine's disguise, the second seduction scene asserts this point with comic force. As Beauplaisir ravishes "Celia the Country Lass," the narrator describes the seduction in tones which are decidedly tongue-in-cheek: "His wild Desires burst out in all his Words and Actions; he call'd her little Angel, Cherubim, swore he must enjoy her, though Death were to be the Consequence, devour'd her Lips, her Breasts with greedy Kisses, held to his burning Bosom her half-yielding, half-reluctant Body, nor suffer'd her to get loose, till he had ravaged all, and glutted each rapacious Sense with the sweet Beauties of the pretty *Celia*, for that was the Name she bore in this second Expedition" (269–70). Beauplaisir masters neither his desires (which "burst out" uncontrolled) nor the basic facts of the situation (his country lass is, after all, the same "Fantomina" in whom he believes he has lost sexual interest). His incongruous use of standard romance clichés ("he must enjoy her, though Death were to be the Consequence") only highlights the sense in which the "rapacious" role he plays as "victor" is not as well imagined or creatively controlled as the role of the "victim" who has willed this seduction from start to finish.

The second seduction scene is no "reenactment" of the first. The political dynamics of seduction have altered considerably. In the first seduction, the heroine struggled against the strenuous "Pressure of [Beauplaisir's] eager Arms" because she had failed to recognize the social ramifications inherent in masking herself as a sexual object. In the next seduction however, Beauplaisir's mastery becomes the fantasy created by the fiction of her disguise. Completing the comedy inherent in this pseudo-mastery, Beauplaisir once again mistakenly believes he ought to offer money for services rendered. This time, the heroine has the droll presence of mind to take his gold with an "humble Curtesy." Completely in control of both the role she is playing and her own ironic assessment of the situation, the heroine makes a joke ostensibly at her own expense. Holding the payment in pretended confusion, she asks Beauplaisir "O Law, Sir! what must I do for all this? He laughed at her Simplicity, and kissing her again . . . bad her not be out of the Way when he came home at Night. She promis'd she would not, and very obediently kept her Word" (270). Whereas the first offer of money had shocked the heroine into forgetting her disguise and rendered her discourse similar to the persecuted maiden's, this second offer elicits a joke between the "obedient" heroine and the reader concerning Beauplaisir's belief that the money he offers is compensation for his sexual mastery. In fact, the heroine needs no compensation. Her loss of innocence is purely voluntary (and purely fictitious). By pretending not to understand the terms of Beauplaisir's sexual conquest ("O Law, Sir! what must I do for all this"), she privileges her alternative viewpoint in which money is an incomprehensible compensation for non-consensual sex. Here, mutually satisfied desire is the more sophisticated "Simplicity" that Beauplaisir cannot grasp.

In part, because her perception of her role and her desires are changing under this succession of disguises, the third seduction provides an increasingly sophisticated understanding of sexual dynamics. After Beauplaisir tires of "Celia," he makes arrangements to leave Bath. Undaunted, the heroine dons yet another disguise, this time as the "Widow Bloomer." She stops Beauplaisir's carriage as it departs from Bath and requests his assistance in conveying her as fast as possible to London because, she explains, her brother-in-law is about to abscond with her widow's inheritance. Like the previous two disguises, this one reveals to the reader as much as it conceals from Beauplaisir and operates as a metaphor for the heroine's own perceptions of her role. Her disguise as "Fantomina" allowed her to act upon her desires, naively trusting in Beauplaisir's avowed constancy. The disguise as "Celia" allowed her to embody the pastoral ideal of sexual pleasure combined with innocence. This third disguise as a recently bereaved widow reveals the heroine's sense of loss in the face of Beauplaisir's repeated inconstancy, and also her determination to retrieve what might otherwise be stolen—her ability to define for herself the personal valence of their sexual interaction and the nature of female sexual virtue.

Despite the difference in Beauplaisir's manner in this third seduction (he too plays roles), the heroine's disguise continues to confuse the roles of seducer and seduced. In the carriage on the way to London, Beauplaisir did not

> offer, as he had done to *Fantomina* and *Celia* to urge his Passion directly to her, but by a thousand little softning Artifices, which he well knew how to use, gave her leave to guess he was enamour'd. . . . He now took the Liberty of kissing away her Tears, and catching the Sighs as they issued from her Lips. . . . She said little in answer to the strenuous Pressures with which at last he ventur'd to enfold her, but not thinking it Decent, for the Character she had assum'd, to yeild so suddenly, and unable to deny both his and her own Inclinations, she counterfeited a fainting, and fell motionless upon his Breast. (273–4)

The implication of force, which was painfully strong in the first scene and a subject for humor in the second, is not present at all in this third scene. The "strenuous Pressures" transform themselves into a cautious venture "to enfold" the woman whose tears he has kissed away. In this third seduction, there are still no clear victors or vanquished, and the erotics of seduction have changed again.

Although Haywood is usually associated with an enthusiastic dedication to amatory writing, it is crucial to note that there is often something she prefers to sex. After carefully preparing the reader for the erotic union between the "Widow Bloomer" and Beauplaisir, the narrator interrupts abruptly and refuses to provide the promised climax. Treating the reader instead to a disquisition on the reasons the heroine's disguises have been so successful, the narrator explains that "there are Men who will swear it is an Impossibility, and that no Disguise could hinder them from knowing a Woman they had once enjoy'd" (274). Thus, the narrator makes it clear that this heroine's success is largely due to her ability to manipulate the "amatory codes" that define the process of seduction.[13] Indeed, this heroine's skill at creating herself as a sexual object is nothing short of masterful:

> She was so admirably skill'd in the Art of feigning, that she had the Power of putting on almost what Face she pleas'd, and knew so exactly how to form her Behaviour to the Character she represented, that all the Comedians at both Playhouses are infinitely short of her Performances: She could vary her very Glances, tune her Voice to Accents the most different imaginable from those in which she spoke when she appear'd herself.——These Aids from Nature, join'd to the Wiles of Art, and the Distance between the Places where the imagin'd *Fantomina* and *Celia* were, might very well prevent his having any Thought that they were the same. (274)

Just as Haywood earlier played with the rhetoric of traditional conduct books, here she toys with standard notions of aesthetics. In his *Essay on Criticism* (1711), Alexander Pope advised that "*True Wit* is *Nature* to Advantage drest" (Butt, 1963 ed., 153). Haywood suggests instead that true advantage results from nature dressed by wit. The "Aids from Nature, join'd to the Wiles of Art" are in the service of passion, not Art. While Haywood takes the facts of oppression for granted, she recognizes an amoral, apolitical power in passion to define the aesthetics of seduction. In short, she recognizes the power of desire to create fictions of desire.

As if to underscore the fact that both fictions and readers of those fictions are necessary for seductions, Haywood's abrupt intrusion in the anomalous first person narrative voice draws attention to the reader/voyeur's dependent status in *Fantomina*'s seduction of the reader. By denying the reader's satisfaction at this particular sexual climax, Haywood emphasizes the control exercised by the author of fictions of seduction. In *Fantomina,* both Haywood and the heroine share this role. The fact that the reader never learns the heroine's "true" name (we learn only that she is addressed as "Lady ——") further underscores the manner in which both Beauplaisir's and the reader's sexual satisfactions are dependent upon the personal and political fictions which enable seduction. The reader's pleasure matters, but he controls the objects of desire no more than Beauplaisir does.

As the title implies, the heroine of *Fantomina* pantomimes a self, "masquing" her own desires without masking them. Donning masks that reveal aspects of her own identity, she acts upon desires with which she could not otherwise identify. The relationship between reader and character thus achieves its own delicate metonymy. Once the reader is implicated in the vicarious experience of this heroine's titillating desires, he shares her ambivalent relationship to victory and vanquishment—and, ultimately, to culpability and innocence.

Reading is closely related to the construction of social fictions and as such, readers and writers of those fictions of seduction are an important part of all Haywood's amatory tales. *Love in Excess* begins with Alovisa's letter to D'elmont. Amena discovers she has been betrayed when she finds another letter Alovisa has written. So too, in almost all of Haywood's narratives, seductions are begun, continued, and discovered in an exchange of letters between the participants or interested spectators. *Fantomina* is no exception. The heroine of this novella sends Beauplaisir two notes. One is from "Fantomina" complaining that he has lost his desire for her (he did not write to her the entire time he was in Bath). The other is from the "Widow Bloomer" offering to entertain him at his earliest convenience. Beauplaisir's response to "Fantomina" constitutes its own masterpiece of seductive fiction. He pretends to chide her for her lack of confidence in his constancy by declaring that "*If you were half so sensible as you ought of your own Power of charming, you would be assur'd, that to be unfaithful or unkind to you, would be among the Things that are in their very Natures Impossibilities*" (276). This is more true than Beauplaisir realizes. In fact he has not yet been unfaithful, precisely because the heroine's "Power of charming" is much greater than Beauplaisir understands.

By itself this clever circumlocution might well have fooled someone less skilled in reading amatory codes. However, Beauplaisir's clever fictions cannot fool the woman who creates the fictions of her own desire instead of adopting those of the male who inspires them. Writing to her simultaneously as the "Widow Bloomer," Beauplaisir claims that "*Never was Woman form'd to charm like you: Never did any look like you, —— write like you, —— bless like you; —— nor did ever Man adore as I do.*" Beauplaisir's exaggerated insistence that no woman looks, writes or "blesses" like the Widow Bloomer (when he has in fact failed to recognize her identity in three previous seductions) suggests that Beauplaisir has serious trouble cracking amatory codes, even as he imagines himself a master of them.

Still, Beauplaisir's sense of mastery, however fragile, provides much of the pleasure in this novella and catalyzes its essential tensions. Early in the novel, when he first learns that "Fantomina" was only pretending to be a prostitute, he "did not doubt by the Beginning of her Conduct, but that in the End she would be in Reallity, the Thing she so artfully had counterfeited" (264). At various times throughout this novel, it seems that the heroine may indeed conform to Beauplaisir's description and mistake the mask for reality. After the rape, she almost defines herself in relation to her pathetic predicament. Later, when the heroine reads Beauplaisir's deceptive letters, she once again loses a sense of herself as both subject and object: "TRAYTOR! (*cry'd she,*) as soon as she had read [the two notes from Beauplaisir], 'tis thus our silly, fond, believing Sex are serv'd when they put Faith in Man: So had I been deceiv'd and cheated, had I like the rest believ'd, and sat down mourning in Absence, and vainly waiting recover'd Tendernesses" (277). This moment produces a cognitive dissonance similar to the earlier fustian outburst, however. If he has betrayed her, he has betrayed her for herself. It is Beauplaisir, not "Fantomina," who is not half as sensible as he ought to be of the heroine's "Power of Charming." That power, which is motivated by passion and directed by her new understanding that she can satisfy her own desires by representing herself as "other," is formidable.

As in the earlier outburst, the heroine quickly resumes comic control by renewing her commitment to a re-assessment of female sexual virtues. The heroine's discovery that Beauplaisir is guilty of the two vices commonly attributed to women ("Inconstancy and Levity of Nature"), allows Haywood to suggest that the desire to rove is a kind of sexual handicap. Whereas Beauplaisir's note to "Fantomina" implies a correlation between his inconstancy and her decreasing power to charm, the events of this story and the narrator inform us differently. We learn that Beauplaisir "varied not so much from his Sex as to be able to prolong Desire, to any great length after Possession" (267). Faithful, patient, and constant, the heroine responds to Beauplaisir's "twice-decay'd Ardours" (270) with ever-increasing efforts to "keep his Inclination alive" (267). She helps him sustain what he cannot sustain on his own. Thus the heroine consciously makes the connection between her ability to control her sexual persona and Beauplaisir's inability to maintain his sexual appetite when she reflects "on the Unaccountableness of Men's Fancies, who still prefer the last Conquest, only because it is the last.——Here was an evident Proof of it; for there could not be a Difference in Merit, because they were the same Person; but the Widow *Bloomer* was a more new Acquaintance than *Fantomina,* and therefore esteem'd more valuable" (277). Haywood links this sexual failure with the inability to make moral and aesthetic distinctions—Beauplaisir cannot determine "a Difference in Merit" any more than he is capable of assessing a woman's true "Power of charming." Intent on the "Conquest" of the latest seduction, Beauplaisir is incapable of distinguishing value or merit in the women he seduces, and thus his own sexual "Merit" becomes suspect.

This new understanding of Beauplaisir's incapacity and a sense of the strength inherent within her own sexual desire is apparent in the heroine's fourth disguise that, for the first time, calls Beauplaisir's attention to the fact that he might be objectified by his own desires in a way that she is not. As "Incognita," her disguised character is even more reflective of her "real" identity than any of her previous "disguises." She acknowledges her wealth, her social status, and her sexual desire. Most importantly, she acknowledges the fact that her identity as a sexual object is a masked identity. She tells him: *"There is but one Thing in my Power to refuse you, which is the Knowledge of my Name."* He accepts the provocative invitation. And after vainly trying to persuade her to remove her mask, he spends the night with her in amorous play. At the erotic climax of this seduction, Haywood's narrator once again interrupts the reader's erotic satisfactions by refusing to exploit the simple titillation such a scene might provide. Instead of the explicit details of their physical pleasure, the reader is informed only that "It would have been a ridiculous Piece of Affection in her to have seem'd coy in complying with what she herself had been the first in desiring: She yeilded without even a Shew of Reluctance: And if there be any true Felicity in an Amour such as theirs, both here enjoy'd it to the full" (284).

The erotics of seduction have changed yet again. For the first time the narrator questions the authenticity of sexual pleasure without the pleasures of "coy" resistance. Perhaps this is because the heroine has now discovered a significant difference between her desires and Beauplaisir's. Although much of her pleasure in these seductions was no doubt derived from exercising her own skill at dodging the role of victim in the victor/vanquish'd paradigm, her *jouissance* was never dependent upon her status as victor (only upon her ability to escape the role of victim). The same cannot be said for Beauplaisir. Using language traditionally applied to the impatient rake's desire for sexual intercourse, this fourth seduction scene emphasizes the extent to which Beauplaisir's pleasure is dependent upon what Kristina Straub describes as the desire to dominate a feminized other (3–18). Of course, Straub is including feminized males in her description of "feminized other" to push at the boundaries of this dichotomy, but the general description applies to heterosexual dynamics as well. Despite the satisfaction Beauplaisir "found in her Embraces, nothing ever long'd for the Approach of Day with more Impatience than he did." He becomes "determin'd in his Mind to compass what he so ardently desir'd, before he left the House" (284–85). The language of sexual desire here operates on "Incognita's" mask instead of her body because Beauplaisir associates sexual victory with the signifiers of his status as the dominant spectator rather than physical pleasure. If masks create an image or spectacle for the benefit of a spectator, they also imply a spectator behind the spectacle, implicating the spectator *as* spectacle. He wants to remove her mask to experience the authority it denies him as spectator of his own mastery.

At this point, *Fantomina* has thoroughly unwound Waller's essentially Lacanian Victor/Vanquish'd paradigm. "In Love the Victors from the Vanquish'd fly," but here, Beauplaisir perceives himself as vanquished by the heroine's sexual agency that refuses to recognize victors and victims. Angry, he leaves "Incognita's" house vowing never to return. Vanquished, not victorious, he flies.

Just as the heroine of Fantomina eschews the role of either victor or vanquished, *Fantomina* makes it difficult, even in the end, to identify this text's heroine as victim or victor. After the "Incognita" episode, the heroine's unexpected pregnancy and the arrival of her mother threaten to subsume the text's comedic tendencies into the tragic closure of the traditional persecution maiden scenario. Pregnancy is typically the ultimate trap of the persecuted maiden—it cannot be masked, or even "masqued."[14] A seduced maiden bearing a child out of wedlock is usually cast out from her family and forced into religious seclusion, starvation, or prostitution. In Haywood's *The Rash Resolve,* when the heroine becomes pregnant out of wedlock, she imagines herself "driven to Want, to Beggary—exposed to public Infamy, the Sport of every Slave" (85–86). When Beauplaisir himself predicts such a fate for "Fantomina" he "had good Nature enough to pity the Misfortunes he imagin'd would be her Lot" (264). However, in this text pregnancy and inconstancy both constitute only paradigmatic challenges to traditional notions of the sexual victor and the sexual victim. The narrator reminds the reader that neither pregnancy nor the arrival of her mother alone would have curtailed the successful continuation of the heroine's plans since "she would easily have found Means to have skreen'd even [her pregnancy] from the Knowledge of the World, had she been at liberty to have acted with the same unquestionable Authority over herself, as she did before the coming of her Mother" (287).

That authority reasserts itself after the heroine's mother summons Beauplaisir. The heroine must explain to him how it is that he is the father of her child even though he thinks he has never slept with her. Her moment of "defeat" is concomitant with his realization that all his sexual victories with this heroine have not been the victories he imagined they were. At this point, comedy creeps back in. When she explains her story to him, this heroine presumably narrates a tale of personal desire and pleasurable fulfillment that creates loopholes in the "law of the signifier" just like the story the reader has in front of her. This is the true "climax" of this sophisticated sexual fiction. Much as Haywood herself does throughout her professional career as a writer of amatory fictions in an increasingly conservative climate, this heroine's story transforms notions of female virtue and female sexual desire that render the sexual ideologies of the day inadequate. Perhaps this is why (possibly like the pleasured eighteenth-century readers themselves) Beauplaisir and the heroine's mother both sit "for some Time in a profound Revery" after hearing her story. Silenced, they are incapable of judgement. Far from triumphing at this final unmasking, Beauplaisir leaves the house "more confus'd than ever he had known in his whole Life" (290).

Few negative consequences ensue from this confession. Lady ——'s public honor remains essentially intact. (Her canny mother has every incentive to conceal her daughter's sexual activities. Beauplaisir is sworn to secrecy, and the doctor seems discreet.) The heroine's flummoxed mother does decide to send her daughter to a monastery, but in so doing she relinquishes the personal control that the narrator has just informed the reader is the only thing capable of containing the heroine. There is no reason to believe she will not evade the monastery's abbess (a personal friend of her mother) as well as she did her aunt.

Ultimately, neither comedy nor tragedy dominates this complicated tale, but the pleasures of desire do control it from start to finish. Beauplaisir is so eager to visit the "Lady ——" after the birth of their daughter that the heroine's mother fears "there was nothing likely to ensue from these Civilities, but, perhaps, a Renewing of the Crime" (290). Even the banishment to a monastery holds the promise of further adventures, since Haywood delighted in rescuing her heroines from monastic confinement.[15] Skilled as she is in using disguise to her advantage, the nun's habit might be as popular a disguise for this heroine as it was at masquerade assemblies (Castle 40). Indeed, for Haywood as for Aphra Behn, monasteries are often only exotic locations for further amatory adventures.[16] The second volume of *Love in Excess* ends with Melliora's retirement to a monastery, but she is quickly abducted by a would-be seducer and thus reunited with her beloved D'elmont. Other heroines escape from monasteries or convents in Haywood's *The Force of Nature: or, the Lucky Disappointment* (1724*), The Agreeable Caledonian; or, Memoirs of Signiora de Morella* (1728), and *Idalia: Or The Unfortunate Mistress* (1723). Even the conscientiously didactic Penelope Aubin rescued two of her heroines from a convent in *The Life of Madam de Beaumount* (1721). Thus, in Haywood's works, banishment to convent or monastery was no guarantee of moral transformation, nor was it an effective stopgap to erotic pleasure. This story's ending suggests not a conclusion, but a sequel.

Furthermore, Haywood pointedly ignores the opportunity for didactic moralizing such an ending offers. *Fantomina* never formally chastises its heroine. Her mother is silent after her daughter's "confession," and Beauplaisir is once again enamored. Nor does the narrator introduce any significant moralistic rhetoric. Indeed, as if to comment upon the power of passion to maintain and control the fictions of desire, *Fantomina*'s final lines compliment its capacity to provide delight outside the usual didactic prescriptions: "And thus ended an Intreague, which, considering the Time it lasted, was as full of Variety as any, perhaps, that many Ages has produced" (291). *Fantomina*'s heroine thus eludes characterization as a figure of rare female empowerment or ambiguous patriarchal collusion. Instead, the psychological sophistication of Haywood's politics of seduction flouts the "law of the signifier" with impunity, to replace the traditional dichotomies (persecuting victor and vanquished maiden, desiring subject and desired object) with an alternative understanding of female sexual agency. *Fantomina* ultimately insists upon the irresistible force of desire itself as the "Great Arbitress" of all fictions of seduction.

Notes

I am grateful to Cynthia Wall, Patricia Spacks, Anna Patchias, Jennifer Chylack, Rick Mallen, and Steve Ramsay for their critical comments and encouragement reading earlier versions of this essay.

1. For discussions of Haywood as a precursor to Richardson in this sense, see Richetti, *Popular* 125 (1969 edition used throughout this essay); Doody, *Natural* 149; Beasley, *Novels* 162–63; and Spencer, 107–18. For a sustained

treatment of the trope of the seduced maiden in eighteenth-century British fiction, see Staves's indispensable article on the subject (91–113). I should mention, however that Staves's study specifies the pathos of these stories of seduced maidens as dependent "upon [the female protagonist] being a modest girl who strenuously resists invitations to illicit intercourse, yielding only after a protracted siege and under otherwise extraordinary circumstances" (96). Neither Pamela nor Clarissa is, strictly speaking, a seduced maiden in Staves's sense because the former successfully resists seduction and the latter never consents to it. Richetti uses the term "persecuted maiden" to include any heroine (innocent or not) pursued by a male intent on seduction with or without consent. It is this second definition under which Haywood's heroines are usually considered persecuted maidens.

2. *Les Lettres Portugaises* was translated into English by Roger L'Estrange in 1678 as *Five Love Letters from a Nun to a Cavalier*. For a discussion of the influence of the continental romance tradition on English "amatory" fiction, see Ballaster, *Seductive Forms* 42–49.

3. Limitations of space preclude a comprehensive survey demonstrating the consistency of this dynamic throughout Haywood's amatory fictions of the 1720s. Suffice it to say here, that aside from *Fantomina* and *Love in Excess* (not to mention numerous periodicals, conduct books, and political fiction and almost everything she wrote after 1730), Haywood wrote many amatory fictions in which something else besides female suffering is the central point of interest, including among others *The British Recluse* (1722), *The Injured Husband* (1723), *The Force of Nature* (1724), *The Surprise* (1724), *A Spy Upon the Conjurer* (1724), *The City Jilt* (1726), *Reflections on the Various Effects of Love* (1726), *The Fruitless Inquiry* (1727), *Cleomilia* (1727), and *Philadore and Placentia* (1727).

4. James Sterling praised Haywood as the "Great Arbitress of Passion!" in his prefatory verses "To Mrs. Eliza Haywood on Her Writings" in volume 1 of the four-volume 1725 edition of Haywood's *Secret Histories, Novels and Poems*, which was reprinted in 1732 and again in 1742. Richard Savage also pays poetical tribute to Haywood's abilities to command the conventions of desire, in prefatory matter to *The Rash Resolve* and *Love in Excess*.

5. For a related discussion of another Haywood text in which female desire is not mutually exclusive with female agency, see Bowers's essay on *Love in Excess* in this volume.

6. See, for example, Spacks, "Ev'ry Woman" *(Past)* 50, and Backscheider, "Woman's" 8 for sophisticated analyses of the complicated nature of eighteenth-century female empowerment.

7. I am greatly indebted to Craft-Fairchild's treatment of *Fantomina* in *Masquerade And Gender*. I especially agree with her suggestion that this

text's use of subject-object distinctions destabilizes traditional dichotomies. I am, however, suggesting that the Lacanian paradigm (which I read as analogous to what I call the "victor/vanquish'd" scenario) is another of the dichotomies this text destabilizes.

8. Here it might be objected that Clarissa does indeed experience at least a "glow" of desire for Lovelace early in the novel. But the point is not that Clarissa does not experience sexual desire, but that by-and-large, Richardson's novel equates both male and female sexual desire with moral shame.

9. Warner provides a reading of *Pamela* in relation to *Fantomina* that also questions the practice of reading backward from Richardson to Haywood (*Licensing* 194–95).

10. For example, even the unfortunate Emmaneulla in *The Rash Resolve* eschews the same "extravagancies" for quite a different, but equally authoritative, reason. She "disdain'd those Testimonies of continued Weakness, which however bitter they may appear in the *Expression*, the *Meaning* still is *Love*; for the Indifferent give not themselves the Pains" (65–66).

11. In Haywood's first conduct book, *The Wife*, she herself advises, "I would not be here understood, that a woman should yield a slavish submission to every unaccountable caprice and whim of the man to whom she is married; or on any score give up her reason and judgment to do him pleasure. I would only have her seem to think as he does in trifling and insignificant matters, and endeavour to be silent and passive in those of greater importance" (6).

12. For an applied analysis of this dynamic within the masquerade trope, see Craft-Fairchild, 54–59.

13. See Ballaster's astute reading of Haywood's *The Masqueraders* and *Fantomina* as attempts "to 'plot' a way out of the negative opposition of the unfortunate mistress and the mistress of artifice, proffering in its place the model of a female experimentation with amatory codes" (181).

14. For a sustained analysis of the use Haywood makes of pregnancy in her fictions to provide a "critique of the sexualization of power that is not reducible to the empowering or disempowering of women," see Thorn, "Althea."

15. In his prefatory verses affix'd to *The Rash Resolve*, Richard Savage notes the inefficacy of monastic confinement over the force of desire in Haywood's fiction when he asks, "*Can a cold Convent quench th'unwilling Fire?*" (xii).

16. For a discussion of the nun in amatory fiction, see Ballaster, 100–103. See also Pearson, "History."

"Blushing, Trembling, and Incapable of Defense"

The Hysterics of *The British Recluse*

Rebecca P. Bocchicchio

> *Action was now his business, and in this Hurry of her Spirits, all unprepar'd, incapable of Defence, half yielding, half reluctant, and scarce sensible of what she suffer'd, he bore her trembling to the Bed, and perpetrated the cruel Purpose he had long since contriv'd.*
>
> Eliza Haywood, *The Mercenary Lover:*
> *Or, the Unfortunate Heiresses* (1726)

The process of seduction is typically not easy on women in Eliza Haywood's amatory novellas. Her heroines burn with passion for their would-be lovers; they pour out pages of fervid love letters; they vow never to see the men again. And then, at the point of actual seduction, something strange happens: suddenly their bodies refuse to obey the dictates of their modesty, their throats won't let words of protest pass, their limbs fail to push away the aggressor, and the hapless heroines, half swooning and yet very aware of what is happening to their bodies, yield until "there is nothing left for him to ask, or her to grant." Haywood's early fictions are full of such seductions, but the following passage from *The Mercenary Lover* (1726) in which a married man finally seduces Althea, his innocent sister-in-law, offers a typical example:

But with what words is it possible to represent the mingled passions of Althea's soul, now perfectly instructed in his meaning; Fear, Shame, and Wonder combating with the softer Inclinations, made such a wild Confusion in her Mind, that as she was about to utter the Dictates of the one, the other rose with contradicting Force, and stopped the Accents e're she could form them into Speech; in broken Sentences she sometimes seemed to favor, then to discourage his Attempts, but all dissolv'd and melted down by that superior Passion . . . never had Courage to repel the growing Boldness, with which he every Moment encroach'd upon her Modesty.

Of course, to a certain degree, highly suggestive scenes like this one served to gratify the desires of the growing mass market of the early eighteenth century, which—then as now—happily devoured depictions of sex and seduction even while the literati of the time condemned them as pandering, as of little artistic merit, and even as dangerous. And yet to offer the needs of the market as the sum cause of Haywood's scenes of sexual excess seems to oversimplify these complex texts which appeal to readers even after two-and-a-half centuries; as critics of the past decade have begun to realize, there is much worthy of discussion in Haywood's works, despite the marginal position they have occupied since the middle of the eighteenth century.

What the woman in the opening quotes experiences is clearly, in the terms of Augustan medical understanding, a hysterical attack. The hyperventilation, pounding pulse, confusion of mind, and halting speech are all symptoms of the "hurry of spirits" that early theorists generally believed were the immediate cause of hysterical attacks. In writing of hysteria in the eighteenth century, I am using this term in its generally understood eighteenth-century sense—as a condition that grew out of a disturbance of the "animal spirits" which were conducted through the nerves, rather than in the twentieth-century psychoanalytic sense of a bodily display of conversion symptoms. Nevertheless, the eighteenth- and twentieth-century formulations of hysteria do have much in common; hysteria has always been envisioned as primarily a female disease, arising out of a weakness of female nature, and functioning as a way to categorize female inferiority. This essay establishes a historical context within which to understand Haywood's hysterical characters.

Few critics have commented in any depth about the elements of hysteria, historicized or not, in Haywood's amatory fiction. Patricia Meyer Spacks, in "Ev'ry Woman is at Heart a Rake," discusses the "devious ways" in which eighteenth-century women writers explored the forbidden topic of female sexuality. Haywood's dreaming and hysterical heroines, she argues, have their sexuality disguised under "the artfulness of innocence": "A suggestive adjective here is *unknowing,* which points to the prurient possibilities of innocence. Here, for a change, is a woman panting and heaving and confessing her wish to yield; but it's essential that she doesn't quite know what she's doing. That nightgown flies open without its wearer's conscious intent; her responsibility remains vague. . . . Only under such special circumstances can sexuality be separated from need to moralize" (*ECS* 33). The hysteric's loss of control and her semi-conscious dream state, according to Spacks, are really narrative devices designed to let the woman have the best of both worlds: she can both experience the raptures of ecstasy and be genuinely dismayed when she comes fully to herself, horrified at what has passed and yet guiltless of any "intentional" wrongdoing. It was no deliberate decision that betrayed her virtue; the heroine's step into experience is not really a true loss of innocence, no matter what the judgement of the world.

In *Seductive Forms,* Ros Ballaster offers the most detailed look at hysteria in Haywood's novellas. Using a modern psychoanalytical understanding of hysteria, her study focuses on the ambiguity of the hysterical response of Haywood's characters; Ballaster argues against Spacks' reading of these symptoms as "direct effusions of fantasy . . . that imply the delight of full commitment to the unconscious" (39). For Ballaster, the heroine's inability to protest, to stop the actions of the amorous hero, is far more troubling. She points to the presence of the nightingale, associated through the story of Philomela with "the inability to articulate feminine rage and resistance," in a typical Haywoodian sylvan seduction scene as suggestive of a reading that emphasizes not the heroine's surrender to pleasure but rather to her helplessness. Following Catherine Clement's reading of the hysteric as unable to signify meaning, as able to do "nothing other than to make things circulate without inscribing them" (Cixous 37), Ballaster argues for the ultimate symbolic dispossession of Haywood's heroines: "The uninterpretability of the hysterical body may endow it with a certain effective power, but the hysteric herself has not control over the representational scene her body presents" (173). With the exception of some of Haywood's masquerade fiction, which Ballaster discusses in the latter part of her chapter, she takes a bleak view of the possibilities for women offered in Haywood's works: "I have considered Haywood's representations of the female subject position within the amatory plot as largely negative and disempowering. She offers her female readers either the model of the 'hysterical' virgin who can only 'make things circulate without inscribing them' or the vicious 'masculine' woman, who, like the men she mimics, ceaselessly circulates in the world of sexual exchange without the possibility of securing absolute satisfaction in a single love object" (179). Ballaster's complication of Spacks's early work provides a needed corrective. This essay, however, focuses on an important—and overlooked—facet of any discussion of hysteria in Haywood's works: a historically contextualized understanding of hysteria and that hysteria's relationship to eighteenth-century constructions of "female" and "femininity."

In the late seventeenth and early eighteenth centuries, as writers as diverse as Lawrence Stone, Thomas Laqueur, and Nancy Armstrong have shown, the categories of "woman" and "femininity" were undergoing major structural shifts and redefinitions; as might be expected, there was a corresponding rise in printed works that served to examine and clarify these categories. These works offer useful insight into what it meant to be a woman during these years, both in theory and in practice. Some insight into that historical context can be gained through a discussion of late seventeenth-and early eighteenth-century medical treatises, which exploded in popularity with the advent of print culture. As a whole, these works construct both a woman who is polymorphously desiring, whose more sensitive nerves make her almost naturally hysteric, and a chaste, modest femininity which refuses expression of that innate desire. Haywood's texts argue against this naturalized figure of the female hysteric through an overproduction of hysteria itself: her hysterics wear their hysteria like a mask that belies the construction of the "naturally" hysterical women by revealing the characters' hysteria to be a result of social forces at work.

The "hysterical afflictions" have long confounded the medical profession. The etiology of hysteria has always been the subject of debate, with medical authorities of every era since at least the second century A.D. arguing over its origins, causes, and even symptoms;[1] in

his discussion of hysteria in the classical period, Michel Foucault traces
the "qualitative instability of these hysterical and hypochondrial ill-
nesses," commenting on the strangeness of "the confusion of their
dynamic properties and the secret nature of their chemistry!" (*Madness* 142–43). Even so, as G.S. Rousseau comments, "Throughout
the Restoration and eighteenth century . . . even the healthy woman
was still seen as a walking womb" (149); it is possible to generalize
about the early eighteenth century's understanding of hysteria. Although some writers allowed either that men could suffer from hysterical symptoms, or that hypochondria or melancholy—ascribed
almost entirely to men—had close connections with hysteria, hysteria
was still a "female disease."[2] While the original cause of hysteria was
debated, it was generally agreed that the symptoms were brought on
by a disorder of the "animal spirits," that mysterious stuff which transferred sensation, internal and external, between the organs and the
brain through the nerves. The exact nature of the nerves—whether
they were hollow or solid, for example—and of the animal spirits
were open to question; all conceded, however, that women's nervous
systems were more delicate than men's and more readily transferred
impression. These impressions were so strongly transferred, in fact,
that not only were women the primary victims of hysteria, but their
very ability to exercise reason and will over their nervous impulses
was questioned (Barker-Benfield xviii). Hysteria fascinated physicians of the latter seventeenth and eighteenth centuries, and dozens
of books, pamphlets, and treatises offered varied, sometimes contradictory, explanations for its causes and symptoms. Nor were these
treatises, written for the most part in the vernacular, limited strictly to
a medical audience; there was "a flow of nerve ideas from scientists
and diagnosticians into literature" throughout the century (Barker-
Benfield 15). A brief discussion of a few of the more influential of
these works which describe and categorize hysteria will define the
historical context in which Eliza Haywood created her desiring, hysterical heroines.[3]

William Harvey, who discovered the circulation of blood, was
one of the first physicians to mix extensive clinical observation of
hysterical women with the wisdom of the ancients. Arguing in 1651
that hysteria is caused by unsatisfied female desire, he lists the grave
consequences of letting young girls go unmarried:

... in young women when there uterus grows hot, their menses flow,
and their bosoms swell—in a word, when they become marriageable;
and who, if they continue too long unwedded, are seized with serious
symptoms—hysteria, furor uterinus, &c. . . . In like manner [as
animals] women occasionally become insane through ungratified
desire. . . . And this would certainly occur more than it does,
without the influence of good nurture, respect for character, and
the modesty that is innate in the sex, all of which tend to tranquil-
ize the inordinate passions of the mind. . . . How dreadful, then, are
the mental aberrations, the delirium, the melancholy, the parox-
ysms of frenzy. . . . brought on by unhealthy menstrual discharges,
or from over-abstinence from sexual intercourse when the passions
are strong! (R. Hunter 131–32)

   He relates several case histories, including that of a maid of eighteen who had lost all feeling in her extremities. "For tryal sake" her
doctor pinned her scarf to her neck, and she went about for some
time without noticing. Finally, Dr. Harvey recommended she be married, and "to many Mens wonder, [she was] cur'd of that strange
disease" (R. Hunter 132). Harvey's paradigm is simple: women have
deep sexual desires, and to deny them leads to all manner of cata-
strophic illness; nurture must be aimed at quieting these desires, and
when that fails, female desire must be satisfied within marriage. Harvey,
in effect, "prescribes" the socialization that conduct books will help
provide as they gain in popularity as the eighteenth century approaches.
   Thomas Sydenham's *Epistolary Dissertation* (1681–82) ranks
among the most important seventeenth-century commentaries on hysteria. Sydenham writes, as he explains, because the "the hysteric disorders . . . I own[,] are neither so easily discoverable nor so readily
curable as other diseases" (130). The subject is of great importance,
however, "for few women (which sex makes one-half of the grown
persons), excepting such as work and fare hardly, are quite free from
every species of this disorder" (130).[4] The "true" woman—which
excludes those, of course, who are so unladylike as to have to work
for a living—is, virtually by her nature, hysterical. Although he notes
that the symptoms of hypochondria (seen as a "male" disease) are
similar to those of hysteria, he argues that since the disease has its
causes in "irregular motions of the spirits [which proceed] from the
weakness of their *texture*" and which are occasioned by "violent

motions of the body" or excessive emotion, it primarily attacks women: "Hence women are more frequently affected with this disease than men, because kind nature has given them a finer and more delicate constitution of body being designed for an easier life, and the pleasure of men" (136).[5] The "kindness" of nature, however, might be questioned as Sydenham relates the litany of symptoms that arise from hysterical origins: convulsions which puff the belly up "like a ball," "a copious discharge of green matter, by vomit," pain so severe it feels as though a nail were being driven into the head, night sweats, and crying fits, to name a few. Sydenham eludes the problem of diagnosing a disease that can mimic any other disease by effectively labeling any symptom in a woman that does not have an immediately obvious cause as hysterical: "Upon this account, whenever I am consulted by women concerning any particular disorder which cannot be accounted for on the common principles of investigating diseases, I always inquire whether they are not chiefly attacked with it after fretting or any disturbance of the mind; and, if they acknowledge this, I am well assured that the disease is to be ascribed to the tribe of orders under consideration [i.e., hysterical]" (135).[6] Every disease can be hysterical, Sydenham argues, and every sick woman as well.

In this century, the hysteric, both real and fictional, has usually been read as an almost tragic figure, out of control, unable to give expression to her emotions or even desires other than through the ambiguous symbols of her body. Ros Ballaster, as noted earlier, sees little promise in Haywood's fictional use of hysteria; she argues that the hysteric has "no control over the representational scene her body presents." The "real" hysteric is treated much the same as her fictional counterpart. Joan Riviere argues that the "representational scene" that is controlled by the woman—her "womanliness," as Riviere calls it—is itself a masquerade, a costume, a series of representations enacted by woman rather than a naturalized subjectivity. Stephen Heath, in his analysis of Riviere's theory, pushes even further. He argues that if "womanliness" is nothing but a masquerade, then "hysteria is what? *Failed* masquerade. The hysteric will not play the game, misses her identity as a woman." Because she cannot control "the representational scene her body presents," she cannot present herself *as* a woman.

And yet, as I have discussed, to be hysteric *was* part of "the iden-

tity of a woman" in the eighteenth century when the ideology of the
"hysterical women" was pervasive, especially for women of the middle
and upper classes. Haywood's persistent attention to hysteria seems,
on the surface, to reinforce this constricted and limiting iconography
of womanhood. But Haywood was acutely aware of the rift that can
occur between surface and substance in life or in fiction. In *The Female Spectator,* she comments that "A modest wife should therefore
never affect the virago, and for her own sake be wary even when most
provoked, that nothing in her behavior should bear the least resemblance with such wretches. I have in a former Spectator taken notice,
that it is not only by force our sex can hope to maintain their influence over men, and I again repeat it as the most infallible maxim, that
whenever we would conquer, we must seem to yield" (1993 ed., 179).
The concept is clear: a surface submission opens up the possibility of
resistance, even of power (albeit a surreptitious power), for women.
The places in Haywood's texts where the heroines "seem to yield"
most completely, then, are the places where, as the quote above suggests, we should look for a sub-narrative that questions the very authority the surface text seems to reify.

It is this possibility, played out through a narrative of hysteria,
this essay will explore. Haywood's texts continuously present a repetition of hysterical attacks which in effect "overproduce" that hysteria, bringing it to the forefront of the narrative. In this way, Haywood's
fiction challenges the delimiting iconography that it seems, on the
surface, to reproduce: the narrative can articulate, through repetition,
the protest that the hysterical character, passive by definition, cannot.[7] In her psychoanalytic approach to masquerade, Mary Anne
Doane argues that "the masquerade, in flaunting femininity, holds it
at a distance. . . . To masquerade is to manufacture a lack in the form
of a certain distance between oneself and one's image. . . . It effects a
defamiliarization of female iconography" (25–26). Through the "hysterical overpresence" of her heroines, Haywood's narratives effect just
such a distance between the Augustan image of the hysterical woman
and the characters in the text. The carefully contextualized attacks of
her heroines show the hysterical body not to be a "naturally feminine" one, but rather to be the result of cultural forces at work—the
result of the constructed idea of what it was to be female in the early
eighteenth century.

On first reading, the story of *The British Recluse: Or, the Secret History of Cleomira, Suppos'd Dead* (1722) seems to play into the traditional ideology of naturalized hysterical femininity. Belinda, a young woman suffering from great sorrows, manages to gain a meeting with Cleomira, an enigmatic recluse who has hidden herself in the attic of Belinda's boarding house. The two take an instant liking to each other and exchange their life stories, both of which turn out to be tales of seduction and betrayal by, as they discover at the end, the same rakish man. During the course of the text, the women form a tight bond, and the tale ends with the two taking a house distant from London, "where they still live in a perfect tranquility, happy in the real friendship of each other." Despite the initial trappings of a standard romance, this is really the story of a painful self-making, of two women who experience the worst of the public world and make the decision to retreat into a semi-utopic sisterhood: we learn through a narratival interpolation at the women's first meeting that the two instantly form a "real tenderness" for each other, which "has ever since remained unshaken." Unlike most romances—including many of Haywood's own—which are built upon a model of female rivalry over the attention of men, this story is based on female companionship bolstered by the friends' anger at the perfidy of their mutual lover. Rather than simply using depictions of hysteria to offer a degree of resistance against ideological norms but going no further, *The British Recluse* offers a sort of resolution (though not a particularly satisfying one) in its heroines' voluntary and mutually pleasing retreat from the social world that has caused them so much disquiet.

In their own retellings of their stories, as they use first-person narration to shape their own histories, Cleomira and Belinda focus on their hysterical responses to past circumstances. As in other Haywood novels, the narration's persistent attention to hysteria seems, on the surface, to reify the constricted and limiting eighteenth-century iconography of womanhood. There is another possible reading, however: by having Cleomira and Belinda tell the story of their own hysteria, by having them exercise narrative control to bring hysteria to the forefront of the text, this novel challenges such a delimiting iconography. Here, the hysterics themselves turn the inarticulate mask of hysteria into an articulate narrative; Cleomira and Belinda show the hysterical body not to be a "naturally feminine" one, but rather to be the result of social forces at work—the result of the constructed idea of what it is to be female.

From the opening pages of the novel, as Belinda sits at the table of her boarding house listening to others discuss the elusive recluse who lives in the attic, Cleomira's story is presented as a cipher open to multiple interpretations. It must be ill-requited love that makes her hide from the world, says one boarder; no, says another, "if the Truth were known, I dare swear [this creature] is some wither'd Hag, past the Use of Pleasures, and keeps herself in private, lest her Countenance should terrify" (4). This banter serves both to pique Belinda's curiosity to meet the recluse and to prepare us for Cleomira's own, more definitive, interpretation of her history. This theme of storytelling develops as Belinda tells her landlady how she intends to meet Cleomira. The landlady answers that "This . . . if any thing will do— —and as you have so ingeniously contriv'd the Plot, it must be entirely owing to my want of Ability in carrying it on, if it shou'd miscarry" (7). The landlady's slippage into the metaphor of pregnancy reflects Belinda's incipient control of the "plot" of her own life. This "birthing" of an independent plan, aided in delivery by the midwifery of the landlady, marks the beginning of a shift from Belinda's old life, which (as we learn later) has put her at the mercy of masculine whims, to a new life of self-making and self-control.

When Cleomira and Belinda meet, they take an instant liking to each other. They quickly learn that each considers herself to be the most miserable of wretches; Belinda offers that "whatever the *Effects* may be, the *Cause* of both our sorrows is the same," and Cleomira agrees. The two agree to write down the cause of their sorrows, so as to avoid the "Confusion of speaking first": "On Exchange of the Papers, *Belinda* read in that which the Recluse had writ; *Undone by LOVE, and the Ingratitude of faithless Man.* And the Recluse found in that which the other had writ, these Words: *For ever lost to Peace by LOVE, and my own fond Belief.* As I expected! cry'd they out both together" (12). Unlike in the hysterical attacks they will soon relate, over which (as Catherine Clément and Ros Ballaster argue) the hysteric herself has no interpretive control, in their notes the women take complete control over the meaning and interpretation of their stories. This decidedly antihysterical action contrasts the unmediated presentation of hysteria with the regulated, inscriptive power of writing about that hysteria.

Realizing that they have both been undone by their desire in a society that has no place for female desire, Cleomira laments the state of women: "Why are we not like Man . . . inconstant, changing, and hunting after Pleasure in every Shape?——Or, if our Sex, more pure, and more refin'd, disdains a Happiness so gross, why have we not Strength of Reason too, to enable us to *scorn* what is no longer *Worthy* our *Esteem?*" (13). Cleomira has hit upon a paradox of eighteenth-century ideas of femininity: she cannot hunt after pleasure, and still be a woman; yet, as a woman, she cannot escape the voracious desire of her sex. Desiring yet not allowed to express that desire, the inner life of such a woman must be one of turmoil and confusion. Haywood's narrative, however, does not accept this conception as "natural" or inevitable; rather, it explores the ways in which "female" (a desiring creature) and "feminine" (the inability to act on, or even show that desire) conflict. The narratives of Cleomira and Belinda demonstrate that these conceptions are part of an ideology of womanhood and not innate qualities of women. The text suggests that when these ideas are internalized, as they initially are by Cleomira and Belinda, hysterical passivity is the ultimate result.

It is important to any reading of the hysteria in *The British Recluse* that the women are telling their stories to each other and, as with all of Haywood's novels, to a predominantly female audience. G.S. Rousseau argues in his discussion of the "historical transformations and representations" of hysteria in the early modern period that "language rather than medicine . . . is the medium best able to express and relieve hysteria's contemporary agony . . . subjectivity has been the teleology of the annals of hysteria in Western civilization" (93–94). To tell one's own story of hysteria, then, to resist the interpretations of the medical literature and the conduct books and instead endow hysteria with personally subjective narrative, was an intrinsically antihysterical act for the Augustan woman. In writing of hysteria, not only is Haywood engaging in an antihysterical act, but so are Cleomira and Belinda: as they write their own histories (both literally and in storytelling), making sense of what has happened in the past and transforming emotional crisis and chaos into a linear narrative, they in effect take control of that hysteria, constructing it through the ahysterical medium of words. This act of self-making belies the very definition of the hysterical woman prevalent at the time.

As soon as they have discovered the similar roots of their unhappiness, Belinda begs Cleomira to tell the story of her sorrows. Cleomira is the main focus of *The British Recluse;* the title refers to her, her story comes first and is almost twice as long as Belinda's, and she serves as a sort of "elder advisor" to Belinda, despite the proximity of their ages. We learn that Cleomira, though only of the gentry, was "bred up in all the Pomp and Pride of Quality" at court; her father's sudden death, however, drastically changes her family's circumstances. Her mother, realizing that the thirteen-year-old Cleomira can now never marry any of the courtiers who admire her, whisks her off to the country. Cleomira, of course, sees no harm in innocent flirtations, because "*Love* was a Passion I had so little Notion of, that I consider'd it no more than as a Fiction" (18). Cleomira is wholly unprepared to deal with the overwhelming emotions that accompany sexual desire, and her mother's attempts to shelter her only increase her fascination with life at court. Eventually, friends visiting from the city overcome her mother's scruples and Cleomira returns to the city to attend the gala ball at which she will meet Lysander.

Even from this early stage, Cleomira's narrative makes clear that she is not the "naturally" hysterical woman that contemporary theorists described, her nerves too weak to mediate or hide the effects of powerful influences from the outside world. In fact, she is often surprised at her own ability to *conceal* her inner emotional state, even when she is the most affected by her surroundings, when it is to her advantage. For example, upon first seeing Lysander at a ball, her inner emotions and her physical reaction are entirely distinct: "I Lov'd— was plung'd in a wild Sea of Passion before I had time to know or stem the Danger. I had so many disordered Motions in my heart that I am amaz'd my feet kept any just measure with the musick, or, that so little use'd as I had ever been to disguise my thoughts, my eyes did not betray the Confusion of my soul, and make visible to the whole Company what I was not yet acquainted with my self" (19). As she narrativizes her past, Cleomira can identify the rush of emotions she felt as passionate love; at the time, sheltered from a knowledge of the power of love, she only knows that she feels as she never felt before.

Cleomira expects her reaction to such unaccustomed sensation to be hysterical—that she will betray her feelings to the gathered crowd through her body—and wonders at her own capabilities of self-control. Later, after an illicit exchange of passionate letters, Lysander follows her to the country and arranges to pass by her chamber window, but to Cleomira's distress, her mother chooses that moment to pay her a visit. Seeing him under her mother's acute eye for the first time since the ball, she again remarks that her body doesn't respond as she expects it to: "Transplanted——Ravish'd——I wonder the violent Emotions of my *Soul* did not bear my *Body* out of the Window" (31). Despite almost overwhelming desire, Cleomira can and does control her physical responses, contrary to what medical literature had to say about the capabilities of female nerves in the presence of strong sensation or emotion.

Belinda's upbringing, respectable but modest, was even more sheltered than Cleomira's. Both of her parents died, but not before arranging her marriage with the auspiciously named Worthly. Belinda respected and admired Worthly, not suspecting that there were more violent emotions in store for her: "In fine, all that I knew of Love was his, nor had I the least Notion, there was any thing farther in that Passion, that what he had inspir'd me with.——Happy had I been to have never been undeceiv'd" (93). Undeceived she will be, of course. On the way back from her first public outing since her father's death, Belinda's coach overturns, and the dashing Courtal (really Lysander in a different disguise) stops to assist. Worthly proposes that she invite him in when they arrive at her house, a suggestion which she finds inexplicably pleasing: "I granted this with a Pleasure, which at that Time I knew not the meaning of. . . . it was a Mixture of Delight and Pain, a kind of racking Joy, and pleasing Anguish" (95). Like Cleomira, Belinda has no way to understand these unfamiliar emotions. Even in the retrospect of her narrative, she can only liken them to a disease which, unfeared and undetected, steals into its host. Although oxymorons are traditional in descriptions of love, in this context they serve to emphasize her inability to categorize the tumult of love: In her inexperience, she has no framework of reference for passion, the feeling of which is not quite pleasure nor pain.

Belinda differs from Cleomira, however, in that she cannot hide the effects of her desire. She struggles to overcome what she gradually comes to believe is her love for Courtal; failing, she postpones her marriage. Worthly, completely unaware of any challenge to his love for Belinda, charges Courtal (with whom he has become friendly) to inquire after the source of her hesitancy. When Courtal calls on her on Worthly's behalf, she finds herself completely unable to disguise her emotions. A simple polite greeting turns into a confession: "I design'd these Words no other than a Compliment; but the Confusion with which I spoke them, gave him too much Reason to believe I had a farther Meaning; and looking on me with Eyes which seem'd to read my Soul,——Oh God! (said he) what sweet Enchantment do those Words contain!" (100). Belinda regrets her transparency: "I have often reflected since, how silly my inward Perturbations made me seem: Courtal must certainly guess from what Source the Disorders he perceiv'd in my Countenance proceeded" (100). Where hysteria substituted for language in the other scenes discussed, here it over-whelms language—Belinda's "perturbations" tell the story of the de-sire that she tries to mask with words. And yet Belinda is expressing her desire in the only way open to her. Engaged to Worthly, and rec-ognizing him worthy of her love and esteem, and also very aware of the impropriety of her feelings for Courtal, she has struggled to over-come—or at least conceal—them. When her body tells the truth her sense of feminine honor wishes her to hide, she lets Courtal under-stand her desire without the need for her to speak first,[8] or to betray her respect for Worthly.

Lysander/Courtal, of course, has no scruples about revealing his desire to either Belinda or Cleomira. Belinda's inability to keep her desire out of her voice and her body, and Cleomira's amazement that she is able to do so, stand out sharply against Lysander's professions of transparency. When he first meets Cleomira at the ball, he *tells* her that his passion for her cannot be contained: "[W]hat I feel for *you* bursts out and blazes too fierce to be conceal'd—It is not to be express'd!" (21) The statement is logically false: he has to tell her what his body supposedly shows, which he claims is beyond verbal expression. Cleomira, on the other hand, has no proper and chaste way to let Lysander see her pleasure in this very forward speech other than through the nonverbal medium of her body: "[H]e saw enough in my Eyes to make him know the Pleasure I took in hearing him speak, far exceeded my Confusion at what he said" (21). In these sharply overlaid images of male and female relationships to language, Cleomira struggles under an almost overwhelming burden of shame and fear, unable to articulate her forbidden desire except through the responses of her body. In contrast, Lysander falsely appropriates the hystericized position as his own, claiming—through language—that only his body can speak his desire.

Although Cleomira can and often does control her physical responses in the face of great emotion, there are points in both women's stories where they do suffer hysterical attacks when confronted with powerful sensations: at crucial times, their nerves act exactly as the Augustan ideas of womanhood would suggest. After Cleomira and Lysander have carried on a secret correspondence for some time, Lysander connives a garden assignation with his lover, the first time the two will have met since the ball. Cleomira tells of her response upon seeing him again, and watching him fall to his knees before her: "My spirits were in too violent an agitation to suffer me to raise him from the Posture he was in, till gaining confidence to do it himself, and interpreting my Disorders in his favor, he took me in his arms, all blushing—trembling, and incapable of Defence, and laying his head upon my panting bosom, seem'd to breathe out all his soul in fervent tenderness. He held me thus some moments before I knew what I was doing" (41).

"Agitated spirits" were, as I have discussed, generally thought to be the cause of hysterical symptoms; what immobilizes Cleomira is clearly a hysterical attack. Belinda describes another instance of hysteria when she recounts her first clandestine meeting with Courtal: "He now began to mingle Kisses and embraces with his Vows; my Hands were the first Victims of his fiery Pressures, then my Lips, my Neck, my Breast; and perceiving that, quite lost in ecstacy, I but faintly resisted what he did, far greater Boldness ensued—My soul dissolv'd, its Faculties overpower'd—and reason, Pride, and Shame, and Fear, and every Foe to soft Desire charm'd to forgetfulness, my trembling limbs refused to oppose the lovely tyrant's will!" (113). Although Belinda's raptures are interrupted by a well-timed visit from Worthly, it is clear that without this intervention, her virtue would have ended with the chapter. What causes this "selective" hysteria, as it were?

Why can Cleomira sometimes completely conceal her overwhelming inner feelings, yet at other times collapse under them? Why does Belinda's bodily "confession" of her desire for Courtal sometimes stop at a confusion in her voice, and at other times move into hysteria? A close reading of the episodes of hysteria shows them to be brought on by an intellectual consciousness of shame, not by an inherently female response to extreme sensation. Belinda and Cleomira are driven into hysterical passivity not by their "natural" femaleness, but rather by an inability to reconcile what they actually feel—a strong desire— and what a "true woman" of the eighteenth century is allowed to reveal—only a lack of desire.

Immediately before Cleomira finds herself unable to raise Lysander from his knees, or to resist his embraces, she thinks of the correspondence they have been carrying on under her mother's nose: "But, when I came near enough to see him, no Confusion sure was ever equal to mine!—The reflection that this was but the third time I had seen him— but the second in which I had an opportunity to speak to him—the condescentions of my letters—and that which I now gave of meeting him, came all at once into my head, and I was ready to sink with shame" (41). She doesn't sink, but she is rendered speechless and immobile—at least long enough for Lysander to engage in some very improper displays of his affection.

Belinda's shame, too, interferes with her ability to control her words and actions. Engaged to one man, and passionate for another, she wants to tell her fiancé of the dangers of allowing Courtal into her presence: "A thousand times I was about to lay open all the weakness of my soul, and warn him of so dangerous a guest, but Shame as often depriv'd me of the power" (97). When Worthly interrupts Belinda and Courtal in the woods and the men draw their swords, she "had certainly run between their swords and receiv'd those wounds each designed for the other, but Shame and Horror struck me motionless" (114). Like Lasselia, Belinda has been publicly exposed as a desiring woman, and, torn between her public identity as Worthly's chaste and pure fiancée and her secret one as Courtal's lover, she hangs momentarily immobilized. (Here her hysteria has another, very practical, benefit: if one of the men is killed in a swordfight, her troubles will be mitigated if not ended.) Hardly a "natural" response to overwhelming sensation or emotion, the characters' hysterical passivity results from their enmeshment in the paradoxes of early eighteenth-century womanhood: they are trapped in an ideology which marks "female" as insatiably desiring, and "feminine" as the complete absence of desire. When the women are confronted with this paradigm, their conflicting impulses conflate into the shame each of them feels just prior to their hysteria. A hysterical attack which leaves them sensate and yet unable to exercise their will provides at least some resolution to this conflict, a way to satisfy their desire without having to admit its existence—and, by putting hysteria at the forefront of the narrative, it allows the text to expose this conflict's destructive power.

Haywood does allow Cleomira and Belinda an evasion of this conflict, though not a completely satisfying one. At the end of her story, Cleomira experiences a remarkable, almost literal, rebirth and takes charge of her life. Abandoned by Lysander, she gives birth to a stillborn child. She learns that her lover has married another woman, and she plans a suicide which (she hopes) will make him feel regret at his actions. She takes enough poison to kill herself and sends her nurse to tell Lysander of her tragic end. When the suicide fails (a suspicious apothecary having substituted a placebo for the poison) and she wakes to hear of Lysander's callous response to her supposed death, something changes in Cleomira: "It was now that I began to feel that Resentment which by a thousand barbarities he had long before deserv'd. And, after some little Struggles between departing Tenderness and growing Hate—'Tis done (said I) reason, at last, has gain'd a Conquest over all that Softness which has hitherto betrayed me to contempt—Now I will live, and love alone shall die!" (88). Cleomira has taken control of her history, eschewing the hysterical passivity of her early life to shape her future in a mold of her choosing. As suggested earlier, Belinda's "rebirth" into self-making begins when she "conceives" the plot to meet Cleomira; it is completed when, after her sister's marriage to Worthly, she and Cleomira leave for a private life in the country, taking a house in which "they still live in a perfect Tranquility, happy in the real Friendship of each other. . . . And where a solitary Life is the effect of *Choice,* it certainly yields more solid Comfort, that all the publick Diversions which those who are the greatest Pursuers of them find" (138).

This is a positive ending, in many ways; the women find happiness, sisterhood, and peace. However, this withdrawal into isolation is not an entirely satisfactory one. Much of their relationship is based on their still-lingering mutual love for Lysander: "I neither can forget, nor remember him, as a Woman govern'd by Reason wou'd do," notes Belinda (136), suggesting their almost obsessive concern with the man who jilted them both. "Their common Misfortunes was a Theme not to be exhausted, and they still found something for which to console each other" (137), the narrator assures us. Her comment that the "chosen" solitary life is more satisfying than the pleasure-seeking life of the city has its irony, as well, considering that both women are "ruined" (although Belinda never had sex with Courtal, many know that she was involved with him while engaged to Worthly) and would likely not find any takers on the marriage market. Furthermore, in escaping social pressures, the women must leave behind society as well—the society which provides much of the energy and excitement of Haywood's works. Implicit in this retreat from society is also a retreat from heterosexual romance; and while the narrative approaches female desire with an awareness of the trouble it can bring young, inexperienced heroines, it also seems to value that desire as a part of a balanced human life rather than labeling it a naturally rapacious, uncontrollable appetite. The story's ending does not resolve these issues, but rather replaces a retreat into the passivity of hysteria with a different, more literal kind of retreat. Removed from the immediacy of the conflicting dictates of "female" and "feminine," Cleomira and Belinda have escaped the socially constructed need for hysteria; this retreat, however, is an evasion rather than a solution, and this text can offer no answers for the desiring woman.

Notes

1. See King's "Once upon a Text" for a convincing refutation of the commonly held belief that Hippocrates was the first to discuss "hysteria" as a disease category.

2. See Veith's classic *Hysteria* (which, while dated in some aspects, is still generally regarded as quite strong on the history of hysteria in the eighteenth century) and Mark Micale's very thorough *Approaching Hysteria* for comprehensive discussions of the gendered history of the disease.

3. Athough the many authors who wrote on hysteria throughout the first two-thirds of the century differ in the particulars of their etiologies of hysteria, they are remarkably alike in the connections they make between

hysteria and femaleness/femininity. Thus, while I focus my discussion of medical texts on works that immediately precede or are contemporary with Haywood's early works, I will occasionally refer to a later text where useful. See Veith, chapter 8, for a discussion of the "cohesiveness" of eighteenth-century medical thought.

4. As Sydenham and other contemporary commentators suggest, it was generally believed that working-class women's nervous systems, "coarsened" by manual labor and hard living, were "coarser" than those of well-off women. Interestingly, the associations of hysteria and class change regionally and over time: Evans notes that in nineteenth-century France, working-class hysterics outnumbered middle- and upper-class patients by as many as two to one; both Veith and Micale point out that contemporary theories of "hysterical neurosis" suggest that hysteria survives as a "comparatively primitive defense mechanism" primarily in "culturally, economically, and educationally deprived environments" (Micale 160).

5. Sydenham's far-reaching influence can be seen, for example, in the work of Richard Blackmore. Writing contemporaneously with Haywood in 1725—fifty years after Sydenham—he echoes and elaborates on Sydenham's theory of female nerves: "It is true, that the convulsive Disorders and Agitations in the various parts of the Body, as well as the Confusion and Dissipation of the animal Spirits, are more conspicuous and violent in the Females Sex, than in Men; the reason of which is, a more volatile, dissipable, and weak Constitution of the Spirits, and a more soft, tender, and delicate Texture of the Nerves, in the last, than in the first" (R. Hunter 320).

6. It is interesting to note that some physicians thought it imperative to delve deeper into a case before ascribing a diagnosis of hysteria. Thomas Willis, for example, writing in 1667, argued that "The hysterical passion is of so ill fame, among the Diseases belonging to women, that like one half damn'd, it bears the faults of many other Distempers: For when at any time, a sickness happens in a womans body, so that its Cause lyes hid . . . presently we accuse the evill influence of the womb, (which for the most part is innocent)" (R. Hunter 189). Willis doesn't limit the scope of hysterical symptoms, however; he only wants to make sure that other causes are ruled out before a positive diagnosis is given.

7. Here I differ sharply from Ballaster. She sees Haywood's hysterical characters as only able to "make things circulate without inscribing them"; I argue that this "symbolic dispossession" is itself inscribed in the narrative as a symbol. The hysteric herself may not articulate resistance, but the narrative of hysteria does.

8. Haywood's heroines—like any good girls of the time—are horrified at the idea of being the first to acknowledge desire. In *Love in Excess*, for

example, Alovisa is about to sign her name to a billet-doux when she suddenly comes to her senses: "'No, let me rather die!' said she, starting up, and frighted of her own designs, 'then be guilty of a meanness which would render me unworthy of life; Oh! heavens, to offer love, and poorly sue for pity! 'tis insupportable!'" (1994 ed., 47–48).

Telling Tales

Eliza Haywood and the Crimes of Seduction in *The City Jilt, or, the Alderman turn'd Beau*

Kirsten T. Saxton

*There is certainly an Influence in an artful, tender, and
passionate Way of Writing, which, more sensibly affects
the Soul, than all the Tongue can utter: Words . . . we
may avoid list'ning to, or they may slide from our
Memory, when Letters will remain perpetual monitors.*

Eliza Haywood, *Letters from a Lady of
Quality to a Chevalier* (1721)

*The Life-wrought Tale should ne'er advance
A line that favours of Romance.*

Francis Coventry, *An Essay on
the New Species of Writing* (1751)

In her 1726 novel *The City Jilt,* Haywood revises the familiar plot of
female seduction and ruin to explore a plot of female vengeance and
destruction. In this text, Haywood negotiates female anger and dispossession through a protagonist who slips outside the delimiting con-
fines of heroine and harridan, virgin and whore, to emerge victorious
and socially ambiguous. The novel differs from most eighteenth-century fiction in that, when its heroine's reputation is ruined by a false
seducer, its heroine is not utterly ruined as a result; Glicera's lost inno-

cence and her subsequent turn to deception and vengeance result neither in moral nor literal bankruptcy, but in her satisfied health and
wealth. Haywood leaves the taste of revenge sweet and lucrative, rather
than cold and ashen, in her heroine's mouth. By empowering Glicera
over the deceased body of her seducer, Haywood creates a powerful
fantasy of wish-fulfilling violence in which the victim of unlawful seduction appropriates the patriarchal codes of law and seduction that
ruined her, revamping them into the weapons by which she exacts her
redress. However, Haywood's text not only serves as a corrective to
the didactic masterplot that implies lost maidenhood translates to lost
maiden, it also provides a complicated and subtle investigation into
the function and nature of narration itself. *The City Jilt* exemplifies
an eighteenth-century movement toward narrative fiction: fiction that
manipulates, revises, and revokes familiar generic tropes to new ends.
In *The City Jilt,* Haywood uses and transforms elements from multiple discourses and reframes these elements in a fictional narrative
not bound by the strictures of the tightly predicated forms of classical
ethics or aesthetics.

Until recently, much scholarship on the history of the British novel
has tended to dismiss Haywood, along with her female contemporaries and predecessors, as less able and less innovative than her male
counterparts. For example, Lennard Davis contends that Haywood
"seem[s] to lack ambivalence and a special attitude toward fact and
fiction," traits which render her texts unable "in formal terms . . . to
create or belong to a genre" (121–22). In a more complex analysis,
yet one that still shies away from granting Haywood any real literary
merit, John Richetti explains that Haywood's "swelling prose [is] the
real content of the scene and drive[s] the reader along to the near-
climax. . . . We are conscious not of logical progression but a . . .
repetition of evocative words and phrases—burnings, blazings,
mountings, burstings" (*Popular,* 1969 ed. 201).[1] Davis and Richetti
are astute in their observances on the formal complexities of
Haywood's prose and affect, yet their analyses of these qualities miss
a crucial point: Haywood's hyperbolic prose and formal pastiche of
inflection do not signal her failure to manage her text adequately;
rather, they reveal her astute manipulation of text and context, of
genre and gesture. Careful reading of, for example, *The City Jilt,* reveals a novel fully immersed in the intertextual, cultural moment of

its conception. The novel does not attempt that "transparent" realism or overarching narrative of providential circumstance so long favored by traditional histories of the British novel.[2] Instead, Haywood manipulates multiple discourses to reveal the dangers of unexamined, seamless stories for those whose ends are not best met by expected endings. Writing before the picaresque instructional comedy of Fielding or the domestic didacticism of Richardson, Haywood, like her contemporary Defoe, agilely crafted fiction that resists formal and moral simplicity. Through its use of satire, its plays on familiar literary tropes and genres, and its destabilization of narrative cohesion, *The City Jilt* formally, as well as thematically, unsettles patriarchal fictions of law, heterosexual romance, and textual authority.

The novel opens with the narration of Glicera's innocence and her ruin at the hands of a false seducer and ends with the heroine's transformation from violated victim to vengeful violator.[3] Haywood's text suggests that Glicera learns the arts of deception from her seducer. After being "done in" by his manipulations of her conventional fantasies of heroic masculinity, Glicera appropriates and manipulates conventional fantasies of feminine passivity and seductiveness to gain control of her life and to wreak havoc, not only on the lover who abandons her, but on men as an aggregate. Glicera dons and deconstructs stock feminine roles to control and manipulate what the text defines as a destructive and indulgent male appetite while retaining her own economic, sexual, and social sovereignty.

At the novel's opening, Haywood immediately situates Glicera as a product within a system of masculine exchange. Glicera is a tradesman's daughter, "the reputation of whose riches grew a greater Number of Admirers to his House, than the Beauty of his fair Daughter's person; tho' she was really one of the most lovely and accomplished Women of the Age" (1995 ed., 67). She is wooed by the wealthy and handsome Melladore; while she loves him, their engagement is one arranged by him and her father for economic, rather than romantic, pleasure. Glicera's father approves of Melladore's large fortune and Melladore desires the marriage, not out of feelings for Glicera, but because of "the real Love he had . . . to the Wealth of which he expected she would be posses'd" (70). Glicera, however, like her suitor, is unaware that her father's riches are smoke and mirrors. Here, Haywood takes a neat double jab at both the traffic in women and the baseness she associated with the mercantile class, positioning the hapless Glicera within a familial and social unit that functions according to the shifting sands of economic exchange rather than affection.[4]

We are comfortably within the arena of the romance here: foreign names; hyperbolic discourse; and stock characters—beautiful and endangered innocent versus seemingly devoted, but secretly immoral, libertine. Melladore has "an infinity of affection" for Glicera, "one of the most lovely and accomplished women of the age." These readily recognizable romantic elements suggest that the narrative will proceed according to generic expectations.[5] However, close reading reveals that Haywood is playing with, rather than simply replaying, a familiar tune. On the first page of the novel, after briefly describing the lovers, Haywood abruptly elides their wooing and skips immediately to their engagement, commenting tartly that "Nothing happening between them but what is common to persons in the Circumstances they were, I shall pass over in Silence the Days of their Courtship" (67). Haywood calls attention to the familiarity of the romance script—both literary and lived. By marking these particular characters as stock, she asserts that they and their hyperbolic vicissitudes are common, in life as well as literature. Haywood subtly warns female readers of the rote and well-scripted nature of courtship language, unworthy even of textual inclusion, as well as of the truly common nature of the failed romance she is about to relate. At the same time, she differentiates her text from the traditional romance by refusing to textualize the details of romance itself, moving instead to the crux of the matter—sex and contracts.

When the death of her father leaves Glicera portionless just before the wedding, Melladore feigns indifference to her economic ruin, falsely insists on his love and desire to marry her, and seduces her: "By such kind of Arguments, accompanied with unnumber'd Vows, Sighs, Tears, and Implorations, she was at last subdued, and fell the Victim of his lawless Flame" (70–71). Haywood describes Glicera's own desire not as specific to Melladore as sexual object, but as the longing to be the object of her lover's desire. Glicera's wish to give "Pleasure to the dear Undoer" highlights the ways in which female pleasure may be experienced, not in terms of woman's own sexual gratification, but in terms of the reflected image of herself as the desirous object of an untrustworthy male gaze: her own pleasure subsumed in and defined by his. Melladore articulates a sexist notion of male desire in his explanation to Glicera that "the very word *Desire* implies an impossibility of continuing after the enjoyment of that which first caused its being . . . for who can wish for what he has already?" (71). In this "why buy the cow" comment, Melladore reveals his knowledge of the economy of romance in which a woman's worth depends on her astute management of her "assets," her insistence on contractual marriage before "giving up the goods." Glicera, implies Haywood, is guilty, not for her loss of sexual innocence, but for her innocence of such market machinations, her lack of awareness of her position as a commodity that must be *sold*, not freely given. *The City Jilt* functions as a primer that instructs women on how to negotiate their worth properly. Eighteenth-century women were forced to operate within a socio-legal system that defined a woman's highest position as that of private property—as wife—and that inscribed female worth either according to the worth of her body as "pure" property or to the pure property her body was worth. Glicera misreads and misinterprets the text of sexual exchange: she reads it as a romance, Melladore reads it as a bill of trade.

Glicera's head is full of heady romantic fantasies that preclude her capacity to protect her own interest. When she informs Melladore of her poverty, she unquestioningly believes his protestations of love. According to the conventions of formulaic fiction, her newly discovered poverty simply provides the necessary obstacle all true lovers must face. Yet it is clear that Glicera does not know how to read the scene accurately. In a setting straight out of one of the French romances in which Haywood and her readers were well-versed, the lovers' conversation takes place in "an Arbour at the end of the Garden, so shadow'd o'er with Trees, that scarce could the Sun's Beams at the height of Noon penetrate the Gloom, much less those of the pale Moon, who then shone but with faint and sickly Fires . . . so that unhappily for her she perceived not the shock her Words had given him, nor the Disorders which that moment overspread his alter'd Countenance" (69). This conventional setting for intrigue recalls countless literary moonlit trysts in secluded bowers, and Melladore's assurances of love mimic the extravagant claims of countless fervent lovers. Yet, in Haywood's hand, the scene becomes a travesty, a burlesque of high sentiment and lofty love and a dangerous simulacrum of romance,

one Glicera cannot recognize as false because the players and the setting so perfectly match a romantic script she has uncritically consumed. Haywood subtly critiques the psychologically uncomplicated
text of the romance, highlighting not only Glicera's duped innocence,
but also her complicity in her own deception by virtue of her desire.
Glicera longs to fulfill the role of the romantic heroine, to be loved
and idealized. She pays no attention to sordid economic realities or
even to the specificity of her lover's character. In her representation of
Glicera's complex motivations, Haywood moves *The City Jilt* into a
realm of psychological subtlety we associate today with novelistic discourse; Glicera "hesitated not if she should believe [him], because she
wish'd it so, and had before set down in her own Heart for Truth, all
that he now professed" (70). Glicera has comfortably positioned herself within a plot whose end—marriage—she believes is fixed, already
"set down" as truth. Yet Haywood shows her readers that the text of
the heart—individual or generic—is a specious source upon which to
base action, and suggests that to buy into such fictions is to sell one's
self short and to risk that other familiar denouement: ruin and death.

The novel does not castigate Glicera for having pre-marital sex
per se, but for her willingness to become an object of male desire
without realizing the inherent precariousness of that position. When
Glicera responds to the death of her father with grief tempered by
relief that she has not, at least, lost her lover, the narrator inserts a
seemingly prosaic comment chastising Glicera for her inappropriate
emotion: "How little is Youth sensible of what it owes to Age, and
how far are we unable to conceive of what is due the Care of a tender
Parent, or how greatly we suffer the loss of such a one! But soon was
this fond Maid made sensible of her error" (69). This remark seems
to offer a conventional moral warning, chiding Glicera for her selfish
lack of daughterly feeling. But the plot of the novel dislocates this
apparent moral message: Glicera's father offered no proper "Care of
a tender Parent." Rather, he left her penniless on account of his over-
extension and greed after having engaged her to be married to the
ignoble Melladore under false pretenses. In light of the actual story
line, the narrator's admonition may be read not as a requisition for
dutiful constancy but as an underscore of the powerless position a
woman holds when she lacks male protection, a gesture that calls
attention to the fact that the presence of a "protector" does not entail

protection. The errors of which Glicera becomes sensible are not her lack of appropriate grief for her father, but the presence of inappropriate devotion to her lover, and her own lack of awareness of her status as pawn in a system of male exchange.

A similar warning is present in the delineation of Glicera's actual seduction: having "melted by his Pressures," Glicera gives in to Melladore, swallowing his arguments that to refuse him would be to bow to that "Decorum which enslaves the world" because they are engaged to be married (70). Again, Haywood, here as in other texts, does not castigate female sexual desire, but rather that naiveté that allows women to fall for stale lines and hackneyed pastoral *carpe diem* romantic logic. Glicera's "fall" is predicated on her falling for the appealing, but ultimately sham, status of romantic heroine. While she melts—"in soft Desires dissolv'd . . . Alas! she knew not the meaning of those tumultuous Agitations" (67)—Glicera misreads the language of the body as the transparent key to the text of the heart, interpreting her own and Melladore's active sexual desire and pleasure as proof positive of love and right action. The narrator's reproof of Glicera for having committed "the Crime she had been guilty of to Heaven and to herself" (71) appears a rote nod to didactic notions of female purity. However, that the narrator defines Glicera's yielding as a crime she commits against *herself* counters such a reading. The novel is less concerned with the moral reverberations of Glicera's lost virginity than with the social and psychological consequences of that loss. In a narrative aside that breaks entirely with conventional notions of the duty of the "moral" to police the immoral, the narrator chastises those female readers who might condemn Glicera for her sexual surrender and defines all women as potential victims to male perfidy:

> Some perhaps, into whose hands this little Narrative may fall, may have shar'd the same Fate with poor *Glicera;* like her having been betrayed by the undoing Artifices of deluding Men . . . to Shame, to late Repentance, and Neverending Griefs; and it is those only, who can conceive what 'twas she suffer'd, or know to compassionate the labouring Anguish of a Heart abus'd. . . . The happy *Insensible,* or the *untempted* Fair, are little capable of judging her Distress, and will be apt to say her *Misfortune* was no more than what her folly merited; yet let those pitiless Deriders of her Frailty take care to

fortify their minds with *Virtue,* or they will but vainly depend on the
Force of their own Resolution to defend them from the same Fate she
mourn'd. (72)

Haywood acidly figures morally censorious women as either frigidly
"insensible" to sexual passion or inexperienced in desire because
"untempt'd," presumably owing to lack of male interest. She deems
both sorts "pitiless" women who will have little chance of defending
their own sexual honor if they refuse to fortify themselves with virtue
(virtue the text implies they lack). The reader must associate herself
with either the frigid prude or the "untempt'd," and therefore undesirable, woman—neither a very appealing option—or she is linked,
ontologically if not experientially, not only with the suffering and
undone heroine, but also with the narrator and an entire community
of "fallen" women. Haywood's call for "Virtue" rings doubly, presenting both a surface warning to remain chaste, and an admonish-
ment to all women to approach "fallen" women with virtuous pity, as
any woman is a hair's breadth away from such an ignominious position. Virtue, in this novel, is not something to be sought primarily for
heavenly reward or abstract moral principle, but is a necessary pre-
caution in a world in which yielding to sexual desire may lead to a
very concrete loss of social and economic standing.

In a move typical of amatory fiction, the narrator's address to the
reader breaks the boundaries between the textual and real worlds,
impinging on the illusory realism of fiction by calling attention to the
tale's own fictitiousness. This self-referentiality relocates the fantastical
romance into the drawing room of its English readers, making them
active and imperiled participants in the melodrama of Glicera's predicament and underlining the fact that the stuff of romance and melodrama—lost virginity, lack of portion, ruin—are not so far from the
doors of any woman in a patriarchal society. Glicera's lost virginity at
the hands of a cad is, in fact, an all too possible and probable plot.
The novel resists the strictures of romance and of familiar conduct
book morality by rendering the seduced and corrupted as victorious
heroine, chastising readers who would attempt to dismiss her as merely
a cautionary example. And yet, while the novel resists the standard
conventions of romance fiction, it simultaneously uses the shorthand
of romance—ruined maiden, villainous seducer, luxurious voyeurism—

to decode the fantastical graphology of romance and to reveal an alphabet of prosaic and psychologically complex motivation and misery beneath.

After the scenes of seduction, the novel commences a complex series of rhetorical and plot devices that reveal Haywood's virtuoso ability to shift between, manipulate, and deconstruct multiple genres and fictional expectations. Believing Melladore will marry her post haste, Glicera is shocked when he treats her with indifference and neglect, even after hearing that she carries his child. Invoking his vow to his father to marry only a woman of equal fortune, Melladore refuses to make "reparation" to Glicera; he refuses hastily to marry her to legitimize her pregnancy. Glicera is thus triply victimized: her father has squandered his (and her) fortune on fripperies; her fiancé has falsely seduced and impregnated her and claims his allegiance to a filial debt that he places above his debt to her; and her body has betrayed her by carrying the visible signs of her loss of maidenhood. Haywood's attention to the prosaic realities of her heroine recalls the detailed commentaries offered by criminal biographies and news writings that laid out in dire detail the minutia of gritty "real life" scandal.[6] However, whereas the "news/novel" discourse (as Lennard Davis terms it, in opposition to the discourse of romance) tended to preach messages that reinforced extant social institutions controlling gender, Haywood's novel lays bare the injustice at the heart of social systems that deny women legal subjectivity.[7] As an impoverished unmarried mother-to-be, whose childbirth will be illegal and fix her firmly outside of social propriety, Glicera is left without recourse; thus, the novel calls attention to the inequities of a legal and social system that places women under the umbrella of male guardianship with no recourse when that guardianship proves ineffectual.[8]

Haywood underlines the horror of Glicera's mistreatment and the violence of her righteous anger by subtly shifting the plot and tone to invoke the Southern European revenge novel.[9] Haywood conjures the furies of these bloody novels as Glicera, and the novel, abruptly seem to shift from one familiar type to another. Glicera's new understanding of the "Perfidy" and "undoing Artifices of deluding Men" transforms her from virtuous innocent to enraged avenger. Shedding the role of ingenue for that of would-be murderess, Glicera no longer desires to please Melladore, but longs to send "a Dagger to his Heart"

(72). However, here Haywood again complicates the genre to which she gestures; rather than unfolding into a simplistic scenario of violent revenge, *The City Jilt* remains psychologically acute and circumstantially realistic, for Glicera's pregnancy precludes her transformation into a murderous she-devil. Despite her absolute hatred of Melladore, her status as unwed and pregnant demands that Glicera must plead for him to marry her in order to grant her child legitimacy. As a female criminal could "plead the belly" to avoid execution, so too does Glicera "plead the belly" in her attempt to attain legal recognition for her child and to avoid criminal punishment for birthing out of wedlock. The preclusion of violent revenge by the heroine's pregnancy replaces the unbridled extravagance of the revenge novel with a realistic template of the much more likely result of illicit sex—the saddling of the woman with a bastard with no recourse except the man who impregnated her in the first place.

Glicera's pleas and Melladore's rejections are narrativized through the insertion of letters into the omniscient narrative. In her unpublished essay, "Narrative Interruptus: The Embedded Letter and Sexual Honor," Debra Rosenthal defines the moment when an omniscient narration breaks off suddenly into a letter, allowing the heroine to speak her own words. She argues that these "interruptions" create an erotic swelling of narrative space, anticipating the inevitable pregnancy that results from seduction. Glicera's letters exemplify Rosenthal's claims that such letters inevitably concern the heroine's sexual honor and that they emblematically "stand in" for the heroine's body. However, rather than being precursors to seduction, as Rosenthal argues such letters invariably are, in *The City Jilt* they are the *results* of seduction. Glicera's letters swell, not with desire, but with rage and despair. The expansion of narrative space they accomplish does not subtly anticipate pregnancy, but insists upon the recognition and manifestation of pregnancy within the seduction narrative.

Glicera's first letter to Melladore argues logically for her rights as his wife, citing his false promises and the weight of their covenant, and appealing to his duties to his unborn child. She threatens to commit suicide, to kill herself and their unborn child, if he does not legally recognize their relation. Melladore's lack of response to her letter nullifies Glicera's and his child's existence; his refusal to acknowledge receipt of her epistle and to acknowledge that he is the creator of her

issue (in both senses of the word) erases her arguments and her pregnancy and tacitly supports Glicera's suicidal threat literally to erase
herself and her child from the narrative. With her status as lover,
mother, and writer blatantly disregarded, Glicera again writes to
Melladore; she challenges him at least to admit his crimes and informs him she longs for death. Neither the body of her text nor the
body that bears his child has any effect, and Glicera yearns to afflict
him with her haunted (disembodied) spirit, declaring that heaven will
revenge her wrongs "tho' it denies the power" to her to do so herself
(76). These letters are written from a position of acknowledged powerlessness, and Glicera's authorship has no positive effect. Rather, the
letters present the female author as fragmented and impotent in the
face of male authority. In her second letter, Glicera presents herself as
occupying a split consciousness: "Divided between *Love* and *Rage:*—
Continue with alternate *Soothings* and *Revilings,* as either of the op-
posing passions rise, to weary and *perplex* each future Moment . . . my
Thoughts . . . o'erwhelm my Reason, and drive me into madness" (75).
The inefficacy of her physical and literary insistence upon her rights
results in Glicera's loss of her sense of herself as an intact subject.

Melladore's response to Glicera's final letter dramatizes the ways
in which the claim of reason may be manipulated to reduce female
rage and loss to unnatural and unfounded hysteria. He maintains that
she has misunderstood the logic of love, explaining that he thought
her "Mistress of a better Understanding" than to have believed they
would marry, as "'Tis not in Reason, 'tis not in Nature to retain perpetual Ardours for the same Object," and admonishing her to "lay
the fault on Fate," rather than him, for her lack of fortune (76). He
ends the letter with a postscript stating that her letter deserves no
response as its unsound tone renders it "not worthy of a serious Regard" (77) and informs her that she will not hear from him again.
Haywood not only exposes the price of male romantic deception, a
cost which is borne bodily by the impregnated and abandoned woman,
but denounces the ways in which the script of that abandonment may
be successfully rewritten to assign the blame to the woman. Her lost
virtue, visible in her swelling body, proclaims, according to the logic
Melladore proposes, her unfitness for matrimony. Her anger at her
condition is defined as contrary both to "Reason" and "Nature" and
is thus categorized as socially, logically, and organically unsound.

Melladore's revisionary logic privileges self-serving pseudo-reason and locates Glicera's error in her inability to read correctly. Her misguided understanding and appropriation of patriarchal fictions have led to her production of texts "not worthy of serious Regard." Melladore's censure of Glicera's letters suggestively recalls the censure Haywood herself received as "the Great Arbitress of Passion" and replicates the discursive hierarchy by which Haywood's own texts have been deemed "not worthy of serious Regard" by critics from her era to our own. Glicera's and Melladore's versions of the "truth" of their relationship exemplify the dueling discourses of amatory and "realist" fiction. Through her self-conscious investigation of the ways in which the masculine vision of rational truth-telling precludes the experiential truth of the female's text, Haywood dramatizes the tensions at play in early-and mid-eighteenth-century English conceptions of narrative integrity.

Toward the middle of the eighteenth century, the direct testimonial began to lose power as narratives that obscured authorial presence under the guise of neutral realism became the privileged form of truth-telling.[10] In *The City Jilt*, Haywood anticipates, as well as contests, the critical trend that will privilege the apparently transcendent narrative—that which is objective, distanced, and controlled—at the expense of those texts whose sentiment, extravagance, and focus on the body render them "feminine," and thus untrustworthy, representations of reality. Glicera's letters, like Haywood's fictions, rely on rhetorical strategies of immediacy, direct testimony, emotional appeal, and lavish language. She presents herself as a spectacle of female sorrow and imperiled flesh. Like the amatory author, Glicera seeks a sensational response—the tear—from her reader, yet she seeks that response as a means to another end: that of identification, respect, and legal empowerment from the reader who denies the worth of her body and its issue. Glicera's letters commingle the rhetoric of feeling with the concrete aims of law and economics and mimic the novel's narrative hybridity. These fictional letters, and the fiction that contains them, reveal the ways in which the active female subject must move between discourses in her attempt to articulate her desire within existing narrative structures whose grammar is limited, exclusive either to the personal *or* the political, the sexual *or* the economic.

Glicera's first letter stands as an exemplum of such discursive pastiche:[11] she moves between hyperbolic romantic diction ("Ah! how inhuman, how barbarous has been your Usage of me!" [73]); clear and logical interrogation of Melladore's actions ("If with the loss of my expected Dower I also lost your Heart, why did you not then reveal it?"[72–73]); and an insistent delineation of her contractual rights under the law ("Remember you are mine as much . . . as if a thousand Witnesses had confirm'd our Contract: The Ceremony of the Church is but Ordained to bind those Pairs, who of themselves want Constancy and Resolution to keep the Promise which Passion forms" [73]). This final claim for the status of their relationship is legally accurate as, until the Marriage Act of 1753, marriage in England was based on the proposition that "what creates the married state and constitutes the contract" is "that FAITH by which Man and Woman *bind themselves* to each other to live as man and wife" (Stebbing 5). Historian Eve Bannett explains that "[c]hurch Courts and Justices of the Peace would uphold the claim of a pregnant woman that she had been 'debauched under promise of marriage,' and if necessary, compel the man in question to perform his promise. Seductions . . . were, for all intents and purposes, real marriages" (234).[12] Despite the legal accuracy of Glicera's claim, she is nevertheless disparaged and denied. She has chosen the wrong text for her complaint; the personal text between ex-lovers does not have the weight to compel Melladore into action, and Glicera, fatherless, penniless, and alone, has no access to or knowledge of the language of state and estate within which successfully to frame her demand.

Glicera's response to Melladore's annulment of the validity of her position is "more terrible than Storms of Whirlwinds," and the brutal character of his words is acknowledged by the narrator's comment that his "stabbing Lines" provoke Glicera to "endeavor to lay violent Hands on her own Life" (she is prevented by a servant maid) (77). The text clarifies the violent effects of Melladore's refutations to Glicera's emotional and physical position by making it clear that his letter is responsible for the death of her unborn child. Immediately after Glicera reads the letter, "[t]he unusual force of those Emotions with which she was agitated threw her into a Mother's Pangs long before the time prefix'd by Nature . . . the Consequence of her too easy Love proved no more than an Abortion" (77). Melladore's insistence on the primacy of his own narrative at the expense of hers erases not only her love, position, and reputation, but their unborn child; he aborts the baby as well as her love and innocence. As Glicera recuperates, "languish[ing] in Pangs which were look'd on as the harbingers of Death . . . the perfidious *Melladore* [was] triumphing in a Bridegroom's Joys" to another woman, one worth 5,000 crowns (78).

As she regains her physical strength and "Tranquillity of Mind," Glicera becomes not more mellowed or more chastised by her fall from grace, but hardened in anger at male perfidy, and her anger is configured as reasonable since it is aligned with mental tranquility: "The Memory of her Wrongs . . . left her not a Moment, and by degrees settled so implacable a hatred in her Nature, not only to *Melladore,* but to that whole undoing Sex, that she never rejoic'd so much as when she heard of the Misfortunes of any of them" (78–79). Rather than passively sitting back in misery, however, Glicera commits her life actively to bring about masculine misfortune. Realizing that public knowledge of her lost reputation precludes her from marrying again and deciding that, even if she did receive an offer, she has "already experienced Mankind," Glicera is adamant never to be "deceived again by the most specious Pretenses" (79), becoming "resolved to behave to them [men] in a manner which might advance both her Interest and Revenge" (78). We might now, particularly with motherhood no longer an issue, expect the text to revert to a tragedian's bloody model of homicidal vengeance. Instead, Haywood plots Glicera's revenge as one of self-interest and psychological manipulation, a tactic that both keeps her protagonist well within the bounds of law, if far outside those of conventional morality, as it simultaneously provides another instance in which Haywood transforms standard plot mechanisms to her own devices.

Haywood's attention to quotidian detail, and her concentration on legal, economic, physical, and psychological realism, resembles that which Defoe is lauded as inaugurating in *Roxana*. Glicera's mode of revenge and the profit she gains by it are notably grounded in what will later be deemed the fertile soil of realistic or psychological fiction. Her capacity for heterosexual love smashed, she now does not differentiate between "the most Ugly" and "the Loveliest of Mankind—for all alike were hateful to her Thoughts"—but "feign[s] a Tenderness" for both so as to milk them for their money while teasing them with never fulfilled promises of easy sexual delight from a beautiful and ruined woman: [A]s nothing is capable of giving more Vexation to a Lover, than a Disappointment when he thinks himself secure from Fears of it . . . She received Their Treats and Presents, smil'd on all" and then disappointed them (79). Her goal is not extravagant murder, but a twofold plan: mercenary manipulation to achieve her own economic "interest," while simultaneously debasing would-be male seducers by besting them at their own "specious pretenses." Haywood locates Glicera's retaliation concurrently in the specific detail of economic and legal concerns and that of interpersonal psychology, literary devices defined as cornerstones of the English novelistic fiction.

For the remainder of the novel, Glicera self-consciously inhabits and acts out the feminine roles she has previously accepted as natural in order to use them to her own advantage. Pretending to be a sort of high-class call girl, a woman who will entertain male desire for the right price, Glicera gains authority over her own representation, becoming a subject who manipulates male desire rather than an object who is governed by it.[13] Glicera aptly puts to use her hard-won knowledge of love and masculine ego in an attempt to secure both capital and retribution by playing on men's readiness to believe in the familiar picture of femininity she presents. Glicera accedes to the cover story that defines women as fickle, shallow dupes and, by self-consciously following the script that has previously been the cause of her undoing, she protects herself from the pitfalls of unmediated occupation of the feminine role: "Never did a Woman passionately in love take greater Pains to captivate the ador'd Object of her Affections than did this fair *jilt*, to appear amiable in the Eyes of Mankind" (84–85). Haywood reveals that the only way a woman can succeed in the game of seduction is to treat it as a battle and to arrive armed and knowledgeable of her enemy. She flatters her wooers while keeping them all unsure of where they stand, putting them into competition with one another in attempts to win her favor via gifts and money, for, as Glicera has "as large a Share of Sense as Beauty, [she] knew . . . well how to manage the Conquests she gain'd" (84), and she amasses conquests of both—suitors and silver—with equal proficiency.

Her manipulations are directed most fully at the elderly and wealthy Alderman Grubguard, whose name echoes his physical deformity and ridiculousness, and whose foolish vanity and self-absorp-

tion recall countless similar characters from Renaissance and Restoration comedies. Haywood revels in her mockery of Grubguard and
goes on at length regarding his folly and egotism: he is "immensely
Rich, but so Old that none who beheld his wither'd Face, and shaking
Limbs, would have believed that in those shrivell'd Veins there was a
Warmth sufficient to maintain *Life,* much less to propagate *Desire*"
(79). Haywood uses the stock character of a bumbling ass to shift the
novel from an arena in which male sexual, legal, and economic power
has prerogative to a feminocentric, carnivalesque, household world
in which Glicera and her friend and live-in companion Laphelia turn
the tables and hoist the male characters by their own petards.

Realizing Grubgard's status as an easy mark, Glicera treats him
"with a double Portion of seeming Kindness," while she and Laphelia
secretly enjoy playing him for the fool. Playing to his narcissism and
competitiveness with other men, they convince him to dress the fop to
win Glicera's affections and can barely stifle their laughter when they
see him bedecked, "look[ing] exactly like one of those little Imitators
of Humanity [monkeys] which are carried about the Streets to make
Sport for Children" (81–82). In a scene reminicient of a Shakespearean
comedy, the women pretend to be flighty encouragers of male pomp
in order to indulge in a reversal of gendered power roles by which
they impel the wealthy and powerful alderman to act the ass. However, in Haywood's version, the gendered power reversal does not
revert back, and the heroines do not end up in a happy double marriage after their escapades. Glicera and Laphelia demonstrate that, in
fact, Grubgard's "act" is no stretch at all, and his transformation into
a foppish society lover blurs the lines between categories of maleness,
collapsing the division between the powerful alderman and the preen-
ing fop to reveal them as fundamentally connected by the texture of
male ego and appetite.

The alderman not only plays the fool by adopting airs unsuitable
to his position and age, but he also plays the pawn in Glicera's final
revenge on Melladore who, she learns to her delight, has fallen on
extreme misfortune. His wife, Helena, proven illegitimate and "basely
born," has lost her inheritance and run away with a lover, leaving
Melladore her massive debts.[14] Upon learning that Grubguard holds
Melladore's mortgage, Glicera determines to gain access to it in order
to obtain power over Melladore. Tellingly, the language of Glicera's

response to Melladore's ruin and of her plans to complete his down-fall is as steamily erotic as any of Haywood's sex scenes: that Melladore was "undone, fill'd her with a Satisfaction so exquisite, that for a moment she thought it impossible it could be exceeded; but soon it gave way to an impatient Desire . . . to be the Mistress of . . . the Power of all that *Melladore* was now worth in the world" (91). Sexual ruin morphs into economic as Melladore becomes the "undone" victim of the "impatient" and desiring "Mistress"; his reputation and financial stability become the body to be taken, and she becomes the plotting seducer whose pleasure will only peak at utter, not partial, "ruin." Haywood crafts a sort of inverse seduction narrative here, replacing heterosexual erotics with an erotics of economic control. Glicera gains an "exquisite Satisfaction" by substituting the now dis-solved "dissolving" romantic pleasures she had with Melladore with the salaciously sadistic, almost masturbatory, pleasures of her self-authored, money-based plot of revenge.

In working through Glicera's manipulations of Melladore's es-tate, Haywood goes into considerable detail regarding the legal status of mortgages, adding a level of textual detail rarely commented upon and calling attention to the increasing commodification of 1720s En-glish culture. While it is notable that Haywood has largely been de-nied credit for her textual forays into the economic strata of her society—credit amply given, in contrast, to her contemporary Defoe—it is also important to note that her use of the language of contracts is particularly gendered. While her Tory affiliation may inform Haywood's distaste for commodities exchange, mercantilism, and contracts *ad passim,* her textual examinations of these subjects reso-nate within a gendered, rather than a gentried, political economy. Having realized that her value is that of a commodity, Glicera does not fade away in shock, but rallies to manage her exchange of that value on the common market for her best interest, becoming the sole proprietor and vendor of that which was previously managed by men. Unlike Roxana or Moll Flanders—whose mercantile skills rely on a prostitution that ultimately endangers their "natural" femininity, a quality in which Defoe's texts remain vested—Glicera learns the les-son that femininity itself is a sham, a bum deal that she bought hook, line, and sinker, but one that she can still "sell" to make a profit. Haywood's detailed inquiry into the machinations of mortgages reveals not only her text's participation in a literary move slated as "novelistic" but her text's implicit assertion that the text of romance fantasy needs to be replaced with that of financial and legal reality.

Glicera and Laphelia convince Grubguard that once he parts with the mortgage of Melladore's estate Glicera will become his mistress, and the two women work to present Glicera as a maid sighing and blushing with desire for the alderman, but in need of tangible, and expensive, proof of his affections to allow him to win her favors over other suitors. Glicera represents herself as available to the highest bidder, and Grubguard jumps at the bait, remarking to himself that, once she is in his "Possession, I will so revenge myself for all her Coyness" (94), a threat that underlines the accuracy of Glicera's summation of masculine desire as dangerous and vengeful if not managed appropriately. Grubguard expects Glicera to desire fawning attention, to be foolishly impressed by his attempts at youth, and to be bought "by way of a bargain" (95), and she masterfully plays up to his expectations. On gaining Melladore's mortgage, Glicera at once drops her guise as mistress-on-the-make, and adopts another familiar role, that of the moralistic prude. She feigns outrage that he assumes she will have sex with him and declares that she has only encouraged him to teach him a moral lesson, claiming: "[A] Man who truly *Loves* me would *Marry* me; that is not in thy power, already art thou wedded . . . If I encourag'd thy Address, or accepted thy Gifts, 'twas but to punish thy impudent Presumption" (100). While Grubguard is astonished, he never guesses Glicera's true design, believing her act as injured feminine moralist as a recognizable and plausible, if disappointing, feminine type. The narrator wryly dismisses Grubguard and his grubby lechery, commenting, "'tis highly probable that after this he made an attack on no other Woman" and informing us that he died soon after Glicera's rejection.

With his estate in Glicera's hands, Melladore writes to Glicera begging her forgiveness and mercy. Here Haywood figures the pleading letter's "narrative interruptus" in terms of *male* submission and desire: Melladore articulates his desire—for forgiveness, blessing, and the love of Glicera—to the author of his fate, and his textual pleas position him at the mercy of the female subject. In a feminocentric fantasy of male supplication, not of sex, but power, Melladore is fully aware of and wretched about his mistreatment of Glicera: he praises her as "[t]he most deserving, yet most injur'd of her Sex," with "so much of the divine Nature" in her, and he is "now sensible of, and acknowledged in Agonies not to be express'd, the Justice of the divine Power in subjecting him to one he had so greatly wrong'd" (101). Gratified by Melladore's reversal of fortune and his acknowledgment of her absolute goodness and his base wickedness, Glicera is "fully satiated" in her revenge. She ceases her active undoing of, but not her hatred for, men and grants Melladore the chance to pay off his debt, rather than having him arrested for foreclosure. However, she refuses to forget his cruel mistreatment by "receiv[ing] the Traitor into Favour" as "some of her weak Sex would have" after his entreaties (102). In a reversal of earlier power dynamics, she continually refuses Melladore's letters of romantic entreaty, nullifying his attempts to alter the script she now has fully in hand. Melladore is forced to join the regiment to earn money and "is mortally wounded in the first Engagement," news Glicera hears with "happy indifference" (101–2). The irony of the double meaning of the phrase "first Engagement" is not subtle; it was his first engagement to Glicera, and the wounds she suffered from it, that ultimately led to his death in battle.

Glicera's rejection of "proper" or "natural" feminine behavior, and her subsequent careful orchestration of the gestures of this be- havior, are supported by a level of female friendship and solidarity more frequently associated with Jane Austen or Fanny Burney than with amatory authors. In her depiction of the closeness and essential nature of the relationship between Glicera and Laphelia, Haywood treads new ground in English fiction, situating the female/female rela- tionship as more valuable than that between the sexes. The two women's relationship is the only one in the novel with any emotional validity: Laphelia is "let into the Secret of her Thoughts" (80), and knowledgeably helps Glicera with all of her plans. She is the harbin- ger of the change in Glicera's fate from destroyed and debauched to solvent and serene: it is Laphelia "to whose Friendship and ready Wit she was chiefly indebted for her good Fortune" (103). In an ironic twist on the marriage plot, after Melladore's death, Laphelia and Glicera retire together in what was once Melladore's "fine House" (103). The two women happily supplant the site of male authority and economic power as a same-sex couple reoccupying the patriar- chal mansion. After moving in with Laphelia, Glicera ever after rejects male attention, "publickly avowing her Aversion to that Sex; and admitting no Visits from any of them, but as she was very certain had no Inclinations to make an amorous Declaration to her, either on honourable or dishonourable terms" (103).

While Haywood retreats from her initial gesture toward lesbianism by informing us that Laphelia eventually leaves Glicera and marries, the phrasing of this information bears noting. We are told that Laphelia "had been a long time contracted" to her husband and that his marriage offers her the "Opportunity of . . . exchanging the Pleasures of a single life, for the more careful ones of a married state" (103). There is no mention of love, simply contract, in a phrase that recalls the contractual nature of Glicera's engagement to Melladore, and the "careful" state necessitated by marriage reads as an opaque warning of the incipient dangers Haywood observes to be present in any heterosexual romantic union. The novel ends with a commendation of Glicera, stating that "Few Persons continue to live in greater Reputation, or more endeavor by good Actions to obliterate the memory of their past Mismanagement, than does this Fair Jilt; whose Artifices cannot but admit of some Excuse, when one considers the Necessities she was under, and the Provocations she received from that ungrateful Sex" (103). In a bold reworking of the marriage/death masterplot, Haywood rescripts Glicera's out of wedlock sex and manipulation of would-be lovers for personal gain not as sin—but simple "mismanagement."

The City Jilt defines heterosexual passion as dangerous for women, not because it is unhealthy or unnatural, but because it necessitates surrender to the fickle will of a sex and a society that Haywood defines as arbitrary and potentially deadly. The novel suggests that only by creating a simulacrum of desire, in which the woman is in total control, can women have a fighting chance in heterosexual romance. That this fighting chance necessitates the adoption of disguise rather than honesty is troubling, as is the fact that Glicera remains defined by stereotypically feminine imagery and roles. However, Glicera secures concrete gains in Haywood's text: she does not feel guilty; she is not killed or ruined despite her "fallen" status; and she is economically and verbally empowered, having taken charge of her own life.

At a formal level, the novel's lack of the "convention of transparency" has precluded its inclusion in canonical top-drawer literary circles.[15] Literary historian John Bender explains that "novelistic realism is marked by its self-representation as a transparent medium, a mode of writing that one sees through rather than a form one looks at" (67).[16] The transparent novel does not call attention to its machinations at a formal level, in contrast to its "unrealistic" cousins, whose concerns often mark the intersection between private and public worlds and muddy the lens of authorial invisibility. To accept that realist novels are transparent, or as Watt has suggested, "ethically neutral," requires prior acceptance of the abstract premise that realist (or, one might simply substitute "real" versus "ersatz") narratives are intrinsically fair and evenhanded.[17] Watt assumes this point of neutral authority in his classic definition of the realist novel:

> The narrative method whereby the novel embodies this circumstantial view of life may be called formal realism; formal, because realism does not here refer to any special literary doctrine or purpose, but only to a set of narrative procedures which are so commonly found together in the novel, and so rarely in other literary genres, that they may be regarded as typical of the form itself. Formal realism, in fact, is the narrative embodiment of a premise . . . which is implicit in the novel form in general: . . . the primary conviction, that the novel is a full and authentic form of human experience. . . . Formal realism is, like the rules of evidence, only a convention . . . [but] [t]he novel's air of total authenticity, indeed, does tend to authorize confusion on this point. (32)

The successful narrator, then, while effacing himself to hew to the neutral, inevitable values of formal realism, shapes our judgment, leading us along and supplying or withholding information so as to dictate our perceptions and to disguise the fictionality of the tale, thus dictating the "primary conviction, that the novel is a full and authentic form of human experience."[18] In the world of the realist novel, providence equals plot, and narrative manipulation is aesthetically superior when it least calls attention to itself or to those conventions of plot, prosody, and public discourse that necessarily and intrinsically inform it.

Haywood's novel *The City Jilt,* like her other fictions, does not fit Watt's categorical template for novelistic worth. Until recently, the rules of evidence for literary authority have dismissed those narratives shaped as self-conscious and self-referential, in which desire is extravagant and immediate, in which language exceeds the realistic space of diction and spills into hyperbole, in which plots move outside of master-narratives, and in which subjective consciousness is self-consciously female. From the middle of the eighteenth-century on, "authentic" and authoritative narratives—which obscure their ideologies through the transparency of their control of the plot, the invisibility and seeming "neutrality" of their narration—are the favored texts. Unlike Bender, I am not convinced that what Watt would deem traditional realist novels always "assume an assent to regulated authority" (Bender 72) as I find plenty of radical content and context in, for example, Defoe and Fielding. Yet, in terms of the critical inheritance that the British novel has spawned, I believe that *criticism* of these favored novels, rather than the novels themselves, often represses or denies those counternarratives which threaten it.

Critics have recently begun to judge the terms by which narratives such as those by Haywood have been dismissed as trifles, worthy only as eccentric precursors to the novel proper, useful background for establishing the age's socio-literary climate, or as historical evidence of feminine authorship as an *ipso facto* accomplishment—the work perhaps ignored, but the biographical existence of the writer applauded. I am committed to, and participate in, the critical enterprise whose aim is to defamiliarize and question traditional standards of aesthetics that have worked to mask the subjective and politicized terms by which texts and genres have acquired legitimacy. At the same time, however, I wonder if this inquiry, this re-evaluation of styles and subjects does not, in some ways, also work to elide the ways in which texts such as *The City Jilt* not only differ from canonically privileged novels, but resemble them. Since I wish to take issue with this argument as well, it is worth some, regrettably cursory, exploration here.

For example, Watt's seminal, if much contested, criterion of "managed circumstance," in which "providence equals plot" and constitutes "diffused authority," provides a productive lens through which to view *The City Jilt*. In fact, the novel's deployment of providence and circumstance, as managed by Glicera and the narrator, fit Watt's measure, albeit probably not to his desired aesthetic ends. The narrator observes "how severely did the unerring hand of Providence re-

venge the Injuries he [Melladore] had done *Glicera!*" (90). While providence was ably assisted by Glicera and Laphelia, we may read the
narrator's statement as a double-edged commentary on the nature of
providence, rather than a tropic, if ironic, move to place agency and
guilt away from Glicera and onto the Fates. On the one hand, the text
distinctly follows the rules of providential plot in its inevitable progression toward Melladore's death and ruin according to an
eschatological narrative of sin and punishment. On the other hand,
the novel rescripts the role of providence and the contextual notion of
circumstance by shifting sin and punishment outside of the normative
Christian conduct book morality that will soon become so popular
with Richardson. Haywood thus allows us to become aware of the
authorial wresting of plot: the hand of providence so carefully constructed in fiction is, of course, always that of narrator, a narrator
whose authority is diffused here by her claim to counterproof: that
the novel's conclusion is just (in both senses of the term) fate.

It is useful briefly to gloss this discussion of *The City Jilt* with
some of Haywood's comments from *The Female Spectator,* a journal
often used as an exemplum of Haywood's movement away from early
fictions (such as *The City Jilt*) to chaste moral piety. In fact, in *The
Female Spectator,* Haywood's referential irony, critiques of gender
inequity, sly wit, and investigations into the machinations of heterosexual romance remain intact, not much different from her fiction of
decades before. In a commentary that recalls Glicera's predicament,
Haywood decries the ways in which "generally . . . Romances, Novels, and Plays . . . dress Cupid up in Roses" (1744–46 ed., 1:10).
Haywood's concern is not one of prudish anti-fiction morality, but
rather of the danger of sensual syntax to young women ill-educated in
the realities of sexual and social congress. She addresses her female
readers: "It is not, therefore, from that Inconstancy of Nature which
the Men charge upon our Sex, but from that romantic Vein which
makes us sometimes imagine ourselves lovers before we are so . . .
nothing but a long continued Series of Slights and ill Usage . . . can
render him less dear" (*Female Spectator* 1:13). She relocates inconstancy as a result of male perfidy and critiques the plots that uncritically
imply that love is a woman's highest goal without instructing her about
its particulars. Haywood follows this exposition with the story of

Martesia, which, while presented as fact instead of fiction, is clearly an imaginative narrative, one that has much in common with her early fiction. Briefly, the moral of this tale of lust and woe is that women who are too tightly constrained and controlled will "fall" more quickly and harder than those who have more liberties and independence: "Woman is in far less Danger of losing her Heart, when every Day surrounded by a Variety of gay Objects, then when by some Accident, she falls into the Conversation of a single one.—A Girl, who is continually hearing fine Things . . . regards them but as Words of course" (1:24). Haywood suggests that women should be exposed to multiple encounters with romance, in life and in literature, so as not to be gullible to those words, like those of Melladore, that without warning could ensnare her. Her retort to men who argue with her claims for women's access to books, experience, education, and authority delightfully skewers moralistic patriarchal pedants: "[Men say that] Learning puts the Sexes too much on an Equality, it would destroy that implicit Obedience which it is necessary the Women should pay to our Commands:—If once they have the Capacity of arguing with us, where would be our Authority?" (*Female Spectator* 2:247).

The City Jilt's vision of a financially successful unmarried woman who is the author of her own fate and has, with the help of her female companion, taken over the male estate may be read as a testament to Haywood's own position as a woman writer whose powerful economic and popular success enables her to "take over" the male house of literary success with the help of her female readership. Haywood, as successful woman author, like Glicera, deconstructed and adapted the guises of femininity and female sexuality to manage Grub Street just as her fictional heroines dispatch Grubgard, the similarly named, similarly lucrative, and similarly ludicrous icon of male pomposity. As a narrative, *The City Jilt* investigates the sagacity of received fictional forms and reframes such forms in novel ways. As Haywood states in the epigraph that frames this essay, "letters will remain perpetual monitors," and so we must ingest them critically. Haywood's tale is not simply one of revised plot, but a telling investigation into narration itself. Haywood reveals the telltale fictionality at the heart of those social and cultural institutions that deny female authority and that attempt to confine women and their tales to the realm of fantastic romance.

Notes

1. In his groundbreaking study, *Popular Fiction Before Richardson,* Richetti argues that Haywood's seductive fictions were instrumental in the constitution of "the myth of female innocence destroyed by a world of male corruption" (169). His thoughts on Haywood have shifted in the past years, as evidenced by his contribution to this collection, and his arguments, with Paula Backscheider in their collection *Popular Fiction by Women, 1660–1730* (1996), that early eighteenth-century fiction by women does not simply create a paradigm of female victimization, but constitutes a more complex body of texts, in which the woman is often actually imagined as aggressor. Certainly, *The City Jilt* fits this latter description; however, I hesitate to separate the positions of victim and aggressor too cleanly or to mark them as fixed poles. In Haywood's fiction, as in the complex social moment in which she lived, personal and political modes and moments of power and powerlessness were fluid and dynamic, despite real experiential disparities of victim and aggressor.

2. Cf. Hammond's recent essay, "Mid-Century English Quixotism," which opens with a compact and useful overview of the current schools of critical thought on the rise of the English novel, including those critical studies that "effectively accept Watt's thesis about the rise of the novel . . . [although] seek to extend or qualify its terms" (247). Hammond notes that "some very recent approaches. . . [stress] that Watt's thesis is itself determined by ideological battles fought in the eighteenth century and won by the nineteenth, about how the novel's history should be represented" (247). Feminist literary historians tend to be far more attentive to works by women authors in their studies, and yet, Hammond argues, often end up reproducing a linear narrative of the progression of the female-authored novel that is "perhaps, just as fictive in its linearity as its brother" (248). While such a charge may have some merit, feminist critics have been those who have attended to the real import of the immensely popular fiction written by eighteenth-century English women (with the exception of John Richetti's previously mentioned early study, which while feminist in effect is not, I think, in specific theoretical intent). Such critics have also investigated the ways in which Watt-inspired dicta excluded women's writing from the arena of successful novelistic production. Cf. feminist studies including Ruth Perry's *Women, Letters, and the Novel* (1980), Jane Spencer's *The Rise of the Woman Novelist: From Aphra Behn to Jane Austen* (1986), Nancy Armstrong's *Desire and Domestic Fiction: A Political History of the Novel* (1987), Janet Todd's *The Sign of Angellica: Women, Writing, and Fiction, 1660–1800* (1989), Laurie Langbauer's *Women and Romance: The Consolations of Gender in the En-*

glish Novel (1990), Ros Ballaster's *Seductive Forms: Women's Amatory Fictions from 1684–1720* (1992), Catherine Gallagher's *Nobody's Story: The Vanishing Acts of Women Writers in the Marketplace, 1670–1820* (1994), Toni Bowers' *The Politics of Motherhood: British Writing and Culture, 1680–1760* (1996).

3. When Glicera transforms from victim to violator, she does not become what Ballaster described as a failed dystopic "masculine" prototype (175–179); rather, she prospers, escaping from the master plot of seduction and demise.

4. In a gesture of Haywood's distaste for mercantile Whiggery, she includes an epigraph to the novel that frames the text within the issue of the negative effects of monetary interest on true feeling, informing the reader that the tale will be a cautionary one regarding the dangers of commerce as they influence romance: "Virtue now, nor noble Blood,/Nor Wit by Love is understood; Gold alone does Passion move: Gold monopolizes Love" (66). See Toni Bowers's essay, "Sex, Lies, and Invisibility," in *The Columbia History of the British Novel* for more discussion of Haywood and Tory politics. Also see Bowers's essay "Collusive Resistance," and Ballaster's "A Gender of Opposition," in this collection.

5. By "romances," I refer to seventeenth-century French amatory texts written by authors such as Mm. de Scudery, La Capranede, and D'Urfe, as well as to the scandal fictions of Delarivier Manley. Until the mid-eighteenth century, with the typological definitions of Fielding, Johnson, Coventry, and others, the terms "novel" and "romance" were virtually interchangeable. While the distinct elements of the French romance were recognizable to Haywood and her audience, the novel/romance was flexible, and Haywood referred to her works as novels.

6. While he does not attend specifically to issues of gender, see Lincoln B. Faller's *Turned to Account: the Forms and Functions of Criminal Biography in Late Seventeenth- and Early Eighteenth-century England* (1987) for a discussion of the ways in which the criminal biography functioned largely as an apologia for extant social systems. In addition, my forthcoming book, *Deadly Plots: Narratives of Women and Murder in Augustan England,* explores the ways in which female criminality is narrativized in novels, newspapers, criminal biographies, and law.

7. *The City Jilt's* delineations of the economic perils of abandoned womanhood resemble Defoe's similarly pragmatic attention to the economic peril of women without male protection, particularly in *Roxana* (1724), without, however, the shading of domestic didacticism that hovers over Defoe's text.

8. Had she a male guardian, he could have pursued Melladore in Church Court to insist that he follow through on his promise to wed Glicera, a promise

considered legally binding in England until 1753. Alone, to have taken him to court herself would not only have been outside of her realm of knowledge and access, but also would have resulted in her highly inappropriate public presentation of her case without a suitable male mouthpiece.

9. I am indebted to Paula Backscheider's essay, "The Story of Eliza Haywood's Novels: Caveats and Questions," included in this volume, for her thoughtful attention to Haywood's use of the Southern European revenge novel.

10. In his book, *Strong Representations: Narrative and Circumstantial Evidence in England* (1992), Alexander Walsh argues that, as courts began to privilege legal narratives based on circumstances versus direct testimony, so did literary aesthetics begin to privilege "realist" fictions over more immediate testimonials.

11. While I used the term "pastiche" before reading her essay, my understanding of its resonances has greatly benefited from Andrea Austin's original and productive use of the term in her essay, "Shooting Blanks: Potency, Parody, and Eliza Haywood's *The History of Miss Betsy Thoughtless*," included in this volume.

12. Bannett states that, "[i]f the couple's promises were expressed in words of the future tense . . . the marriage became binding as soon as consummation occurred . . . the marriage would in principle be sustained by the courts against any subsequent marriage" (234). In his introduction to Defoe's *Conjugal Lewdness*, Max Novak explains that "Defoe's attack on intercourse before marriage was leveled against a practice that was practically universal before the Marriage Act of 1754" (x). Haywood's readers would have been aware of the civic, as well as social, wrongdoing of which Melladore was guilty.

13. In her brief discussion of the novel in her book *Masquerade and Gender: Disguise and Female Identity in Eighteenth-Century Fictions by Women*, Catherine Craft-Fairchild reads Haywood's *The City Jilt*, as well as *Fantomina*, in terms of masquerade. However, Craft-Fairchild's analysis is more indebted to contemporary psychoanalytic understandings of the term than my own (68–73). In her article, "Descending Angels: Salubrious Sluts and Petty Prostitutes in Haywood's Fiction," Mary Anne Schofield contends that Glicera "prostitutes her body in order to gain wealth, power, and most especially, control which she exercises over the duped male . . . Glicera vows to get even. She does so by selling her body to all men" (193–94). I disagree entirely with this contention (as does Craft-Fairchild). Glicera would have no power over her admirers, as she has been well taught by Melladore, if she gave up sexual favors; her power relies on her teasing promise of such favors with no delivery, a promise she extends in exchange for "plate and presents."

Her comment to her aging and wealthy beau, Alderman Grubguard, sustains this reading; she admonishes him that "[i]t is not in the power of the loveliest, wittiest, and most engaging of all of your Sex to tempt me to an Act of Shame" (99).

14. In another textual moment that reveals Haywood's concerns with contract and realistic detail as inseparable from the machinations of romance, she goes into great detail about the legal particulars of Helena's case (see particularly page 86).

15. John Bender describes realist narrative as being identifiable via "its dense particularity, its rules of cause and effect, its mastery of consciousness" (166), and associates this movement in fiction with the impersonal supervision offered by the new penitentiary system which arose at the same time. Romance or amatory fictions have often been denied fully vested status as novels at least in part because they tend not to fulfill the conventions of narrative transparency.

16. Flaubert condensed the basic principle of realist representation in a comment later echoed by Joyce: "The illusion (if there is one) comes from the *impersonality* of the work. . . . The artist in his work must be like God in his creation—invisible and all-powerful: he must be everywhere felt, but never seen" (Steegmuller 1:230).

17. In other words, to accept, as the eighteenth-century courts did, narratives of circumstance and providential plot in which the individual subjective authority of the manager of the "facts" remains obscured "requires the unacknowledged acceptance of a certain kind of authority diffused throughout the text" (Bender 69–71).

18. Watt, like Davis and McKeon after him, cites Fielding as the master of this particular and authoritative realist discourse.

A Gender of Opposition

Eliza Haywood's Scandal Fiction

Ros Ballaster

In 1992 I characterised Eliza Haywood's early fiction as a retreat into "romance proper" from the "[t]he allegorical duplicity of scandal fiction, its complex double movement between the amatory and party political plot" that had been the distinguishing feature of the work of her female predecessors in "Tory" fictionalizing, Aphra Behn (*The Love-Letters between a Nobleman and His Sister* [1684–87]) and Delarivier Manley (*The New Atalantis* [1709] and *Memoirs of Europe* [1710]).[1] Haywood's scandal fictions of the 1720s, I claimed, lacked the directness and oppositional definition that had made Manley's work so influential and threatening in the campaign against the Whig politicians and society figures of Anne's court. The political climate of the 1720s saw a more fluid and shifting set of political alliances around the loose definitions of "Court" and "Country" than the political categories of Whig and Tory that had held sway from the Exclusion Crisis through the first decade of the eighteenth century (*Seductive Forms* 156–77). Moreover, Haywood's departure from the feminocentric strategies of narration I identified in Manley's best-known fiction seemed to give evidence of a retreat from the attempt to figure (female) party political agency through sexual political narrative. Where Delarivier Manley deploys an all-female circuit of narration and consumption of "factional" texts in her *New Atalantis* (the goddess Astraea is "guided" by the female allegorical figure of

Intelligence and later the midwife, Mrs. Nightwork), Haywood's scandal fictions—indeed, the majority of her fictional writings, scandal, amatory or otherwise—are narrated either by an "ungendered" narrator, as in *The Secret History of the Present Intrigues of the Court of Caramania,* or a male narrator (Cupid is the main narrator of scandalous tales of court intrigues to a male visiting the island of Utopia in *Memoirs of a Certain Island Adjacent to the Kingdom of Utopia,* and *The Adventures of Eovaai* are told by the Anglicized son of a mandarin). However, I overlooked the possibility that Haywood might be treating a masculine narrator satirically, a technique I had noted in the work of Manley. *The Adventures of Rivella,*[2] Manley's "autobiography" of 1714, uses a male narrator (Lovemore) and a male consumer (d'Aumont) of her life's "story" to assault the "appropriation" by the publisher, Edmund Curll, and scandalous biographer, Charles Gildon, of the female writer as amatory icon rather than political agent. In the first volume of her *Memoirs of Europe,* Manley uses a male narrator, the Count de St. Gironne, to expose the unthinking misogyny at the heart of his scandalous court tales (see chapter 4 of *Seductive Forms*). These earlier instances in her predecessor's work should perhaps have alerted me to the possibility that Haywood chooses an aesthetics consciously and satirically signposted as "masculine" for political effect.

Brean Hammond, in an excellent recent study, has challenged my own attempt to make a case for psychological depth and complexity, if not political sophistication, in Haywood's early work. He argues that Haywood and Defoe offer alternative and powerful models for "novelization" in the early eighteenth century, the former structuring narrative around "plot-event" and the latter structuring narrative around "relationships"; "the happy instability of reader's response to story," Hammond claims, "is what she offers in place of psychological investigation."[3] Employing Hammond's insights into what he terms "novelization" enables my own reconsideration of Haywood's tactics and purchase as satirist; I aim to trace in Haywood's scandal fiction both a shrewd critique of the gendered cultural and political poetics of the 1720s and 1730s and an attempt to "configure" a rival aesthetics more hospitable to the imagining of agency for women as writers and political "plotters."

Hammond glosses "novelization" as "the set of material, cultural

and institutional changes responsible for the promotion of prose narrative to its undisputed preeminence as the most widely consumed
form of imaginative writing, a process that extinguished the long poem,
marginalized all other poetic forms, and rendered the theatre a mi-
nority interest" (303). The signs of "novelization" are first, "a tendency . . . towards a hybridization that breaks down traditionally
observed generic boundaries" and second, an "aspiration . . . on the
part of many disparate forms of writing toward the condition of narrative" (250). In his account, Haywood becomes for her high-cultural
contemporaries—the Scriblerian circle of Pope, Swift, and Gay in particular—the exemplary figure of the decline of culture through "novelization," the departure from classical ethics and aesthetics into a
hybridized, market-led circulation of promiscuous textual bodies for
financial profit. Scriblerian or Patriot allegories of Walpole and his
ministry, with the exception of Jonathan Swift's *Gulliver's Travels*
(1726) and Fielding's *Jonathan Wild* (1743), incline to poetry or drama
as the vehicle for satire, more often than not presenting the "fictionalizing" of political relations as an expression of "court" interests and
harnessing the diagnosis of a degraded culture (the symptom of which
is the novel) to the critique of philistinism, financial self-interest, and
preferment in Walpole's government.[4] Hammond's work, and that of
Christine Gerrard and Colin Nicholson before him, has done much to
undermine the myth that appears to have underpinned such early studies as Bertrand Goldgar's *Walpole and the Wits* (1976): that the opposition to the "Great Man" Robert Walpole, "Prime Minister" to
the Hanoverian kings from 1721 to 1742, could be characterized as a
"country" grouping advocating landed property, monarchical prerogative, and country retreat as the basis for "good" government by contrast with a "modern" "court" grouping around Walpole wedded to
urban complexity, credit, commerce, and protocapitalism.[5] Gerrard
demonstrates that by the late 1720s the active Patriot opposed to
Walpole was not necessarily a country gentleman but more likely a
tradesman living in London, Manchester, or Bristol defending the
national interest by arguing for a return to the expansive trade and
empire of the Elizabethan period by contrast with the parochialism
and expense of Walpole's standing armies and high taxes.
　　Such reassessments of the shifting political allegiances and aesthetics of the early eighteenth century have made it possible to see

how Haywood, pre-eminent representative of the "hack" writing for bread and looking for a niche market, may have been harnessed to the hydra-headed opposition to Walpole's ministry. The fact that she joined Henry Fielding's troupe, known as the Great Mogul's Company, at the Little Theater in the Haymarket in the 1730s invites us to speculate that she, like Fielding, was stepping up her satirical attacks on the Walpole ministry at this time. In particular, she capitalized on the public unrest of 1736 in her most focused attack on Walpole, *The Adventures of Eovaai,* first published in that year.[6] In 1733 she collaborated with her lover, William Hatchett, in revising Fielding's anti-Walpole play of 1731, *The Tragedy of Tragedies* (itself a more specifically satirical version of the earlier *Tom Thumb* of 1730), as *The Opera of Operas.* In 1737 she took the role of Mrs. Screen in Fielding's play *The Historical Register for the Year of 1736,* the satirical attack on Walpole that led to the latter's amendment of the licensing act so as to bring Fielding's (and Haywood's) dramatic career to a halt.[7]

Unlike Fielding, however, Haywood could not seek association with the "Scriblerus" club—the title assumed in 1713 by the Tory wits Swift, Gay, Pope, Parnell, and Arbuthnot to designate a shared project burlesquing pedantry and bad writing—since she already loomed large as a representative of Grub street promiscuity in Alexander Pope's 1728 *Dunciad.* Fielding's *Covent-Garden Tragedy* of 1732 was attributed to "Scriblerus Secundus" and took Colley Cibber as its chief "fool," a move Pope was to imitate in replacing Lewis Theobald with Colley Cibber as the king dunce in the 1742 revision of the *Dunciad.*

Another acquaintance of Eliza Haywood's, Aaron Hill, also unsuccessfully sought recognition as a Scriblerian from Pope. In her estrangement from Aaron Hill's circle of the 1720s (known as the Hillarians) as a result of her scandalous treatment of Martha Fowke Sansom and Richard Savage in her *Memoirs of . . . Utopia* in 1724,[8] Haywood lost her connection to the only cultural circle of the early eighteenth century that was hospitable both to female artistic endeavor and to the social and partisan politics of benevolence and constitutional monarchy we can trace in her scandal fiction. The Scriblerian "mock-epic" productions of the first two decades of the century (Pope's *Dunciad* and Swift's *Gulliver's Travels*) and the Patriot poetry of the

1730s advocated an aesthetics of an heroic masculinity identified with the "epic" as a means of fending off the dangers of an encroaching and engrossing effeminacy associated with the "romance" and the female-authored novel, symbolically embodied in the luxurious and supine Hanoverian monarchy and its exploitative ministry. Hill's periodical, the *Plain Dealer,* by contrast, had included a poetic tribute from a female friend to Delariver Manley on the latter's death as a preface to a claim for the "the superiority of our Women's Talents" in Britain (no. 53, 21 September 1724) and argued that romances and novels provided "Gallant and Heroick Examples, of Male and Female Virtue" for young female readers (no. 62, 23 October 1724).[9]

Despite her material and intellectual connections with Aaron Hill, Richard Savage, and later Henry Fielding, in the history of Haywood's ventures into scandal fiction and her textual practices, we can trace an uncanny mirroring of the trajectory of the writer who sought to put the most distance between his work and her own, Alexander Pope. Like Pope's *Dunciad* of 1729, Haywood's *Memoirs of . . . Utopia* (1724–5) sets up those who may have considered themselves friends and allies of the author as representatives of types of vicious behaviour and false wit. Haywood's opposition partisanship is, like Pope's, hard to diagnose: the extent of her sympathy for Jacobitism in the 1715 and 1745 rebellions seems to have been considerable and yet, like Pope, in the 1730s she seems to have been attracted to the alternative "rival" prince in the shape of Frederick, Prince of Wales.[10] Indeed, the textual relationship between Haywood and Pope may have been initiated well before Pope's representation of Eliza as the prize in a pissing competition between rival booksellers in the second book (lines 149–158) of the *Dunciad* (1728).[11]

Haywood imitates the supernatural machinery of Pope's popular *Rape of the Lock* in at least two places in the first volume of *Memoirs of . . . Utopia*. When Bellario (Eustace Budgell) carelessly throws down his love letters from women, a sylph snatches them up and takes them to Olympus.[12] In the apocalyptic closing scenes of the first volume, when the Genius of the isle causes the shrine of fortune to come crashing down so that the crowd around the magical well sees clearly its fabricated nature (a satirical representation of the financial crash that resulted from massive public and parliamentary speculation in the South Sea Company in 1720), coquettes and beaus remain unmoved, since "Nature sent 'em into the World animated only by a little Spirit of her own—they have no Souls, are incapable of discerning any thing farther than the Senses direct them—Thought, Penetration, Reflection, are what they know nothing of—they are a sort of *Butterflies;* pretty, little, unhurtful, insipid Insects, who when they have play'd away their Season here, are translated into some other World to buz about, incapable of meriting either Heaven or Hell" (286). Haywood's coquettes and beaus are decorative, superficial, and ineffectual presences that invoke the image of the coquettes transformed into sylphs and prudes transformed into gnomes of Pope's 1714 version of the *Rape of the Lock.*[13] In a seemingly conscious imitation in mock-heroic prose of the 1714 *Rape of the Lock* card-playing scene of the third canto, during which Belinda's lock experiences its "rape" at the hands of the Baron, volume 2 of *Memoirs of . . . Utopia* offers a scene of a society gambling parlour:

> At *Ombre* some were busily engaged,—at *Basset* others.—In one
> part of the spacious Room a Crowd of *Beaus* and *Belles* were
> attracted by the musick of a rattling Dice-box—in another, a well-
> match'd Pair, more politely, were beating Time to the brisk Measures
> of the sprightly *Violin.*—*Here,* might be seen a Youth, inspir'd with
> tender Passion, breathe out his Soul in Vows of everlasting Love at
> the fair Shrine of some admir'd *Coquette;* who, vain of her new
> Conquest, laughs out aloud, and by a thousand Affectations takes
> pleasure to proclaim his Pains, and her Disdain.—*There,* the Sport of
> the disengaged part of the Assembly, stood a forsaken Nymph,
> bursting with jealous Rage to see the roving Swain address elsewhere
> those Sighs which once were her's—At rich *Beausetts* the Votaries of
> *Bacchus* quaff'd reeling Worship to the drunken God; while the more
> thinking Heads sipp'd *Coffee, Tea,* and luscious *Chocolate.* (58–59)

If the *Rape of the Lock* surfaces as an important intertext, it is worth speculating that Haywood is also offering a critique of the work of her Scriblerian predecessor. *Memoirs of . . . Utopia* takes the form of a repetitive series of accounts of seductions and rapes of court and country ladies by rapacious politicians and aristocrats. Pope's figurative and mocking account of the "rape" of a lock of hair targets the trivializing imagination of women and chastises its heroine, Belinda (and behind her Arabella Fermor, the original "victim" of Lord Petre's attentions), for overreacting to a chivalric game. Haywood literalizes the "rape" of the lock into an account of the sexual predatoriness of a "corrupt" court. Alongside the use of narratives of sexual seduction and betrayal as vehicles for the representation of political seduction and betrayal (in both the exercise of arbitrary power is "masked" as an expression of passionate love for the mistress/state), Haywood pursues yet another concealed interest: the exposure of the misogynist underpinnings of the aesthetics deployed by the masculinist satires that she imitates.

Karen Hollis has highlighted this critical slant toward Scriblerian satire in Haywood's fiction in the context of another work by Haywood, her *Secret History of Mary, Queen of Scots* (1725), a novella which charts the abuse and forgery of Mary's letters by her half-brother and secretary, revealing the appropriation of the figure of women's writing for scandalous public display by male authorities for state political ends. Hollis concludes:

> For Pope and Swift, popular print culture could be constructed as monstrously female, disfiguring the purity of male letters; simultaneously, they endeavored to preserve a masculinized, elite, and public literary preserve by aligning women's writing with an idealized private sphere. The *Secret History,* in contrast, genders print as male, characterizing it as controlling both Mary's story and the means of production of writing. Haywood identifies her history as an intervention into the male appropriation of the content as well as the circulation of women's stories. If Mary's letters prove pathetically vulnerable within the text, open to manipulation and misinterpretation, Haywood's book will compensate for that weakness through publication, proving a final, authoritative statement of the truth of the matter. Her story will intervene in what is represented as a male domination and manipulation of print, which gives male authors control over the construction of female sexuality. (48)

The traffic in the figure of the female body in satirical writing is not, however, one way. In the light of Haywood's imitation of *The Rape of the Lock* in her *Memoirs of . . . Utopia,* Pope's *Dunciad* might be seen as evolving his representation of Dulness, as a feminized and debased form of "imagination," through his reaction to Eliza Haywood's scandal writing.

The specific instance of Pope's antagonism to Haywood lay in her scandalous portrayal of his neighbor and friend, Lady Henrietta

Howard (mistress to the Prince of Wales and patron to Pope's
Scriblerian ally John Gay) as the designing and power-hungry Ismonda,
mistress to the married Theodore, King of Caramania, in the 1726
Secret History of the Present Intrigues of the Court of Caramania.[14]
Yet Pope's apparent chivalry in defense of one woman (Henrietta
Howard) at the hands of another (Haywood) masks a gendered aes-
thetics in which the female imagination is presented as a counterfeit
that debases the currency of an authentic masculine creativity.
Haywood appears as a "mother" of two illegitimate children with
"Two babes of love close clinging to her waste" (*Dunciad* 2.150).[15]
Her promiscuous scribbling (the reference is to her two scandal fictions of the 1720s) is equated with her pursuit of sexual liaisons outside of the formal legitimating structures of marriage which guarantee
lineage. Pope's footnote comments that "In this game is expos'd in
the most contemptuous manner, the profligate licentiousness of those
shameless Scriblers (for the most part of That sex, which ought least
to be capable of such malice and impudence) who in libellious Memoirs and Novels, reveal the faults and misfortunes of both sexes, to
the ruin or disturbance, of publick fame or private happiness"
(*Dunciad*, 2 n. 149). Dennis Todd clarifies the gendered nature of the
aesthetics of imagination at work in Pope's poem in the context of
early modern theories of reproduction and the idea of maternal "impress" on fetal form through acts of imaginative creation:

> The Dunces are born as featureless repetitions of each others' works
> . . . or blank slugs on which are stamped the identities of their
> forebears. . . . And all of them, fathers, sons, and works, revolve
> back into the mother. For "She marks her Image": meaning not
> simply that she sees herself in her children but that she sees herself in
> them because she "marks" them with her image in the way that a
> mother . . . disfigures her offspring in the course of monstrous birth
> by impressing on them the forms of her imagination. Lineage, instead
> of being a succession of individual identities, becomes a kind of
> tautological genesis, the production of a line of repeatable, indistin-
> guishable objects, the endless replication in matter of the mother's
> imagination. (Todd 215–16)

Yet, Pope's account is disingenuous. His own "original" creative
imagination lies in the appropriation of the novelizing energies of

Haywood's writing, monstrous mother to his own. Indeed, the cyclic apocalyptic structure of the books of the *Dunciad* might seem to owe much to the two volume structure of *Memoirs of . . . Utopia,* both of which conclude on ironic visions of the possible sweeping away of the corrupt state. The scandal chronicles of Haywood, and Delarivier Manley before her, might be cited as the shadowy forebears, the "mothers" of Pope's own scandalous writing which, even as it tries to lay claim to the quality of masculine "epic," finds itself spawning keys and imitations that "frame" the poem as a manifestation of the very print cultural profligacy and promiscuity that it seeks to satirize.[16]

The peculiarly "double" nature of Haywood's satirical enterprise, both imitation and critique, is particularly evident in the history of her novelizing treatment of the notorious "Prime Minister," Robert Walpole. She marshalls the same arguments against the "Great Man" offered by her male contemporaries in the more or less orchestrated opposition campaigns of the 1720s and 1730s and also offers a critique of the structuring misogyny in the available discourses of such "opposition" satire: a misogyny which, her novels reveal, tends toward the exclusion of women from politically instrumental positions. This "double" practice is most visible in the *Adventures of Eovaai* of 1736. Haywood's *Memoirs of . . . Utopia* and her *The Secret History of . . . the Court of Caramania,* written and published in the 1720s, do not take Walpole as their central and single target. Rather, they provide a series of scandalous accounts of members of the circle around George, Prince of Wales, and Princess Caroline before the former's accession to the throne in 1727, including Walpole. The key to the London second edition of the *Memoirs of . . . Utopia* (1726) identifies the necromancer Lucitario as "C—gs" (James Craggs or Craggs the Younger, Secretary to Aislabie at the time of the South Sea Bubble). Margaret Rose alerts readers to a separately published 1725 Dublin key to the *Memoirs of . . . Utopia* which gives "Mr. W–l—e" as Lucitario, placing the *Memoirs* in a group of writings that represent Walpole as a financial and political wizard, following his masterly "screening" of the effects of the South Sea crash.[17] The Dublin key and the London key identify a figure who is celebrated at the end of the first volume, Cleomenes, as "Mr. Walpole" and "Mr. W—e" respectively. Cleomenes is presented as a possible saviour of the isle, "a greatly noble *Patriot*" (277), but Rose convincingly demonstrates the irony of this representation, summarizing the description of Cleomenes as a "paradoxical encomium, recalling Dryden's *MacFlecknoe,* [which] ironically treats each of Walpole's vices through extolling their opposites" (*Political* 42). The familiar signposts of opposition complaints against Walpole are present: preferment of his relatives and allies regardless of merit, avarice, opportunism, impiousness, and long-standing infidelity to his wife with his mistress, Molly Skerritt:

> The truly Meritorious ne'er sued to him in vain, nor did the Undeserving, tho' ne'er so near ally's by Blood, meet advantage by his Favour.—The humble Virtuous need but to be known, to be exalted high as his Interest can raise them, but the proud Vicious meet his utmost Scorn.—With him no Recommendations but intrinsick Goodness and known Abilities are of force—no secret Bribes, no Flatteries, no Insinuations, ever mov'd him to a forgetfulness of what he owes to Heaven, or to his Country.—Nor is his *Capacity* inferior to his *Zeal*—with a Penetration almost infallible, he sees Events long e'er they happen—looks into the Source of things, and turns, with admirable and virtuous Policy, intended Evils on the heads which form'd them—Dear to *Minerva* and *Astrea,* their Aid he constantly invokes, and reaps the Benefit of his pious Orizons—Then for his strict Obedience to thy Laws, Joy-giving *Cupid*! well thou know'st his Faith, so often tempted, and yet never false to his first Vows, his sacred *Hymeneal* Contract. (277–8)

The second volume of *Memoirs . . . of Utopia,* published in November 1725, sees a similarly ironic resurfacing of the figure of Walpole. Earlier in the year, Walpole had revived the Knighthood of the Bath in order to secure honors to confer on his aspiring supporters, overseeing the investiture of thirty-eight new red-ribboned knights, himself included. Haywood draws a scene in which Cupid stands at the doors of the Houses of Parliament bemoaning the sexual and political corruption of its members, when the Genius of the Isle enters, full of smiles, with the news that he has been visited by the goddess Fame; she has informed the Genius that

> A Troop of noble Youths, by me inspir'd, thirst to reform the Manners of the Age: With solemn Vows they bind themselves to right the Injured—defend the Widows and the Orphans Claims,—rescue assaulted Chastity,—and fight the Cause of all that are defenceless

and forlorn. To my Protection are the gallant Band committed, under my Banners do they list themselves: Each on the Badge of his sacred Order bears this Inscription in Capital Letters engrav'd,

A KNIGHT OF FAME

By that Title are they enrolled in Heaven's immortal Court, and thus must be distinguish'd here below. (276–77)

The following year Walpole was delighted to receive the Order of the Garter from George I, plastering the ceilings and chimney piece at Houghton with the star and garter image and earning him another of his many nicknames, that of "Sir Blue-String."[18] In the *Adventures of Eovaai*, Haywood ironically picks up the motif. Atamadoul, the maid of honour in love with Ochihatou, elopes with him by pretending to be her mistress under cover of a veil of "the finest blue Net in the World, embroider'd all over with silver Stars" (29). In the concluding stages of the novel the young prince Adelhu diplomatically covers Eovaai's nakedness with a blue robe embroidered with silver stars he is wearing (53).

In the sections that conclude both volumes of *Memoirs of . . . Utopia*, Walpole is summoned as a political "hero" who claims to offer salvation to his people, the restoration of a balance of government between Commons, Lords, and Sovereign. Here Haywood, in tune with numerous other opposition writers, presents Walpole as disguising his own hunger for advancement and arbitrary power in the language of Lockean principles of contract and good government. As Jerry Beasley succinctly puts it, "while Walpole himself invoked Locke as the authority for his policies and his manner of governing, others saw in him the very embodiment of the greed, dishonesty, and arbitrary power that Locke had condemned. By the wicked manœuvrings of his administration (so the Opposition argument went) the first minister had usurped all power in Parliament, upsetting the balance of government and reducing the monarch to a cipher. He was a devious hypocrite who had made himself master of the land" (*Portraits* 415). Margaret Rose locates Haywood firmly in this opposition discourse, claiming that "[t]hroughout her life, she upheld the Lockean precepts of constitutional government with the correct balance of power between King and Parliament" (*Political* 15).

Haywood's political position is most clearly stated in the later scandal novel, *The Adventures of Eovaai* (1736), in which she abandoned the serial narrative structure of Manley's scandal chronicles that she had imitated so closely in *Memoirs of . . .Utopia* for the dystopic single history favored in the separate books of Jonathan Swift's *Gulliver's Travels*. This shift was in keeping with the narrowing of her satiric focus from the many targets she located in her own acquaintance and that of George, Prince of Wales, to the single figure of Walpole, who miraculously survived as prime minister in the Prince of Wales's transition from rival monarch-in-waiting to sovereign in 1727.

By the mid 1730s not only had the administrative balance of power shifted, but the nature of the opposition had altered. The most vigorous and vocal opposition to Walpole and his ministry did not emanate from Scriblerian cultural political quarters but from the "Patriot" Whigs who took as their political figurehead the dissident Frederick, Prince of Wales. Haywood's novel, on the surface, offers an unproblematic fictionalizing of Patriot political argument in favour of a broad-based, non-partisan resistance to "arbitrary" power in government, advocating royalist rather than republican solutions. The evil prime minister of Hypotofa, Ochihatou (Walpole), has enchanted the king Oeros (George II) with a magic feather into supine acquiescence to the extent that no enquiry has been made into the apparent death of his heir, the young prince Adelhu (Frederick, Prince of Wales, or possibly, but more unlikely, the Young Pretender).[19] The depiction of Ochihatou clearly signposts him as a representation of Walpole, triggering all the conventional associations touted in opposition writing. Introduced as the "great man" (62), but described as physically deformed, he has discharged all civil and military appointments and preferred his own creatures. Seizing public treasure into his own hands, he has built palaces for himself and his concubines and employed "a kind of Civil Army" (66) to raise taxes, laying waste the country's traditional agricultural resources (in 1733 Walpole was obliged to back down on his proposal to transfer customs duties on tobacco and wine to inland excises due to backbench opposition that saw it as a means of making all tax fall on land). Ochihatou, like Walpole (who resisted campaigns for war with Spain in the 1730s), evades involvement in foreign wars, failing to support his country's ally, Habul, against the threat of "engrossing universal Monarchy" by the states of Narzada and Fayoul (90).

Ochihatou's exercise of arbitrary power extends from his state political to his sexual political behaviour. Eovaai, princess of the kingdom of Ijaveo, has lost a magic jewel which protected her and her nation from the influence of evil spirits and hence becomes vulnerable to the expansionist political and lustful sexual ambitions of Ochihatou. Without the magic jewel Eovaai can no longer see Ochihatou's real deformity and corruption (his powers of necromancy enable him to adopt the guise of an attractive man), and when he rescues her from imprisonment in her own country she seems likely to succumb to his seductive overtures. Ochihatou, after subjecting her to scenes of sexual revelry at court, is about to enjoy her when he is called away on urgent political business, and Eovaai is visited by the female genii, Halafamai (Truth), who gives her a magic perspective that allows her to see Ochihatou for what he really is. Halafamai spirits Eovaai away to the borders of Hypotofa where she is sheltered by Alhahuza (Patriotism) in his austere castle dedicated to Patriot heroes. Her ideas of constitutional monarchy now revive, displacing Ochihatou's attractive creed of arbitrary power, but bringing her perilously close to succumbing to the alternative creed of republicanism, literalized in Alhahuza's letting down a drawbridge from his castle to enable her to enter the republic of Oozoff. Here she engages in lengthy discussions with an old man who advocates republicanism as the only means to prevent tyranny. Ultimately, Oozoff cannot protect Eovaai, and twenty of Ochihatou's men succeed in abducting her and returning her to his clutches.

Ochihatou now plans to rape his victim if she will not give her consent but leaves her alone briefly to try and reconcile herself to submission. A chained monkey brings Eovaai some wooden tablets; her reading of the tablets transforms the animal into an aging beauty named Atamadoul, who, it transpires, is Ochihatou's prisoner. She tells her story of her hopeless love for Ochihatou and her substitution in place of her mistress, the princess Syllalipe, with whom Ochihatou had planned to elope. He discovers her real identity and punishes her by transforming her into the shape of a monkey and confining her to his bedchamber so that she must watch his sexual encounters without hope of satisfying her own lusts. Atamadoul substitutes for Eovaai on Ochihatou's return and Eovaai, rather than Atamadoul, becomes the reluctant yet titillated observer of sexual riot; the cheat is discovered when servants break in with lights to announce a public uprising led by Alhahuza and his Patriot cohorts. Ochihatou transports Eovaai in a magic chariot to the kingdom of Huzbib, whose sovereign is an ally of Oeros, and here they enjoy temporary sanctuary while Ochihatou tries to convince Eovaai that he regrets his previous aggression. When his magic arts reveal to him that the spell over Oeros has been broken, he once again spirits Eovaai away, transforming her naked person into the shape of a dove and his own into a bird of prey to carry her in his talons. They return to Ijaveo where he plans to rape her and force her to make him king; however, she escapes his grasp, seizes his wand and breaks "it in sunder before his Face" (151). He ties her by her hair to the bough of a tree and prepares to beat her to death with a switch of nettles and thorns, but a beautiful young man rushes forth to prevent him. Ochihatou recognizes Adelhu and beats his own brains out on a tree to avoid becoming the young man's prisoner. Eovaai is restored to her capital and her throne, where she suspects Adelhu of usurping her authority but soon discovers he has acted nobly to save her country. She agrees to marry him, thus uniting the two kingdoms.

Haywood's use of an oriental fiction to satirize Walpole is by no means unusual. George Lyttelton, popular Patriot writer and nephew to Lord Cobham, leader of the Patriot circle known as Cobham's Cubs, had used the device of the foreign traveler commenting on the contemporary political scene in his *Letters from a Persian in England to his Friend in Ispahan* of 1735. Lyttelton's narrator argued Patriot positions in favor of freedom of the press to check corrupt ministers, warned against bad administration, and advocated that the distinction of Whig and Tory be abandoned in favor of a single national standard. Haywood herself had experimented with the technique in her 1727 *Letters from the Palace of Fame,* which, like Lyttelton's *Letters,* modelled itself on the popular translations of Marana's *Turkish Spy* and Montesquieu's *Persian Letters.*[20] In the third letter of Haywood's collection, Walpole is figured as Alim, the Sultan's evil first minister whose corruption is revealed by Ariel, a minister in the regions of the air, to Alla, his correspondent and an inhabitant of the world.[21] However, Haywood complicates and deepens the allegory in the book-length *Eovaai,* not least by developing a complex narrative frame that allows her to pass comment on the opposition positions rehearsed, but not necessarily endorsed, in the narrative.

Haywood's irony is indicated in her dedication of the novel to Sarah Churchill, Duchess of Marlborough, whom she had subjected to fierce scandalous allegory in the second volume of her earlier *Memoirs of . . . Utopia.* Sarah Churchill appeared as Marama, "of a Disposition so perverse and peevish, so designing, mercenary, proud, cruel and revengeful that it has been a matter of debate, if she were really Woman, or if some Fiend had not assumed that Shape on purpose to affront the Sex, and fright Mankind from Marriage" (249–50). The dedication to *Eovaai* contrasts Sarah's husband, the Duke of Marlborough, Whig favorite of Queen Anne and principal target of Delarivier Manley's *New Atalantis,* with Walpole, describing the latter as an "ambitious, or avaritious Favourite, void of Abilities as of Morals" who has "spread a general Corruption thro' the Land, and destroy'd all the Blessings that Godlike Man bestow'd" (45). Given Marlborough's own reputation for avarice and the extravagance of his palace at Blenheim at huge cost to the public purse, it seems that Haywood is in fact paralleling her own opposition writing with earlier opposition representations of court favorites or chief ministers. The specific and obvious parallel would lie with Manley, principal purveyor of the prose romance satire as a vehicle against Sarah Churchill and her husband in her *The Secret History of Queen Zara* (1705) and *New Atalantis* (1709).[22]

The parallel with Manley is extended in that, like Manley in the *New Atalantis* and *Memoirs of Europe,* Haywood "frames" her text in a complex fictional history of its translation. The translator is a Chinese speaker, the "Son of a Mandarin" according to the subtitle of the 1736 edition; he resides in England, and his text is a translation itself of a translation from a much larger text, the annals of the first ages written in a pre-Adamitical language, the language of nature. The "translation," or rather "interpretation," of this lost language used in the annals, he tells us, was undertaken by seventy philosophers in the fifth century at the commission of an illustrious Chinese emperor of that period. When the emperor died and his patronage therefore ceased, the philosophers' labours came to an end, having produced versions of only three of the twenty-one histories. The English translator has worked from *"a very correct Copy of that which is esteem'd the best"* (51) and promises to undertake more.

The instability of the act of "translation" is central to the narrative machinery of the novel. The names of the protagonists are "interpreted" rather than "translated" by the cabal of seventy philosophers undertaking the work and are, the English translator consistently reminds us, up for dispute. In the mold of the Scriblerian annotation of Pope's *Dunciad,* footnotes punctuate the text, allowing the English translator to comment on the ambiguity of the text and criticize the cabal's interpretative choices as well as the arguments of a scholar named Hahehihotu, a "commentator" on the cabal's "translation." In the course of the novel Hahehihotu is revealed to be a committed republican as well as an out-and-out misogynist. Hence, in a footnote relating to the divine "Aiou," who originally gave Eovaai's father the magic jewel, the English translator comments that "the Cabal differ'd very much concerning the Signification of this Name, and at length left the Matter undetermined" (55); the name "Eovaai," a footnote records, means "By Interpretation, *The Delight of the Eyes*" (55). The textual machinery not only encourages readers to look to "interpret" the meaning of the text in some other context than that of a pre-Adamitical history not known to them—that is, in their own historical moment—but it also alerts them to the "instability" of such acts of translation and interpretation.

In the metacommentary, also conducted in the footnotes, relating to the cabal's political, social, and moral judgments on the text and, in particular, its protagonist, the princess Eovaai, Haywood further destabilizes the allegorical enterprise, the search for a direct correspondence between text and referential world. The English translator is not, it appears, in sympathy with the positions held by the cabal nor with those held by Hahehihotu, who is himself, it appears, often at variance with the cabal's interpretation of the text. The young English translator quarrels early with the commentary on the text. When Eovaai's curiosity leads her to ponder the inscription on her magic jewel, taking it out of its case so that it can be snatched by a passing bird, a long footnote tells us that

> The Commentator will needs have it, that these Words imply a
> Vanity, or kind of Self-sufficiency in *Eovaai;* and infers from thence,

that it's an Error to trust Women with too much Learning; as the Brain in that Sex being of a very delicate Texture, renders them, for the most part, incapable of making solid Reflections, or comparing the little they can possibly arrive at the knowledge of, with the Infinity of what is beyond their reach. But as old a Man, and as rigid a Philosopher as he was, I am apt to think, he wou'd have spared this Part of his Animadversions, had he been honour'd with the Acquaintance of some *European* Ladies. (57)

At numerous subsequent points in the narrative the English translator chivalrously intervenes to defend Eovaai and her sex from such animadversions. When Eovaai succumbs to the compliments of Ochihatou's servants, despite having had the benefit of an education from her worthy father in the dangers of listening to favorites, the monstrosity of arbitrary power, and the avoidance of vanity, he considers the commentator unjust in concluding that education is wasted on women (73). When Eovaai finds herself subject to "unusual Thrillings thro' every Vein" as she listens in on the rapturous sexual pleasures of Ochihatou and Atamadoul, the English translator notes that "The Commentator employs no less than three whole Pages in the most bitter Invectives on this Propensity, which, he will have it, is only natural to Woman-kind" (35).

The commentator's misogyny is linked to his republicanism, which the English translator calls to our attention in the passages relating to Eovaai's encounter with the patriot Alhahuza and the republic of Oozoff. Eovaai is impressed with the qualities of the heads of the commonwealth in Oozoff and wonders why they do not designate one of their number king, prompting a footnote that reads: "The Commentator, who I shrewdly suspect to have been a Republican in his Principles, lays hold on this Passage, to lash, with a good deal of Severity, that Veneration which weak Minds, as he calls them, pay to Kings merely as Kings" (10). Eovaai's query is answered, not only by the commentator and the English translator's comment upon him, but also by an old man from Oozoff who extends the arguments voiced by Alhahuza against arbitrary power into a critique of all systems of monarchical government in that they encourage the propensity toward tyranny in all men. His comments in turn spawn a series of footnotes. One footnote contextualizes the reasons for the people of Oozoff's dislike of monarchy: they experienced extreme tyranny at the hands of the kings of Narzada at an earlier stage in their history. Another opens up a gap between Hahehihotu and the cabal members. Hahehihotu, we are told, considers the cabal to have "grossly misinterpreted" a passage concerning the abuse of authority by kings, when they substituted the phrase "many kings" for the phrase "all kings," which he considers more accurate (113). The following footnote on the same page points out that, since the cabal was engaged in a work of translation for an emperor, they were obliged to mitigate the critique of monarchical power, offering a critique of the exercise of "arbitrary will" rather than sovereign power itself (113).

Here, Haywood faces squarely the fine distinctions that opposition writers were forced to draw, both exposing Walpole's apparent defense of constitutional monarchy as a "cover" for the exercise of arbitrary power by a minister and avoiding the imputation of republicanism and the refusal of monarchical government that might be implied by opposition to his ministry. This is partly achieved by designating the advocates of republicanism, the old man of Oozoff and the aged commentator, as spokespersons of "old" and worn-out ideologies, contrasting them with the "new" and vital prospects held out by Eovaai's slow, and not always sure, trajectory toward the wise exercise of her own constitutional monarchy, confirmed in her eventual marriage and political alliance with the young and virtuous rightful heir of Hypotofa.

The satirical treatment of Bernard Mandeville's *Fable of the Bees* (1714) is instrumental in this process of differentiation of patriot from republican sentiment.[23] In an explicit reference to Mandeville's influential treatise of the benefit of private vices to public virtue and the development of a strong and enterprising trading culture, Oozoff is described as a state in which the people suffer "no Drones to eat up what the others laboured for. Thus every Individual, like the industrious Bee, while he acted for his own Interest, acted also for that of the Public" (109). Oozoff is a successful trading republic with expanding commercial interests throughout the globe maintained by the industrious virtue of its inhabitants; in Mandeville's notorious fable it is the Hobbesian pursuit of self-interest and vainglory on the part of the bees within a constitutional monarchy that makes them into a powerful imperial and trading capitalist nation. Haywood here establishes an imitative relationship to Mandeville's text similar to the one I have argued we can trace to Pope's *Rape of the Lock* in her earlier work. She both invokes and transforms her source text, implying a "hidden" logic (in this case the incitement to republicanism) behind the apparently innocuous playfulness. Even on its own terms, however, Oozoff is seen to fail; Haywood indicates that a republican state can succeed only in trade, not imperialism or militarism. Ultimately, the republic cannot protect Eovaai from the incursions and arbitrary lusts of its neighbour, Hypotofa. Oozoff's impartiality and wisdom—a footnote says that the cabal are in dispute as to which term is designated by the word "Oozoff" (108)—reduce it to a nation so reliant on foreign trade that it cannot, or will not, exercise political or public influence on other states.

Where Haywood is distinctive as an opposition writer is in her critical association of republican with misogynist sympathies, leading to a distinctively "feminocentric," if not "feminist," argument for constitutional monarchy. She carefully develops the figure of Eovaai, shifting her representational significance from the familiar iconographic status of the state as embattled virgin into a model for the importance of women's practical education and involvement in matters of state and the exercise of power. Margaret Rose accurately summarises the sexual and state politics of Haywood's novel as follows:

> Through Eovaai's developing maturity and growing political consciousness, the author would seem to advocate a constitutional monarchy, such as the one the Patriot Opposition wished to see working in Britain. It is significant that the staunchest upholder of constitutional principles turns out to be a woman, who having undergone many trials, grows politically adept. Through the intelligent and dynamic Eovaai, Haywood also enters into the eighteenth-century debate concerning the innate differences between men and women and suggests that a woman is as fit to rule as a man, if she receives a suitable education. (*Political* 103–4)

In the course of the novel, Eovaai is "translated" from the object of tyrannous political desire into the subject of political action, acquiring an education in the interrelationship of private virtue and public responsibility.

In the process, Haywood uncovers the misogyny underpinning the critique of arbitrary power—whether republican and directed

against the abusive monarch and his favorites, or monarchical and
directed against the encroachment of the political administration into
the exercise of sovereign authority; for both, the chaste wife or the
embattled virgin stands as sign of the suffering state. Female "virtue"
is confined to this symbolic role. Behind the allegorical figure of Eovaai
stands that of Lucrece, the chaste Roman wife whose rape and subsequent suicide results in an uprising against the exercise of arbitrary
power in the shape of the tyrant Tarquin and the institution of the
Roman republic in 510 B.C. Haywood's novel makes us aware that
the translation of the female protagonist from the iconic status of
idealized virgin or chaste wife sacrificed for the future of the state—
and also symbolic of that state's resisting but virtuous suffering— into
the role of thinking political subject can only be interpreted by
masculinist commentators as a sign of the degeneracy and corruption
of the female sex. When Eovaai responds intellectually or sexually to
her "adventures," the commentators can only "reframe" her within a
counter image of an intrinsic feminine propensity toward vice, mani-
fested as a fascination with corruption, triviality, self-interest, and
sexual pleasure, and imperviousness to the exercise of reason. In the
masculinist critique of arbitrary power, "woman" stands either as the
sign of virtuous and uncomplaining resistance around which Patriot
heroes can congregate in her defense (and by extension, defense of
their country), or as a sign of the luxuriousness and decadence of self-
interested domination against which the patriotic boy-hero must pit
his own martial and virile virtue. Either role precludes women as subjects from rational political agency. It is significant in this context that
it is Eovaai who breaks Ochihatou's wand in front of his face, even if
she must subsequently be saved from his (now merely) human powers
of aggression by the young hero, Adelhu.

The conclusion to Haywood's *Adventures of Eovaai* should, however, give the proto-feminist reader pause for thought. Eovaai determines to marry Adelhu and make him king "*as she said,* to recompense
him for what he had done for herself and People, but *in reality* to
gratify the Passion she was inflamed with for him" (158). Haywood
is careful to include a footnote by the English translator, again highlighting the misogyny of his source, having him observe that "The
Historian, methinks, might have spared giving his Opinion in this

Matter; but, if it were as he suggests, that Passion cou'd not be blame-able in *Eovaai,* which had Gratitude for its Source, and was encour-aged by an appearance of the greatest Virtue and Bravery in the Object" (158). Given the preceding story in which Eovaai's sentiments of sexual attraction to Ochihatou have been carefully demonstrated as built on principles of gratitude and the apparent virtue and bravery in their object, a cloud of suspicion must lie over the seeming "rationality" and "maturity" of Eovaai's choice at the end of her long and educa-tive adventures.

In this respect, Haywood's anti-romance can be paralleled with a similar strategy of apparent retreat from uncomplicated advocacy of an ideal of sexual, social, and political order maintained through ra-tional government of both self and state in the final book of Jonathan Swift's *Gulliver's Travels.* Here too, the main protagonist is ironically treated, revealing himself to be subject to those very passions he has ostensibly rejected. Gulliver's unequivocal commitment to Houyhnhnm rationality and rejection of his own people as Yahoos results in a form of madness in which he displays the very vice that he claims to repu-diate. On his reluctant return to England, Gulliver is only partially reconciled to his Yahoo-kind, spending much of his time with his be-loved horses; he declares that "when I behold a Lump of Deformity and Diseases both in Body and Mind, smitten with *Pride,* it immedi-ately breaks all the Measures of my Patience" and entreats "those who have any Tincture of this absurd Vice, that they will not presume to appear in my sight" (1941 ed., 280). Eovaai also finally submits to the self-gratifying passion that the text has throughout identified as destructive to all forms of government, private or public.

We need not view this interpretative paradox, where the reader doubts the seriousness of the text's overt message that reason should govern passion, as a retreat from the radical position outlined earlier that claims political agency for women. Rather, like Swift in *Gulliver's Travels,* Haywood appears to be pointing to the dangers of over-in-vesting in the power of rationality and reminding her readers that all acts of power, whether performed by women or men, are "interested"; indeed, they may be self-deluded, governed by passions that the agent does not necessarily recognise in her- or himself. Eovaai's passions are now in tune with the interests of state rather than running counter to them (the choice of Adelhu as sexual and sovereign partner will prove politically advantageous), but we are reminded this is by happy accident rather than the result of mature judgment. This paradoxical pattern of advocating prudential reason and yet acknowledging the "ungovernable" nature of sexual passion is discernible in all of Haywood's fiction.

Like *Gulliver's Travels, Eovaai*'s conservative politics of sexual and social economy is frequently undercut by anarchic and perverse comic energies. Haywood invites us to take seriously the pluralizing interpretative tendencies of the text's machinery, not least in recognizing that the name of the much-reviled commentator (Ha-he-hi-ho-tu) points to the text's comic purpose. Put simply, readers are encouraged to snigger not only at her satiric targets, but at the allegorical seriousness of satire itself. Part of the process of "novelization" in the early eighteenth century to which Haywood contributes so significantly is just such a hybridizing tendency. The *Adventures of Eovaai* provides its readers as well as its protagonists with opportunities for titillation and perverse pleasure that exceed its ostensible moral purpose. Haywood fills, indeed crams, the novel with humorously-treated sadomasochistic instance, never missing an opportunity to comically foreground sexual symbolism: Eovaai's seizing of Ochihatou's "wand" and breaking it before his face and his subsequent attempt to beat her to death with a birch made of stinging nettles and thorns as she hangs from a tree; the absurd prudery which makes her require him to turn his back on her as she strips off in order to enable the enchantment that will spirit them away as dove and bird of prey to Ijaveo; her embarrassing enjoyment at listening in on the joys of sexual congress between Atamadoul and Ochihatou. Haywood reproduces the distinctive sexual voyeurism and specularization of the female body found in prose romance from the Renaissance onward,[24] but also undercuts and makes comic the seriousness of romance as a mode of representation. *Eovaai* might then be classified as a mock-romance, the feminocentric inverse of Scriblerian mock-epic. If the mock-epic identifies a feminized "romance" as undercutting the heroic potential of masculine agency associated with the epic, Haywood's "mock-romance" identifies a masculine force of "rigid" interpretation as restricting, perverting, and containing the wayward libidinal affections of female romance.

Notes

1. *Seductive Forms,* 154; vol. 2 of *Works of Aphra Behn; Memoirs* rpt. in vol. 2 of *The Novels.*

2. *Adventures of Rivella* rpt. in vol. 2 of *Novels.*

3. *Professional,* 227.

4 . Beasley identifies Haywood's *Eovaai* and Lyttelton's *Court* as the "best of the orientalised political romances" directed against Walpole and his ministry ("Portraits" 421).

5. Gerrard, *Patriot Opposition;* Nicholson, *Writing.*

6. *Eovaai* was published anonymously in July 1736. In 1741 it was reprinted as *Unfortunate Princess* under Haywood's own name. All subsequent references are to Wilputte ed., *Adventures of Eovaai* (1999), which is based on the 1736 edition. The year 1736 saw the Porteus riots in Scotland and civil unrest in London resulting in the militia firing on rebellious mobs; Parliament passed a bill designed to abolish bribery and corruption but this seems to have only inflamed opposition feelings. On Fielding's political sentiments and writing in the 1730s, see chapters 2 and 3 of Cleary.

7. See Blouch, "Eliza Haywood" and Elwood, "Stage Career." For the later reinstigation of the antagonism between the two authors in the 1750s, see Elwood, "Henry Fielding."

8. A series of anxious letters from Hill to Pope and evasive responses from the latter in January and February 1731 relate to Hill's apparent appearance in the second book of the 1729 *Dunciad* as an unnamed champion in the diving contest who does not sink in the mud but "mounts far off, among the swans of Thames." The 1728 *Dunciad* note designated the champion merely as "H—"; in 1729 two asterisks suggested "Aaron." See *Correspondence,* 3:164–77. For an account of Haywood's treatment of Martha Fowke Sansom, who appears as the monstrous "Gloatitia" in *Memoirs of Utopia* and is accused therein of alienating the affections of both Aaron Hill and Richard Savage from their "true" friends (presumably Haywood), see Fowke, *Clio,* esp. 28–30.

9. *The Plain Dealer* was published every Monday and Friday from Monday, March 23, 1724 to Friday, May 7, 1725. On Aaron Hill's circle, Haywood's role within it, and the references to the *Plain Dealer* mentioned here, I am indebted to Christine Gerrard who provided me with a copy of an unpublished chapter of a forthcoming biography of Hill.

10. On Pope's possible Jacobitism and flirtation with Patriotism see Downie, "1688," 25–44, and and Gerrard, "Pope," 9–24.

11. All references to the *Dunciad* (book and line number[s]) are to the *Twickenham Edition.*

12. 2nd ed. (London, 1726) 131–2. All subsequent references are to this edition.

13. *Twickenham Edition*, 1.63–66. All subsequent references (canto and line number[s]) are to this edition.

14. A second edition of *Secret History* was published with a prefatory key in 1727; all subsequent references are to this edition.

15. Blouch has convincingly demonstrated that Haywood may well have been the mother of two illegitimate children, suggesting that they may have been the product of liaisons with Richard Savage (around 1723–24) and William Hatchett (in the late 1720s). Blouch points to a letter seeking patronage from Haywood (B.M.Add. MS. 4293 f.82) in which she refers to "the melancholly necessity of depending on my Pen for the support of myself and two children, the eldest of whom is no more than 7 years of age" (quoted in Blouch, "Eliza Haywood" 537).

16. Pope's 1729 *Dunciad Variorum* included a list of "Books, Papers, and Verses" abusing the author of the 1728 *Dunciad*, including Edmund Curll's *A Compleat Key to the Dunciad* (1728), which transforms the text into a "roman à clef" along the lines of Haywood's scandal fictions, and *The Female Dunciad* (1728), published by Curll, to which Haywood contributed a novella entitled *Irish Artifice*. See *Dunciad* (210–12).

17. Rose, *Political Satire* 40–41.

18. See J.H. Plumb, *King's Minister* 101.

19. Whicher considers the prince Adelhu to be a "cautious allusion to the Pretender"; see *Life and Romances* 104. The identification of Adelhu as Frederick, Prince of Wales, is more likely, given Haywood's apparent commitment to constitutional monarchy (a position rarely associated with the Stuart kings in exile), and given her dedication of a 1729 play, *Frederick*, to Frederick. The play is reprinted in *Plays*, ed. Valerie C. Rudolph. Like other opposition writers, Pope included, Haywood appears to have been attracted to the cause of Frederick in the 1730s and reverted to a Jacobite position in the subsequent decade. Thomas Lockwood has provided evidence of her later interest in Jacobitism in a 1749 pamphlet entitled *A Letter from H— G—*. See Lockwood, "Eliza Haywood."

20. Giovanni Paolo Marana's *L'Espion Turc* (1684–6) was translated into English as *Letters Writ by a Turkish Spy* in eight volumes between 1687 and 1734. Charles Montesquieu's *Lettres Persanes* (1721) was translated into English by John Ozell as *Persian Letters* in 1722.

21. Haywood, *Letters from the Palace*.

22. Note, however, that Sarah Churchill was a Patriot toast in the 1730s and hence the dedication may be a means of signposting *Eovaai* as a Patriot

text within opposition writings. With thanks to my graduate student, Maddie Rowe, for pointing this out.

23. 1989 Penguin Classics edition cited here. Of Dutch extraction, Mandeville expanded his Hudibrastic poem, "The Grumbling Hive, or Knaves turn'd Honest" (1705) into *The Fable of the Bees* in 1714 by adding a series of prose essays pursuing the same Hobbesian political and economic theory. In the fable, the hive thrives so long as the principle of allowing the individual the maximum freedom to pursue private self-interest is maintained: "Thus every Part was full of Vice,/Yet the whole Mass a Paradise" (67). In the constitutional monarchy of Mandeville's hive, a corrupt ministry does not diminish national success: "Their Kings were serv'd; but Knavishly/Cheated by their own Ministry" (66). The hive declines when a Puritan moralist camp institutes moral behaviour and social responsibility.

24. See in particular Hackett, "'Yet Tell Me.'" There are striking parallels between the scene Hackett cites as an instance of a critique and indulgence of specularisation of the female body (57) in Wroth's *Urania*, in which we encounter Limena stripped to the waist and tied by her hair to a pillar as her husband whips her, and the scene of Ochihatou's attempted beating of Eovaai.

"A Race of Angels"

Castration and Exoticism in Three Exotic Tales by Eliza Haywood

Jennifer Thorn

Among the eight tales that comprise the prolific Eliza Haywood's 1727 collection *The Fruitless Enquiry* is the fantastic "History of Montrano and Iseria," which focuses on an adoring husband's plea for readmission to happy domesticity after eight years absence in "some part of the Indies." That which requires forgiveness is not Montrano's long silence, not his mere absence. Rather, the obstacle to reunion is castration, the unhappy culmination of eight years' refusal of the amorous advances of the queen whose captive slave he had been. Such husbandly loyalty is as unusual as castration in Haywood's repertoire. Ironically, the one exception is inextricable from the other: the consequence of Montrano's self-identification as "husband" was, he tells Iseria, that "from that cruel Moment, [he] had no more the power of being so" (75).

The suitably dramatic terms in which Montrano mourns his mutilation remind us of specifically eighteenth-century inflections of both "race" and reproduction. "[D]epriv'd for ever of the dear Names of Father and of Husband; robb'd of his Sex, and doom'd to an eternal Sterility" (75), Montrano does not describe his castration as an amatory loss. His "sexual identity," a modern designation of limited applicability to this period, is thus a matter not of "sexual orientation" alone but of reproductivity as well. As Jonathan Ned Katz has written, "The operative contrast in this society was between fruitfulness and barrenness, not between different-sex and same-sex eroticism" (38). The form of Montrano's lament also reminds us of a second, closely related eighteenth-century presumption that differs from our own: "racial identity." Begging Iseria to accept him, he laments that he can now only "condemn thy charms to cold sterility: Thou, who mayest bless the world with a race of Angels" (83). This use of "race" to indicate lineage is entirely in accord with the definitions offered by the *Dictionnaire de l'Academie Francaise* in 1694 ("lignee, lignage, extraction") and, soon thereafter, by both Samuel Johnson in his *Dictionary of the English Language* (1755) and the first edition of the *Encyclopedie* (1765) (Hudson 247). While beauty is undoubtedly associated with pallor in Haywood's fictions, here self-description in terms of "race" references reproduction more directly than phenotype.[1] "Sexual" and "racial" identity are thus aspects of a single mode of being: producing offspring, preserving family lines.

Montrano asks Iseria to forgive not the lovemaking they will not do, but the beautiful children he will not sire and, by implication, their offspring as well, as a later part of the "race." This lament valorizes both Iseria's fertility and generationality per se, presuming male fulfillment in, and fidelity to, marriage and family life. Late-twentieth-century readers of Haywood may well find be surprised by this deviation from the "myth of female innocence destroyed by a world of male corruption" (Richetti, *Popular* 1992 ed., 169) in terms of which her work has variously been examined. The exotic tales I examine here—*Letters from the Palace of Fame . . . from an Arabian Manuscript*, "The History of Montrano and Iseria," and *Philidore and Placentia; or, L'amour trop delicat* (all 1726 and 1727)—are perhaps unique in Haywood's vast oeuvre in their valorization of male domesticity and their celebration of female reproductivity. I seek in this essay both to describe the distinctiveness of these tales and to relate them to Haywood's career-long interest in the implications of reproductive sexuality for individual autonomy. William Warner has recently characterized early-eighteenth-century formula fiction in terms of its reliance upon "the continuity of received formulas as the matrix for pleasing variation" (*Licensing* 114). The recurrence of castration and exoticism in these tales is "continuous" and "various" in just this way, a working through of the cluster's relation to the themes and situations for which Haywood was already well-known. Attending to

Haywood's narrative reuse of castration and exoticism in these three tales thus affords an ideal vantage to examine in small the recycling of motifs and situations that was so vital a part of her astounding productivity and has been so consistently a rationale for her later critical denigration.

Both senses of reproductive identity—the production of offspring and the preservation of familial lines—are implied by Haywood's weirdly utopic use of castration and exoticism to reimagine autonomy. In many of Haywood's fictions, illicit amorous dalliance results in conception, a burdensome consequence that women alone cannot evade.[2] In two of the three tales under review, castration not only protects women from conception; it also is imagined as freeing men to emotionality and loyalty. The intergender sympathy thus imaginatively facilitated by castration relies equally upon the tales' exoticism.[3] "Away" is where castration happens and where it can even be imagined as utopian, enabling male interiority and male-female equality. The denizens of "away"—"barbarians"—psychically underwrite this fantasy, the conditions of which might be summarized thus: if European men are castrated, and if "barbarians," against whom Europeans can define themselves, are present, then European men and women can experience the pleasures of sameness. As indefinite as Haywood's uses of exotic locales has seemed to some—George Whicher, for example, wrote disparagingly of the vague "Bengall" in which Haywood set *Cleomelia, or the Generous Mistress* that "[t]he scene might equally well have been laid in the Isle of Wight" (63)—these tales thus can be grouped with works such as "Vision of Mirza," *Rasselas,* and *The Citizen of the World* in which "the Orient" is used as a screen onto which social arrangements at home were projected for critique and imaginative reconfiguration.

These three exotic tales are utopian in their muted meditation on the allegedly biological source of social inequality. In so doing, they call to mind recent revisionist attention to the traditional understandings of the Enlightenment achievement of the rights-bearing individual. Thomas Laqueur, for example, focuses on the transition through the seventeenth and eighteenth centuries from a scientific understanding of the female body as an inferior version of the male body to an understanding of the two as distinctly different. Laqueur has emphasized the ways women's civic disenfranchisement was cast as the natural analogue of their relation to reproduction: "The tendency of early contract theory is to make the subordination of women to men a result of the operation of the *facts* of sexual difference, of their utilitarian implications," Laqueur writes. "What matters is the superior strength of men, or more important, the frequent incapacity of women because of their reproductive functions. Bodies in these accounts are not the sign of but the foundation for civil society" (157). Elizabeth Fox-Genovese similarly notes the interdependence of Revolutionary-era individualism, with its "vision of society as composed of impersonal and interchangeable units of sovereignty with a model of human beings as rational, accountable, and autonomous" and a "new concept of motherhood" (123). Here again the universalist potential of abstraction was undercut by reproduction: this new ideal "confirmed the new centrality of the individual, . . . not by endowing mothers with individualism," Fox-Genovese writes. "The purpose of motherhood was, rather, to nurture the individual" (125).

Laqueur's argument suggests that it would be fruitless for women to avoid motherhood by way of seeking status as an "individual"; the mere potentiality for conception is what matters, not the reality. In eighteenth-century England, the distinction between potential and actual pregnancy was moot in the face of the presumption of a normative reproductivity. Throughout the century, of course, the Book of Common Prayer enjoined procreation as the purpose of marriage. Reproductivity "justified" the double standard, for without a cultural insistence on women's chastity, men could not be sure they were the fathers of their wives' children, their heirs; hence, Samuel Johnson's well-known response to Boswell's inquiry about the basis of the double standard, "Confusion of progeny constitutes the essence of the crime." In the early eighteenth century, a national duty to procreate was voiced with increasing frequency and intensity, as in the 1728 sermon by Richard Smalbroke, the Bishop of St. David's, asserting that "whatever has a direct Tendency to lessen the Number of Subjects, and to weaken or dishonour the Government, or bring it in to Confusion, falls under his [the Magistrate's] immediate Cognizance" (McLaren 22). Abortion was similarly understood as an explicitly political, as well as moral, offense, as in Joseph Addison's *Guardian* of 11 July 1713, in which he damns as "Monsters of Inhumanity" those who foil God's plan by attempting abortion and "by Unnatural Practices do in some Measure defeat the Intentions of Providence and destroy their Conceptions even before they see the Light," which crime "robs the Commonwealth of its full Number of Citizens" (McLaren 61).[4]

Not only women were urged to reproduce; men, too, were enjoined to distinguish illicit sexual pleasure and appropriate reproduction. Haywood's contemporary Daniel Defoe made female subordination the correlate of reproduction even as he claimed to argue against it in his *Conjugal Lewdness; or, Matrimonial Whoredom,* printed the same year, 1726, as the fictions under scrutiny in this essay: "Love knows no superior or inferior, no imperious Command on one hand, no reluctant Subjection on the other" (26). The limited equality of this kind of marriage is, however, problematically predicated upon mutual devotion to family, indeed, to reproduction, for, as Defoe repeatedly asserts, "Matrimony was instituted for the regular Propagation of Kind" (*Conjugal* 123). Perhaps cognizant of the rising rates of bastardy, Defoe writes that any man who has sex with his fiancée before wedlock "makes a Whore of his Wife": "[H]e defiles his own Bed, pollutes his own Seed, spreads Bastardy in his own Race, and shews a most wicked vitiated Appetite" (65). Such depravity exceeds even "the more rational, more moderate and better governed Savages of the Indies, East or West, to the Negroes of Africa, the Poigraura's of Brazile, nay, . . . the very Hottentots of Monomotapa, and the Cape of Good Hope" (67). Defoe's attack upon sex-as-pleasure, in opposition to intercourse as solely the means of legitimate reproduction, is especially pointed in the full chapter he devotes to those craven beings who marry and "then publickly profess[] to desire they may have no children, and . . . us[e] Means physical or diabolical, to prevent Conception" (123). But the vividness of Defoe's depiction of the conjugal inequality that typically accompanies childbearing redounds not to his point but to those who resist reproduction, even perhaps creating sympathy for the abortion-seeking married women he describes. He cannot understand how a woman could want to marry but not want children: "To present to all this Aversion for Children, to nauseate the Nursing, the Watching, the Squaling, the fatigue of bringing up Children, which, as they call it, makes a Woman a Slave and a Drudge all her Days; to be perpetually exclaiming against this, and then MARRY, what must we call this?" (133). "In a word," he concludes of such "preposterous" cases, "she would have the Use of a Man, but she would not act the Part of the Woman" (133).[5] Thus, in Defoe's horrified presentation, men who separate reproduction from pleasure are barbarous, and women who do so verge upon murderers in the temptation to abortion they cannot but feel.

In many of her fictions, Haywood dramatizes precisely this abyss between sex-as-pleasure and reproduction, reminding her readers that "having the Use of a Man"—or a woman—not infrequently results in conception. Typically, female fertility is a liability in Haywood's works, a tilting of the playing field of amatory contest to which she so regularly attends. Women who get pregnant in Haywood's tales are generally jilted, or about-to-be jilted, lovers, a view of pregnancy as vulnerability of a piece with Behn's witty deprecation of "a cradle full of noise and mischief" as the end to sexualized fun in *The Rover*.[6] Perhaps uniquely in Haywood's oeuvre, *Letters,* "Montrano and Iseria," and *Philidore and Placentia* do not represent their female protagonists' capacity for conception as disempowering. Of course, the utopian vision of ungendered individualism evinced by these three tales is ironic. Women can be imagined as empowered by fecundity here only because of castration: conception and reproduction cannot, will not, happen.

In the brief analyses of the entwining of castration and exoticism in *Letters,* "Montrano and Iseria," and *Philidore and Placentia* that follow, I foreground the proximity of "race" and reproduction with which I opened. All three tales represent travel in the East in terms of wealth, which in two of the three tales imaginatively enables filial escape from paternal control. One can track a progression from feigned castration as sexually and materially empowering to a European *(Letters);* to castration as disabling to one of two men, whose friendship and wealth both derive from "Ceylong" ("Montrano and Iseria"); to castration as one of several ways in which the sexual and material promise of "Persia" is divided between two men friends *(Philidore and Placentia).* When castration is real, in other words, it becomes a kind of payment by means of which others are freed to happy mercantilism and true love. This progression begins in *Letters,* in which castration is only pretended and the relationship of male to female is as polarized and adversarial as in most of Haywood's fictions.

Montesquieu's *Persian Letters* reached England in 1721 and started a fashion to which Haywood may well have been deliberately contributing with her 1726 publication of the overtly fictitious letters from Ariel, a servant of the princess of the celestial realm of Fame, to Alla, attached to the court in Constantinople. The multiple points of view that characterize Montesquieu's satiric tour de force are not in evidence here. Instead, Haywood's *Letters from the Palace of Fame*, only sixty pages long, consists of five letters, all from Ariel, peppered with "Janizaries," the "Alcoran," and "the Ottoman dominions," a vocabulary Haywood first deployed in her unsuccessful play *The Fair Captive* (1721). Ariel and Alla are both of indeterminate gender, and the revelations about motivation and causality that Ariel offers from her/his superior vantage attribute to men and women an identical inability to identify and follow the way to happiness.

Unlike the tales to which I turn shortly, which focus upon Europeans abroad, *Letters* is set in "Arabia" and concerns "Mussulmen" almost exclusively. Apart from a few denigratory and stereotypical references to "subtile Mussulmen," Haywood assimilates Muslims to her usual amatory model of motivation and causality. The domesticity of her exoticism—the ease with which it can even now be entirely overlooked—recalls the anonymous and hugely popular Grub Street translation of Antoine Galland's *Les mille et une nuits* (1704–17), the progenitor of widespread literary taste for Oriental tales, which rendered its exotic protagonists in terms of the very unexotic "Flambeaus" of their "Apartments" and their appreciation of "Instruments of Musick" and other "Diversions of the Court" (5, 3). *Letters* may owe another debt to France in its evocation of Haywood's 1726 translation of Mme de Gomez's *La Belle Assemblee*, which follows a group of youthful aristocrats who have retreated to the country for the recreation of nature, solitude, reading, and conversation, discussing ideals of kingship, methods of commanding loyalty, and romantic love. *Letters* also resembles *The Spectator* and, indeed, Haywood's own later *Female Spectator* in its basic structure: letters on aspects of human nature and society in which general assertions are illustrated with brief case histories. The gender neutrality of these anecdotes—men and women alike are blind to their best interests and subject to chance—resembles less Haywood novellas-in-miniature than *Spectator* papers or tales from *La Belle Assemblee*.

Letter 1 focuses on the falseness of reputation: the exemplary Cosmelia married only as a cover for her infatuation with an undeserving gallant; the learned Alsatus depends upon a ghostwriter for the much-praised "Orations" he has made in "the Divan"; the able military commander Ruzaras loses to "the Christians" in Adrianople as a reflection only of his lack of "the art of insinuating himself into the favour of the Divan" (6). Letter 2 teaches the lesson that individuals are not responsible for, or capable of controlling, their reputations, a lack of control that should teach reliance on "the Will of that supreme Power who is the Creator of both [the Stars] and you" (10). Thus Narzolphus deems himself fortunate in the possession of the virtuous Ximeme only to discover after their marriage that she's not a virgin; Bellzara is thought lucky to have married the rich Oxyartes, but his diseases privately disgust her. Letter 3 pushes the lesson of human helplessness still further, listing examples of those who pursued their desires only to be made ridiculous or unhappy, even in success: Almeria wanted to be a court lady, but is so "aukward" there that she will "probably" be "kept in a State of Celibacy much longer than is agreeable either to her Inclinations, or Circumstances"; Boanerges chose to become "an Expounder of the Alcoran" but would have been more successful as "a Leader of the Spahi's"; Artaxus "neglects the study of something that might raise his broken Fortunes" by stubbornly persisting in his plan to marry money though he has been rejected by "a hundred different Women" (18).

It is Letter 4, the first in which a recognizably Haywoodian sexual politics of assertion and desire is evident, that initiates the entwining of castration and exoticism on which I focus here. In its vividness and length, this letter dominates the entire collection, unbalancing its five-part structure. Ariel opens by offering to "make amends for the perhaps too serious Entertainment of my last Letter" by "let[ting] [Alla] into a Secret" (25), the unknown means by which Forzio revenged himself upon Alla's own enemy, Benhamar, "the present Bashaw of Astrachan" (25). The tale shifts to present tense as we follow three characters through a characteristically Haywoodian story of intrigue, desire, and revenge. Forzio purchases as a slave "a young Christian, of so compleat and perfect a Mould, that he seem'd form'd by Nature for no other purpose than to charm the Fair" (27). He names him Ozmin (a sterotypically "Oriental" name Haywood had used in *The Fair Captive*), teaches him Arabic, and has him introduced to the Bashaw's household as a eunuch, promising him his freedom if he will seduce the Bashaw's wife, Aspatia, and obtain proof of the crime.[7]

If, as earlier discussed, formula fiction relies on both "the continuity of received formulas [and] . . . pleasing variation" (Warner, *Licensing* 114), the emphasis in this first story of castration is squarely on "continuity" rather than "variation." Castration and exoticism are not (yet) accompanied by formal or thematic innovation. "Persia" requires no alteration to Haywood's usual plots and modes, and castration functions simply as a disguise not unlike those Fantomina assumes in her own exploration of autonomy and desire. Its primary dramatic purpose is to exempt Ozmin and Aspatia from responsibility for acting upon their desires: he wants to go home and practice "that Faith which here I must renounce," and she, of course, thinks she is safe from violation with him. When the two soon-to-be lovers meet, Aspatia's beauty motivates Ozmin to "a warmer Passion" than piety in his pursuit of her. The pleasures afforded to the reader depend upon superior knowledge of motivations and bodily abilities: we know, as Aspatia does not, what is going on as Ozmin begins "looking on her with those sort of Glances which are generally the fore-runners of an amorous declaration; kissing her Gloves, Robes, or whatever she bad him reach to her, with a fervor which nothing but believing him an Eunuch could have left her any room to doubt was an infallible Demonstration of a Lover's Zeal" (32). This vantage both protects the reader from Aspatia's vulnerability and makes it safe to imagine her desire.[8] She asks "Whether you who are Eunuchs ever feel any Emotions at the sight of a beautiful Woman, which make you wish yourselves in another condition?" Ozmin's reply, given the reader's superior knowledge, is both suggestive and ironic: "Had any other but Aspatia, answer'd he, ask'd me that Question, I should have reply'd in the Negative.—It must, indeed, be Charms of an uncommon quality, and such as only she is mistress of, which can convert Frigidity to Burnings—call Nature back, when in the bud destroy'd, and make the sapless Trees again shoot forth" (33). When Aspatia permits "the imagin'd Eunuch" to hold her hand, he declares his wish to kiss and hold her. "Where would be the offense to Virtue," given his state, if the mistress were to permit herself certain liberties with her slave? Readers of Haywood will not be surprised that moments later Aspatia is "quite dissolv'd, and melted with his Indearments," "unreluctant[ly] suffer[ing] him to rove o'er all her Beauties, to take every Freedom that Curiosity or Desire could wish" (36).

The consequences of the lovers' sexual satiation are also familiar to readers of Haywood. That Aspatia is "strangely surpriz'd" at the turn of events is not unlike the surprises faced by many a Haywood heroine on discovering that she has had sex. A typically self-centered Haywood male, Ozmin is soon telling her "that he had some Effects in Europe, which if she wou'd permit him to go and dispose of, he would return again with all convenient speed" (41). A normative gender polarity is enforced, as the aggression with which Aspatia now demands sexual satisfaction—she would have him continue "a Slave" for her "pleasure" (42)—disgusts Ozmin and reconciles him to the final step of the plan. He sends her a letter, and takes her passionate reply immediately to Forzio, who "loaded him with rich Gifts, and conducted him himself to the Sea-side" (46) for his voyage home. The guise of castration that Ozmin assumed, but did not invent, thus affords a European male both sexual gratification and financial remuneration: linkages of sexual and financial self-assertion, and sex with payment, that will recur in the exotic tales to which I next turn.

Letter 4, the second longest in the collection, similarly seems to abandon, as if exhausted, the claim of illustrating universal self-deception variously evinced by the first three letters. It, too, focuses upon a single history and themes—forbidden love across class lines and paternal involvement in the amorous disposition of offspring—that recur in tales under study here. Young Jehura's infatuation with Zimrac flouts the wishes of her loving father Kenneth Zipporo. The besotted Jehura would rather "indulge a criminal Pleasure in private, with this low-born Minion, than to shine out as one of the Stars of the Seraglio" (50). Zimrac sweet-talks her into elopement when Kenneth is away visiting a friend, and then rapes and abandons her, leaving her "dead, or dying" in the woods where Kenneth luckily is thrown from his horse soon thereafter. Though the dichotomy between Zimrac's selfish aggression and Jehura's blind victimization is familiar Haywood territory, Kenneth's paternal fidelity is not. Indeed, the reader's sympathy is directed, as the tale closes, not to the abandoned and miserable Jehura but to the "still tender Father," who cannot revenge himself upon Zimrac because so doing would "expose the Crime of a dear Daughter, whose Reputation was of more estimation with him, than all he had lost by her Folly" (58). *Letters'* donnée thus comes full circle as it closes: only Alla knows the secret truth behind the "Fame" that Kenneth enjoys for a well-ordered household.

Thus *Letters* offers no revision of "the facts of sexual difference," reinforcing the association of female impregnability with a victimizing vulnerability that is evident in other works by Haywood. The disguise of castration only reinforces the gender dichotomous norms of the nondisguised world. Exoticism, too, is superficial even on the nonrealist scale in which Haywood worked, informing character and place names but not narrative structure or causality; the "Mussulmen" that populate the collection behave just like Haywood's European protagonists. But the dramatic potential of castration and exoticism seems to have lingered in Haywood's imagination, emerging in fantastically utopian ways in the tales of the following year, 1727, to which I now turn. Here, rather than accommodating castration to her usual modes, Haywood seems to accommodate her usual modes to reimagining castration.

Both *Philidore and Placentia* and "Montrano and Iseria" open up a fantastically utopic model of nonreproductive selfhood, imagining with special pointedness passive masculinity and aggressive femininity. These gender reversals require juxtaposition to "savages" and enable homosocial passion and heterosocial commonality for Europeans. The narrative structure I map here for "Montrano" recurs in *Philidore,* to still more finely wrought ends: intensely affective doubled male protagonists, one of whom "masters" the Orient and one of whom returns from it castrated, and doubled female protagonists, one of whom aggressively asserts her sexual will and one of whom is rewarded for genteel restraint.

George Whicher, considering Haywood's place in the genealogy of collected tales identified with *The Decameron,* singled out *The Fruitless Enquiry* for special praise, finding in it "the best examples of her brief, direct tales" (30). The collection links eight tales within the frame tale of one Miramillia's search for a woman "so compleatly contented in mind, that there was no wish but that she enjoy'd" (3), for a fortune-teller has told her that only a shirt made by this woman can ensure the safe return of her lost son. Miramillia sets off to visit the happiest women she knows, only to discover, and report sympathetically, the secret sadness of each. Though castration is represented in *Fruitless Enquiry* in two tales, "The History of Clara and Ferdinand" and "The History of Montrano and Iseria," only in the latter does the additional component of exoticism correlate with an ambiguous utopianism.

"Clara and Ferdinand" experiments with the castration as a means of disrupting the "facts" of sexual inequality, but, without an exotic elsewhere into which to project so violent an act, the pleasures of the tale are insufficient to mitigate the anger with which castration is associated. In this darkest of the tales within *Fruitless Enquiry,* the virtuous Clara, left wealthy by her father's death, is raped by her cousin Ferdinand at her sister's wedding. He binds her hand and foot with plaited rushes, a detail that the cold eyed narrator provides only to discourage readerly sympathy for her: "A Woman must be at least half consenting to her own Rape, that would suffer herself to be confined by such as these" (242). After the rape, Clara attempts suicide with Ferdinand's sword. He stops her with glib endearments of the kind that "Men on such a Score are never at a loss to form" (243); and she forgives him, believing his passion for her was so excessive that he couldn't control himself, and in the years that follow gradually regains her serenity. But when Clara hears the story of her own rape, with only the names excluded, told by a visiting lady who had heard it from her husband, she is filled with "Hatred" and "Revenge." Cousin Ferdinand arrives that night for a visit, and Clara welcomes him, inviting him for a little walk. There she in her turn binds him hand and foot with plaited rushes, "laughing all the while, and crying, now I will ravish you" (249). She castrates him with her penknife: "Live, but no more a Man" (249). When Ferdinand dies soon thereafter, having sent her a deathbed letter declaring that he did indeed love her truly, she inherits all his money. Wracked with guilt, Clara retires to a nunnery, where she is reputedly still living at the story's end.

Where castration in "Clara and Ferdinand" is both brutally material and punitive of aggressive desire in men and women alike, the exoticism of "Montrano and Iseria" offers its readers instead the pleasures of sympathy for the male and female victims of an abstracted exotic elsewhere. As in *Letters* and "Clara and Ferdinand," castration is associated with the acquisition of wealth, but the "magic" of exoticism in "Montrano and Iseria" renders this transformation guilt-free. The tale begins, as Haywood's tales involving eastern climes often do, with the long shadow of paternal failure. Montrano's father squandered his fortune on a mistress, leaving him with no inheritance and under the guardianship of an uncle, Polusino, who has forbidden Montrano to marry his beloved but impecunious Iseria. When the young couple marries secretly, Polusino bursts into their bedroom on their wedding night, drags Montrano from the bed, and ships him off to "some part of the Indies" (50) against his will, with the intention both of curing him of his ill-advised love for Iseria and putting him in the way of easy money. Within a paragraph, then, readers are removed from a domestic Europe and relocated in an "Orient" in which the usual rules of intergenerational and intergender conduct don't apply and thus can be reimagined.

Montrano meets Alcestus on the ship, and the two men "began an Intimacy there" that would be lifelong (56). They are separated when, after the ship is wrecked in the Maldives, they are sold to different local rulers by the natives who find them, "a People, who we easily perceiv'd, to be wholly Unciviliz'd" (58). Montrano, purchased for the so-called Incas of Alsoore, is given to his wife, Elphania, who falls in love with him and tries for five years to seduce "the accomplish'd Slave" (53). When at last she sees through the madness he is feigning to avoid her, she has him castrated by "six lusty slaves": "[A]s you slight the joys of love, when proferr'd you by her," her servant tells Montrano, "she will taken effectual care you will never taste them with another" (74). Having thus assured the impossibility of the consummation of her desires, Elphania frees Montrano, giving him the money that enables his return to "Ceylong," where he joyfully finds Alcestus. The two friends become wealthy in the two years they must wait before they can get a ship to Europe. Montrano brings Alcestus home to act as an eyewitness to his captivity. Can Iseria find it in herself to take back her now impotent husband? She can: "Unkind Montrano, answer'd I, think you my Love was sensual! . . . [T]hus will I cling about you" (84). The tale ends with affirmations of their love against the backdrop of their wealth, derived both from Montrano's trading in the East and the repentant death of the patriarch-as-villain, Polusino, in Montrano's absence.

As this brief sketch suggests, the love story—"The History of Montrano and Iseria"—is the least of the pleasures offered by the tale. The pairings that are imagined more dramatically are Montrano's friendship with Alcestus and his fraught refusal of Elphania. Focusing on the emotionality of men, "Montrano and Iseria" provides an exception to the "cultural inability to envisage men except in terms of rational success" that Margaret Doody sees proliferating after the late seventeenth century: "[I]n colonialist, militaristic, and expansionist societies such as France and England of the time, male experience was in some respects becoming officially much smaller" (*True* 279).[9] Travel in the East, willed or involuntary, affords European men freedom from an oppressive and limiting domesticity, associated with both fathers and reproductivity. Both men, not simply the castrated Montrano, are granted the freedom to feel in their travels—to cry, talk of their love, pledge their loyalty. Montrano "could not forbear giving [his troubles] vent in tears and exclamations whenever he was alone" (71); and Alcestus laments his five years service primarily for the separation from Montrano it requires (59). So irrelevant to the tale is Iseria, and so firmly present is Alcestus at its conclusion, that we are left at the tale's conclusion with a psychic, if not sexual, ménage à trois, with the range of human experience divided among them: female domesticity, male adventure, and a kind of androgny identified with both.

Montrano is feminized in the East even before his castration renders his maleness problematic:[10] he has learned what it means to be powerless to shape one's fate, and his only virtue is loyalty in love. Like Pamela, Montrano suffers from the lusts of a superior who would control him sexually; and like Pamela, he repudiates the financial gain his would-be seducer offers as part of the assault. "[I]f you receive me not with the extremest Pleasure," Elphania tells Montrano, "you are not only ungrateful, but also perverse; blind to your own interest, and deserving of the misfortunes you have already fallen under" (64). Montrano is a helpless traveller, and his Orient is a world turned upside down. His uncle chose "Ceylong" as his destination in kidnapping because a former servant lived there now "in great repute"; his marriage to the widow of a Dutch merchant had "put him in possession of all her effects, which were very considerable" (56). The failure of traditional gender, class, and familial hierarchy to function in Montrano's "Ceylong" calls to mind Aphra Behn's *Widow Ranter,* which disapprovingly surveys an America in which men who were criminals in England have become powerful and wealthy statesmen and true aristocrats rule no more, as well as Daniel Defoe's *Moll Flanders,* in which a similar America is viewed much more positively.[11] The readerly pleasure most obviously offered by the Elphania plot, then, is that of imagining a helpless and loyal man.

Haywood rings variations on the standard juxtaposition of lustful exotic to chaste European in her characterization of Elphania, who is in fact an enslaved European who had been forced into prostitution by controlling parents and bad luck. Though she is denounced hyperbolically as "a cruel and revengeful woman, restrained by no principles of honour, religion, or generosity" (68), one can easily imagine her as the heroine of another Haywood tale. Too gay as a girl, Elphania was sent to Brussels "to be made a Recluse" against her will. She eloped to Holland with a Dutch officer she met on the journey. When he died, she and her companion-servant, an old woman, were "reduced to very great Hardships, which compelled us to do something contrary to the Laws"; soon thereafter, Elphania was "sent to Ceylon, to expiate, by an eternal slavery, a sin, which nothing but necessity could have made us guilty of" (63). Haywood's projection on the Orient of desired but disavowed sexual passion thus differs strikingly from the nineteenth-century "colonial desire" anatomized by Robert Young.

"Imperial cross-referencing," the mapping of masculinity onto the West and femininity onto the East against which Homi Bhabha has warned us, is equally absent in the dramatization of European male interaction with "Ceylong." Joe Snader has characterized the Oriental captivity narrative in terms of its male protagonists' "mastery of self and alien land[,] enabl[ing] their escape from cultures which . . . can only temporarily subjugate them" (277). Here, Montrano's castration, however fantastic, makes any such assertion of ultimate triumph impossible. But Alcestus's story is not unlike that Snader describes; it is a kind of Defoe-plot of enterprise rewarded. Alcestus travels as a trader confident of his connections and abilities. He embarked for "Ceylong" as a delegate for his father, to collect a debt;

"the Governor of the Fort, being a particular friend of our family, we judged he would have interest enough with the Dutch factory there, to compel the villain to do us justice" (56). Where Montrano's release and subsequent enrichment comes about not for any action on his part but as an almost fatalistic reward for "feminine" suffering, Alcestus saves the life of his master, the sovereign of the Maldives, and is abundantly rewarded for his valor. Doubled plots thus protect readers as they imagine female aggression and male helplessness, and differentiate Haywood's uses of exoticism from those that would predominate in later eras.

Telling his story to Alcestus, so Alcestus can retell it to Iseria, Montrano is at a loss to convey the horror of his subordination to Elphania: Alcestus "must make use of [his] own Imagination to conceive, what kind of fury it was that seiz'd the soul of this most vile woman, and sparkled in her eyes" (73). The pleasures of "Montrano and Iseria" are those of this imagining, safely contained as it is in "the Orient," and they are those of the comradeship that the telling, and retelling, enacts.

Philidore and Placentia represents a culmination of the stages in the representation of castration and exoticism that we have tracked in *Letters* and "Montrano and Iseria."[12] As in "Montrano and Iseria," the love story announced in the title contends with more vivid pleasures of reimagining masculinity and disassociating maleness with willed "individual" autonomy. Bellamont, this tale's victim of castration-in-the-Orient, is introduced in terms that suggest he will be only a subordinate character, an opportunity for the protagonist Philidore to display his courage and generosity. Dressed as a Persian, he is being flogged by other Persians when the valiant Philidore sees and rescues him. But Bellamont, like the Persia with which he is closely associated, only seems subordinate: for the promise of social regeneration with which the tale happily concludes rests squarely upon his castration and the "Persia" to which the tale pays a sustained, and "magical," visit.

Both elements sustain the dream of *Philidore and Placentia,* the elevation of the poor but genteel Philidore into a nobler, wealthier "race." The tale's opening again informs us of ancestral inadequacy to push the presently-living forward into the future. Philidore's forebears, "indolen[t] or unfashionabl[y] honest[]" (157), have left him too poor to court his beloved Placentia, and he will not work to better his condition because he lives only to be near her. Darkening his skin with walnuts to appear rustic, Philidore takes work as a menial servant in Placentia's grand household, content simply to kiss the pillows where she has sat. Soon enough he is rescuing her from robbers, unknowingly forcing his beloved's reexamination of her presumption that birth correlates predictably with worth. She worries that "it cannot be that he is the son of a peasant; a boor could never produce so angel-like a form, nor could a homely cottage inspire him with a behavior so elegant, a courage so undaunted, and a mien and voice so languishing and delicate" (166). Introduced thus as the common-sense defying end of a familial line, Philidore becomes, through the "magic" combination of castration-and-exoticism, not simply an "angel" whose beauty argues the nobility of his "race" but the assimilated newcomer to a still more noble lineage whose reproductivity will preserve it.

Seeing through his darkened skin to the "true gentleman" within, Placentia tries to promote Philidore to allow them to speak alone more freely, but he selflessly declines both such elevation and the intimacy it would afford. Soon thereafter, Placentia dresses herself seductively and summons the seeming servant whom she has realized she loves. When his refusal of her proposal of marriage causes her to swoon, it is all the passionate young Philidore can do to resist kissing the lovely bosom thereby exposed. To keep her from tainting herself by unbecoming alliance with him, Philidore banishes himself from Placentia's presence, shipping off to live with a trader uncle in "Persia."

As in "Montrano and Iseria," the doubled characters of *Philidore and Placentia* enact oddly parallel actions—European men succeed or fail in the exotic East, and European women are chaste at home or lustful abroad. It succeeds beyond "Montrano and Iseria" because of an additional doubling, the delicately schizoid deprecation and celebration of male selflessness voiced by the narrator. Of Philidore's astonishingly un-Haywoodian refusal of amorous dalliance, the narrator exclaims admiringly, "How few of those who call themselves lovers shall we find of this description? They swear, indeed, that nothing is so dear to them as the satisfaction of the beloved object; but if we look into their hearts, we shall easily discover that a blind gratification of their wishes is all they aim at, and to obtain that, no matter what becomes of the fortune, fame, and reputation, nay, the very life of the woman they pretend with so much ardency to adore" (169). Philidore is thus framed as a wonderful, even miraculous, exception to the rule of male sexual aggression. But he is not comfortably ideal, because he is—by virtue precisely of his exceptionalism—not recognizably manly. "But if most men are agitated by too gross a passion," the narrator continues ambivalently, "Philidore was certainly by one as much too nice" (169). This doubled admiration and damnation of Philidore's repudiation of aggression, be it directed toward making love or money, is of a piece with the tale's overall use of "Persia" as both utopia and dystopia, welcome release from a reviled domestic stasis and mutilating banishment from a desired domestic fulfillment.

The challenge Philidore poses to common sense social arrangements is double. He happily eschews his class position, dressing like a rustic, "whet[ting] knives for the butler . . . and such like servile employments." His patience in doing is almost inexplicable, suggesting to the narrator "the most abject meanness of spirit to have borne [this] even to have preserved life" (159). More pervasively, if less tangibly, Philidore defies common-sense notions of maleness. Even when his beloved later begs him to make love to her, he will not: "[S]ure he was the first lover that ever regretted such a discovery" (177). The shift of the plot to "Persia" answers both these implicit questions by affording Philidore scope for manly self-assertion in chivalric violence and by offering as contrast the more literal effeminacy of Bellamont with his castration.

Exoticism, the relocation of protagonist and plot to "Persia," marks the first significant mode of transformation of Haywood's familiar amorous plots. "Persia" holds no fainting maidens unwittingly exposing their breasts, no titillating accounts of desire enacted or restrained. Instead, it imaginatively dislocates reproductivity by representing both intense male-male bonding and castration as the punishment for aspiring to interracial dalliance. Philidore's ideal masculinity is burnished in juxtaposition to exotics, a consolidation further intensified by the fortune he eventually will amass through (exotic) trade. He is granted exceptional physical prowess in "Ceylong": his ship is seized by pirates, and he alone of his shipmates survives wandering in a desert, contact with "a great number of men armed with bows and arrows" (185), and attack by a tiger. As he makes his way to the "kingdom" of Persia, he comes upon "a young man of a most beautiful aspect, though disguised in blood and dust, who, with his back against the trunk of a large tree, was defending himself against three that attacked him." "'If you are a man of honor and a European,'" calls the stranger, "'assist an unfortunate Christian oppressed by these barbarians'" (187). The chivalric prowess Montrano evinced defending his mistress from robbers on her estate is here recast as a "racial" duty.

Moved "by an impulse which he could not at that time account for" (188), Philidore defends "the beautiful stranger," killing the three "barbarians." Freeing him, Philidore "burn[s] for the knowledge of who he was . . . with a greater impatience than he had ever done for anything since the time he had quitted the presence of his adorable Placentia" (188). When the stranger faints after victory, Philidore feels "a disappointment more touching than he could have imagined he could have been sensible of after the loss of the dear-loved Placentia" (189). This grief, the narrator tells us, is "wonderful from a stranger" (188). Philidore's attraction continues through the stranger's convalescence, even as doctors examine him and discover his recent mutilation.

Meanwhile, back in England, the days pass, and the heartbroken Placentia hears from her older brother, who had vanished while on a grand tour twelve years ago. He is returning home. Overjoyed that his reclamation of the position of head of the family means she will now lose the fortune that so intimidated her "too delicate" beloved, Placentia and her maidservant set out for Persia to find him. The captain of the ship conceives a "brutal passion" for Placentia—"Enjoyment any way was what he aimed at" (216)—and gives her a deadline, after which he will marry or rape her. Her plans to commit suicide are foiled only by the arrival of an "Algerine corsair." All passengers are taken as slaves, a fate Placentia prefers to rape (219). She is purchased in the marketplace of Baravat by an unknown benefactor who has heard of her despairing efforts to kill herself with a scimitar, a clear reworking of Clara's efforts to kill herself with Ferdinand's sword after he raped her. Of course, this benefactor is Philidore, on his way home to claim her, having amassed enormous wealth in Persia of his own efforts and as his now-dead uncle's heir.

Inset within this tale of European empowerment abroad is "The History of the Christian Eunuch" rescued by Philidore. We learn in due course that he is in fact Placentia's brother Bellamont, shipwrecked and taken captive by Persian privateers on his way home to England from Constantinople and sold into slavery in "the Oguzio" to the Bashaw of Liperda, who had "taken a fancy to [his] person" (197). Like a trophy wife, Bellamont's subsequent captivity at first evinced "nothing but the name of slave," he tells his rescuer.[13] He was given only light duties, was permitted to continue painting as he had learned to do in Italy, and enjoyed conversation with his host-master. "Such a slavery had been a glorious future for some men" (198). Bellamont rises to grieve his lost autonomy (read masculinity) only when another slave equates his value to the Bashaw with "a fine garden, a place, a rich jewel, or any other thing which affords him delight." Freedom is a matter of access not to possessions but to self-possession: in language evocative of Mary Astell's earlier comparison of wives and property, Bellamont's fellow-slave awakens him to his own imprisonment: their master "thinks on those whom ill fortune has reduced to be his slaves but as part of the furniture of his house, something he has bought for his use" (198).

No longer a happy slave, Bellamont embarks upon a rivalry with the master he had thought of as a friend, conceiving a violent passion for Arithea, "the most loved and beautiful of all the numerous train which crowded [the bashaw's] seraglio" (199). He paints her portrait, he pines for her, and, when she sends him a letter seeking an illicit assignation, he joyously goes to her. Where Philidore's strange restraint was described as defying common sense models of masculinity and class prerogative, Bellamont's unconsummated adoration from afar is given a nationalist cast. Arithea scolds Bellamont for "the coldness of you Europeans, who can content yourselves with so little when you so much merit all" (204). Though Haywood failed even to comment on the inter-"racial" sex she imagined in *Letters,* here it functions symbolically as the ultimate taboo, a desire that cannot be tolerated. Bellamont is captured, and his punishment, to be the more humiliating, is not death but castration. The bashaw's slaves "deprive[] [him] of all power of ever injuring their lord or any other person in the manner [he] was about to do and left [him] nothing but the name of man." If only he could have taken pride in being a "cold" European! He wishes for death, not wanting to live as "the scorn of both sexes and incapable of being owned by either" (206), but when Arithea sends him some jewels and a pitying letter, he follows her admonition to "fly this barbarous place" (207) and makes his way home. The "Janissaries" who had been flogging him when Philidore arrived on the scene were servants of the bashaw sent to return him to service.

Bellamont is castrated as punishment for aspiring to self-determination, marked by the attempted amatory conquest of an exotic woman. In a sense, then, he is castrated for being normatively masculine—for answering Philidore's mysterious unwillingness to acknowledge or act upon his lust. The two amours are in many respects identical: a well-born man, cast as a servant, worships a woman elevated beyond his reach. The two women's behaviors are also described similarly. "'Must I then make use of force to draw you to me?'" (175), Placentia demands; "it was only the want of a necessary boldness which brought you into any misfortune" (204), writes Arithea. It is Bellamont who sensibly, from the point of view of the narrator, responds to such feminine "force" with manly "boldness," and it is Bellamont who is disenfranchised from the happy ending and from the social regeneration that it implies. The "magical" difference, of course, is race. A white slave invading the harem is not, the conclusion suggests, comparable after all to a (feigned) manservant adoring his mistress at home.

Bellamont's castration in the exotic East, coupled with the wealth Philidore accrues with his trader-uncle and by means of his death, directly enables Philidore's promotion. Philidore is made a man—the wealthy and reproductive co-head of a noble family—by his "feminine" endurance of degradation. Throughout the tale, the narrator laments in equivalent terms his lack of financial and amatory will. His ancestors' failings need not have ruined him, for "[h]e had qualifications . . . which might have raised his fortune in some employment worthy of his birth and genius": "But alas! he labored under the pangs of an unhappy passion which was not only infinitely more grievous to him that all he had to fear from a narrow fortune, but also entirely took from him the power of attempting anything for himself or in the least answering the expectations the world had of him" (157). His departure to the potentially lucrative arena of Persian trade is similarly described. "[H]e was in reality embarked for Persia, not out of any hope of making his fortune with an uncle, who could easily have put him in the way of doing it; for he, alas! was dead to all considerations of interest" (184). Philidore's financial success is thus ironic, accrued "femininely," by accident. His amatory success depends, of course, upon his financial success; he can be rewarded for restraint in love only because he has, however unintentionally, eschewed restraint in money-making.

Overall, the exoticism and castration plots in *Philidore and Placentia* reward a nostalgic interpretation of aristocratic delicacy by keeping it magically separate from commerce.[14] Philidore may act as if the "employment [most] worthy of his birth and genius" is self-less love, but the plot shows us that it is foreign trade. Without that trade, he would not have been "restored" to the nobility his behavior evinces. He "submits" to debasement—service, clothed even to his skin as "a country boor"—"with a patience which would have argued the most abject meanness of spirit to have borne even to have preserved life" (159). This same submission informs his travel; it is not willful travel, like Bellamont's grand tour, but a kind of passive chivalric masochism, to protect both his beloved and his exalted conception of love. It is Bellamont, unable to conceive of submission in love and protected by ancestral wealth and privilege from the degradation of work, who is left debased on both counts at the end of the tale. He will have no love, and he will have no heirs. At home, Bellamont is no longer the lover, no longer the "beautiful stranger." The tale's concluding paragraphs cast him instead as a "generous brother and faithful friend" whose goodness is evidenced, at last, by repudiation of personal power. He "settled the remainder of his vast estate on them and their heirs after his decease, being well assured he should have no children of his own to inherit it" (230). Thus, via castration-and-exoticism, a male ideal is constructed of fantastic restraint and magical power, of "feminine" elevation into "masculine" prerogative.

"European culture gained in strength and identity by setting itself off against the Orient as a sort of surrogate and even underground self" (3). While the three exotic tales I have surveyed here evince the "Orientalism" described thus by Edward Said, they do not display the "peculiarly (not to say invidiously) male conception of the world" in terms of which he further characterized the phenomenon (207). Rather than the "playground for chosen and powerful white men" (115) that Jane Miller sees reified in *Orientalism,* Haywood represents the Orient as liberating for certain European men and women by their evasion of reproduction. Haywood combines an equally fantastic castration and exoticism to imagine an ironic utopia in which European men and women can escape enlistment in generation and generationality—self-constitution in relation to family name or property—and thus can abandon amatory battle. Such a "racial" context—the corporeality, reproductivity, and status-marking pallor of the amatory bodies that populate these fictions—is crucial to understanding the meaning of castration in her exotic tales, for the fantasy Haywood offers there is of a sexuality that is ungendered and thus fully "individual"—mobile, self-determining, and unconstrained by patriarchy.

While these tales certainly do not achieve the liberatory utopias to which they aspire or on which they comment, they offer an important vision of decentered and diffuse subjectivity that forces reexamination of the conventional association of the valorization of autonomy and the colonial period.[15] The culmination in Philidore of the three-tale sequence I have tracked dramatizes the desirability of freedom *from,* as well as *into,* willed individualism. Appreciation of the tales as a kind of social criticism is, however, complicated by the fact that the utopian gender fluidity they model requires a correlate rigidity in European/non-European interaction. Haywood's "individuals" may be, in a sense, freed from gender dichotomy, but they achieve this freedom only by defining themselves against non-Europeans who are, fittingly, almost without exception described as if in herds. The shipwrecked Montrano and Alcestus are greeted by "two or three of the Natives, who sending forth a loud Cry, they ran up farther into the Country, and before we could well resolve in what manner we should behave among a People, who we easily perceiv'd, to be wholly Unciviliz'd; we saw here a Hundred of them coming toward us; some arm'd with great Branches torn off the Trees, some with Axes, and a few with Bows and Arrows, and we now repented that we had taken no Care to bring our Guns from on board" (58). The luckier Philidore faces a less martial "barbarian" collective, being met on shore simply by "some poor people, who on sight of these strangers, ran frighted into the country, making a most terrible noise as they went" (185). Only after following these "poor people" for some time do the stranded

Europeans face "a great number of men armed with bows and arrows coming out against them" (185).

Fox-Genovese's criticism of "individualism" rests upon the falseness of its promise of "universality": "To insist upon the self's universality means to submerge woman in man" (118). In just this way, Haywood's dream of non-gendered, because non-reproductive, individual autonomy rests on a presumption of European, if not yet "white," universality. "Astrachan," "Ceylong," and "Persia" absorb European anger, lift obstacles to loving European union, and fill even unwilling Europeans' pockets. "Race" figures specifically in these tales in the preservation of bloodlines that proper reproduction is to assure. But a later sense of "race," close to "nation," hovers here, too. Here is yet another way in which Haywood, whose works have so often been read as predictors of the novel, can more usefully be read with an eye to liminality: early-eighteenth-century England's varied references to, and reliance upon, "race."

Notes

1. See Hall: "[T]he English/European division of beauty into 'white' or 'black' not only served aesthetic purposes but supported an ideology that still continues to serve the interests of white supremacy and male hegemony" (4).

2. See McKeon for discussion of "the modern system of sexuality," in which "the category 'gender' works to discriminate not only socialized behavior from natural fact, but also masculine from feminine" ("Historicizing" 301). See Ballaster for discussion of Haywood's career within the context of popular associations between women's textual production and promiscuity: "[I]t is Haywood whose textual production was most consistently identified with sexual promiscuity" (158).

3. My focus upon exoticism in Haywood's exotic fictions should not suggest that considerations of Orientalism, race, or nation-making are extraneous to those fictions in which her characters stay home in England or in Europe. So, too, though I will emphasize the aspects of these tales that, to my mind, differentiate them from Haywood's other works, I do not claim that difference is absolute. See Armstrong and Tennenhouse's *The Imaginary Puritan* for the related argument that the early modern appeal of American captivity narratives in England lay in the way they offered the opportunity to imagine being English abroad.

4. It is worth noting in this regard that humanitarian outrage at the

abandonment and murder of unwanted children was insufficient to see
England's first foundling hospital funded by the state. Only with the Seven
Years War and the state's need for cannon fodder was the London Foundling
Hospital funded by the state. Such a view of "foundlings as potential soldiers and colonists" had characterized the Continent since the late seventeenth century, as is evident in Louis XIV's Edict of 1670 to that effect:
"[C]onsidering how advantageous their preservation really was, since some
of them might become soldiers, and be usefull in Our Armies or Troups,
some to be Tradesmen, or Inhabitants in Our Colonys, which we are settling
for the advantage of the Trade of Our Kingdome" (cited by McClure 15).

5. This impossible ideal of reproduction correlates with ironic appropri-
ateness to the economic individuals of Defoe's novels: the acquisitive and
isolate Crusoe, whose individualist asexuality extends to his report that the
supplies he brings on his return to the island include wives; and Moll and
Roxana, both abandoning mothers and self-made women. For suggestive
readings of Defoe in terms of these contradictions, see Bowers, *Politics*, 98–
123; and Brown. Max Novak notes in his introduction to *Conjugal Lewdness* that "Defoe's attack upon intercourse before legal marriage was levelled
against a practice which was practically universal before the marriage act of
1754" (x).

6. Pregnancy is represented as disabling in other Haywood tales of this
period. Glicera, in "The City Jilt," succumbs to "the lawless Flame" and is
immediately abandoned by her beloved Melladore. "To enhance the Misery
of her Condition, she found herself with Child, with Child by a Man who
was already tired with her Embraces" (Willputte 71). Cleomira in *The British Recluse* makes a similar discovery as she is coming to recognize Lysander's
deviousness: "To add to my Affliction, I was with Child, and every Motion
of the unborn Innocent increased at once by Tenderness and Grief"
(Backscheider, *Popular* 180). The eponymous Fantomina first finds that "the
Consequences of her amorous Follies would be, without almost a Miracle,
impossible to be concealed" and then has the misfortune to go into labor
before her deceived and trusting mother's eyes: "She could not conceal the
sudden Rack which all at once invaded her; or had her Tongue been mute,
her wildly rolling Eyes, the Distortion of her Features, and the Convulsions
which shook her whole Frame, in spite of her, would have revealed she
laboured under some terrible Shock of Nature" (Backscheider, *Popular* 246).
See also Thorn, "'Althea,'" *Eighteenth-Century Women*, forthcoming.

7. See Nussbaum, "Feminotopias" in *Torrid Zones*, for a discussion of
eighteenth-century narrative uses of "eunuchs" per se.

8. Ballaster argues similarly, though with recourse to different primary
materials, that "Haywood's heroines are both indulged and punished for

succumbing to sexual desire": "Through this paradoxical movement Haywood's fiction sets about constructing the modern female reader of romance fiction. Erotic fantasy on the part of the woman reader, a heterosexual fantasy of subjugation and self-abandonment, is encouraged in the secure knowledge that ultimately female sexual pleasure will be punished or tamed" (170).

9. That Doody associates this restriction of male emotionality with the eclipse of Mme de Scudery offers a new venue for investigation of that staple of Haywood criticism, her relationship with her declared model.

10. Armstrong and Tennenhouse's analysis of the rhetorical authority presumed by early modern male-authored accounts of captivity by Native Americans considers the effeminizing helplessness with which captivity was regarded. "Captive men owned neither their labor nor their bodies, according to the legal theory of the period. Under such conditions, there is reason to think an eighteenth-century readership would not have considered them men" (*The Imaginary Puritan* 393).

11. See Hendricks: "In creating *The Widow Ranter*, she unconsciously exposes the principal contradiction of her class-based discourse of civility: aristocratic civility is incompatible with colonialism and imperialism" (238).

12. See Schofield for a different reading of *Philidore and Placentia* as the fulfillment of Haywood's previous work: "The integration of mood and setting, perhaps naively and superficially achieved [in *Idalia*], reaches its climax in *Philidore and Placentia*" (*Eliza* 28). See also McKeon's reading of the tale as "a gentle critique less of romance idealism that of the new idealism of progressive ideology, which says personal merit when it means cash, and replaces the old ideology of status with the new reification of money" (*Origins* 261).

13. McBurney tells us that the Oguzio is "presumably a section of the Mediterranean coast occupied by the Oghouz Turks, original founders of the Ottoman Empire. A check of the bashaws during the sultanate of Achmet III (1703–30) reveals no Bashaw of Liperda. Mrs. Haywood's lascivious and cruel Turk is, however, a familiar romantic and novelistic stereotype. Baravat, where Placentia is sold into slavery, must be in 'the dominions of the Grand Sultan,' though it appears to be the novelist's invention" (195).

14. See Sedgwick, *Between Men*, for discussion of representations of the aristocracy as feminized in which such delicacy is a liability.

15. See, for example, Azim: "The novel is an imperial genre, not in theme merely, not only by virtue of the historical moment of its birth—but in its formal structure—in the construction of that narrative voice which holds the narrative structure together" (30).

Speechless

Haywood's Deaf and Dumb Projector

Felicity A. Nussbaum

In the early eighteenth century a cluster of publications, some of which have been falsely attributed to Daniel Defoe, centered on the life of Duncan Campbell, a deaf-mute secular prophet who flourished from 1710 to 1730. Campbell is the subject of *The History of the Life and Adventures of Mr. Duncan Campbell, A Gentleman, who, tho' Deaf and Dumb, writes down any Stranger's Name at first Sight* (1720); *Mr.Campbell's Packet, for the Entertainment of Gentlemen and Ladies* (1720); Eliza Haywood's *A Spy upon the Conjuror* (March 19, 1724) and *The Dumb Projector* (1725); *The Friendly Daemon; or the Generous Apparition* (1726); and *Secret Memoirs of the Late Mr. Duncan Campbell* (1732).[1] The Scotsman Campbell attracted a parade of the curious and the lovelorn to his door with claims of possessing second sight and foretelling the future (see fig. 1). Eliza Haywood was among those who frequented his home, as well as Susannah Centlivre, Martha Fowke, Aaron Hill, Richard Savage, and Richard Steele. When his story was first published it became so popular "that even before the first edition was exhausted, the sanguine publisher Edmund Curll ordered a second" (Baine 144). According to the *Spectator* for 28 June 1714, "the blind *Tiresias* was not more famous in *Greece* than this dumb Artist has been for some Years last past in the cities of London and Westminster" (4:512). Campbell himself boasts in his memoirs, "But I was once in such a Vogue, that not

Hill Pinx.   Price Sculp.

The Effigies of

M.ᵣ Duncan Campbell

the Dumb Gentleman

Duncan Campbell, frontispiece from *The History of the Life and Adventures of Mr. Duncan Campbell, A Gentleman, who, tho' Deaf and Dumb, writes down any Stranger's Name at first Sight; with their future Contingencies of Fortune* (London 1720). Later versions attempt to remedy Campbell's concern that he appears too corpulent here. It is noteworthy that Campbell's hands, by which he communicated, are not visible. By permission of the British Library.

to have been with me, was to have been out of the Fashion; and it was then as strange a Thing not to have consulted the *Deaf and Dumb Conjurer*, as it is now not to have seen the *Beggars Opera* half a dozen Times, or to admire *Polly Peachum*" (*Secret Memoirs* 13–14). Realizing the benefits of being à la mode, he enjoys being a man of the moment whose advice is advertised as more valuable than new fashion. For women, soliciting Campbell's advice allegedly competed with expenditures on newfangled clothing for their pocket money. His fame was such that an advertisement in William Bond's *Weekly Medley*, 31 January to 7 February 1719, admonishes female masquerade-goers: "I would therefore advise most Ladies, who are at so much Cost for their Habits, to lay out as they may with much more Prudence and Benefit One Piece of Gold more to see him for so much previous wholesome Advice; or if they are so silly as not to follow my Counsel, they would be at least so wise to themselves" to impersonate Campbell as a mute and to affect being dumb only when they are solicited by strange masked men.[2]

Taking advantage of the popular taste for the odd, Campbell commodified his own person to become the equivalent of a London tourist site, thus avoiding the usual dislocation of the disabled to the margins of the marketplace as beggars or ballad-hawkers. Instead Campbell evolved into something of a cultural icon, and he functioned, in the way that disabled figures so often do, as a corporeal node that tellingly reveals social and historical tensions. The deaf predictor blurs the boundaries between the mysterious and the perverse, and his differences, like those represented more generally by the "defective," are a cultural means of locating the universal, the dominant, the metropolitan, the national, and the present through the aberrant and strange. Articulating these differences produces the normal, a word that apparently is used as a common standard of measure for person first in 1759, even as the culture seeks to locate the abnormal in place and time, as elsewhere and other.[3]

In this essay I will place Eliza Haywood's two contributions to the Duncan Campbell stories, *A Spy upon the Conjuror* (1724) and *The Dumb Projector* (1725), in the context of anomalous beings of both sexes and of women writers in particular. The Duncan Campbell myth provides secular conversion stories that inspire awe as well as the irrational belief that there may be some connection between uncanny abilities and disability. Eliza Haywood makes use of this intertwining of imaginative power and physical defect to connect implicitly Campbell's predicament to that of early eighteenth-century women writers, and she may well be responding to pervasive fears reflected, for example, in Alexander Pope's *The Dunciad*, about the mercenary nature of the burgeoning group of writers of both sexes who sell the product of their imaginations. Haywood was of course characterized by Pope "with cow-like udders, and with ox-like eyes," and her works were compared to "two babes of love close clinging to her waste" in *The Dunciad* (*Poems* 2: ll. 149–58; and see Ballaster, *Seductive Forms*). This enduring image of the paradigmatic woman writer, the monstrous and repulsive prize bestowed on the winner of a pissing contest, should be given equal weight, I think, with the more familiar epithets applied to women writers of the period such as whore, heteroclite, and bluestocking. Haywood's Campbell resembles these early eighteenth-century female authors as someone who finds locating a confident and authentic voice difficult; and like writing women, he is an anomaly in relation to gender expectations. In spite of being perceived as monsters, Campbell and able-bodied women who publish support themselves through intellectual labor and make their "disability" commercially viable.

Gender cannot be isolated from other regnant cultural and political values, and Campbell challenged other kinds of assumptions as well. Campbell violated expectations of the deaf as isolated, economically dependent, and lacking in sexual desire. I am also arguing here that the fashionable Campbell has such peculiar cultural resonance because he represents both past and future. As a freak of nature, a human being who employs sign language and a mute who writes, Campbell sits precariously on the cusp between prehistoric time and the unknown future as a cultural embodiment within whom the conflicts between past and present intersect. Figured as a remnant of the barbaric and uncivilized past, he is also nearly contemporaneous with Linnaeus's division of man into *homo sapiens* and *homo monstrosus* in *Systema Naturae* (1735; 10th ed., 1758; translated into English in 1802), representing both a being who evolved from ancient creatures and an analog to the noble savage, a marvelous brute. The popular literature of the period, including *The Spectator*, draws associations, for example, between Campbell, "A Dumb Oracle," and a chattering

magpie who is taught to speak. Yet in spite of seeming to derive from
the past, he made his living as an emblem of the speculative and of its
promise for the future.

In the eighteenth century defective beings were often associated
not only with a location at the edge of European geographic knowledge, but also with an earlier "less civilized" period of history. By
defective beings, I mean those with exceptional morphologies such as
giants, pygmies, and dwarves, as well as those with physical and cognitive disabilities including the deaf, the blind, and the retarded.
Campbell, then, is an example of monstrosity's temporal location in
the prehistoric. Mutant forms are, like race, given geographic specificity; often indicative of a species apart, abnormality is relegated to
remote and intemperate climates: the defective, then, are easily inter-
mingled and made synonymous with the racialized since dwarfs, giants, and blacks together compose "deformed races." A "geography
of monstrosity" places the monstrous at the edges of what is known
and beyond, just as the racialization of space took shape in climatic
theories that ascribed low intelligence and lax morals to torrid zones
populated largely by people of color. Ancient writers such as Pliny
and Herodotus, notes V.Y. Mudimbe in *The Invention of Africa*, are
among the first to create this "spacial mythography" that distinguishes
the savage, black, and strange (the headless, satyrs, cave-dwellers without language) from the "civilized" (71). Pollution, deviation, and degeneration of the "race" created social disorder and contamination of
the larger social body, and it was popularly accepted that an environmental cause could take root in physiology to become heredity. An
hereditary cause was sometimes believed to possess a somatic quality
after originally being termed environmental. That is, coldness and
moistness are bodily conditions influenced by the environment, and
they may take sufficient hold in the body to be transferred from generation to generation; similarly, skin afflictions that first appear as
disease may become hereditary in a second generation as race, like
defect, develops a mythological history.

The notion of the monstrous, when taken together with the geography of race, complicates what Charles Mills takes to be inherent
within the racial contract: that it "norms (and races) space, demarcat-
ing civil and wild spaces" (41). In Rousseau's *Discourse on Inequality*, as Mills points out, "the only natural savages cited are *nonwhite*

savages, examples of European savages being restricted to reports of feral children raised by wolves and bears, child-rearing practices (we are told) comparable to those of Hottentots and Caribs"; and because the state of nature was deeply racialized, savages were universally defined as nonwhite (68). This leap from monstrosity to racialization is also compatible with other conceptual frameworks in the Enlightenment. *Spectator* 17 contends that odd creatures are found in "the woody Parts of the *African* Continent, in your Voyage to or from *Grand Cairo*" (1.76). David Hume's famous racist footnote singles out a Jamaican man of learning as a rare exceptional being who is akin to a speaking parrot: the Negro who is aligned with a parrot can be trained to imitate language, and his hybridity is both bestial and freakish. In a similar instance, Robinson Crusoe taught his parrot to speak well enough to startle him awake by imitating human sentiments: "Poor *Robin Crusoe*, where are you *Robin Crusoe?*" just before locating the puzzling footprint (Defoe 142). The parrot is also a familiar means to mock women's alleged talkativeness. Haywood herself adopts the persona of the glib, gossiping parrot in the periodical *The Parrot,* published from 2 August 1746 until 4 October 1746 as a reverse satiric device, and Kim F. Hall aptly notes that in another earlier historical context, the Renaissance, "the parrot figures in misogynist treatises as well, in which women are said to be incapable of autonomous speech, able only to mimic the language of *man*kind" (244).[4]

Campbell's borderline test case on the fringes of civilization determines whether only humans speak, even as he refuses to remain voiceless by writing and gesturing for profit. The deaf and dumb also more generally arouse contemplation of the question of the relationship between animal sounds and the gesticulations and noises that other speechless creatures employ. Such distinctions among modes of communication in various species also have a racial resonance: "Thus a category crystallized over time in European thought to represent entities who are humanoid but not fully *human* ('savages,' 'barbarians') and who are identified as such by being members of the general set of nonwhite races. Influenced by the ancient Roman distinction between the civilized within and the barbarians outside the empire, the distinction [arises] between full and question-mark humans" (Mills 23). Speech and the capacity to create speech distinguishes men from brutes;

and beyond the mere imitation of articulation characteristic of crows and magpies, it is crucial to definitions of the origin of the human race. Jean Coenrad Amman, an eighteenth-century Swiss physician who tutored a deaf Dutch girl, claims that whole nations of the speechless can be found in Africa: "I have oftentimes heard from some Persons, that it was little beneath a Miracle, that God should give Men, to express the Thoughts of the Mind, rather by Motions, which are effected by the Lips, the Tongue, the Teeth,&c. Than otherwise, and that so universally, that there is no Nation so Barbarous, no not excepting the *Hottentots,* which cannot speak in a Language" (3). This is a particularly telling distinction since speech was believed to distinguish man from animal, the civilized from the savage, and it also confounded the difference between an oral and a written culture. Lord Monboddo remarks, "And I have made it, at least, highly probable, that it does at present actually exist in the woods of Angola, and other parts of Africa, where races of wild men, without the use of speech, are still to be found"(Burnet 1:v). Wondering at the extraordinary effort that Thomas Braidwood (1715–1806) painstakingly exerts to teach the deaf, Monboddo uses these examples to demonstrate that articulation is a learned rather than an innate skill. Demonstrating that language is not natural to man, in his account deaf people resemble men in a state of nature who "have inarticulate cries, by which they express their wants and desires" (1:190).

Similarly, gesturing instead of speech was also given exotic flavor in its presumed transmission from Turkey. George Sibscota was among those who reported that the exotic, disabled mutes assigned to the harem, communicated through hand motions: "The Emperour of the Turk maintains many such Mutes in his court; who do express the Conceptions of their minds one to another, and as it were interchange mutual discourse, by gesticulations, and variety of external significations, no otherways than we that have the faculty of signifying our own thoughts, and conceiving those of other Persons by outward Speech. Nay the Turkish Emperour himself, and his Courtiers, take great delight with this kind of Speech shadowed out by gestures, and use to employ themselves very much in the exercise hereof, to make them perfect in it" (41–42). Sibscota's early linguistics manual shows how the mutes retain their own languages and speak only with gestures at a dinner.[5] According to these theories, civilized man speaks while monsters who do not communicate in the conventional way exist precisely on the boundary of what is humanoid to define the limits of the human. As Nick Mirzoeff has noted, "In this sense, sign language becomes the unstable mark of simian similarity and difference with the hearing/human"("Paper" 82).[6] The disabled and racialized Other is figured as a means to truth through becoming the object of scientific experimentation, yet also as a sign of obfuscation in the sense of continuing to pose insoluble mysteries.

Being taken for a prehistoric being who survives in a modern time, yet able to perceive events in the future as if they were in the present, Duncan Campbell exemplifies this double temporal disjunction. Duncan's father, Archibald Campbell, who allegedly derives from the legendary home of second sight, the Shetland islands, married a Laplander woman after having been shipwrecked.[7] In one version of the story, a letter ostensibly from Archibald Campbell to *his* father recounts his experience in Lapland: "When first I enter'd this Country, I thought I was got into quite another World: The Men are all of them Pigmies to our tall, brawny *Highlanders*: They are, generally speaking, not above Three Cubits high; insomuch that tho' the whole Country of *Lapland* is immensely large, and I have heard it reckon'd by the Inhabitants to be above a Hundred *German* Leagues in Length, and Fourscore and Ten in Breadth: Yet I was the tallest Man there, and look'd upon as a Giant" (*The Supernatural Philosopher* 18–19). Frequently presumed to be diminutive people,[8] Laplanders were sometimes exhibited for profit. For Oliver Goldsmith, in *An History of the Earth,* extreme climates, like those in Lapland, may contribute to the degeneration of an entire population, "as their persons are thus naturally deformed, at least to our imaginations, their minds are equally incapable of strong exertions. The climate seems to relax their mental powers still more than those of the body; they are, therefore, in general, found to be stupid, indolent, and mischievous"(2:228). Accident, heredity, mutation, and climate all breed the potential for deformity. In addition, Campbell's birth apparently confirmed the Laplanders' superstitions surrounding the maternal imagination as represented in Laplander folklore: "If a Star be seen just before the Moon, we count it a sign of a lusty and well grown Child, without Blemish; if a Star comes just after, we reckon it a token that the Child will have some defect or deformity, or die soon after it is Born" (*His-*

tory of the Life 25). The unknown commentator for *The History of Duncan Campbell*, perhaps William Bond, is the only one who tells this part of the story that relates to Lapland. Others, especially Eliza Haywood (who resists making his mother's imagination the cause for his deafness), are more especially interested in Campbell's status as a speculator for the lovesick who makes a living from his special gift.

When Campbell first learned the Scots' language, according to *The History of the Life*, he learned "to leave off some Savage Motions, which he had taken of his own accord, before to signifie his Mind by, and to impart his thoughts by his Fingers and his Pen" very intelligibly and swiftly (36) (see fig. 2). In reality, after Campbell was orphaned at twelve, the precocious deaf and dumb boy became a soothsaying phenomenon who marketed his disability to counter serious debt. The evidence is compelling that Campbell was truly hearing-impaired, though he may have possessed some modicum of hearing. But fortune-telling is a questionable skill, and the validity of the disability (even for modern commentators) is sometimes confused with skepticism concerning Campbell's second sight. Campbell foresees the future with second sight, which Samuel Johnson later defines in *The Journey to the Western Islands of Scotland* as "an impression made either by the mind upon the eye, or by the eye upon the mind, by which things instant or future are perceived, and seen as if they were present. . . .Things distant are seen at the instant when they happen" (107). Haywood's *Spy Upon the Conjuror* begs the question of his credibility as a fortune-teller while remarking on his amazing capacity to write the names of people he met for the first time, along with those of their former or current spouses. In Haywood's version there is no answer to the letter from an acquaintance inquiring why Campbell makes people write down their questions if he can already read their minds.

Campbell defies the usual picture of a bereft and infantilized person with a disability and is instead figured as a man who also resembles a woman and is thus a third sort of hermaphrodite being. One observer of Campbell describes an adulatory gathering:

> As soon as I enter'd the Room, I was surpriz'd to find myself
> encompass'd and surrounded by a Circle of the most beautiful
> Females that ever my Eyes beheld. In the Centre of this Angelick
> Tribe was seated a heavenly Youth, with the most winning comeli-

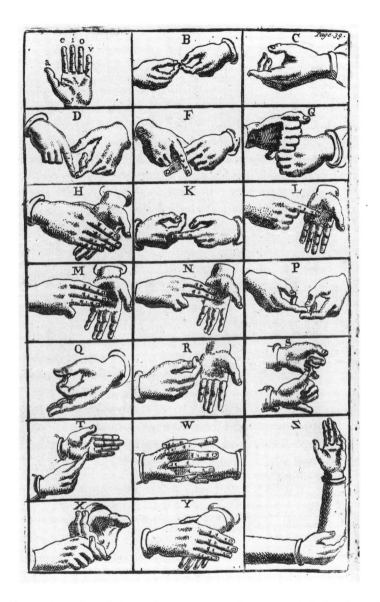

Engraving of an eighteenth-century sign language alphabet from *The History of the Life and Adventures of Mr. Duncan Campbell, A Gentleman, who, tho' Deaf and Dumb, writes down any Stranger's Name at first Sight; with their future Contingencies of Fortune* (London 1720). Sign languages for the deaf originated in the seventeenth century with such publications as John Bulwer's *Chirologia: or the Natural Language of the hand. Composed of the Speaking Motions, and Discoursing Gestures thereof* (London 1644), and a literature of "surdo-mutism" flourished among physicians and scientists. By permission of the British Library.

ness of Aspect, that ever pleased the Sight of any Beholder of either
Sex; his Face was divinely Fair, and ting'd only with such a sprightly
Blush, as a Painter would use to Colour the Picture of Health with,
and the Complexion was varnish'd over by a Blooming, like that of
flourishing Fruit, which had not yet felt the first Nippings of an
unkind and an uncivil Air; with this Beauty was join'd such a smiling
draught of all the Features, as is the result of Plesantry and good
Humour. His Eyes were large, full of Lustre, Majestick, well set, and
the Soul shone so in them, as told the Spectators plainly, how great
was the inward Vivacity of his *Genius*: The Hair of his Head was
thick and reclin'd far below his Shoulders; it was of a fine Silver
Colour, and hung down in Ringlets like the curling Tendrils of a
copious Vine. He was by the Women entertain'd, according to the
Claim, which so many Perfections joining in a Youth just ripening
into Manhood, might lay to the benevolent Dispositions of the tender
Sex. One was holding the Bason of Water, another washing a Hand,
a Third with a Towel drying his Face, which another Fair had
greedily snatch'd the Pleasure of washing before, while a Fourth was
disposing into order his Silver Hairs with an Ivory Comb, in an
Hand as White, and which a Monarch might have been proud to
have had so employ'd in adjusting the Crown upon his Head; a Fifth
was setting into Order his Cravat; a Sixth stole a Kiss, and blush'd at
the innocent Pleasure, and mistook her own Thoughts as if she kiss'd
the Angel and not the Man; and they all rather seem'd to adore than
to love him, as if they had taken him not for a Person that enjoy'd
the frequent Gift of the Second Sight, but as if he had been some little
Prophet peculiarly inspired, and while they all thus admired and
wonder'd they all consulted him as an Oracle. The surprize of seeing
a young Man so happy amidst the general concurring Favours of the
Fair, made me be for a while lost in a kind of delightful amazement,
and the consideration of what Bliss he was possess'd, made me scarce
believe my own Eyes, when they told me it was *Duncan Campbell*,
who I had left an unhappy Orphan at *Edinburgh*. (*History of the
Life* 128–29)

In this extraordinarily visual passage, Campbell captures the observer's
gaze as well as the attention of the beautiful angelic women who sur-
round him. He is pleasing to either sex, "divinely fair," a blooming
virginal youth ripe for the picking who with his silver shoulder-length
hair resembles a prelapsarian Adam, a prophet, or Christ himself. His
body parts are aligned with nature, his hair tendrils like a vine, his

complexion like fruit. The attending women fawn over his toilet, each
contributing to bathing and dressing a part of him in turn. He is monarchical and majesterial, but also feminized as a sexual object in the
loving attention devoted to his body. Campbell, "just ripening into
Manhood," inspires a dressing ritual which resembles nothing so much
as a royal prince with his English harem, in which the attending women
are emboldened to kiss him. His vibrant nature exudes a luscious sexuality. A regal yet approachable androgynous creature, he is a gorgeous if somewhat peculiar specimen who will ripen into more, and
his capacity to prophesy magnetically draws the women to him. In a
curious gendering, Campbell seems to rise beyond a mere man or
woman, and yet he becomes aligned with an androgynous being rather
than an amphibious bestial creature.

Incarnating the latest fashion, Campbell is associated with femininity both as a beautiful spectacular object and as an aberration or
defect, a connection common to the eighteenth century (see Nussbaum,
"Dumb Virgins"). Disability is characteristically linked with effeminacy, as in Jean-Nicolas Bouilly's play *Abbé de l'Epée*, when Theodore
was played by Madame Talma: "It is noticeable that the character of
the signing deaf boy was considered an appropriate role for a woman
to play" (Mirzoeff 75). Campbell is also feminized because of his epi-
lepsy, a condition that he blames on the extraordinary concentration
required for fortune-telling: "[A] Flirt of a Fan has made me sudden
drop down in the most terrible Convulsions, and rendered me wholly
incapable of answering any Questions that Day . . . I cannot but look
on it as a Womanish, or at best, a Pedantick one, but all I can do has
hitherto been ineffectual" (*Secret Memoirs* 16). Thus Campbell is a
figure who embodies enfeebled and enervated masculinity while at
the same time in other accounts he is regarded as sexually desirable.
In either case his potency is unstable and very much at issue. By his
own account Campbell is at pains to disassociate his hearing impair-
ment from effeminacy, and he displaces impotency onto blindness instead. Campbell recounts his meeting with a famous blind man who
claimed that he could distinguish colors by touch, and who relished
playing card games. After twice losing at cards, Campbell discovers
that the blind man's squire marked the cards with pinpricks so that he
could distinguish them by touch. The deaf man teaches the blind man
some sign language with great relish: "In fine, no two Persons in Com-

pany could be more conversible with each other, than we were within the Time prefixed; on which, said the blind Man, *I see by Feeling, and you hear by your Eyes.*" The two engage in a debate over the hierarchy of disabilities, each claiming that his is the more highly valued. Campbell insists on the superiority of sight over speech and hearing: "I told the Company, *That I would not lose the Sight of the Sun, and a fine Woman, to be Emperor of the whole globe; and, that I would be deprived of Legs and Arms, nay, endure* Castration *itself, rather than quit so valuable a Blessing as that of Sight*" (117). Sight is equated to his sexual organ: to be able to see is to have a penis, and Campbell, like his commentators, tries to make manly what had been in the past associated with "credulous Nurses and old Women" (*Supernatural Philosopher* 6). To be deprived of his eyes would be *worse* than losing sexual prowess, and, curiously, to gaze upon a woman, to see her, in this logic, is more significant than bedding her. In Campbell's formulation, as long as he possesses sight he is manly.

Campbell is not emasculated in Haywood's account, in spite of his occupying a cultural location that is akin to that of old women and shiftless beggars. Haywood is careful to distinguish Campbell from ignorant fortune-tellers who are fearmongerers or who provide love charms, "and a thousand other fantastick, ridiculous Spells, which rather would excite Derision, than raise Belief in the thinking Part of the World" (*Spy* 126). Campbell's misogyny also serves to counter any charges of a masculinity at risk: "He would often smile and write to me," Haywood reports, "*O Woman! Woman! Woman! The Sin of Eve taints thy whole Sex*" (73). Obviously Haywood hoped to cash in on the extraordinary popularity of Campbell's story. Though her biographical narrative reveals little plot, it becomes an occasion for the narrator to expose Campbell's misogyny and even to participate in it: "Heavens! That Women can be mad enough to publish their own Disgrace, and swell the Triumphs of him that has undone 'em! Yet so it is with our inconsiderate Sex!—to vent a present Passion,—for the short-liv'd Ease of railing at the Baseness of an ungrateful Lover,—to gain a little Pity,—we proclaim our Folly, and become the Jest of all who know us" (*Spy* 75–76). Both Haywood and Campbell take women to task for their refusal to heed warnings about men's casually ruining their reputation, and Campbell appears to have had unusual prescience in regard to virgins and their future ruination.

For Eliza Haywood, Duncan Campbell, the deaf and dumb seer, is both eroticized and exoticized as an *au courant* forecaster of the future who, in spite of being voiceless, wields cultural power through translating his imaginative visions into writing. In Eliza Haywood's version, more romantic and scandalous than other accounts, her pose as a voyeur anticipates her later posture as the Female Spectator (Baine). Haywood writes in the person of Justicia, the "spy upon the conjuror," who visited Campbell regularly, stole some of his papers that constitute the book in which he is featured, and seems to be slightly in love with him herself, a posture she encourages the reader to share. *The Spy Upon the Conjuror: Or, A Collection of Surprising and Diverting Stories, with Merry and Ingenious Letters* (1725) defends Campbell (also called the "Dumb Predictor" and the "Dumb Oracle") against those who question his second sight and the validity of his deaf and mute condition. Haywood's collection of tales and letters, not quite a biographical narrative, emphasizes Campbell's communicating through writing in the presence of his clients much more than his deafness or communicating through sign language. While Campbell makes of himself a sexual object and acknowledges his own peculiarities as a deaf person, Haywood also produces purported letters that engage questions of courtship, rape, sexual harassment, and jealousy. Haywood focuses on his ability to tell stories of love that enrage the auditor, yet command sufficient respect to allow him to make a living by fortune-telling. In Haywood's version, and in the *Secret Memoirs of the late Mr. Duncan Campbell* (1732), Campbell is accused of appealing to women who are more easily duped because of their sex and who constitute the preponderance of paying customers; however, among other clientele were the manly members of the Royal Cabinet who also sought his prophecies.

The section of twenty-five letters concluding *The Spy Upon the Conjuror* appeals to Campbell for his advice, for example, for a woman who had been raped, a forsaken lady, a common woman unhappily married to a rich old man, a widow, a young gentleman in the country, and others who seek wisdom from an eighteenth-century counselor. In fact, it seems to me that Haywood cleverly skirts the conventional voyeuristic Orientalism popular in the early eighteenth century, and that she also manages to avoid representing her narrator as the normative human being against whom we should judge the irregular

Campbell. In short, Haywood skillfully eludes the narrative stance
that would align itself with a "normate" vision, Rosemary Garland
Thomson's pejorative term for the hegemonic subject position that
assumes the power to determine social norms surrounding the body's
configurations (8–13). Campbell's disabled body is a cultural reposi-
tory for political and social contradictions in the early eighteenth century concerning modernity and the body it engenders, and Haywood
takes the high ground in her sympathy with him.

Haywood also emphasizes the violence and rage directed against
Campbell as if to underscore her personal understanding that the culture refused to accept the body it insisted on judging to be defective.
From the first she portrays him as the object of scorn: "I believe no
Man on Earth has ever met with more ill Treatment, Injustice, and
Barbarity" (*Spy* 144). Skeptical customers attack him to prove that
he is faking his disabilities: one woman catches his fingers (his means
of communication) in a door to trick him into crying out, a man who
had never before met him beats him with a cane to get him to protest,
and another customer marvels that though he lances Campbell's fis-
tula (a pipe-like sore or ulcer), he does not utter a syllable. Describing
a situation analogous to the predicament of various women writers,
Haywood tells stories of a culture that tested and tortured Campbell,
even though he had no voice to articulate his pain:

> I was one Day at a Lady's, where Mr. *Henry Vaughan*, a Surgeon
> of very good Repute . . . told the Company, laughing, that he was
> going to make the *Dumb* to speak: I ask'd him what he meant; and
> he reply'd, He was that Afternoon to perform that sad Operation of
> cutting a *Fistola*, which he assured me was worse to the Patient who
> endured it, than cutting off Legs or Arms.—*The Person,* said he, *that
> is to undergo it, is the famous Fortune-Teller,* Duncan Campbell, *who
> pretends to be Deaf and Dumb; but I'll engage I make him speak
> before I have done with him.* All the Company was impatient to
> know the End of this Adventure, and engaged him to come back and
> give us an Account; which in about an Hour after he did, but in a
> Humour very different from that in which he left us. He acknowl-
> edged his Mistake; and said, he was now convinc'd that Mr.
> *Campbell* could not speak, since he had endured as much as ever
> mortal Man went through, and had not utter'd the least Syllable, and
> in his Agonies vented the Sense he had of them, by a Noise which

sufficiently testified he was really denied the Benefit of expressing what he felt any other Way." (147–48)

Campbell's inarticulate but heartfelt noise communicates his agony, shames those who would disbelieve his disability, and turns potential mockery into sympathetic understanding. Unquestionably, Campbell's status as a hot commercial property motivated Haywood's opportunistic desire to capitalize on the popular rage that made his conjectures marketable. But she may also have found in his condition an emblem of women writers' struggles to be heard and their difficulty in articulating that condition.[9]

Haywood's attitude is largely one of respect, admiration, and celebration rather than pity-mongering. She emphasizes Campbell's second sight more than his disability and admiringly notes that much of what he sees is not easily predicted. Further, Haywood defends him against charges of being mercenary by pointing out that he refuses to talk to certain offensive women in spite of turning away potential customers in making that decision: "This more amaz'd me, having always thought that Money made every Body welcome" (136). She includes a letter from a gentleman who subscribes to the theory of nature's compensating for his disability "by doubling the Vigour of those Senses you are possess'd of, the Deficiency of those she has denied you. The Want of Hearing and Speaking would to another Person be an inconsolable Affliction; yet you, methinks, appears as gay and unconcerned as those who labour not under either of those Defects.—I guess that you will answer, That that supernatural Gift, called the second Sight, abundantly compensates for what is denied you by the Want of those more common Blessings"(238).

In her discussion of Campbell, Haywood also reports some of the ways that visitors questioned, sometimes cruelly, whether Campbell was a sentient being; such questions have erotic connotations:

It was of a young Woman who really by her Dress, and Manner of Behaviour, appeared to be not of the lowest Rank of Life; she happened to come when our *Dumb Oracle* was abroad: But being told he would come in soon, she chatted away an Hour or two with Mrs. *Campbell*; and being of a pretty pert Humour, ask'd her how she cou'd be brought to like a Man that could not speak.—*Good God!* said she, *How did he make Love?—Lord! I wonder whether he*

can feel or not?—She persecuted her with a thousand such-like idle
Questions, telling her she wonder'd how so fine a Woman as she
could venture on a Monster.—To all which Mrs. *Campbell* made but
short Replys. At last, his coming home cut off any farther Conversation of this kind; but having never seen Mr. *Campbell*, it was not
without a great deal of Difficulty she was persuaded it was he,
imagining, as she afterwards confess'd, she should have seen something very deform'd, and miserable in his Aspect; . . . but by writing
her Name, and several Particulars of her Life, he soon made her
sensible he was really the Person she came to consult. But the Jest is,
that this fine Lady, who was so full of Wonder before, became so
diligent in learning the Art of talking on her Fingers, that in a little
Time she grew a perfect Mistress of it, and made use of it to invite
Mr. *Campbell* to come to see her at her Lodgings by himself. . . .
Some Letters afterwards found among those Papers, which I stole out
of his Closet, give indeed a too great Demonstration that she liked
him but too well. (154)

The curiosity that the young woman shows upon first being confronted
with difference is soon supplanted by her adoption of his method of
communication, and an erotically charged liaison between them ensues. She and other skeptics puzzle over his status as a thinking and
feeling human being, and as a sexual man, affording Haywood an
opportunity to titillate the reader.

Haywood's narrator, Justicia, purports to test Campbell's abilities
by interrogating those who consulted him. In Haywood's account,
Campbell's divining powers repeatedly assume more significance than
his disability. Here as elsewhere his "supernatural Gift" (238) compensates for his inability to hear or speak: "The naturally deficient
Organs in so noble a Temperament, indeed, demand Commiseration
from all generous Humanity; yet the superabundant Retaliations of
Providence in your many unparalell'd Endowments, almost puts me
to a Stand whether I ought not, in some Measure, conclude even those
very Defects a Blessing, amidst the universal empty Noise and Depravity of Conversation" (257). This is a benevolent picture of a man,
admirably compensating for his disability, whom Justicia rages against
as she would against any man whose vision of her unhappy future is
antagonistic. She was disordered, distracted, and furious, making *her*
the peculiar one: "How my own Character was made ridiculous, by
the Wildness of my ungovernable Rage" (75). Campbell fully partici-

pates in print culture literally by writing predictions rather than re-
sembling a stereotypically beastlike being who communicates with
hand gestures. She does not discuss signing with the hands until the
end of the first volume, and then only incidentally when she characterizes him as civil, sociable, and possessing good sense. Haywood's
Campbell, unlike the hero presented in some of the other accounts, is
a modern citizen rather than a residual being from an ancient and
oral past. *The Spy upon the Conjuror* also seems to be a veiled lament
that Campbell may be going out of fashion, and that lesser modes of
fortune-telling such as reading tea and coffeegrounds are gaining
greater vogue, thus making his skills less marketable. The products
that come from economic speculation and imperial trade may put the
more primitive second sight out of business. Yet Campbell's
prophecying for profit about an uncertain future, and the cultural
imperative to speculate and invest in the promise of the future is made
most visible in the nation's South Sea Bubble stock venture (1722)
and provides a compelling national fable for the new credit economy.[10]

Haywood, herself the spy upon the conjuror of the title, predictably exploits passion and love more than the other commentators
since her version of Campbell makes him seem ordinary except for his
very unusual gift of second sight. Misdirected passion creates monstrosity, and Campbell, the very center of reason in Haywood's account, risks the venom of his clients, chiefly women, who like Haywood
herself perversely transform *themselves* into monsters when faced with
the "truth" of Campbell's prophecies: "But I had scarce Time to finish it, before a Woman burst into the Room in a very rude and abrupt
manner; and by her Way of Behaviour, shew'd me, as in a Glass, the
Transformation I had been under when I was there before, and how
monstrously Passion disfigures the *Person*, as well as *Reason*, of those
who harbour it. She who, when her Fury was a little abated, I perceiv'd
to be a Woman of singular good Sense, and what one might call
extreamly handsome, appear'd at her first Entrance, the very Reverse
of both.—She had quite forgot all Decorum; lost, for some Moments,
all that belongs to a Woman of Discretion, or good Breeding.—Her
Eyes shot Fire; her Cheeks bloated with Fury; her Lips trembled; every Feature was distorted; her Voice was big, hoarse, and masculine;
and her Expressions such as are ordinarily made use of by Fish-Wives,
Market-Women, and others of the same Degree of Gentry"(81). Fail-

ing to accept his prophecy sends this woman catapulting into the loss of femininity, beauty, and class status. The woman who distorts her beauty with rage at Campbell's accurate prophecy regarding her lover's deceit provides a mirror image for Justicia. She becomes an emblem for the literal ugliness that misplaced passion evinces when it rails against the inevitable betrayal by men that Campbell predicts. Such violent anger also diminishes her social class and makes her indistinguishable from ordinary sellers of goods in the street, unlike Campbell who prophesies from the domestic space of his home. Paradoxically, too, Campbell is reputed actually to make the crooked straight, defying his own categorization as disabled, as he does when a deformed woman comes to him. Haywood explains his inability to forecast his own future as self-neglect rather than a failure of powers (170). She is not much interested in his personal history, his Jacobitism, or his Laplander or Scottish origins; instead he is a fashionable yet manly figure whose perception of Englishwomen's present and future is uncanny and whose misogyny is excused as his recognition of the realities of a sexual double standard.

Though Haywood seems to erase the importance of Campbell's Scottish heritage in order to normalize him, Scotland also evokes for English readers an archaic past which Campbell embodies, a theme that Johnson echoes in his description of Braidwood's school for the deaf in the *Journey to the Western Islands* (1775). Braidwood formed a special academy for the deaf and dumb in Edinburgh that he moved to London in 1783 when it became a public institution supported by George III, a man who struggled with mental disability himself. In the *Journey,* Samuel Johnson famously compares the Highlanders' culture to those of the Eskimeaux and the Hottentots, and the sign language of the deaf inspires hope after a tour of a nation that Johnson finds to be backward and vacuous: "[W]hatever enlarges hope, will exalt courage; after having seen the deaf taught arithmetick, who would be afraid to cultivate the Hebrides?" (164). Scotland, a nation primitive and disabled, deserves "cultivation" since its elusive oral history defies the written narration that he is attempting. Johnson's metaphor of cultivation also justifies England's usurpation of that role. Johnson found instructing the deaf and dumb to be a sign of emergence from the past into a commercial future and a print culture.

Scotland, then, in Johnson's account is "ignorant and savage," a disabled nation requiring special education and happily anticipating "cultivation," a metaphor for colonization by the English who are, in the terms of the *Journey*, the able-bodied (51).[11] Clusters of metaphors adhere to Scotland as a nation that first learns to speak and then to think, paralleling the evolution from child to adult, individual to collective, barbarous to civilized. In Col, Johnson remarks, "The uncultivated parts are clothed with heath, among which industry has interspersed spots of grass and corn; but no attempt has yet been made to raise a tree" (124). Braidwood's school instructs the deaf to speak, to write, and to read lips, gestures, and print: like Campbell, "they hear with the eye"(163). Johnson's witnessing their achievement gives him hope: "I have seen so much, that I can believe more." The scholars greet their master "with smiling countenances and sparkling eyes, delighted with the hope of new ideas" and exemplified in the young woman who, "quivering her fingers in a manner which I thought very pretty, but of which I know not whether it was art or play, multiplied the sum regularly in two lines, observing the decimal place; but did not add the two lines together, probably disdaining so easy an operation. . . .It was pleasing to see one of the most desperate of human calamities capable of so much help" (164). Recent critics of the *Journey* have emphasized Johnson's personal identification with Braidwood's pupils as "an image of himself as writer, as well as struggling with the problem of self-inscription and (provisionally) solving it," and Johnson's inability to bridge the gap between recovering an ancient national Scottish myth that had not been articulated on one hand, while documenting it as Scotland's authoritative historian on the other (Sherman 207; Wechselblatt 143). Like the deaf and dumb, Johnson is unable to translate into print what he foresees for a material and commercial culture: "He portrays himself as writing from a position of silence and solitude (he is 'deaf' and bereft of 'conversation')" (Sherman 197), and thus appropriates the women writers' predicament as his own. Johnson remarks on the absence of trees, history, written language, of a naked landscape, emigration, and land of superstition. But if Scotland arouses fears of vacuity and the mental instability arising from the mind's inability to fix on an object, it also represents the hope that "cultivation," a word as important to the *Journey* as "vacuity," inspires. Cultivation, something that Scotland must depend on England to provide, is associated with Englishness, concerning everything from turnips that will produce fodder for hungry sheep and cows, to the language: "The great, the learned, the ambitious, and the vain, all cultivate the English phrase, and the English pronunciation, and in splendid companies Scotch is not much heard, except now and then from an old lady" (162). The ancient unwritten language is feminized and antiquated, most characterized by a withered specimen of the sex. In contrast, Haywood's Duncan Campbell defied the expectation that fortune-tellers were doddering old women and was instead sexy, manly, imaginative, beautiful, powerful, and deaf.

In *The History of Sexuality,* Michel Foucault posits that the regulation of children in the eighteenth century extends to the publication of popular medical advice directives that correct the physical impairments in young bodies. As Ann Laura Stoler puts it, "In the making of a bourgeois 'class' body in the eighteenth century, a new field of discourse emerged concerned with 'body hygiene, the art of longevity, ways of having healthy children and of keeping them alive as long as possible'"(53). Along with this aim to regulate the corporeal, the aberrant are pushed increasingly to the margins in order to "civilize" the social body as a category of the normal evolves. Rosemarie Garland Thomson has demonstrated in relation to American literature that "without the monstrous body to demarcate the border of the generic, without the female body to distinguish the shape of the male, and without the pathological to give form to the normal, the taxonomies of bodily value that underlie political, social, and economic arrangements would collapse" (20). The aberrant are akin to all those who inhabit the margins—"races" other than European, women, those of uncertain gender, the laboring classes—as European nationalisms and the modern body associated with them begin to cohere. Haywood's depiction of the deaf-mute clairvoyant is truly radical: the conjurer, an individual evocative of erotic attention and possessed of economic self-sufficiency, is also a Scot neither needing nor commanding pity, prejudice, national chauvinism, or imperial opportunity in the guise of cultivation. We might speculate that for Haywood, Campbell's predicament shares some affinities to the plight of that other intellectual monstrosity, the woman who writes for money. Though she herself benefits from selling his story, Haywood resists treating the conjuring

deaf man Duncan Campbell as a freak of nature who resembles a
woman preaching, a dog walking on its hinder legs, a talking parrot,
or a learned black man. Haywood instead explores the terms by which
an impaired human being who, though voiceless, speaks through writing and gesture and even dares to warn of a future that antagonizes the
very customers who willingly paid for the unfavorable forecast.
Campbell's voiceless struggle to construct a personhood, a subjectivity,
parallels that of other aberrant beings and offers an alternative to nor-
malcy as a means to claim an articulate humanity within modernity.

Notes

1. For a convincing refutation of the attribution to Defoe, see Baine,
who believes that William Bond authored *The History* and *The Friendly
Daemon*. Publisher Bond's *The Supernatural Philosopher: or, the Mysteries
of Magick, In all its Branches, clearly Unfolded* (1728) appeared as a "second edition" to *The History*. This book, according to Baine, "reissued sheets
of both of the 1720 editions . . . with a new title" (145). *Secret Memoirs* is, I
believe, inaccurately assumed to be a reprint of *Friendly Daemon*.

2. *The Weekly Medley,* 31 January / 7 February 1719, is cited in Baine
from the Bodleian microfilm record.

3. Canguilhem remarks that "Between 1759, the date of the first appearance of the word *normal*, and 1834, the date of the first appearance of the
word *normalized*, a normative class conquered the power to identify the
function of social norms with its own uses and its own determination of
content" (246).

4. See also Nussbaum, "Difference," for a discussion of analogies between the bestial and the savage as related to racial assumptions in the eighteenth century.

5. In addition, Jean Baptiste Tavernier's *A New Relation of the Inner-
Part of the Grand Seignor's Seraglio* notes that mutes in the seraglio communicated through sign language, which functioned to avoid distracting the
monarch with the sound of servants speaking.

6. For the definitive work on the relationship between sign language and
the aesthetic/visual arts in France in this period, see Mirzoeff, *Silent Poetry,*
who quotes Perier, one of Sicard's deputies, as saying: "The Deaf-Mute is a
savage, always close to ferocity and always on the point of becoming a monster" (62). Mirzoeff also reports that anthropologists were encouraged "to
learn sign language in order to communicate with the native peoples they
encountered" (68).

7. According to Baine, information relevant to the parentage of Campbell's mother in Lapland was cribbed from Johannes Scheffer's *History of Lapland* (150).

8. Jean-Jacques Rousseau writes that "There have been, and there perhaps still are, Nations of men of gigantic size; and apart from the fable of the Pygmies, which may well be only an exaggeration, it is known that the Laplanders, and above all the Greenlanders, are well below the size of man. It is even claimed that there are whole Peoples that have tails like quadrupeds" (80).

9. Epstein argues that within patriarchy, "women physically retreat . . . and can use only speech—the polite speech of self-command—to countermand violation" (149). In particular Frances Burney's later writings are characterized by inarticulate pain, "speechless agony" (89).

10. As such, Campbell seems to be the personification of "a society now living to an increasing degree by speculation and by credit" who possesses "the image of a secular and historical future." Fortune-telling exemplifies the way that "property . . . has ceased to be real and become not merely mobile but imaginary" (Pocock 98, 112).

11. Midcentury brings the beginning of institutionalized special education, according to Winzer.

"Haywood," Secret History, and the Politics of Attribution

David Brewer

The World, I know, pay but little Regard to a Writer's Promises . . . I hope, however, if they will now and then lay a little Dulness at my Door, they will at least require very good Evidence before they convict me of Abuse: Since I never yet was, nor ever shall be the Author of any, unless to Persons who are, or ought to be infamous; and it is really hard to hear that scandalous Writings have been charged on me for that very Reason which ought to have proved the contrary, namely because they have been scandalous.

—Henry Fielding, *The Covent-Garden Journal*

Tucked away in the second appendix to *The Dunciad Variorum* (1729), amidst "A List of Books, Papers, and Verses, in which our Author was abused," may be found a curious addition to *our* author's *oeuvre*. According to Pope, the anonymously published *Memoirs of Lilliput* (or, more accurately, *Memoirs of the Court of Lilliput*) are actually the work of "Mrs. *Eliz. Haywood*" (92), an attribution which implicitly provides Pope with yet another excuse for including Haywood among the Dunces in the poem proper.[1] Few twentieth-century Haywood scholars have accepted Pope's attribution or even taken it particularly seriously. The founder of academic Haywood studies,

George Frisbie Whicher, simply notes that "the style of the book is unlike that of her known works" (119). Seventy years later, Mary Anne Schofield echoed Whicher's dismissal: the *Memoirs* are "no longer attributed to [Haywood] because the style is unlike that of her known works and because the narrator indulges in far too many sarcasms at the expense of women to acknowledge Haywood's hand in the production" (*Eliza* 82). Those Pope and Swift scholars who have even commented upon the attribution's existence have all accepted Whicher's pronouncement as definitive.[2]

Yet the question remains open: whether or not the *Memoirs* are actually the work of Haywood, why should Pope have claimed that they were? Whicher's and Schofield's ears may well be unerring in their ability to detect Haywood's style; Schofield could easily be correct in her assertion that Haywood would not possibly have indulged in so many sarcasms at the expense of women. Certainly no documentary evidence has come to light to link Haywood—or anybody else for that matter—to the *Memoirs*. In short, there is no reason, other than Pope's word, to attribute the *Memoirs* to Haywood. And anyone who has studied the *Dunciad* knows that Pope's word is not always to be trusted. Yet scholars have verified most of Pope's other attributions in the appendix in which the *Memoirs* are given to Haywood.[3] The problem seems insoluble: one must either rely upon the uncertain tools of connoisseurship, such as those employed by Whicher and Schofield, or one must presume (with equal uncertainty) that Pope knew whereof he spoke and that Haywood was versatile enough to produce a narrative that did not sound like her other work. Who shall decide when doctors disagree? Rather than let the question slip away as unanswerable, however, I propose that we suspend dispute over the accuracy of the attribution, asking instead what does it mean for Pope to attribute the *Memoirs* to Haywood? What does "Haywood" herself mean for Pope? And how does her meaning—loosely speaking, her reputation—shape the practice of attribution itself?

In this century, attribution has moved from its origins in connoisseurship to become a largely positivist venture. If nineteenth- and early twentieth-century scholars made attributions based upon their sense of an author's biography and style and what he or she would or would not have written, more recent scholars have combed the archives in search of documentary evidence, such as records of payment from booksellers, to link authors to texts.[4] As the prestige of documentary evidence has grown, attributions by contemporaries, such as Pope, have been increasingly regarded as hearsay—useful, perhaps admissible, but to be treated with considerable skepticism since, in the absence of demonstrable personal knowledge, such attributions amount to little more than literary gossip. But despite this generally salutary skepticism, a presumption remains that while attributions made by contemporaries are often incorrect, the practice of attribution itself is (and has been historically) quite straightforward: one simply pins an anonymous or pseudonymous text onto the author one thinks responsible. No provisions are made, except ad hoc, for dealing with attributions undertaken on any basis other than reasonably sincere conviction regarding the veracity of the attribution.

Yet one need only remember the sheer frequency of anonymous and pseudonymous publication in the eighteenth century (which necessitated almost constant guessing at authorship on the part of readers) and reflect upon a few of the best documented cases of readers' attributions to be convinced that attribution is a far messier and more self-interested practice than most scholars have allowed; veracity is only one of a host of aspects to be taken into account.[5] Even an incorrect attribution can tell us a great deal about the attributer, the attributee, the text(s) in question, and the politics surrounding the practice itself. This essay will explore one such (probably incorrect) attribution, that of the *Memoirs,* to illustrate just how much can be teased out of Pope's seemingly uncomplicated act and what it can tell us about the far-better known portrait of Haywood in book 2 of the *Dunciad.*

Far from straightforwardly ascribing an anonymous text to the author he thought responsible, Pope, in his attribution of *Memoirs of the Court of Lilliput* to Haywood, performs an act of self-definition on behalf of the Scriblerians more generally. In conjunction with the depiction of Haywood elsewhere in the *Dunciad,* Pope's attribution attempts to redefine what "Haywood" meant as an author in order to distinguish the Scriblerian practice of personal satire from the genre of amorous and political scandal-writing, or "secret history," to which it was unwillingly indebted. By representing Haywood not as the "Great Arbitress of Passion" (as she was generally regarded in the

1720s), but as Delarivier Manley's successor in the role of "Scandalosissima Scoundrelia," Pope tries to create a conviction in his readers that an unmistakable difference in kind exists between the tactics of the Scriblerians and those practiced by the authors of amorous "secret histories," including whoever wrote the *Memoirs*.[6] Scriblerian satire, Pope implies, was motivated wholly by honorable feelings of outrage at the moral and aesthetic atrocities of modernity. Ideally, the Scriblerians would lash the vice but spare the man; if naming names became necessary, it would be done solely for the sake of the public good. "Secret history," on the other hand, was nothing but (sometimes thinly veiled) partisan slander undertaken to gratify the spite, envy, and lust of its readers.[7] Such readers, by virtue of their choice of reading matter, if nothing else, were necessarily so far beyond the pale as to be incapable even of hoping to emulate the virtues of the brave and noble men whose motives were so basely maligned by the secret historians. But as with all such efforts at self-distinction, in his portrayal of "Haywood" as undeniably and unambiguously "other," as clearly un-Scriblerian in every aspect, Pope protests too much. Strategies and techniques drawn from the "secret history" that "Haywood" supposedly embodies (both literally and figuratively) have a distressing habit of betraying their origins, giving the lie to Pope's self-fashioning. Perhaps counterintuitively, I suggest that one of the best places to hear the strain is in Pope's apparently slight gesture of attributing *Memoirs of the Court of Lilliput* to Eliza Haywood.

As their subtitle suggests, the *Memoirs* present themselves as a supplement to *Gulliver's Travels:* they "contain an Account of the Intrigues, and some other particular Transactions of that Nation, omitted in the two Volumes of his Travels." In an elaborate preface from "The Publisher to the Reader," one Lucas Bennet recounts how he came into possession of the manuscript of the current text: Gulliver gave his additional papers, "which he believ'd might be of advantage to the Publisher" (vi), to Bennet, a childhood friend, in order to relieve his poverty. While Bennet professes to be uncertain as to why Gulliver held these papers in reserve, he suspects that it may have been because Gulliver "thought it improper to mingle with an account of the Manners and Customs of the several People he had been among, any Histories of their Amours" (vi). As such, the *Memoirs* would seem to reproduce Gulliver's own distinction between what he chooses to relate in his *Travels*—only "such Events and Transactions as happened to the Publick, or to my self"—and the less pressing material (such as ethnographic descriptions) that he reserves for his forthcoming "general Description of this Empire" (34).[8] The *grand récit* of public affairs comes first and appears as a distinct bibliographic unit. Only afterward, and as a separate publication, should an account of the minutiae of Lilliputian private life appear, such as "their Plants and Animals . . . with other Matters very curious and useful" (34).

Yet, in a move familiar to deconstructionists, the seemingly extraneous or peripheral, not to mention trifling (the "Amours" of the Lilliputians), turns out to be central, an absent presence at the heart of the originary narrative of the *Travels*. Time and time again in the *Memoirs,* Gulliver confesses that in the *Travels* he misrepresented the actual motives driving the Lilliputians (and so, presumably, the assorted English courtiers for whom they stand). For instance, according to the *Memoirs,* the real reason why Flimnap turned against Gulliver was not the jealousy and ingratitude inherent in being a minister—and particularly marked in Walpole's treatment of Oxford and Bolingbroke—but rather Gulliver's happening upon Lady Flimnap *in flagrante delicto* with her lover. To revenge herself, Lady Flimnap "incens'd" her husband against Gulliver and thereby brought about his persecution (and so, if we follow the allegory proffered in contemporary "keys" and by most modern scholars, the downfall of the Tory ministry in the last years of Queen Anne).[9] Accordingly, the *Memoirs* suggest, specific illicit "amours," rather than timeless verities about the corrupting effects of power or broad-based condemnations of modernity, are the best explanatory category with which to analyze recent English politics. Indeed, the *Memoirs* imply that "exemplary history" of the sort Swift writes is necessarily distorted because in order to distribute "applause and reproach for the purpose of promoting virtue and discouraging vice" (Varey 46), it must suppress the private, often sordid springs of action underlying public events. "Secret history," on the other hand (such as that practiced in the *Memoirs*), thrives upon the disclosure of such causes: private affairs, especially women and the sexual desire they inspire, are shown to be

"the prime movers of history" (DeJean 137) and supposedly prin-
cipled political decisions are revealed to have hung upon "private ca-
balling, hole-and-corner intrigues, [and] backstairs diplomacy" (Rogers
193).

Perhaps not surprisingly, Swift seems to have been somewhat irked
at the ways in which the *Memoirs* undercut his historiography of
Lilliput. In "A Letter from Captain Gulliver, to his Cousin Sympson"—
first published in the 1735 Faulkner edition of the *Travels*—Gulliver
bemoans not only the English Yahoos' failure to be reformed but also,
and for our purposes more tellingly, all of the Gulliveriana that had
appeared in the wake of the *Travels:* "You are loading our Carrier
every Week with Libels, and Keys, and Reflections, and Memoirs,
and Second Parts; wherein I see myself accused of reflecting upon
great States-Folk" (xxxvii).[10] Since the only piece of extant Gulliveriana
calling itself "Memoirs" that had been published by 1735, much less
by 2 April 1727 (the supposed date of Gulliver's letter), was *Memoirs
of the Court of Lilliput* (first advertised 7 January 1727), we can be
reasonably certain that Gulliver's complaint refers to the same text
that Pope ascribes to Haywood. Obviously, we must be careful in
attributing to Swift anything Gulliver says—we know, for example,
that Swift never entertained such sanguine hopes of reforming the
Yahoos as Gulliver professes to have had upon first publication of his
Travels—but considering other complaints Swift made about the reception of the *Travels,* I think we can be fairly confident that he both
knew and disliked the *Memoirs.*

From my brief description of the *Memoirs* and Swift's likely reaction
to them, it should be apparent that while the *Memoirs* are chock-full
of "amours," the affairs in question are recounted in such a way as to
suggest that they are thinly veiled anecdotes *à clef,* rather than the
timeless tales of seduction and betrayal that feature in most of
Haywood's known work.[11] Furthermore, simply because they supplemented *Gulliver's Travels* at a time when the *Travels,* especially the
first voyage, were (rightly) regarded as in large part a highly partisan
exercise in Tory historiography, the *Memoirs* signal that they should
be read in the context of recent politics, that the scandals recounted
not only have actual—and presumably recognizable—referents, but
also consequences for the public. Indeed, Gulliver's complaint in the

letter to Sympson suggests as much: the *Memoirs* are lumped in with various efforts to identify (and often denounce) the political intervention made by the *Travels*. So far as we can tell, Gulliver—and Swift?—seems to consider the *Memoirs* as part of the same ilk as the "keys" produced by the ever-opportunistic Edmund Curll or the "reflections" and "libels" (and charges of libel) leveled by Walpolite pamphlets like *A Letter from a Clergyman to his Friend* (1726). That is, all of these varieties of Gulliveriana capitalize upon the same aspects of the *Travels,* those most thought to "reflect . . . upon great States-Folk" (xxxvii).

Given all of this, the seemingly obvious presumption when guessing at the authorship of the *Memoirs* would be that they are the work of a practiced political writer or polemical historian, most likely one who specialized in "secret history" of the sort discussed above: a latter-day Delarivier Manley or Mme de Villedieu, or one of their male imitators, such as John Oldmixon. Eliza Haywood, despite all of the tales that she entitled "secret histories," would not seem a likely candidate, for not only does she frequently "ma[ke] it clear that the discovery of the real identity of a character would not illuminate interpretation of the text" (Ballaster 155), but her authorial reputation at the time of the *Memoirs'* publication, so far as it can be reconstructed, was not primarily that of a scandal writer, much less a meddler in politics. Even her two experiments with writing *à clef—Memoirs of a Certain Island Adjacent to the Kingdom of Utopia* (1725–26) and *The Secret History of the Present Intrigues of the Court of Carimania* (1727)—seem to have only bolstered her prior reputation as the "Great Arbitress of Passion," the figure who most embodied amatory fiction in all its sprawling apolitical, nonreferential glory. In order to understand how Haywood could even seem plausible as the author of the *Memoirs,* therefore, we must first survey, as best we can, what "Haywood" meant in the 1720s.

Mentions of Haywood in the 1720s fall into two broadly defined camps: those who admired her talent as a chronicler of all the glowing sensations of love, and those who sided with the Scriblerians in seeing her as the epitome of scandal-writing. Most critical discussion of "Haywood" in this century has echoed the Scriblerians' valuation of her.[12] Yet the former camp seems to represent better most pre-Richardsonian readers' conceptions of "Haywood," even after Pope's attack (and the allied sorties made by Richard Savage). At the very least, Pope left enough readers unconvinced that Haywood was still able, as an actress, to capitalize upon her pre-*Dunciad* reputation well into the 1730s, playing roles that prominently advertised her in terms that could equally well describe the amorous heroines of Haywood's early novels.[13]

So let us consider for a moment "Haywood" as Eliza, "Great Arbitress of Passion," rather than Eliza, prize for urinating booksellers. Our best evidence for this alternative perspective upon "Haywood" are the prefatory poems to her collected *Secret Histories, Novels and Poems* (first published 1725). Obviously, like all such front matter, the poems are overwrought to the point of idolatry and so can hardly be trusted as transparent evidence of Haywood's reputation. But if we regard the terms upon which "Haywood" is flattered, rather than the magnitude of the flattery per se, I believe we can get a reasonably representative sense of the non-Scriblerian camp's conception of its author. Consider James Sterling's "To Mrs. Eliza Haywood, on her Writings." Sterling professes to "glow with Zeal" and "melt in soft Desires" at the amorous perils undergone by the lovers in Haywood's texts; his body responds involuntarily with "throbbing Breast, and watry Eye" until his "captive Spirit ebbs and flows" through the "dire Labyrinths" of Haywood's narratives. He attributes the "vast Effulgence" of Haywood's "pow'rful Ray" of Love to her own "fair Female Mold" (which his readers may see for themselves in the frontispiece printed five pages previous). That is, the desirability of Haywood's body serves as the source of her near-divine power to override her readers' self-possession, thereby causing their bodies to yield to her "charming Page."

Other prefatory poems echo these categories of praise. Haywood's then-lover Richard Savage exalts the ways in which her body and text collapse into one another: "What Beauty ne'er cou'd melt, thy Touches fire/And raise a Musick that can Love inspire." Are these "Touches" Haywood's caresses or simply the "Stroaks" of a painter superior to the "young Artist" whom Savage claims to be? Savage's poem, like Sterling's, refuses to make any hard and fast distinctions between the two. Praise for the female author seems to require simultaneously objectifying her and personifying her work, blending the two into a "Soul-thrilling" amalgam "each succeeding Page" of which "still boast[s] those Charms." And both Savage and Sterling, as well as "an unknown Hand," marvel at Haywood's power to move her readers in ways that transcend the usual limits of gender and sexual orientation. Savage inquires "when thy Count pleads, what Fair his Suit can fly?" He obviously expects an answer of "None," which, given his emphasis upon Haywood's "Touches" as the source of her narratorial power, would require that the suitor to whom her "Fair" readers are submitting is in fact Haywood in textual drag ("thy Count"), rather than any male lover. Similarly, the "unknown Hand" extols Haywood in terms unmistakably reminiscent of penetration, but with the usual roles reversed: "Love's Shafts" fly "with sweet, but powerful Force" from her "Words" and "Looks" into the male reader's "Charm-shot Heart," which "receives th' Impressions of the Conqu'ring Dart,/And ev'ry Art'ry huggs the Joy-tipt Smart!"

If we consider the presumptions underpinning all of these poems— namely, that Haywood's power as the "Great Arbitress of Passion" stems from her own desirability (and vice versa) and that her "swelling" language overwhelms her readers, both male and female, in a manner reminiscent of the seducers in her work—it seems difficult to see why Pope would attribute the *Memoirs* to her. Certainly, a hostile reader could claim that there was something indecorous, even "unnatural" about the "Haywood" of the prefatory poems, but surely that unseemliness would have come off as wholly apolitical. After all, the "secret histories" included in the same volumes as these poems make no sustained efforts to signal topicality, much less any partisan intentions.[14] Even the two *romans à clef* for which Haywood is singled out in the *Dunciad Variorum* betray none of the "interest in direct political intervention or allegiance to . . . opposition figures" (Ballaster 156) that so characterized Manley's work in the genre. How do we get from "Haywood" as arbitress of passion to "Haywood" as latter-day incarnation of the *fin de siècle* French *historiennes galantes* who supposedly "saw *galanterie* everywhere . . . because they were themselves so *galantes*" (DeJean 140)? As so often seems to be the case when dealing with this period, I suggest that the best way to explain the revaluation of "Haywood" is to look about for the injured parties. Richard Savage seems a good place to start.

As we saw above, so long as Savage was Haywood's lover he wrote of her in extremely glowing terms. In *Love in Excess* she could "meet" "Scorching Phoebus['s]" "Fierce Beams, and dart him Rays for Rays,"

so powerful were her descriptions of love. Whole countries ("Spain
. . . in Fiction, in Politeness, *France*") yielded to her as "Love's powerful Queen" in *The Rash Resolve* (Savage 50–51). But sometime around
1724, after fathering a child with Haywood, Savage left his queen.[15]
Perhaps in an effort to revenge herself, Haywood includes both Savage and his new mistress, Martha Fowke, in *Memoirs of a Certain
Island Adjacent to the Kingdom of Utopia* (1725–26), the first of her
two 1720s experiments in writing *à clef*. The portrayal of Savage as
"Young Riverius" is quite sympathetic and supports his claim to be
the bastard son of "Masonia" (Anne Mason, formerly Lady Maccles-
field) and "*Count* Riverius" (the Earl of Rivers). Haywood's account
of Fowke is not as flattering. She first appears as "Gloatitia," an in-
cestuous, promiscuous, and spendthrift would-be poetess. Later she
crops up again as the mistress of "Young Riverius," leading him down
the primrose path "not only to mean Actions, but such also as are
unjust and wicked" (1:183).[16] Not surprisingly, Savage (a man not
known for measured response) counterattacked quite viciously in *The
Authors of the Town* (1725), a poem that anticipates the *Dunciad* in
many ways, including its portrait of Haywood.

I propose that *The Authors of the Town* inaugurates the Scriblerian
revision of what "Haywood" meant, redefining her as a "cast-off
Dame" who "Writes Scandal in Romance" (and so a likely candidate
to write *Memoirs of the Court of Lilliput*). Driven at least as much by
personal pique as by outrage at the ways in which "Bright Arts, abus'd,
like Gems, receive their Flaws," Savage turns his previous acclaim of
Haywood on its head. Where formerly she derived her near-divine
authority regarding love from the desirability of her body, now she is
"a cast-off Dame, who of Intrigues can judge" because she has had
multiple lovers, all of whom have thrown her out (Savage implies
with good reason). Her textual production is still intimately tied up
with her body and her private life, but her agency has been redefined.
Once upon a time, "Nature's self," not to mention all of Haywood's
readers, responded to Haywood's "beamful Fires." Now her actions
are merely reactive to the men around her. Had she not been cast off
by a series of men (beginning with her husband and ending, most
recently, with Savage), had her personal life not been scandalous as a
result of this string of lovers, she would not have been able to write
scandal or romance, much less "Scandal in Romance." Similarly, if

the bookseller William Hatchett had not deigned to pick her up after Savage left her—making her into "A Printer's Drudge"—she would never have had the temerity to continue to write. But "Flush'd with success" at Hatchett's condescension, "for Stage-Renown she pants,/ And melts, and swells, and pens luxurious Rants." Note that now Haywood herself supposedly "melts" and "swells" (as a result of her licentious "Success" with Hatchett), rather than inducing such effects in her readers. Rather than "dart" Phoebus "Rays for Rays," Haywood now only exudes "a sulph'rous Flame," a glow of Lust, and "Envy's Blaze." Even her sexual desirability, the former basis of her power and near-divinity, is now denied by Savage, both as a fact and as a source of agency: "Some Black Fiend, that hugs the haggar'd Shrew,/ Hangs his collected Horrors on her Brow!" Quite deliberately, it seems, Savage redefines "Haywood" as the antithesis of everything he formerly claimed her to be: reactive, rather than the font of action; scandalous, rather than inspirational; hellish, rather than celestial; a "cast-off Dame," rather than "Love's pow'rful Queen." Intriguingly, though, Savage did not abandon his previous categories of praise, he simply transferred them over to his new mistress, Martha Fowke. Fowke's readers now supposedly respond the way Haywood's did, back when Savage was her lover: "Tears fall, Sighs rise, obedient to thy Strains,/And the Blood dances in the mazy Veins!" If formerly for Haywood "the Myrtle's Leaves with those of Fame entwine,/And all the Glories of that Wreath are thine!," now Savage knows much better and sees that Fowke is the one "Crown'd with the Palm, Bays, Myrtle, and the Vine." All this suggests that Savage has but two ways of classifying women writers—one laudatory, one derogatory—and that the occupant of a given category depends upon his current relationships, rather than any particular, much less disinterested, critical judgment.

What seems to have happened next was simply that Pope accepted Savage's vindictive valuation of "Haywood," perhaps as a favor to Savage or some of his other friends, and then transmuted "Haywood"-according-to-Savage into a means of Scriblerian self-definition. For there is nothing about Haywood per se, or her relationship with Pope himself, to make her appearance in the *Dunciad* particularly necessary or unavoidable. If, as the "Publisher" of the 1728 *Dunciad* claims, "*The Poem was not made for these Authors, but these Authors for the Poem.* And . . . they were clapp'd in as they rose, fresh and fresh, and chang'd from day to day, in like manner" (vii), then it would seem that what Pope needed was a woman writer to serve as the prize in one of the games of book 2, a modern authorial analog to the slave girl/fourth prize of *Aeneid* 5:285 or the woman offered as a first prize, along with a vase, in *Iliad* 23:262ff. That is to say, Pope had a position to fill, rather than one to create for Haywood specifically. Elizabeth Thomas or Susanna Centlivre (with whom, respectively, Haywood was paired as a "never wash'd" "glor[y] of [her] race" in the 1728 and 1729 versions of the *Dunciad* [3:152–53; 3:144–45]) would have done just as well.[17] Like Haywood, Thomas and Centlivre had worked with Pope's old antagonist, Edmund Curll.[18] Like Haywood (and most other writers of the time), Thomas and Centlivre had attacked Pope or his friends in print. Indeed, Thomas's and Centlivre's attacks were considerably more malicious and personal (and Thomas's more recent) than anything Haywood ever wrote.[19]

Yet Haywood is a star in the *Dunciad,* the only woman writer to receive such billing. Not only is she the prize in the central episode of the central book, not only is she the subject of some of Scriblerus's most virulent commentary (as well as his suggestion that "Our good poet" has pulled his punches in order to maintain generic decorum), but she also has the dubious distinction of having twice as many of her works depicted in the frontispiece to the 1729 *Dunciad Variorum* as any other author. Two of the seven volumes depicted as the ass's burden are Haywood's, and, as Elias Mengel notes, they are in the lowest position, particularly the *Court of Cariman[ia]* (167). In the anti-hierarchy of Dulness, the work that sinks the lowest would seem to be Haywood's most recent experiment in writing *à clef* (although the results are still considerably less political and scandalous than those of any of her predecessors in the genre). The fact that this title is singled out—and designated as even lower than Haywood's "Nov[els]" and the writings of Oldmixon, presumably including his "secret histories"—suggests that Pope has adopted wholesale Savage's redefinition of "Haywood" as the licentious author of "Scandal in Romance" *par excellence,* rather than the "Great Arbitress of Passion."

Sure enough, if we turn to the other mentions of "Haywood" in the *Dunciad,* especially the 1729 *Variorum* edition (to which the frontispiece in question belongs), Savage's valuation seems ubiquitous. In the famous portrait in book 2, Pope highlights "Eliza['s]" irregular sexual history—she has "Two babes of love close clinging to her waste" (2:137; 2:150)—even as he denigrates her desirability. Rather than celestial "Looks" that "inspire," she has "cow-like-udders" (2:145; 2:155). Rather than a "fair Female Mold" (a term that would presumably include the décolletage depicted in the frontispiece to *Secret Histories*), she displays her "fore-buttocks to the navel bare" (2:141; omitted in 1729). And rather than sending out rays of light, causing the bodies of her readers to "melt," or otherwise instigating any action, she is wholly passive: "the pleas'd dame soft-smiling" awarded to Curll for his "smoaking" arc of urine (2:169, 161; 2:182, 174). Scriblerus, in his *Variorum* notes, amplifies Pope's depiction of "Haywood" as reconfigured by Savage: according to our learned commentator, so far as could be done within the generic decorum of epic, Pope denounces "Eliza" as a "shameless scribler," whose "profligate licentiousness" is made worse by her gender, "which ought least to be capable of such malice or impudence" (35). She is singled out for her "most scandalous books, call'd *The Court of Carimania* and *The new Utopia*" (36). All in all, it would seem that the "Eliza" of the *Dunciad* is essentially Savage's "cast-off Dame" writ large, and so, as Christine Blouch puts it, Haywood's "prominent place in the *Dunciad* seems not so much the inevitable result of aesthetic felonies as it is the result of a real, biographical accident," namely, her break-up with Savage (Blouch, "Questions" 146–47).

Yet the question remains: why should Pope have undertaken such a portrait of "Haywood"? He may have done so, as Blouch suggests, as a favor to Savage, who has long been suspected of being Pope's "native informant" regarding Grub Street.[21] Or he may have wished to revenge himself upon Haywood for her "implausibl[e]" slur upon "Patty" Blount (Marthalia) in *Memoirs of a Certain Island,* as Rumbold conjectures (162). Certainly the two theories need not exclude one another; Pope could be quite tenacious in the service of his friends. But I would like to contend that more work is being done by Pope's depiction of "Haywood" (and his attribution of *Memoirs of the Court of Lilliput* to her) than can be accounted for by simple score-settling.

For Pope's "Haywood" is not just the biographical Haywood filtered through Savage's spite. She is also, and I find this very telling, the supposed exemplar of an entire category of dunce. That is to say, Scriblerus seems to be speaking for Pope more transparently than usual when he claims that Pope "styleth *Eliza*" as the representative of a "vile class of writers," "the libellous Novellist[s]" (25). Similarly, Scriblerus tells us that in the game in book 2 "is expos'd in the most contemptuous manner, the profligate licentiousness of those shameless scriblers (for the most part of That sex, which ought least to be capable of such malice or impudence) who in libellous Memoirs and Novels, reveal the faults and misfortunes of both sexes, to the ruin or disturbance, of publick fame or private happiness" (35–36). All this suggests that "Haywood" is at least as much of a figure for "libellous Novellist[s]" or "shameless scriblers" considered *tout ensemble,* as she is an individual singled out for her own "aesthetic felonies." And lest we dismiss this classification as merely Scriblerus's own hobby-horse, Edward Young confirms it in a letter written shortly before the publication of the 1728 *Dunciad* (Young saw the poem in manuscript): "The 5th Book of Virgil is burlesqued in Games in which Booksellers . . . p-ss for Authoresses" (quoted in Sutherland, *Dunciad* xvii). For Young, the *Dunciad*'s "Eliza" signified "Authoresses" in general, not just Haywood. I suspect that she functioned much the same for Pope. Her presence in the *Dunciad* may well be the result of "biographical accident," but her referentiality extends far beyond the biographical Eliza.

Given all of this, the "Haywood" of the *Dunciad* (and so the "Haywood" supposedly responsible for *Memoirs of the Court of Lilliput*), can be best understood as something of a scapegoat, a figure pilloried in an attempt to distinguish categorically the kind of writing "she" embodies from that engaged in by the Scriblerians.[22] As with all scapegoats, the process of casting out involves an effort to establish (or reestablish) difference where sameness threatens, undeniable distinction where boundaries seem disturbingly fluid.[23] But why should scapegoating be necessary? After all, received literary history (both old-fashioned and "new") puts the Scriblerians in one box and Haywood in another. The valuations upon a given box may change— one generation's whorish dunce is another's pioneering woman novelist—but on the whole the possibility that "Haywood" would seem too similar to the Scriblerians for their own comfort seems beyond the pale.[24]

Yet if we look anew at the work of the Scriblerians with "libellous Novellist[s]" or "shameless scriblers" in mind, I suggest that we can see a will to distinction from such writers pervading the canonical texts. Consider Gulliver's pointed vindication of Lady Flimnap—that exoneration which, as I detailed above, *Memoirs of the Court of Lilliput* works so hard to undermine. According to Gulliver, not only did Lady Flimnap not "take a violent Affection for my Person," and never "came privately to my Lodging," but her visits were always public and always supervised both by her family and his servants (52). Furthermore, given the disparity in their sizes; of course, we can surmise that the possibilities for physical intimacy between the two were rather restricted. Indeed, Gulliver defies the Lilliputians "to prove that any Person ever came to me *incognito*, except the Secretary *Reldresal*" (53). Critics have long found Gulliver's protests a bit shrill, and some have gone so far as to cite the mention of a "very private" visitor in the next chapter as proof that Gulliver must be lying about his relationship with Lady Flimnap. But cataloging the specifics of Gulliver's mendacity seems beside the point. Even if we are to take the inconsistency as evidence of a lie, and therefore evidence that Lady Flimnap was attracted to Gulliver and perhaps even had some sort of liaison with him (an inverted preview of the scene with the Brobdingnagian maids of honor?), the sheer vehemence of Gulliver's denial still begs for an explanation, especially in the context of the political allegory being developed throughout the first voyage. That is, even if we should see a size joke in Gulliver's protesting too much, Swift too protests too much. He insists as best he can without dropping the mask of irony, that whatever else the voyage to Lilliput may be, it is not "Scandal in Romance," not "secret history" of the sort written by his former collaborator Delarivier Manley, with all of the latter genre's insistence upon illicit love as the explanatory category *par excellence*.[25] But, of course, the *Travels* are necessarily and unavoidably affiliated with Manley's kind of writing (which is also "Haywood's," according to Scriblerus), for they chronicle recent English politics under the intermittently transparent guise of a naive traveler going about exotic lands. Prior to the *Travels*, fictionalized partisan narrative, as a genre, was inextricably bound up with amatory fiction. Both kinds of writing were the work of authors like Swift's "Corinna," who, since she was visited at birth by both Cupid and a satyr, "Of love shall always speak and write . . ./The world shall feel her scratch and bite" (*Poems* 120).[26] In order to write allegorical satire that was not amatory, therefore, Swift had to clearly distinguish his work, make it manifest that not only was love as a subject conspicuously absent from the *Travels*, but as an explanatory category it was illegitimate and ridiculous (as a liaison between Gulliver and Lady Flimnap would have to be).

Pope's work also bears the traces of what I have been calling the Scriblerians' will to distinction, their collective effort to deny any kinship between the personal satire in which they engaged and the "shameless" revelations made by "Haywood" regarding "the faults and misfortunes of both sexes, to the ruin or disturbance, of publick fame or private happiness" (35–36). In the 1728 preface from "The Publisher to the Reader" of the *Dunciad*, for example, we learn that while the names of most of the dunces are dashed out (e.g., H— for Haywood in 3:153): "We judg'd it better to preserve them as they are, than to change them for fictitious names, by which the Satyr would only be multiplied; and applied to many instead of one. Had the Hero, for instance, been called *Codrus*, how many would have affirm'd him to be Mr. W— Mr. D— Sir R— B—, &c. but now, all that unjust scandal is saved by calling him *Theobald*, which by good luck happens to be the name of a real person" (vii). Where would one find "fictitious names" of the sort the "Publisher" rejects? Just look in either of the Haywood texts singled out by Scriblerus a year later. Or in any of Manley's scandal chronicles. Circa 1728, signaling the presence of satiric, topical writing through the use of Italianate or classical names was one of the hallmarks of "Scandal in Romance." Furthermore, as an examination of annotated copies of Haywood or Manley reveals, the problem of proper referentiality that the "Publisher" notes was very real indeed. To whom does "Miranda" refer in Haywood's *Memoirs of a Certain Island* (23)? The separately published "key" has her as "Mrs. M—r—n." In one copy, now at the Clark Library, a reader has filled in the blanks so that the key now reads "Mrs. Martin." In another Clark copy, a reader kept a list on the flyleaf of persons he or she thought concealed by the allegory. According to this second reader, "Miranda" is "Mrs. Morton" (or perhaps "Mouton"—the handwriting is difficult to decipher). And a copy at the Huntington claims, in the margin, that Miranda is "Mrs. Moreton."[27] Obviously, the "Satyr" is here "multiplied," both through the "fictitious" names and the dashing out of vowels in the key.

In order to avoid similar difficulties—and to try to make it strenuously clear that his satire was not merely personal, although it certainly included personal attacks—Pope printed in full the names of all the dunces, not just Theobald, in the 1729 *Dunciad Variorum*. Now readers could feel secure—or disappointed—in the knowledge that "Smedley" unequivocally referred to the bearer of the proper name Jonathan Smedley, although it might also take in other members of "Smedley's" "vile class" of "dark and dirty Party-writer[s]" (25). Thus the Scriblerian form of personal satire, unlike Manley's work (or that of Haywood in the two *romans à clef* for which Scriblerus singles her out), ostentatiously asserts its non-proliferation, its refusal to engage in "the inflationary tendencies of political allegory" (Gallagher 125). Just as the *Travels*, whatever else they were, were emphatically not about love, so too the *Dunciad Variorum*, whatever else it is, is not the sort of text where readers could misapply what they were told about Mrs. Martin's scandalous behavior to the wholly respectable Mrs. Morton (or vice versa, depending on which reader we trust).

I have only touched upon the myriad ways in which we can see traces of the Scriblerian will to distinction from "Haywood" pervading their texts. Yet it should already be apparent that these various efforts at distinction work in conjunction with the portrait of "Haywood" in book 2 of the *Dunciad*, along with those in *The Authors of the Town* or Savage's later *An Author To be Lett* (a title which sets itself against Haywood's 1723 comedy, *A Wife To be Lett*), in order to induce in the Scriblerians' readers a sense of an unmistakable difference in kind between the tactics of the Scriblerians and those employed by the authors for whom "Haywood" serves as synecdoche. That is, not only do the Scriblerian texts proclaim themselves insistently (even stridently) not "Haywood," but the Scriblerians themselves strive to "cast-off" "Haywood" as a scapegoat through the representation of "her" as always already different from them, not only in subject matter or literary tactics, but in her very approach to writing. Thus Pope denies even her authorial power to annoy (relegating complaints about her work to Scriblerus's notes) and simply depicts her as "pleas'd" and "soft-smiling" at Curll's urinary prowess

(2:169; 2:182), a "woman . . . more genuinely interested in sex than in writing" (Rumbold 163). Thus Swift claims, in a letter written a few years later, not even to have seen, much less read "Haywood" (despite the frequent reprinting of her works in Dublin): "Mrs. Heywood I have heard of as a stupid, infamous, scribbling woman, but have not seen any of her productions" (*Correspondence* 501). And thus, I propose, Pope credits "Haywood" with the authorship of *Memoirs of the Court of Lilliput*. Who better to be assigned responsibility for a text that so gave the lie to Scriblerian denials of indebtedness to "libellous Novellist[s]" than the figure whom the Scriblerians so insistently built up as the scandalous and contemptible antithesis of all that they stood for, namely "Haywood"? How else could potential readers of the *Memoirs* so effectively be dissuaded than by casually attributing the work, in an appendix no less, to the single most vilified dunce in the poem, one whose very existence seemed an affront to the values the *Dunciad* tries to instill in its readers?

We will probably never know who actually wrote *Memoirs of the Court of Lilliput*. Haywood could have done so, and so Pope's attribution, like many of his other attributions, may well be based upon evidence that, if extant, would satisfy the most doctrinaire of positivists. On the other hand, Whicher and Schofield are right to claim that the *Memoirs* do not really "sound" like Haywood's other work from the period. But in either case, far more is at stake in Pope's attribution than simply its veracity. Attribution is a literary practice, and so has its own set of politics at least as fraught as those of any other practice. By considering accuracy as but one of a host of factors surrounding an attribution to be pondered, by remembering that in an age of anonymous publication, authorial reputation can determine an authorial canon (like tends to be ascribed to like), by keeping in mind that authorial reputation itself can be amazingly contested, by doing all of these things, we can begin to write literary history across the "vortex" created by the received accounts, literary history that is not always already written upon the victors' terms, or within their categories (Warner, "Elevation" 589). We can pose anew Foucault's famous question, although without his "stirring of . . . indifference": "What difference does it make who is speaking?" It matters, I submit, a great deal, even, perhaps especially, when we do not know who is doing the speaking.

Notes

I am grateful to Rebecca Bocchicchio, Helen Deutsch, Catherine Gallagher, Kathi Inman, Kirsten Saxton, Patrick Spedding, James Grantham Turner, and, of course, Rebecca Morton for their suggestions regarding earlier versions of this essay. I would also like to acknowledge the generous support provided me during the research and writing of this essay by the William Andrews Clark Memorial Library and the Mabelle McLeod Lewis Memorial Fund.

1. All quotations from the *Dunciad* will parenthetically refer to book and line numbers in the case of verse or page numbers in the case of prose and will cite the 1728 (if relevant) and 1729 editions, in that order.
   The full title of the putative Haywood text in question is *Memoirs of the Court of Lilliput. Written by Captain Gulliver. Containing an Account of the Intrigues, and some other particular Transactions of that Nation, omitted in the two Volumes of his Travels. Published by Lucas Bennet, with a Preface, shewing how these Papers fell into his hands.* The Memoirs ran into two second editions, one in Dublin, the other in London. Both are dated 1727.

2. See, for example, Welcher and Bush's introduction to their reprint of the *Memoirs* (ix-x) or J.V. Guerinot's bibliography of attacks upon Pope (99).

3. By my count, twenty out of Pope's thirty-five attributions of book- or pamphlet-length attacks upon him have been confirmed by modern scholars and only five have been disputed outright, either by contemporaries or modern scholars (see the relevant entries in Guerinot). Guerinot claims that "very few of Pope's attributions of Popiana can be proved to be wrong" (29).

4. Haywood's own canon has recently been expanded through just this sort of documentary evidence. On the basis of manuscript receipts dated March and April 1742, the William Andrews Clark Memorial Library now attributes to Haywood and her lover, William Hatchett, the translation into English of Crébillon *fils*'s *Le Sopha* as *The Sopha: a moral tale. Translated from the French original of Monsieur Crebillon* (1742).

5. Consider, for example, Lady Mary Wortley Montagu's practice of attributing to Sarah Fielding, her poor cousin, far more novels (mostly hackneyed ones) than any single writer could produce. If one compares the novels in question, Lady Mary comes off as either extraordinarily tone deaf or else wholly uninterested in the questions of style and ideological consistency that have traditionally preoccupied connoisseurs. She does, however, seem extremely concerned with excusing (on account of Fielding's poverty) the shoddiness of her cousin's putative literary production. Accordingly, I suspect,

her attributions have far more to do with family dynamics (and Lady Mary's interest in maintaining a self-image of magnanimity) than with any interest in knowing who actually wrote *The Female Quixote* or any of the other works that Lady Mary ascribes to Fielding.

6. Manley is called "Scandalosissima Scoundrelia" in the 27 September 1709 issue of the *General Postscript,* quoted in Gallagher 131.

7. For a sensible recent discussion of secret history (in its several varieties), see Mayer 94–112 and 147–54.

8. All quotations from *Gulliver's Travels* will be drawn from Turner's 1971 edition.

9. The notes in Turner's edition of the *Travels* provide a good summary of the allegorical decodings proposed both by contemporaries and twentieth-century scholars. See also Goldgar 52–62.

10. The letter is dated 2 April 1727, but Williams insists that it was "almost certain[ly] . . . written in 1734 . . . or 1735" (49). For an exhaustive survey of Gulliveriana (over 330 items in the 1726–35 period alone), see Welcher, *Annotated List.*

11. The two works for which Haywood is singled out in the notes and frontispiece to the *Dunciad Variorum—Memoirs of a Certain Island Adjacent to the Kingdom of Utopia* and *The Secret History of the Present Intrigues of the Court of Carimania*—are obvious exceptions to this general tendency (and are the only works of Haywood's for which "keys" seem to have been published). As such, they will be discussed below.

12. See, for example, George Sherburn's "More pity has been wasted on Mrs. Haywood than her character warrants" (quoted in Sutherland's edition of the *Dunciad* 443).

13. See Heinemann on the roles Haywood played in the 1730s and how they played off of her reputation as arbitress of passion. See too the depiction of Haywood as "Mrs. Novel" in Henry Fielding's *The Author's Farce and the Pleasures of the Town* (1730). Fielding gently mocks "Haywood," but in terms reminiscent of the pre-*Dunciad* camp: in Hades, she relates how she "died for love" (57)—which turns out to mean death as a result of giving birth to the illegitimate child of Signior Opera, after he cruelly abandoned her. Mrs. Novel could be a Haywood heroine, seduced and betrayed by a charming foreigner whom she trusted. But Fielding's raillery never crosses over into the hostility that so characterizes the *Dunciad.* At the end of the farce, she remains an object of desire, more sinned against than sinning. She is also responsible for enticing the Constable to permit one more dance (and thereby further contributes to the audience's play-going pleasure).

14. Guskin has recently argued that "Montamour" in *The Injur'd Husband* stands in for Martha Fowke (30), and so gives the lie to Haywood's

preface in which she pointedly denies "expos[ing] the Reputation of an English Woman of Quality." In general in this period, such denials often, perhaps even usually, invite readers to be on the lookout, "keys" in hand, for topicality. Consider, for example, the inscription beneath Hogarth's *A Midnight Modern Conversation* (1733): "Think not to find one meant Resemblance there/We lash the Vices but the Persons spare." Several faces in the print are clearly recognizable contemporaries of Hogarth. In Haywood's case, however, little beyond the name (putatively an allusion to Fowke's relationship with Aaron Hill) invites such a reading *à clef*, and no key seems to have been published to aid readers not already acquainted with the details of Fowke's amours. Accordingly, while Guskin may well be right about "Montamour," I find it difficult to believe that many readers outside the Hill circle would have known that scandal was being peddled in *The Injur'd Husband*, much less whom that scandal involved.

15. All of the biographical details in this essay are drawn from Christine Blouch's trenchant revision of Whicher in her dissertation and in "Romance of Obscurity."

16. For further details regarding Fowke and Haywood, see Guskin 28–31 and Tracy 62–65.

17. On Thomas and Centlivre, and their inclusion in the *Dunciad*, see Rumbold 163–66. For further evidence of the potential interchangeability of women writers in the *Dunciad*, see Rumbold 162: "[I]n an earlier manuscript version the first line ["Lo next two slip-shod Muses traipse along" 3:149; 3:141] had specified 'Pix and slip-shod W—,' i.e. Mary Pix and Lady Mary [Wortley Montagu]. In addition, 'meditating song' [3:150;3:142] echoes words that Gay had used of the Countess of Winchilsea and may therefore be a concealed allusion to her."

18. Thomas, in particular, might seem well suited to play "Haywood's" role in book 2, as she too could be called, somewhat unfairly, a "Printer's Drudge": Thomas was Curll's "Corinna" (the leaky vessel from whom spills the excremental "lake" in which Curll slips during the race after the phantom poet [2:53; 2:65]). Rumbold argues that unlike Ovid and his Corinna, Curll and Thomas do not seem to ever have been lovers (163–65).

19. Pope insisted that Centlivre was partially responsible (along with Oldmixon) for *The Catholick Poet*, a 1716 ballad attacking Pope and his translation of the *Iliad*. Thomas and Curll apparently collaborated on *Codrus: Or, the Dunciad Dissected*, a 1728 faux-biography of Pope that rather cruelly mocks his family. See Gucrinot 38–40 and 153–56, respectively. Haywood, on the other hand, does unjustly criticize "Marthalia" (keyed as Mrs. Bl[oun]t) as "the most dissolute and shameless of her Sex" in *Memoirs of a Certain Island* (1725–26), but otherwise does not mention Pope or his friends with

any particular hostility, unless he objects to the fairly flattering, even admiring portrayal of Henrietta Howard as "Ismonda" in the *Court of Carimania* (1727).

20. On Savage's role as "informer" for the *Dunciad*, see Sutherland's introduction to the *Dunciad* xxv-xxvi, his introduction to *An Author To be Lett*, Tracy 105–8, and Johnson 50.

21. Helen Deutsch has pointed out to me that "it's not just [Haywood's] difference/similarity to male authors that is rewritten" through the figure of "Haywood," "but also her difference from other women." That is to say, "Haywood's real difference from Manley and others is elided in the process of making her synonymous with 'authoress'" (e-mail to the author, 23 November, 1997). Regrettably, space will not permit an exploration here of the questions Deutsch so shrewdly raises, but they certainly deserve consideration in the near future if we are to move beyond the increasingly staid methods of conventional literary history. For an interpretation intriguingly analoguous to the one being developed here, see Hammond's account of how Pope "anathematized Centlivre, but . . . also used her" (*Professional* 214; published, alas, after the completion of this essay).

22. My thoughts on scapegoating and what it involves are deeply indebted to many years of conversation with John Vignaux Smyth about the work of René Girard.

23. We may be witnessing a breakdown in these separate spheres of literary history. The recent work of William Warner on the presence of Behn, Manley, and Haywood in that of Richardson and Fielding promises a new, more productive way of thinking about cross-gender literary relations, as does Hammond's latest book, and Carole Fabricant's essay on Manley and Swift in Donald Mell's new collection on *Pope, Swift, and Women Writers*. Somewhat surprisingly, however, work on Haywood is conspicuously absent from the latter collection.

24. Hammond independently arrives at a similar point: "When [Gulliver] comes under suspicion of conducting an affair with a six-inch-high court lady in Lilliput, there is surely a satire intended on the metaphorical 'littleness' of the sexual intrigue that is the stuff of 1720s romance; in particular of the 'secret history' variety favored by Haywood" (*Professional* 270).

25. Traditionally, "Corinna" has been read as referring to Manley, based in large part upon a note in Faulkner's edition that the poem was "written in the year 1712" (soon after Swift's collaboration with Manley on the *Examiner*). Yet the mention of "Memoirs of the New Utopia" in the last line of the poem opens up the intriguing, if utterly unprovable, possibility that "Corinna" may refer to Haywood. So far as we know, there was no personal relationship between Swift and Haywood (as the poem would seem to require, with

its opening mention of a birthday), but *The new Utopia* is what Scriblerus calls *Memoirs of a Certain Island* and Swift's poem was not published until 1728 (when work on the *Variorum* was well underway), so an allusion to Haywood, though unlikely, is possible. See Rogers's notes (in his edition of the poems) for a summary of these issues (650).

26. The copies in question are, respectively, Clark *PR 3506 H94 M3 (the 1726 London 2nd ed.), Clark Temp C 95 503–2 (the 1725 Dublin ed.), and Huntington 244972a (also the 1726 London 2nd ed.).

Histories by Eliza Haywood and Henry Fielding

Imitation and Adaptation

John Richetti

Haywood's and Fielding's careers intersected on the stage and on the page. A sometime actress, Haywood was among the players Fielding assembled in 1736–37 at the New Theater in the Haymarket in a company that performed, among other plays that year, a revival of his "Pasquin" and his new "The Historical Register for the Year 1736," a harshly critical satire of the Walpole government, with its companion piece, the farce, "Eurydice Hiss'd, or, A Word to the Wise." As Martin Battestin notes, Haywood must have forgiven Fielding for satirizing her as "Mrs. Novel" in "The Author's Farce" in 1730 (*Henry* 84, 215). But years later, as Fielding's rival novelist in *The History of Miss Betsy Thoughtless* (1751), she attacked him and the theatrical company of which she had been a part. Early in the narrative, one of Betsy's brothers arrives in London during "a season of the year in which he could not receive the least satisfaction." The king, it seems, is in Hanover with the court, and fashionable London has dispersed to country seats:

> There were no plays, no operas, no masquerades, no balls, no
> public shews, except at the little theatre in the Hay-market, then by
> the name of F—g's scandal shop; because he frequently exhibited
> there certain drolls, or, more properly, invectives against the ministry;
> in doing which it appears extremely probable, that he had two views;
> the one to get money, which he very much wanted, from such as

delighted in low humour, and could not distinguish true satire from
scurrility; and the other, in the hope of having some post given him
by those whom he had abused, in order to silence his dramatic talent.
But it is not my business to point out either the merit of that
gentleman's performances, or the motives he had for writing them, as
the town is perfectly acquainted both with his abilities and success;
and has since seen him, with astonishment, wriggle himself into
favour, by pretending to cajole those he had not the power to intimi-
date. (*Betsy Thoughtless* 45–46)[1]

Haywood's retrospective scorn for her old employer may well have
had a particular cause of which we are ignorant, but this attack can
also be seen as her long-meditated response to his contempt in *Tom
Jones,* two years earlier, for the authors of "foolish Novels, and monstrous Romances." In this introductory chapter to book 9, Fielding
writes "Of those who lawfully may, and of those who may not write
such Histories as this," and in his best mock-dictatorial manner ridicules and disqualifies the culturally deprived authors of novels and
romances: "For all the Arts and Sciences (even Criticism itself) require some little Degree of Learning and Knowledge. Poetry indeed
may perhaps be thought an Exception; but then it demands Numbers,
or something like Numbers; whereas to the Composition of Novels
and Romances, nothing is necessary but Paper, Pens and Ink, with the
manual Capacity of using them. This, I conceive, their Productions
shew to be the Opinion of the Authors themselves; and this must be
the Opinion of their Readers, if indeed there be any such" (1:489).
Fielding goes on to outline the qualifications for writing a "history,"
and they encompass not only "a good Share of Learning" but experience in the world as well as knowledge of books: "Conversation . . .
with all Ranks and Degrees of Men" (1:491, 494). But Fielding calls
the first requisite for the historian "Genius" and divides that into two
attributes, "Invention and Judgment." Romance writers, he remarks,
are ignorant enough to assume they have plenty of the former, but a
little Latin would teach them that "by Invention is really meant no
more, (and so the Word signifies) than Discovery, or finding out; or to
explain it at large, a quick and sagacious Penetration into the true
Essence of all the Objects of our Contemplation" (1:491). Fielding's
special meaning for "invention" derives from the Latin verb, *invenio.*
"To find out, discover" is the primary meaning, although its mean-

ings even then included "devising" and "inventing" in our modern sense. His polemical and pedantic gloss on the term derives from the rhetorical term "invention," which "is the devising of matter, true or plausible, that would make the case convincing," in the words of the pseudo-Ciceronian *Ad Herennium* (7).

In his first two novels, at least, Fielding invokes these classical rhetorical values in order to avoid what he identifies by his practice, as well as his critical precepts, as two morally and aesthetically dangerous features of the market in modern narrative: mere fantastic imagining and mere particularized and literal-minded rendering of contemporary life and manners. Indeed, in the first of the opening chapters of *Tom Jones*, Fielding simultaneously recognizes and satirically rejects these undiscriminating extremes of romance and vulgar mimesis. An author, he jokes, is like the keeper of a "public Ordinary, at which all Persons are welcome for their Money." His history will feature a menu or bill of fare, for the novel as a whole and for the individual books, so that readers may choose whether they wish to buy, or in fact, in Fielding's suggestive metaphor, to consume. The "Provision" he offers is "Human Nature," which will be offered to the reader's "keen Appetite" in all its varieties, from the "plain and simple Manner in which is found in the Country" to "all the high French and Italian Seasoning of Affectation and Vice which Courts and Cities afford" (1:34). As readers of the rest of *Tom Jones* can testify, this promise to please the consumer is ironically qualified by a narrative that also pleases its author and hopes mainly to please only a particular kind of informed and alert reader of a book that is selective and exquisitely structured, that, in its explicit conversations with ideal readers, extracts the general and the universalized out of a host of contemporary particulars. Rhetorical arrangements and discovery (*dispositio* and *inventio* are the Latin terms) characterize his fiction from the start, and the reader that *Tom Jones* continually projects is a connoisseur of tone and style, delighted by parody, satire, and a presiding sense of emerging form and implicit structure that plays against what Fielding projects as the vulgarity of mere representation or romantic imaginings.

As every student of her remarkable career knows, Haywood responded energetically to the new narrative fashion in the early 1740s for extended, morally complicated, and representationally varied fiction. She was, as Jerry Beasley puts it, "rejuvenated" by the new novel of the day ("Politics" 233), although Ros Ballaster calls her transformation and moral conversion a matter of economic necessity: "Haywood could no longer make money by selling her short romances of passion" (197). Beth Fowkes Tobin summarizes this second phase of Haywood's career: she was "able to adjust to her readers' changing tastes and expectations by mastering genres as different as the scandal chronicle, the novel of seduction, the comic romance, the moral essay and the conduct book" (ix). Works such as *Anti-Pamela: or, Feign'd Innocence Detected* (1741), *The Fortunate Foundlings* (1744), *Life's Progress Through the Passions: Or, The Adventures of Natura* (1747), *The History of Miss Betsy Thoughtless* (1751), and *The History of Jenny and Jemmy Jessamy* (1753) resemble Fielding's, Smollett's, and even Richardson's novels from those years in their energy and variety of closely observed social scenes and situations, as well as in their claims to moral seriousness. *Anti-Pamela,* an amusingly vicious attack on Richardson's book, features Syrena, a clever and amoral reversal of his priggish paragon. But Haywood's next four books are serious attempts to experiment with new forms of fiction, the last two achieving authentic status as novels of domestic realism more or less in the style of Fielding and Richardson. In Mary Anne Schofield's summary of Haywood's reformed manner, "sensational material has given way to moralistic reporting," and she insists in these novels that "she is dealing with real, not fictitious characters who can therefore be considered as good, moral, object lessons" (*Eliza* 87). This essay traces those experiments and moral claims and examines their results; however, the discussion will have to exclude *The History of Jenny and Jemmy Jessamy* for reasons of length.

    The Fortunate Foundlings is an original and extended exercise in popular narrative, true to its subtitular menu of promises: "Containing Many wonderful ACCIDENTS that befell them in their TRAVELS and interspersed with the CHARACTERS and ADVENTURES of SEVERAL PERSONS of condition in the most polite Courts of Europe." Although Haywood is very attentive to chronology and the book features a variety of specific historical settings (London, the wars against the French in the Low Countries, Paris, Vienna, Venice, Warsaw, St. Petersburg), romantic melodrama propels this energetic and totally extravagant narrative, which looks back as much to Aphra

Behn's romantic fictions as to the new novel of the 1740s. Instead of the vaguely dehistoricized settings of her many amatory novellas in the 1720s, Haywood places her characters in a timeline that begins "in the memorable year of 1688" when Dorilaus discovers two infants under a tree on his estate, along with the following note: "Irresistible destiny abandons these helpless infants to your care.—They are twins, begot by the same father, and born of the same mother, and of a blood not unworthy the protection they stand in need of; which if you vouchsafe to afford, they will have no cause to regret the misfortune of their birth, or accuse the authors of their being—Why they seek it of you in particular, you may possibly be hereafter made sensible—In the mean time content yourself with knowing they are already baptized by the names of Horatio and Louisa" (3). Although this note is a more or less transparent riddle to any reader of romances (Dorilaus is pretty obviously their father, as is revealed at the end), he suspects nothing and raises them on his estate. Circumstantiality and particular historical references are strewn about: Horatio is sent to Winchester School under the famous Busby and rejects Oxford to join Marlborough's army in Holland, where he meets the duke and is captured by the French at the Battle of Hockstadt. However, these details are more than overbalanced by Haywoodian melodrama: Dorilaus proposes to Louisa, who rejects his advances and runs away to London; Horatio falls in love with Charlotta, an attendant of King James's daughter at the English court in exile; Louisa works as a milliner in London and is solicited sexually by a nobleman and retreats (ill with consumption) to Windsor, where she becomes a traveling companion to a rich widow, Melanthe, who takes her to Vienna; Horatio is refused by Charlotta's proud father and joins the army of Charles XII of Sweden as his aide-de-camp in Warsaw; after fighting gallantly, he is made a lieutenant-colonel but captured by the Russians and sent to prison in St. Petersburg; Louisa, meanwhile, goes to Venice with Melanthe and is pursued amorously by the Count de Bellefleur but falls in love with the young M. du Plessis, part of the count's entourage.

The difference between all this hectic activity and Haywood's 1719 bestseller, *Love in Excess,* lies precisely in the lip service paid to historical particularity, with Haywood's parade of real places, glamorous and famous persons, and actual events. Action-packed, bursting with passion, martial glory, gallantry, and sentimentality, *The Fortunate Foundlings* is an amalgam and extension of Haywood's earlier style, a narrative manner necessarily free of irony or moral analysis in its pursuit of glamour and excitement. For example, when Horatio tells Charlotta (sent by her father to a monastery to keep them apart) of his plan to enlist with Swedish Charles, Haywood's narrative voice fairly revels in the emotional and ideological intensities of the moment, encouraging simple participation and excited assent in the reader as Charlotta is both distressed by love and exalted by the thought of her lover's military glory: "[S]he listened to him with a mixture of pleasure and anxiety:—she rejoiced with him on the great prospects he had in view; but the terror of the dangers he was plunging in was all her own. She was far, however, from discouraging him in his designs, and concealed not her admiration of the greatness of his spirit, and that love of glory which seemed to render him capable of undertaking anything" (143).

Pervasive energy and a wild variety of scene and situation are accompanied by agony and exaltation, by melodrama and pathos, by the formulaic difficulties and resolutions of romance at its most intense. Thus Louisa, near the end, thinking her lover, young du Plessis, may be dead, escapes from an Italian convent in mendicant's costume. On the road to Paris, she is caught in a freeze-frame of delicious pathos: "A young creature of little more than eighteen years old,—wholly unacquainted with fatigue,—delicate in her frame,—wandering alone on foot in the midst of a strange country,—ignorant of the road, or had she been acquainted with it, at a loss where to go to get any intelligence of what she sought, and even doubtful if the person she ran such risques to hear of, yet were in the world or not" (309–10).

Alert and opportunistic, ready to exploit emotional moments for absolutely all they're worth, Haywood the narrative presence subordinates herself as of old to the projected needs of clearly implicit readers who want to be swept away by crisis after crisis, and her persona is simply an efficient means of delivering her romantic fable. *The Fortunate Foundlings* is a new and improved formula fiction, but Haywood's writing has, most of the time, the rhetorical transparency and efficiency of her earlier work as it delivers the thrills she assumes her readers want. Recent history and particular geography, obtrusive markers that might modify that efficiency and complicate melodrama, are simply the narrative equivalents of name-dropping, part of the glamorizing aura the book throws around its materials. What is truly striking in Haywood's next two novels is her adaptability, her shifting away from this tried and true formula of extravagant romance, and her searching for new relationships between her narrative voice and her subjects as she seems to try to find what will work best. An entirely new and distinct narrative persona appears in *Life's Progress Through the Passions: Or, The Adventures of Natura* (1747). Unexpectedly, Haywood promises in her opening page a *roman à thèse*. Declaring herself "an enemy to all romances, novels, and whatever carries the air of them," she strikes a pose of intellectual curiosity and skeptical, disinterested empiricism: "The human mind may, I think, be compared to a chequer-work, where light and shade appear by turns; and in proportion as either of these is most conspicuous, the man is alone worthy of praise or censure; for none there are can boast of being wholly bright" (*Natura* 2).

Encompassing a wide range of emotional changes and moral developments, *Natura* traces its hero's life from birth in the middle ranks, to his school days at Eton, and dwells, of course, on his sexual coming of age, including his youthful seduction by a cunning courtesan, Harriot, into a marriage contract. Doting on Harriot, quarreling with his father over her, going into ruinous debt for the money she demands, Natura is shocked to find her in bed with another man and he resolves to leave England. But he and his father are reconciled, and Natura is sent on the grand tour of Europe. The events that follow on the continent are varied: most amatory, some military, some, on his return to England, political, as Natura is elected to Parliament, and some domestic, as he marries (unhappily). But these events are accompanied by regular commentary by the narrator, some of it the familiar Haywoodian theorizing about the psychology of passion, but a good deal of it more broadly concerned with the general human nature that her hero is supposed to exemplify. Most of this commentary is intelligent, if conventional. One passage is especially relevant to the attractions both travel and fiction can offer. When Natura rambles through France and lingers to look at Roman ruins in Lyons, Haywood, through him, displays an interest in geography, history, and culture, and she offers some thoughts on the pleasures of variety and new experiences:

The drive of novelty is inherent to a human heart, and nothing so much gratifies that passion as travelling—variety succeeds variety:—whether you climb the craggy mountains, or traverse the flowery vale;—whether thick woods set limits to the sight, or the wide common yields unbounded prospect;—whether the ocean rolls in solemn state before you, or gentle streams run purling by your side, nature in all her different shapes delights; each progressive day brings with it fresh matter to admire, and every stage you come to presents at night customs and manners new and unknown before. (101–2)

And yet just a few pages later, Natura, at the opera in Rome, has an outrageous, sexually scandalous adventure that looks odd next to these serious observations. In a friend's box he meets a young woman who becomes so enraptured by the music that he is able, literally, to make love to her. Caught up by the music, the lady "was so much dissolved in extasy, that crying out. O God, 'tis insupportable," she embraces Natura, who "seized the lucky moments;—he pressed her close, and in this trance of thought, this total absence of mind, stole himself, as it were, into the possession of a bliss, which the assiduity of whole years would perhaps never have been able to obtain" (105).

Taken together, these two scenes mark Haywood's ambitious fusion of narrative formulas: the modified picaresque of progressive personal development is punctuated by the scandalous and amatory intensities for which she was notorious. The reader, like the tourist hero, craves variety, and the mixture of narrative attractions in *Natura* is consistent with its theory of human nature. Haywood's narrator is less than scandalized by Natura's rape of the enraptured music lover; she offers a libertine defense of the scene, cynically shifting the blame to the victim, who we learn "had the reputation of a woman of strict virtue" (106). Only religion and morality, the fear "of offending against law and custom" prevent such encounters, "and it is not therefore strange, that whenever reason nods . . . the senses ever craving, ever impatient for gratification, should readily snatch the opportunity of indulging themselves, and which it is observable they ordinarily do to the greater excess, by so much the longer, and the more strictly they have been kept under restraint" (107). To be sure, subsequent events in Natura's story, especially his amatory and marital failures, qualify such libertinism on the thematic level, as he subsides from sexual adventures and politics into domestic tranquillity with a young French widow. But as a spirited and indeed original rehearsal of popular narrative formats, *Natura* serves its implied readers' need for variety and excitement, both sexual and intellectual, and in fact articulates throughout a subversive, almost Sadeian view of personality. As the narrator meditates at the end on Natura's action, this is her startling conclusion: "Man is a stranger to nothing more than to himself;—the recesses of his own heart, are no less impenetrable to him, than the worlds beyond the moon;—he is blinded by vanity, and agitated by desires he knows not he is possessed of" (206). In her shorter and more tightly formulaic amatory tales in the 1720s, Haywood dramatized a similar attitude toward sexual desire, compulsive in men and mysteriously obsessional in her heroines, but here in *Natura* desire is generalized as well as intellectualized, tested and explored in a variety of specifically rendered social and historical settings. In his contradictory impulses, Natura illustrates human nature, and Haywood appeals to her readers' own experience of their natures to validate her narrative.

Haywood's next and, by common consent, her best novel, *The History of Miss Betsy Thoughtless* (1751), is a retreat from this promising balance of psychosexual realism and intellectual analysis. Traditionally, this novel marks for most commentators Haywood's most mature phase as a novelist. Jane Spencer notes the "new feminine modesty and morality" that Haywood came to display in *Betsy Thoughtless,* and she finds in it and its successor, *The History of Jemmy and Jenny Jessamy,* "more detailed and naturalistic rendering of both inner and outer realities, the heroine's environment and her thought processes" (147). Thanks, I suppose, to her eye for the main chance in the narrative market, she produces what is in some ways a perfectly good imitation of Fielding and, as Spencer shrewdly notes, an interesting anticipation of Jane Austen's methods and themes (Spencer 152). In proposing to show us in Betsy "the secret springs which set this fair machine in motion, and produced many actions, which were ascribed, by the ill-judging and malicious world, to causes very different from the real ones" (*Betsy Thoughtless* 13), Haywood is attempting a version of Fielding's deeply ironized mock-inquiry into mid-century moral and social structures and reproducing in preliminary comments like this one his understanding of character and behavior as a matter of comically predictable recurrences, a pattern which gains its comic force from its insertion in a variety of detailed specifics of contemporary life. *Betsy Thoughtless* is a Fieldingesque exercise in social/moral commentary, as Haywood seeks to ground our understanding of the flirtatious Betsy's personality in a comprehensive survey of upper-middle class female circumstances that shape her destiny. She traces her heroine's fatal fondness for serial but chaste conquests to her upbringing as an impressionable teenager at her guardian's London house after the death of her father. Mr Goodman has fallen in love with a widow, Lady Mellasin, and he has been swayed by doting affection to indulge his bride in anything she wants.

> Never did the mistress of a private family indulge herself, and those about her, with such a continual round of publick diversions. The court, the play, the ball, and opera, with giving and receiving visits, engrossed all the time could be spared from the toilet. It cannot, therefore, seem strange, that Miss Betsy, to whom all these things were entirely new, should have her head turned with the promiscuous enjoyment, and the very power of reflection lost amidst the giddy whirl, nor that it should be so long before she could recover it enough, to see the little true felicity of such a course of life. (18)

This corrupting and quite specifically social/moral background is supplemented by several Haywoodian amatory plots that are at work in her guardian's house. In a separate and complicated subplot that parallels Betsy's own marital history, Lady Mellasin is an adulteress who will eventually be caught *in flagrante delicto* by Mr. Goodman. Of more immediate relevance is the matching of the innocent but wayward Betsy and her half-sister, Flora Mellasin. Right next to Betsy's technically innocent flirtations (as well as her unfortunate first marriage) is Flora's sexual obsession and actual carnal involvement with Trueworth, who loves Betsy but marries someone else when she thoughtlessly spurns him. As Haywood develops matters, Flora's hysterical infatuation with Trueworth clarifies Betsy's moral failure, rendering it a relatively harmless hedonistic self-absorption when considered next to Flora's destructive obsession, which is beyond mere pleasure in its melodramatic excess. Thus, Flora writes to Trueworth when he shuns her: "Be assured, I cannot,—will not live, without you!—Torture me not any longer with suspence!—Pronounce my doom at once! But let it be from your own mouth that I receive it, that

you, at least, may be witness of the death you inflict, and be compelled to pity, if you cannot love, the most unfortunate, and most
faithful, of her sex" (332–33).

The relationship played out between Flora and Trueworth illustrates in its blend of sex and power (including treachery and near violence when Trueworth discovers a letter Flora has written to his fiancée,
Harriot, denouncing him) what Betsy is spared by her innocent vanity.
Or, to put it another way, Betsy's sexual relations are carried out under
another narrative dispensation in which comic and domestic realism
produces a vain but virtuous coquette who is reformed in due and painful course to the error of her ways and is rewarded with (by this point)
the conveniently widowed Trueworth, the Mr. Right she had foolishly
spurned. As Haywood, straining for epigrammatic summary, puts it
early on in the novel, Betsy "was far from setting forth to any advantage, the real good qualities she was possessed of:—on the contrary, the
levity of her conduct rather disfigured the native innocence of her mind,
and the purity of her intentions" (189).

Flora and Trueworth's brief affair, in contrast, evokes another and
indeed more convincing realism that is attentive not only to sexual
inevitabilities but to their social context. The narrator reflects that
Trueworth's dalliance with Flora was, after all, "no more than any
man, of his age and constitution, would have done, if tempted in the
manner he had been" (320). Although full of remorse for this sexual
lapse, Trueworth also understands the necessity for self-protection
and tactical reserve: "[H]e considered Miss Flora as a woman of condition,—as one who tenderly loved him, and as one who, on both
these accounts, it would not become him to affront" (321). He reflects, however, that Flora having violated "all the rules of virtue,
modesty, and even common decency, for the gratification of her wild
desires" might well seek to expose herself in order to ruin him with
Harriot: "[H]e found it therefore highly necessary to disguise his sentiments, and act towards her in such a manner as should wean her
affections from him by degrees, without his seeming to intend, or
wish for such an event" (321).

In the social and psychological world Haywood evokes, even so
noble and upright a man as Trueworth follows two inescapable rules
that govern personal relationships: male sexual privilege and self-pro-
tective masculine reserve. Trueworth, as a man, is allowed to act like

flesh and blood, but the double standard means that a woman who
yields (or worse, actually pursues a man and offers herself) inevitably
produces moral disgust. As Flora presses him to renew their amour
and as he comes to desire the virtuous and modest Harriot, his state
of mind illustrates the principle that it "little becomes a woman, whose
characteristic should be modesty, to use any endeavours to enforce
desire, that those who do it are sure to convert love into indifference,
and indifference into loathing and contempt" (333). But such emotions, as Trueworth's predicament also illustrates, need to be kept in
check for tactical reasons, just as the sexual and economic motives for
seduction that govern the rest of the male characters in the novel are
both assumed by everyone else and in practice disguised or left implicit and unstated. In context, Betsy's ingenuous desire to be admired
(desired) by many men marks her as so essentially modest and delicate that she is necessarily unaware of what in another narrative world
could only be seen as her own sexual motives and of the complex
social situation and economic privilege that help form and focus them.
      Pressed by her brothers, Betsy drifts into an unhappy marriage
with a Mr. Munden, which through her indifference and his tyranny
and infidelity Haywood satirically renders as a commonplace occur-
rence. The low point of this marriage-à-la-mode is the attempted seduction of Betsy by Munden's patron, Lord ——, which she repulses
with a virtuous indignation that displeases Mr. Munden: "'Tis true,
my lord's behaviour is not to be justified, nor can yours in regard to
me be so; you ought to have considered the dependance I had on him,
and not have carried things with so high a hand . . . but that cursed
pride of yours must be gratified, though at the expence of all my expectations" (493). Clearly, as Haywood explains, the profligate
Munden "stood in need of some addition to his revenue," and she
ironically leaves it to readers to wonder why his reaction to his wife's
virtue is disgust rather than the "highest love, tenderness, and admiration" (494). For her part, Betsy is full of self-reproach, looking back
with horror on the pleasure she had in "appearing amiable in the eyes
of that great man" (495). The incident inspires nothing less than her
conversion from coquetry and provokes a proto-Austenian eclaircisse-
ment, for "she now saw herself, and the errors of her past conduct, in
their true light" (495). Astonishingly, Haywood expects her readers
to think that until now, Betsy had no notion of the sexual implica-

tions of her coquetry, even when she was single. So she soliloquizes in rather stilted fashion: "The pride of subduing hearts is mine no more;—no man can now pretend to love me but with the basest and most shameful views.—The man who dares to tell me he adores me, contradicts himself by that very declaration, and while he would persuade me he has the highest opinion of me, discovers he has in reality the meanest" (495). Put this improbable innocence (and its awkward eloquence) next to Haywood's smoothly ironic rendition of the deplorable Mr Munden's acquiescence in the amorous lord's plot. The satiric point of all these sordid doings is complicated by the contrast between her naive heroine and the corrupt world of power and privilege Haywood evokes in this sequence in a skillful mimicry of Fielding's manner of self-interested idiom: "Ill-natured and perverse as Mr Munden was, it must be confessed, that his present situation nevertheless merited some compassion:—he had a great share of ambition;—loved both pleasure and grandeur to an excess; and though far from being of a generous disposition, the pride and vanity of his humour made him do many things through ostentation, which his estate would not well support" (493).

Haywood saves Betsy from a degraded (and boring) future as loyal wife to the feckless and treacherous Munden by bringing on stage another sexualized female opposite: Betsy befriends a mysterious foreign lady only to find that she is her elder brother's French mistress, cast off when she is caught in bed with her mercer. Thanks to a servant who observes Munden and this Mademoiselle de Roquelair hurrying "together, arm in arm, into a bagnio" (527), Betsy realizes the full extent of their perfidy and leaves Munden, although "the vows she had made him at the altar were continually in her thoughts . . . whether the worst usage on the part of the husband could authorize resentment in that of a wife" (536). Munden's death, brought on in short order by his dissipation, rescues Betsy from this quandary, and since Trueworth has (thanks to smallpox) become a widower, it is not very long until a rapturous happy ending is arranged:

"Oh, have I lived to see you thus!"—cried he, "thus ravishingly kind!"—"And have I lived," rejoined she, "to receive these proofs of affection from the best and most ill-used of men:—Oh, Trueworth!—Trueworth!" added she, "I have not merited this from you."—"You merit all things,"—said he; "let us talk no more of what is past, but tell me that you now are mine;—I came to make you so by the irrevocable ties of love and law, and we must now part no more!— Speak, my angel,—my first, my last charmer!" continued he, perceiving she was silent, blushed, and hung down her head;—"let those dear lips confirm my happiness, and say the time is come that you will be all mine." The trembling fair now having gathered a little more assurance, raised her eyes from the earth, and looking tenderly on him,—"You know you have my heart," cried she, "and cannot doubt my hand." (564–65)

Like all such happy endings, Haywood's in *Betsy Thoughtless* is very much worth waiting for, since the preceding hundreds of pages are crowded with varied and entertaining obstacles to marital happiness, including that most relevant of hindrances, an unhappy first marriage. Usually, women's novels of courtship and marriage do not include second chances, and Betsy's sufferings as a wronged wife share narrative space with many other sorts of experiences. *Betsy Thoughtless* is a rollicking romp through high life, with a heroine whose only fault is that consumerist curiosity for new pleasures and objects of desire that readers of the novel must, if they are to enjoy it, share with her. As a young (and attractive) woman with a substantial fortune, Betsy has only one conceivable destiny—marriage—and her flirtations occur in the extended period between sexual/financial maturity and the delayed fulfillment of that fate. Although such adventures are formulaically condemned by Haywood, they are obviously for character and reader alike the whole pleasurable point of the narrative, a series of eroticized encounters and excursions that describe and traverse a space of fantasy and freedom in which the woman enjoys her status as a desirable object and postpones her transformation into a domestic acquisition by a male as a financial and biological asset. So Haywood's tracing of Betsy's moral development from coquette to grimly faithful wife to blushing widow/bride is entirely adequate to her readers' implicit needs: she can be in this sequence a moral lesson about vanity, a champion of integral female virtue in the face of conventional male morality, and a happily wed romantic heroine. For within the world of genteel privilege it evokes, Haywood's novel celebrates individual, if delayed, moral agency, marking with appropriate condemnation the schemes for power and pleasure of its interesting villains and noting with satisfied approbation the achievement of moral integrity and happiness by its central couple. To that extent, the novel is a pleasant fantasy of leisure-class independence in which society's moral balance is unthreatened by the various male and female profligates who inhabit it, as well as by the potentially subversive lesson its heroine learns about male oppression. Naive and vain as she is, Betsy is quite capable of heroic feminist questioning when one of her brothers warns her that her virtue is less important than her reputation:

> She assumed the courage to tell him, his way of reasoning was neither just nor delicate.—"Would you," said she, "be guilty of a base action, rather than have it suspected that you were so?"—"No," answered he; "but virtue is a different thing in our sex, to what it is in yours;—the forfeiture of what is called virtue in a woman is more a folly than a baseness; but the virtue of a man is his courage, his constancy, his probity, which if he loses, he becomes contemptible to himself, as well as to the world."
>
> "And certainly," rejoined Miss Betsy with some warmth, "the loss of innocence must render a woman contemptible to herself, though she should happen to hide her transgression from the world."— "That may be," said Mr Francis; "but then her kindred suffer not through her fault:—the remorse, and the vexation for what she has done, is all her own.—Indeed, sister," continued he, "a woman brings less dishonour upon a family, by twenty private sins, than by one public indiscretion." (335–36)

Taking such passages as the moral center of Haywood's novel, some recent commentators have detected a subversive, feminist strain in the plot of *Betsy Thoughtless,* and I think they are, on their own terms, exactly right. Beth Fowkes Tobin sees Haywood's originality at mid-century as a matter of continuing her attack on "patriarchal power," but now "within the new moral bourgeois codes" by exploiting the "reformed coquette" plot to "criticize masculine authority." For Tobin, Betsy challenges the sexual double standard, and through her "rebellious spirit and energetic refusal to relinquish control over her life to the men who act as her guardians and advisors" Haywood "exposes the inconsistencies that abound in the moral codes that proscribe female conduct" (xxxiii). Deborah J. Nestor calls Betsy's first marriage a revelation of the "injustice of the bourgeois domestic ideology that perpetuates such unequal relationship," and she correctly identifies this part of the story as "one of the most intimate and painful chronicles of the decline of a marriage found in the early English novel" (Nestor 584). These feminist revisions challenge the traditional view, stretching back to Clara Reeve's literary-historical dialogue, *The Progress of Romance* (1785), that Haywood in *Betsy Thoughtless* had been converted to the side of virtue. That Haywood probably intended her perky and feisty heroine's career to illustrate patriarchal injustice is clear enough, but it is equally clear that the novel's plot and its accompanying authorial commentary defend a conventional bourgeois ideology of female subordination and sexual suppression. *Betsy Thoughtless* is a good enough novel, in one sense, to support both positions, as Tobin points out when she says that such interpretations "depend upon the reader's sexual politics" (xxxiii). It is in fact, I would argue, Haywood's best novel precisely because it highlights these contradictions in eighteenth-century sexual ideology. The novel's single most resonant scene occurs during the early days of her marriage to Munden, and it will serve to show how, occasionally, Haywood can very effectively descend from the heights of romantic melodrama and conventional conduct book female morality to a startling and significant domestic realism that is much more penetrating than Betsy's merely conventional questioning of male privilege. This scene can also serve to illustrate what I want to label a productive looseness in Haywood's narrative manner. Haywood's interesting ambiguity and exposure of ideological contradiction are the result of her lack of full narrative control, of her failure to sustain, with any coherence, her imitation of Fielding's "historical" approach. Betsy is a creature of contradictions, of course, and in elaborating her exciting and varied escapades even as she extracts their moral and social meanings, Haywood achieves a satisfying double effect. Fairly naive mimesis collides with the cautionary tale; moral ideology and gossipy reportage cooperate to produce what looks like real insight into the conditions of female existence in the leisure classes.

Munden's estate is modest. Betsy is oppressed by his demands for economy (for example, that she use her own "pin money" to pay one of her servants) and by his tyrannical manner. In this precisely detailed rendition of domestic unhappiness, Haywood's novel is convincing by virtue of occupying the middle range between comedy and high seriousness, Betsy's fate as a disillusioned consumer of the innocent satisfactions of female vanity is Haywood's alternative to the comic exhilaration or tragic exaltation of the moral novel of Fielding and Richardson. I use the loaded term "consumer" deliberately. Betsy is fully and particularly immersed in a world where young women of the leisure class acquire lovers along with other luxury goods, and it is wonderfully appropriate that the Munden marriage is irrevocably fractured in a memorable scene that is the climax of Betsy's separation from carefree consumption, of lovers and other toys, and her painful insertion into brutal domestic realism. Infuriated by Betsy's resistance to his economizing, resolved "to render himself absolute master," bursting with resentment and malice at her resistance, he expresses all these emotions in a shockingly violent gesture:

> The reader may remember, that Mr Trueworth, in the beginning of his courtship to Miss Betsy, had made her a present of a squirrel;— she had still retained this first token of love, and always cherished it with an uncommon care;—the little creature was sitting on the ridge of its cell cracking nuts, which his indulgent mistress had bestowed upon him;—the fondness she had always shewn of him put a sudden thought into Mr Munden's head, he started from his chair, saying to his wife, with a revengeful sneer, "Here is one domestic, at least, that may be spared."—With these words he flew to the poor harmless animal, seized it by the neck, and throwing it with his whole force against the carved work of the marble chimney, its tender frame was dashed to pieces. (448–49)

Betsy's pet squirrel, a love token from another sort of man, evokes a lost world of idyllic female leisure in which there is an implicit equation between the pet and its pampered mistress. Munden's violence is especially frightening within that implication. In its striving for domestic realism, *Betsy Thoughtless* has various interesting moments of focus on such particular artifacts of leisure-class existence, but this is one of the most coherently brutal in its dramatization of male rage. Consider again the comparison of Fielding and Haywood with which I began, and Betsy's squirrel may recall the young Sophia's pet bird. But particulars in *Tom Jones* are, obviously, subordinated to Fielding's controlling comic and moral symmetries, and details function quite precisely most of the time as part of the comic structuring of the narrative: the pet bird exists so that Blifil can display his smooth hypocrisy in releasing it because he "thought there was something cruel in confining any Thing" (1:160), so that Tom can display his gallantry in climbing a tree after it, and so that Square and Thwackum can gloss the incident, each in his comically fatuous and self-serving way. Haywood's novel has no such comic structural project in mind, and Betsy's squirrel is both less and more than Sophia's bird. The squirrel scene is an insertion and eruption of a randomly chosen fact; it is peculiar to Betsy's emotional and amatory history but also evokes the social-economic world that contains and explains her marital and emotional dilemma. Haywood's rhetorical flatness and her structural simplicity become, in select moments like this, specifically novelistic (rather than rhetorical) strengths as she inserts contemporary materials into her narrative. Such a scene owes nothing to the learning Fielding required of a "historian"; its materials are copied from life rather than "invented" in his special rhetorical sense, and the scene is observed and reproduced, in a sense, rather than constructed or manipulated toward clearly visible moral ends. I have no way of knowing, of course, if the squirrel incident is taken from life, but in Betsy's history it has a gratuitous circumstantiality, a paradoxically enabling lack of generalized meaning. The history of the squirrel is simply an instance and illustration of the artificial and gratuitous variety essential to leisure-class life as Hayward's novel evolves it. Trueworth's characterization of the gift squirrel bears on this issue, as he sends it to Betsy with these words just after meeting her for the first time:

> I remember (as what can be forgot in which you have the least concern) that the first time I had the honour of seeing you at Oxford, you seemed to take a great deal of pleasure in the pretty tricks of a squirrel, which a lady in the company had on her arm:—one of those animals (which they tell me has been lately catched) happening to fall in my way, I take the liberty of presenting him to you, intreating you will permit him to give you such diversion as is in his power,—Were the little denizen of the woods endued with any share of human reason, how happy would he think himself in the loss of his liberty, and how hug those chains which entitle him to so glorious a servitude. (111)

A clever reading of this passage would find in Trueworth's dedication of his gift an ironic anticipation of what the married Betsy will become in the loss of her liberty, and by extension what she will still be as Trueworth's blushing bride. But such meaning requires extraction and retrospective critical exertion, and Haywood doesn't ask her readers to make such efforts or to think about such implications, just to look back and remember the existence of the squirrel, which is nothing more nor less than an interesting prop, part of the scenery that used to define Betsy and her world, and whose violent destruction serves to illustrate her new marital and economic situation.

Haywood's novel is like this episode, loose and opportunistic, stringing together interesting or striking incidents and scenes, noting persons and places that give readers glimpses of an attractive but also occasionally dangerous world of sexual and domestic relationships. The old Haywoodian melodrama lingers in the Flora plot (and in the story of her adulterous mother, Lady Mellasin), but domestic and marital realism of a sober sort eventually dominates in the long account of Betsy's marriage to Munden. That realism derives precisely from a narrative perspective Fielding doubtless would have disdained as literal-minded and vulgar, lacking true inventiveness: Haywood's incremental elaboration of the stress points in sexual and marital reality, her focus on sharply rendered particular moments of social and moral contradiction and conflict. The result is an evocative string rather than an expressive structure. Munden's outburst is improvised and random, and in this regard it imitates Haywood's narrative method as she chooses, in effect, from a whole range of equally possible events and things to illustrate her heroine's life. *Betsy Thoughtless* is thus crudely, sometimes powerfully, effective in isolating moments of intensity and subversively clear-eyed examinations of female fate. Its virtues in this regard are inseparable from its limitations as a history in Fielding's sense.

Note

1. All references in the text are to the 1997 Oxford paperback edition of *Betsy Thoughtless*.

Shooting Blanks

Potency, Parody, and Eliza Haywood's *The History of Miss Betsy Thoughtless*

Andrea Austin

Eliza Haywood's abrupt transition from writing steamy, scandal novels to penning more decorous fiction after the phenomenal success of Richardson's *Pamela* has often been characterized as a "mid-career conversion."[1] To some, both contemporaries and more recent critics, Haywood has seemed a veritable reformed rake; to others, she has seemed a literary mercenary, able to adopt whatever viewpoint was most lucrative. Indeed, this image of Haywood as stopping and taking stock of her work points to some self-reflexive literary function, and yet the majority of criticism dealing with *Betsy Thoughtless*, the first of her novels in the new style, stops short of examining it as a formal attempt at parody.[2] The reason for this reticence has its origins, I suspect, in the same complex of gender and genre associations that began to solidify and gather force in the mid-eighteenth century. Significantly, parody has, as a critical term, undergone a masculinization from the eighteenth century through to the postmodern period insofar as it is aligned with metaphors of aggression, sexual potency, and with the parodist's oedipal struggle to mark distance from the parodied text. Because women writers' parodic strategies have not always been similar enough to those of their male counterparts to warrant critics' inclusion of them in histories/theories of the genre, parodic works by women are often unrecognized or misread. *Betsy Thoughtless*, in the context of parody, suggests something more at work in Haywood's maturation as a writer than a bowing to public pressure or the profit motive. Far from opportunistically exhibiting a more didactic style only to suit a change in popular tastes, *Betsy Thoughtless* shows Haywood turning toward parody in order to promote a simple, central message not very different from that of her earlier works: the inequity of woman's lot.[3] In making this turn, Haywood grapples with the not inconsiderable mechanical difficulties of writing women's parody and forges innovative parodic techniques that become, in her hands, powerful tools of feminist criticism.

During the eighteenth century, English authors begin in earnest to work toward a definition of the term "parody," begin to show a concern for distinguishing it from related forms, and begin to consider the ramifications of having their works labeled as parodies. As Richard Terry notes in "The Circumstances of Eighteenth-Century Parody," "the Augustan Age was the first great age of parody, the period in which it became both prolific and mainstream" (76). Importantly, parody came to be overwhelmingly construed as a form of literary attack. Dictionary entries from early in the century, for example, emphasize the element of ridicule. In his *Dictionarium Anglo-Britannicum* (1708), John Kersey defines parody as "a Poetick Sport, which consists of putting some serious Pieces into Burlesk."[4] Nathan Bailey's *Dictionarium Britannicum* (1736) glosses parody as "a poetical pleasantry, consisting in applying the verses of some person, by way of ridicule, to another, or in turning a serious work into a burlesque by endeavoring as near as can be to observe the same words, rhimes, and cadences."[5] Along with the lexicographers, several of the major literary figures of the day conceived of parody as a form of aggression.

Pope referred to *The Dunciad* as a "parody,"[6] and Swift, master of vituperation, made much of parody's potential for biting exposition and ridicule in his Apology prefixed to *A Tale of a Tub*: "[T]here is one Thing which the judicious Reader cannot but have observed, that some of those Passages in this Discourse, which appear most liable to objection are what they call Parodies, where the Author personates the Style and Manner of other Writers, whom he has a mind to expose" (12). Addison's description, in the extremely influential *The Spectator*, distinguishes between two types of "burlesque," both of which are motivated by ridicule: "[T]he two great Branches of Ridicule in Writing are Comedy and Burlesque. The first ridicules Persons by drawing them in their proper Characters, the other by drawing them quite unlike themselves. Burlesque is therefore of two kinds, the first represents mean Persons in the Accoutrements of Heroes, the other describes great Persons acting and speaking like the basest among the People" (no. 249, 1711; 467–68). Though he does not use the word "parody," he offers by way of example, as Margaret Rose points out, references to both ancient and modern parodies (*Parody* 57). Likewise, Dryden's descriptions in *A Discourse Concerning Satire* (1693) of "verses patched up from the great poets . . . and turned into another meaning," followed by "songs . . . turned into burlesque" (2:103) suggest that he, too, recognized ridicule as a prime motive of parody.

Definitions that were less restrictive in scope nonetheless did not rule out an underlying belief in parody as a form of attack. Henry Home, in his *Elements of Criticism* (1762), speaks of parody in a noncommittal way, taking in a range of stances in observing that "ridicule . . . is no necessary ingredient in a parody, yet there is no opposition between them." However, he offers by way of example *Le Lutrin*, stating that it "lay[s] hold of a low and trifling incident, to expose the luxury, indolence, and contentious spirit of a set of monks. Boileau the author turns the subject into ridicule, by dressing it in the heroic style, and affecting to consider it as of the utmost importance; and though ridicule is the poet's aim, he himself all along carries a grave face, and never once bewrays [*sic*] a smile" (1:359, 351). Similarly, Johnson officially describes parody in his *Dictionary* (1755) as "a kind of writing, in which the words of an author or his thoughts are taken, and by a slight change adapted to some new purpose." He may, though, personally have thought of parody as a more ridiculing form. Terry believes that he did, pointing to Johnson's uneasiness about its use for mean-spirited attacks on esteemed writers, as in Johnson's comment in the "Life of Prior" ("Semantics" 68).[7] Of Prior and Montague's *The Hind and the Panther Transvers'd*, a parody of Dryden, Johnson comments: "There is a story of great pain suffered and of tears shed on this occasion by Dryden, who thought it hard that 'an old man should be so treated by those to whom he had always been civil.' By tales like these is the envy raised by superior abilities every day gratified: when they are attacked every one hopes to see them humbled; what is hoped is readily believed and what is believed is confidently told" (*Lives of the English Poets* 2:182). Note that Johnson considers envy to be the primary motive for attack. In this respect, Johnson shares with Shaftesbury a prefiguring of Bloom's work on the "anxiety of influence." Shaftesbury, as well, attributes to the parodist an expression of jealousy and desire to challenge the great masters, and claims parody to be "no more than mere burlesque or farce" combined with "a concealed sort of raillery" (1:130).

Undoubtedly, such views owe much to the Hobbesian theory of humor as an exultation in superiority, the earliest forms of laughter being, according to Hobbes, expressions of ancient warriors' triumph over fallen enemies. This association of parody with ridicule, together with the parodist's stance towards major literary predecessors, would tend to militate against the identification and/or practice of parody by women writers. Writing, already a suspect occupation for women, could be considered specifically unnatural for the woman writer when it found expression as parody, a form of pointed literary attack. Eighteenth-century ideologies of femininity, promulgated by conduct books, periodicals, memoirs, and a large number of novels, urged women to be non-competitive, modest, charitable, and selfless, or, as Mary Poovey has so aptly put it, urged women to conform to the "ideology of the Proper Lady." Furthermore, references such as Johnson's and Shaftesbury's mention of envy focus on parody as a type of literary ambition, a "taking down" of the great masters, and so an act particularly publicly inappropriate for the woman writer. Self-effacing prefaces and dedications that accompany so much of the fiction by women in this period stress the inappropriateness of any form of literary ambition for women, as in, for instance, Haywood's dedication of *The Fatal Secret*: "None can tax me with having too great an opinion of my own *Genius*, when I aim at nothing but what the meanest may perform." With these words, Haywood hardly displays exultation, revels in superiority, or pretends to any but the most humble compositional talent.

At the same time that parody was becoming implicitly masculinized, conceptions of literary practices best described as pastiche came to share many features with stereotypes about women's writing, and to take on an implicitly feminine character. The much more modern term "pastiche" was not in general usage in the eighteenth century, but certain literary practices are clearly its forebears: "medley," "mixture," and "miscellany" are all terms designating essentially the same techniques that we have now come to call "pastiche." Rose provides several definitions of the form: pastiche is not necessarily comic or critical of its source; it is "a neutral practice of compilation," deriving from the Italian "pasticcio," a pastry or pie dish combining a number of different ingredients; a "medley," "hotchpotch," "farrago," "jumble," or "miscellany," it consists of "fragments pieced together or copied with modification from an original, or in professed imitation of the style of another artist" (*Parody* 72–74). It is worth noting that contemporary readers complained that Betsy was too much of a mixed character in eliciting contradictory emotions, an ambiguity they apparently found unsettling in the face of Haywood's claimed desire to "condemn two decades of her own fiction" (Ross 69).[8] Like her story, Betsy is something of a patchwork. One atypical early usage of "pastiche" perfectly describes *Betsy Thoughtless*; the *OED* includes a statement from *The Art of Painting* (1744), where pastiche is denoted as "those pictures that are neither originals nor copies, which the Italians call *Pastici* . . . because as the several things that season a pasty are reduc'd to one taste, so counterfeits that compose a *pastici* tend only to effect one truth."[9] Atypical in attributing to pastiche a certain unity of purpose, this reference to *pastici* begins to get at the central problem of the female parodist. *Betsy Thoughtless* tends to promote "one truth" and, in so doing, challenges the conventional distinctions between parody and pastiche.

Haywood's *Anti-Pamela; or, Feign'd Innocence Detected* (1741), in reprising her "sensually stimulating . . . earlier type of story," as Mary Anne Schofield comments (*Eliza* 84), and as a direct response to Richardson, makes an interesting transition between her early and later fiction and attests to an interest in parody at this crucial phase in her career. However, the simple comparison between Richardon's Pamela and her own heroine, the prostitute Syrena Tricksy, proved too slight and static a vehicle to satisfy the burgeoning talent of the parodist. In *Betsy Thoughtless,* Haywood further explores the potential of parody by pushing the envelope of conventional definition, offering a version of the education novel which presents a challenge to the parody/pastiche dichotomy in the asymmetry between its appearance and its purpose or message. The distinguishing characteristic between parody and pastiche in the foregoing definitions is that of critical intent: parody intentionally targets other texts and comments critically on them; pastiche merely makes use of or borrows from other texts and does not make a critical comment. Haywood's experimentation in *Betsy Thoughtless,* though, works out a parodic method which resembles both. Distinct features of Haywood's parodic method include a wide range of source materials and a willingness to move beyond the targeting of a particular text or group of texts to a more flexible use of intertextuality that does not necessarily involve an attack on the borrowed form, but may certainly involve multiple, even contradictory stances, lending the work the appearance of pastiche. At the same time, this use of intertextuality is not random or purely ornamental, but is the vehicle for pointed, critical comment, giving the work the effect or purpose of a parody. Four techniques in particular form the bulk of the novel's parodic thrust: characterization, repetition, imitation or mimicry, and quotation.

Whether in imitation of Fielding, or simply due to her experience with comic theatre, Haywood's use in this work of descriptive character names like Betsy Thoughtless, Miss Forward, and Mr. Trueworth immediately indicates its humorous nature. Yet naming in this novel also signals a hyper-awareness of generic convention, suggesting a parodic intention to rework such stock romance figures as the naive heroine, the false friend, and the true hero. Within the first five pages, Haywood further establishes a parodic tone by introducing a comic romance in miniature with the story of Sparkish and Forward. "Master Sparkish," we are told, "had read the story of Piramus and Thisbe;—he told his mistress of it, and in imitation of those lovers of antiquity, stuck his letters into a little crevice he found in the garden-wall" (10).[10] The casual and transient emotions of the young Forward and her adolescent beau, not to mention the mock-tragic conclusion of the affair (Sparkish is sent off to university), contrast with the tragedy of Pyramus and Thisbe so as to burlesque the mythological love story. Frivolous and light-hearted in treatment, the Sparkish-Forward affair is disarmingly deceptive in its trivialization of the subject of love. Haywood's parodic characterization insists on the disparity between the ideal and the real and deepens into a sustained interrogation of the role of the romance suitor and an explosion of the myth of the romantic hero when it comes to Betsy's beaus. Skillfully deploying Sir Frederick Fineer and Captain Hysom as parodic doubles, Haywood allows these two extremes to comment both on each other and on the hero, Trueworth.

An account of how Sir Frederick has fallen in love with Betsy alerts us to the Fineer thread's comic content. Mrs. Modely relates the silly story of how Fineer catches but one glimpse of Betsy in the street and faints dead away in a swoon with love for her. Not as naive as we might have thought, Betsy parades Fineer in front of her guests as an object of merriment since she finds his romantic encomiums risible in the extreme, and then laughingly takes him to task for his mythological comparisons. When he calls her a "Graecian Venus," she replies: "If you mean the compliment to me, Sir, the Graecian Venus's are all painted fat, and I have no resemblance of that perfection" (282). Betsy's first love is entertainment, and while Fineer provides her with this sport, she demonstrates that she is in no danger of taking his rhetoric seriously. What we discover, however, is that Fineer does in truth have a serious motive for his behavior. He turns out to be a fraud and a fortune-hunter, more interested in Betsy's money than in her person.

The plain-spoken naval officer, Captain Hysom, forms a violent contrast to the simpering Fineer. Also something of a stock character, the rough old gentleman refuses to adopt romantic rhetoric, overlooks even to the basic niceties of wooing, and proceeds to court Betsy in the most business-like way imaginable. His manner, along with his advanced age, provoke in Betsy and any other company who happen to be present when he calls as much levity as Fineer's exaggerated addresses. Although Hysom's method of wooing is in every respect the opposite of Fineer's, his motive is actually not so different. He, too, is a businessman, and has weighed into the bargain of a young, pretty wife the material considerations of her fortune and the convenience of having her for a housekeeper. Like all parodic doubles, Fineer and Hysom figure sameness as well as opposition, but Haywood has a point to make with this comic pair: they reveal the tragic truth that, whether courted by suitors from one extreme or the other, the marriage market is dehumanizing in treating women only as commodities.

It would also seem that the message of these characterizations is that the wise girl will choose the suitor who does not woo either with overblown romanticisms or with gruff imperatives. Instead, she will choose the porridge Goldilocks ate, accepting the suitor who blows neither too hot nor too cold. But is Trueworth really "just right"? The structure of the novel's plot implies so, introducing Trueworth as a suitor recommended to Betsy by a brother who is quite fond of her and has her interests at heart, and ending with Betsy's eventual marriage to her hero. Nor does the narrator allow us to forget that Trueworth is the one true suitor in a series of many, as we find on page after page the warmest descriptions of Trueworth's courage, integrity, goodness, and real affection for Betsy. Yet Haywood includes a miscellany of episodes, heaped up in insistent detail, that undercut Trueworth's role by subtly contradicting the narrator's view of him.

To begin with, Trueworth's patience leaves something to be desired. Betsy fervently believes that the man who would win her should suffer long and patiently, and although the overtly didactic narrator presents this belief as part and parcel of Betsy's wrong-headedness, still, we might expect Trueworth to have rather more fortitude than he shows in being so quick to lend credence to the slander against Betsy and to call off their courtship. To be sure, the credibility of the narrator's advice to Betsy on patience in love is suspect. Very early in the novel, the narrator interjects: "But I will not anticipate that gratification which ought to be the reward of a long curiosity. The reader, if he has the patience to go through the following pages, will see into the secret springs which set the fair machine in motion, . . . To proceed therefore gradually with my history" (13–4). The narrator affects to tell a love story, but apparently expects more patience of readers than Betsy is to expect from her suitors.

Not stopping there, Haywood mercilessly plays up Trueworth's affair with Flora, and not just the sordid details of the liaison; as well, she provides thorough narration of the messy breakup. Several protracted scenes in which Flora confronts him with her grief and anguish interrupt the main plot events. Believing Flora to be a friend of Betsy's, Trueworth becomes involved in a sexual affair with Flora anyway, a fact which does not convince us of his integrity. That he carries on the affair after he has already begun to court Harriot is still another strike against him. Flora, for her part, does really seem to love Trueworth, at least to the degree that she is capable of loving anyone. In this matter, the fashion in which Trueworth spurns her is cruel in the extreme, in spite of Flora's shortcomings. He has enjoyed her, tired of her, and now he no longer wants her—all well before he discovers the true extent of her deceptions. Notwithstanding the narrator's pronouncements concerning Trueworth's pity for Flora's condition, or the portrayal of Flora as a vicious character, there is some truth in the girl's words when she confronts her lover with the epithet "Most cruel and ungenerous Man!" (332). Finally, Trueworth's decision to marry Harriot, even though he still loves Betsy, caps the series of his unlaudable actions. In the context of his behavior, then, Trueworth's name gains even more subtly parodic proportion and the novel's conclusion reads as a sly gibe at the conventional marriage ending.

A repudiation of romance is not the result of these portrayals, though, as Haywood, in poking fun at the beaus, also discloses that the reality the romance masks or opposes is not an attractive alternative. If these men fail to live up to the ideal of romantic behavior, she insinuates, that is not the fault of the romance. Specifically, the romance is not so much impugned in this parody as is the injustice of men's ill conduct towards women. Rather than illustrating a profound change of direction for Haywood, *Betsy Thoughtless* thus shares with Haywood's earlier works a common theme: "the tragic axiom," comments Deborah Ross on the scandal novels, "that women who love are doomed" (69). An inevitable effect of this apparent exposition of and simultaneous investment in romance, mixed with the pitting of story detail against narrative voice, is a contradictory expression that, by conventional definitions, resembles the schizophrenia of pastiche. Compounding the effect, Haywood creates similar contradictions with her strategic use of repetition, imitation, and quotation.

As Dale Spender remarks, plot incidents in *Betsy Thoughtless* may not be boring, but they are repetitious (ix). There is no denying the repetition of scene in this novel, especially those scenes in which women find themselves powerless in the face of men who mean them harm. Betsy experiences a series of near rapes, while various interpolated narratives tell comparable stories of women raped, seduced, and abandoned. Unsurprisingly, these repetitions lend the work a picaresque or episodic feel as well as a degree of titillation value, opening Haywood to the criticism of hackneyed rehearsal of a motif found to be extremely successful in the early part of the century—a criticism, basically, of bad writing. According to Terry, it was exactly this issue of literary quality that helped to "foster . . . an efflorescence of parodic activity" in the eighteenth century because it was not simply the proliferation of writing that created so fertile a ground for parody in this period, he argues, but the amount of poor writing produced ("Circumstances" 76–77). Terry connects an awareness of poor literary quality with a cultural sense of literary congestion and concludes that "where literature gains a sense of its own congestion, it invariably turns self-reflexive." He uses the example of Pope's *The Dunciad,* a parody which takes aim at the "apocalyptic inundation" of inferior writing" (77). Bad works, apparently, were as or more likely to be parodied as the works of the masters, and a key hallmark of poor literature was its formulaic and repetitive nature.

Pope suggests as much in his relentless lampoons of Cibber and others as offering the same substandard material again and again. While the example of Cibber and the many other male writers Pope attacks illustrates the obvious point that men wrote badly, too, the image of Haywood in *The Dunciad* actually giving birth to bastard fictions literalizes the contemporary conviction that women were the wellspring of inferior works.[11] Male literary reviewers often evinced the opinion that, while some men could write badly, almost all women were assuredly bad writers—and the more scribbling women there were, well, the more literary trash would accumulate. Moreover, the modes of fiction thought fit for women to publish in—those which emphasized women's experiential authority and centered on domestic themes, such as love and the home—already ensured the type of faint but damning praise that became so common, "'t'is well writ, for a lady."[12] Women, therefore, are more likely to be the butt of the parody, its target rather than its practitioners. Cautioned against unseemly literary ambition, as in parody of the masters, or lumped together as a group of poor writers, women come to be doubly excluded from dominant critical conceptions of the parodist.

Even Spender is somewhat apologetic about the repetition in *Betsy Thoughtless.* Instead of comprising a flaw, though, I would argue that this repetition in reality functions, to use Linda Hutcheon's definition of parody in *A Theory of Parody,* as a "repetition with a difference." Each time Betsy experiences an attack on her virtue, Haywood replays her powerlessness, yet adds to each incident a greater and more ludicrous reliance on fate until Betsy's preservation of her virtue comes to seem mostly the result of accident, with the repetition of the events functioning as a kind of parodic emphasis. Exaggeration, addition, and incremental repetition are all humorous devices, and while the first of Betsy's close calls makes a straightforward enough beginning (a young Oxford student, a garden, and opportunity), by the time we read of the old peer concocting the most elaborate plots to be alone with Betsy, attempting to chase her around the room, and then stopping short for fear she will expose his designs to the servants (or is he simply out of breath?), we have entered the territory of farce.

Haywood's point is not that rape is funny. Rather, these repeated scenes of Betsy's danger are incrementally juxtaposed with the various interpolated seduction narratives, such as those involving Forward, Thomas's mistress, and Marplus's mistress, in order to underscore that inequity between the sexes drives the action of each sequence. Taken on their own, Betsy's perils might seem merely humorous in the classic sense of comedy as tragedy averted.[13] However, juxtaposed with the seriousness of the seduction narratives, the humor of Betsy's exaggerated and contrived misadventures falls curiously flat. With such vivid depictions as the destitution and desperation of Forward, Flora, and the others, the tragedy Betsy avoids never leaves the stage, as it were, but is continually kept before us. This juxtaposition thus works to fundamentally redirect our notion of the scenes' farcical content— to expose, in the proper sense of the word "farce" as a kind of humorous sham or absurd pretense,[14] that the true sham(e) is belief in Betsy's culpability. In this way, Haywood parodically takes aim at the use of this plot as stock comic theater and prose fare, suggesting that the spectacle of old men and rakes attempting to ruin vain young girls is by no means a funny one after all.

Further, this repetition/juxtaposition calls attention to a profound ambiguity between the concepts of rape and seduction by working with the fact that Betsy's avoidance of ruin is due only to fate. Betsy incontrovertibly muddies the careful dichotomy of the prim and proper Miss Mabels on the one hand and the fallen Miss Forwards on the other.[15] A member of both circles, she links the two, and when even the didactic narrator comments that if Betsy "were not utterly undone, it must be owing rather to the interposition of her guardian angel, than to the strength of human reason" (97), it becomes apparent that Betsy's reliance on fate forms but the thinnest of dividing lines between virtue and ruin. While the Floras and Forwards may be vicious and untrustworthy, Haywood reminds us that in the context of gender inequity, the matter of consent is less material than the final result: these girls are victims, too.

It is no wonder, then, that Betsy undergoes not a reformation, but a series of reformations, as her own confusion concerning the appearance of virtue and the reality of it belies her confidently stated opinion that innate possession, rather than social perception, determines a woman's purity. Connecting the Floras and the Mabels, she rehearses the border crossing over and over, moving easily between the two worlds and demonstrating how haphazard is their differentiation through her repetitive traversal of the boundary dividing them. Each time Betsy is mortified by one of her misadventures, she vows to reform and be less thoughtless from thenceforth. Nevertheless, a fresh complication follows closely on the heels of almost every one of these vows. For example, when she discovers that Flora has forged letters defaming her, Betsy recognizes that her behavior has caused others to give more credit to Flora's scandalous gossip than it deserves. Betsy regrets her coquetry and alters her behavior to include the striking up of a new friendship with the ultra-conservative Miss Mabel. However, this reformation immediately precedes the incident in which a young rake nearly rapes Betsy while escorting her home from a play. Betsy's refusal to give up her friendship with Miss Forward is the ostensible cause of the danger, as the fellow believes that Betsy must be of Forward's profession. Likewise, following her lucky escape after the play, "the most bitter of [Betsy's] enemies could not have passed censure more severe than she did on herself." Betsy is sensible that "by the levity of her conduct she had been thought a common prostitute" (206–7). Again Betsy determines to be more circumspect in the future, but when we come upon the very funny portrayal of Betsy measuring the number of paces in the room out of sheer boredom only some pages later, we begin to suspect that this determination, as well, is doomed to failure. Then again, when Betsy rehearses the same regrets and self-admonitions upon discovering that Trueworth has married someone else, the entire Fineer thread unfolds soon after and culminates in his attempt to rape Betsy and force her into marriage. In fact, this repetitive pattern has the effect of undercutting Betsy's supposed final reformation and, by implication, the happy ending to which her reformation leads. Every fresh start echoes the previous one and presages the next one, until only the parody of reformation remains.

Provocatively, sandwiched between the reformation vows and near escapes is Betsy's repeatedly-offered rationale for her unseemly behavior. She announces time and again her disinclination for marriage, explaining that it is this disinclination from which her coquetry springs. In addition, her resentment toward the haughty manner of the men in her life is what drives her into those dangerous situations in the first place. Trueworth's strong request to Betsy that she give up Forward, his brusque cessation of his courtship of her, Thomas and Francis's decision that Betsy should not have the management of herself, and Munden's mistreatment of her—all of these instances of high-handed authority have a powerful effect in impelling Betsy towards the play, Fineer's rooms, and the peer's study. The entire repeated pattern therefore works to illustrate the double-bind of women in Haywood's society: a woman who desires freedom and an equal share of life's entertainments puts herself in serious danger, but a woman who denies herself these things and maintains the character of a "proper" woman risks giving up all authority over her own life.

This parodic reformation strikes several interesting resonances, extratextually and intertextually. Betsy's parodic attempts to reform, together with the unappealing role into which patriarchy attempts to coerce her, forge an extratextual connection between Betsy and her creator that fascinatingly echoes Haywood's own supposed literary reformation. Intertextually, Betsy's reformation also resonates with amatory and libertine fiction. By reversing the gender roles and presenting us with a heroine who appears to amend her ways, Haywood parodies the reformed rake tradition in literature that usually features male characters changed by the power of love and gestures toward the female rakes of her earlier, amatory novels. Tania Modleski asserts the centrality of Richardson's *Pamela* to the development of twentieth-century forms of mass-market fiction for women, arguing that the idea that libertines given to serious vices could reform and make good husbands helped to enforce women's obedience to the domestic ideal: "[T]he 'reformed rake plot' and the debate that raged around it pointed to women's sense of vulnerability in regard to marriage and hence foreshadowed the critique of the family which would be the covert project of the so-called 'domestic' novelists" (18). Pioneering this project, Haywood's parody strikes another blow against the double standard and points to the illogic of the convention, implying that the reformation of these rakes is no more complete than is Betsy's. To be sure, Richardson's portrayal of Mr. B is as much indebted to Restoration comedy as the domestic novelists are to Richardson, a train of intertextual associations that can gesture towards pastiche. Haywood takes in novelistic traditions as well as comic theatre in mocking the stock figure of the reformed rake as a contrived and unbelievable plot device, as she does with the repetition of Betsy's perils. Again, her chosen parodic method contributes to the work's patchy or mixed appearance, with the addition of other genres helping to derail any sense of a sustained parodic attack on the romance.

Haywood continues to widen her range of intertextual materials while promoting her central message with her use of imitation, a method which finds both thematic and technical expression in *Betsy Thoughtless*. Primarily, parodic imitation accomplishes its work in this novel by questioning the gender associations that were accreting around the idea of imitation. The popular and widespread debate concerning literary imitation versus originality or creative genius, outlines Terry, was another of the major factors influencing the proliferation of parody ("Circumstances" 82–88). Imitating the writings of other authors was a vital part of a grammar-school education, yet at the same time, the concept of genius called for writers to imbue their own words with a sense of uniqueness or originality. The terms of this debate are obvious in Betsy's criticism of the Oxford student's attempt to woo her with lines from Waller: "'O fie upon it,' said Miss Betsy, laughing. . . , 'this poetry is stale, I should rather have expected from an Oxonian, some fine thing of his own extempore, on this occasion; which, perhaps, I might have been vain enough to have got printed in the monthly magazines'" (50). Helping to shape the terms of the debate, Terry explains, were Locke's theories of the psychological origins of language; "the complexion of style [was] referred back to the psychological factors governing it" (83). What Locke's influential work added into the mix was the notion that literature could stand for properties of the mind.

The twist that Lockean theory gave the debate was especially pivotal in terms of gender because it gave new impetus for connecting the style, and even the substance, of a man's or a woman's writing to stereotypes about differences in the way men's and women's minds worked. As Paula Backscheider suggests, the attitude that male writers were more apt to produce original works of genius, whereas female authors could only either repeat others' stories or copy down stories based on the pattern of their own lives—could only offer imitations or relations rather than truly creative works—reveals the degree to which the terms "repetition" and "originality" were already becoming heavily gendered.[16] Women's minds, as far as prominent eighteenth-century male thinkers were concerned, were inherently weaker than men's, not only less rational, but less capable of profound and penetrating thought. Like Betsy, they are essentially thoughtless, lacking in the critical faculty, and therefore, more likely to construct fictions by retelling the same stories, in essence, rehearsing autobiography or compulsively pasting bits and pieces of others' stories together, a mimicry which easily resolves into the blind, endless repetition of stale scene after stale scene and formulaic novel after formulaic novel.

The novel-reading miss could not be expected to show any more critical ability than the novel-writing missus, leading to one of the most prevalent stereotypes of the period: the young woman with puffed up ideas of herself culled from the reading of romances. Johnson ridicules such feminine tendencies with his portrait of Imperia in the *Rambler*,[17] and certainly, the idea of women as naive and uncritical readers fueled the indictment of women's fiction as promoting young women's mimicry of the female characters about whom they read; hence, the intensity of debate over the morality of women's fiction. Betsy's imperious behavior with her suitors, her expectation of long, patient courtship, and her familiarity with the rhetoric Fineer uses demonstrate her kinship with this stereotype. Moreover, Betsy shows herself to be a natural mimic early on, following Forward's lead in the boarding school and receiving from her an education in coquetry, then heedlessly following the fashionable tastes and amusements of her guardian's wife and daughter. Haywood thoughtfully selects her materials, however, so as to parody the idea of the imitative female reader, debunking the stereotype and exposing that a contradiction lies at its heart. When Betsy reacts to a play she has just seen, *The Careless Husband*, Haywood inverts the portrait of Imperia while at the same time making explicit the idea of Betsy as a naive or imitative reader.

Betsy mimics the didactic message of the play: "She was very much affected with some scenes in it;—she imagined she saw herself in the character of Lady Betty Modish, and Mr. Trueworth in that of Lord Morelove, and came home full of the most serious reflections, on the folly of indulging an idle vanity, at the expence of a man of honour and sincerity" (248). A page or two later, she hears an old ballad which, though "merely bagatelle," has exactly the same effect on her. Betsy's mimicry therefore intimates her ability to mould herself, wax-like, to either vice or virtue, an ability which echoes the popular contemporary notion that in order to be led down the correct path to conventional womanhood, a female reader had only to be given appropriately moral literature.

Betsy is not, at this point in the novel, led down the "correct" path. Like the other avowals of reformation, her reflections after the play and ballad are transient, but two in a series. The didactic message of these texts does not take, undermining our belief in Betsy's powers of imitation. In addition, Haywood slips Betsy's reaction to a letter from Trueworth between that of the play and the ballad to provide further context in which to read the failure of Betsy's imitative ability. Quickly reversing their tenor upon receipt of a letter from Trueworth informing her of his decision to leave London, Betsy's thoughts about her own responsibility for the desertion can be guessed at by her exclamation, "ungrateful man!" (248). If the female reader really were blind and uncritical, a piece of wax to be molded, there exists no little difficulty in accounting for the equally prevalent contemporary castigation of the persistence of the young Imperias's headstrong adherence to romantic notions of their own importance. Haywood's presentation of Betsy's parodic transit from one extreme to the other and back again in this way reveals the contradiction inherent in patriarchal ideology's simultaneous belief both in women's malleableness and in their unaccountable stubbornness.

This debunking of blind and uncritical feminine imitation has ramifications for Haywood's own use of imitation as a narrative technique. Luce Irigaray, Joan Rivière, Mary Anne Doane, and Judith Butler, among others, have all made substantial contributions to the concept of mimicry as a feminist method of subversion. The idea that femininity is a masquerade or type of mimicry, or that gender is a sort of parodic performance, provides a rich theoretical basis in which to ground discussion of disguise in Haywood's fiction [18] and, with *Betsy Thoughtless* especially, the way in which Haywood uses the didactic voice of the narrator to imitate or mimic "proper" feminine sentiment. Broadly speaking, theorists like Butler have conceived of mimicry as being like parody in the sense of making a copy. Rather than leaving the connection in such general terms, though, I want to emphasize how literal and literarily explicit that connection is in this Haywood novel. As the parodic nature of Betsy's reformation appears to such great effect in her reaction to other texts, it forms a carefully nested *mise-en-abyme* of imitation as narrative technique and so points to the textual referents of Haywood's own mimicry.

Indeed, to argue that the didacticism which Haywood mimics is not just conventional femininity, but exactly the moralistic narrative tone that so many women writers after mid-century had already adopted in their fiction makes a kind of common sense that hardly seems to need the support of complicated theory. The question of context, though, makes the preceding theoretical detail useful. How do we distinguish mimicry as parodic from a simple intention to copy without critical comment? We cannot make this distinction based on the imitative utterance alone; the clues to its parodic nature lie in the interplay between the utterance and its context. Put another way, of course, this is the same problem as that of the distinction between parody and pastiche. Betsy's imitative ventures provide us with a contextual correlative in which to read Haywood's mimicry of moralistic fiction as something more than a blank or patchy borrowing, but do so specifically by mirroring within the text, in Betsy's responses, the act of critical reading. To mimic in this way is, then, as with repetition, to add a parodic emphasis which draws attention to the enclosed material, almost as if to put quotation marks around it and mark it as the word of another. Betsy's platitudinal mouthing and the narrator's own moralistic tone function almost as a type of quotation.

More manifestly, a multitude of direct quotations in *Betsy Thoughtless* contribute to the rampantly intertextual feel of the work. As with repetition and imitation, however, the distinction between innocent or critical use—between simple quotation and quotation as parodic strategy—is a crucial one. In her thorough study of parody, Rose isolates quotation as a favored parodic strategy in the eighteenth century. "Parodic quotation," Rose states, "connects and contrasts

disparate texts," and may "result in incongruous associations, undermining the seriousness of the piece" (*Parody* 58). Rose conscientiously
differentiates parodic quotation from cross-reading, authoritative
quotation, and cento by pointing to the parodist's recontextualization
as commenting critically on the borrowed words. Similarly, Terry discusses quotation as "the most scrupulously exact and economical form
of parody" ("Circumstances" 79). In the case of quotation, he argues,
the parody arises not from distorting the other's words, but from
recontextualizing them. Yet these formulations of quotation as a parodic strategy can render some parodic practices of women writers invisible because direct quotation may not work to parody, or may not
work only to parody, the quoted material. It may work instead, or in
addition, to criticize some aspect of the main text, such as an overtly
didactic narrator. While to take Haywood's use of mimicry literally as a
form of quotation does reveal criticism of the borrowed material, direct quotation in *Betsy Thoughtless* often does not, though ultimately
both operate toward the accomplishment of the same purpose.

That Haywood's use of direct quotation will work towards the
same central message as her use of characterization, repetition, and
imitation is immediately evident in the fact that twenty-four of the
thirty-three quotations offered, although variously drawn from a wide
range of sources, are explicitly concerned with the relative power relations of men and women in love. The first quotation that appears in
the novel consists of the lines from Waller that the young Oxford
student recites. They are standard romantic fare, idealizing the beloved. Still, there is more to this scene than Betsy taking the student to
task for his lack of originality. Even at this early stage, Haywood uses
reference to other texts to hint that Betsy is less gullible with respect
to suitors' exaggerated protestations than the narrator's description
of her allows. The narrator would have us believe that Betsy's head is
completely turned by romantic rhetoric, but plainly, in this scene, Betsy
recognizes a "pick-up" line when she hears it. Nor is it by any means
clear from the context whether it is Waller's poetry which offends or
simply the student's use of it. With this quotation, it is not so much
that Waller's text is parodied as it is that Waller's lines offer a vehicle
for subverting the narrator's presentation of Betsy's credulous vanity
and pride.

Even so unlikely a source of wisdom as Flora quotes directly with a surprisingly truthful effect. For instance, when Flora pays Betsy a visit after Trueworth has broken off the courtship, she tells Betsy that "nothing is more common than that men should be false." She then offers, by way of authoritative evidence, a quotation, saying, "Remember what the poet says: 'Ingratitude's the sin, which, first or last,/ Taints the whole sex . . .'" (281). These words come from the mouth of an apparently untrustworthy character, one who has lied and attempted to turn Betsy and Trueworth against each other. And yet Flora's words about Trueworth ring with an undeniable validity: Trueworth is false, to Betsy, to Harriot, and to Flora. Again, it is not so much the quoted material that is parodied as it is that the quoted material undercuts the narrator's overt portrayals.

In some scenes, Haywood adopts a recontextualization strategy that is at once more complex and more subtle in its operation. She directly juxtaposes sets of quotations, placing them in dialogue with each other so as to encourage new associations. In the middle of the interpolated narrative of Forward's ruin, we find a pair of quotations reminiscent of the intertextual relationship in the Marlowe and Raleigh "Passionate Shepherd" and "Nymph's Reply" pairing. Direct quotation adds another dimension to Haywood's investigation of the ambiguity surrounding the concepts of rape and seduction. Espousing the carpe diem argument, Forward's seducer recites some romantic poetry and presses her to yield. Forward, in turn, offers a quotation that emphasizes regret and makes much of her own guilt in courting her ruin. On its own, the girl's borrowing might just pass as sincere, an echo of the narrator's severe pronouncements, albeit an incongruous one given Forward's character. In juxtaposition with the first quotation of this set, however, it turns oddly against the narrator's position. By evoking the whole carpe diem literary tradition and gesturing towards exactly the set of power relations that made the nymph's giving in so risky, Haywood highlights the artificial nature of the exchange, reinforcing the idea of Forward's words as convention or mere contrivance and suggesting that we should not believe that the fault is all Forward's any more than we should believe that Forward believes that the fault is all hers. While irrefutably intertextual in form, this strategy of quotation makes it difficult to pinpoint a specific parodic target; instead, it offers a refractory, seemingly contradictory, perspective. The strategy approaches even more nearly the appearance of cento when Haywood strings together sets of three or more quotations in close proximity, as she occasionally does, but attention to the manner in which the quotations comment upon each other and upon the story reveals in this interplay, as with the paired borrowings, simply a more copious and intense form of quotation as an act of critical revision.

A final point I want to make about quotation in *Betsy Thoughtless* has to do with the repetitive fashion in which Haywood introduces borrowed lines. Only in a few instances does she identify the original source. The overwhelming majority of quotations follow the introductory phrase "as the poet says," or some variation thereof. Despite the fact that so general an introduction of quotations is common enough in the period, it is not beyond the realm of reason to draw, on the basis of these introductions, some conclusions about the impact of Haywood's intended audience on her selection of parodic method. Terry, Hutcheon, and Rose all discuss how a growing standardization of education in the eighteenth century influenced the development of parody because it led to a cultural sense of a shared literary heritage and shared values. The greater the number of people familiar with a specific canon of works, the greater the certainty with which a parodist could rely on reader familiarity with the target texts. The problem with this argument, though, in the context of gender, is that women did not, in fact, receive the same kind of education as men, and the standardization of what education they did receive is a vexed issue.

For the woman writer wishing to try her hand at parody and casting about for models, both her own and her expected readers' exclusion from the classical fare of the grammar schools made many male-authored models of parody unsuitable. In *Betsy Thoughtless,* the ornate and detailed references to the classics that figure so prominently in the parodies of such writers as Pope and Dryden are kept to a conspicuous minimum. From Betsy's recollection of Dido's lament, "so elegantly described by the poet" (390), to the by-the-by introduction of a maxim on beauty that "the poet somewhere or other expresses" (459), Haywood's use of direct quotation negotiates these difficulties brilliantly. She incorporates a diverse selection of materials that lend additional resonance in the context of knowledge of the originals, but also downplays any expectations about reader competence and familiarity with the understated phrasing, "as the poet says," that promises in its lulling repetitiveness—playfully, even parodically— the exchangeability of one poet's words for another's.

Frederic Jameson's statements about the difference between postmodern parody and pastiche epitomize the dependence upon gender associations in the dichotomization of the two forms: "[P]astiche is like parody, the imitation of a peculiar or unique style, the wearing of a stylistic mask, speech in a dead language, but it is a neutral practice of such mimicry, without parody's ulterior motive, without the satirical impulse. . . . Pastiche is blank parody, parody that has lost its sense of humour" ("Postmodernism" 65). Pastiche is blank, blind, impotent, while parody is potent and critical. Haywood herself alludes to the pastiche-like nature of her novel in several of the chapter titles, variously referring to the chapter contents as "mixtures," "medleys," and "olios."[19] Possibly, this use of terminology is a more self-conscious one on her part than might at first seem, related to an insincere self-deprecation and strategy of indirection. As Terry details, at least one eighteenth-century book of cutting parodies attempted to veil its libelous content by hiding behind the more innocent motives of the pasticheur, denoting itself with the terms "miscellany" and "imitation."[20] Unlike Betsy Thoughtless, however, it did not fool anyone.

It is perhaps most telling that Jameson describes pastiche as a form that has lost its sense of humor. Regina Barreca has thoroughly documented the stereotype that women have no sense of humor, arguing that it is less a case of women lacking humor than it is a case of men's inability to see it and humor theorists' inability to fit it into pre-existing paradigms.[21] The same situation applies to women's parodic writing, as its strategies are not easily assimilable to standard theories of parody, and even in those female-authored works which advertise their parodic status, there are elements which escape conventional definitions. Austen's Northanger Abbey, or Lennox's The Female Quixote, for example, are overtly parodic in tackling the gothic and the romance, but critics, both contemporary and recent, have often found the loss of parodic thrust and growing sympathy with the targeted form, as well as the contrived tacking on of an abrupt or contradictory conclusion, confusing, and some have gone so far as to consider these aspects technical flaws.[22] That Haywood was able to bend the limits of deliberate intertextuality to hold to a central message consonant with that of her earlier works illustrates that if the Augustan age defined parody as an implicitly masculine pursuit, it was also an age that witnessed a persevering experimentation with parodic strategies uniquely adapted to the needs of the woman writer. In this respect, *Betsy Thoughtless* represents a significant innovation in form and is a more accomplished work than has generally been recognized, marking one of Haywood's important contributions to the evolution of women's literary history.

Notes

1. Green uses the phrase "a mid-career conversion" in the title of the chapter she devotes to Haywood in *The Courtship Novel*.

2. Deborah Nestor, for instance, argues that *Betsy Thoughtless* and *Jenny and Jemmy Jessamy* are both critiques of Richardson, while Mary Anne Schofield suggests that Haywood's use of romance in *Betsy Thoughtless* is self-conscious, noting that in this novel, "it is *the* romance plot, but . . . it is a romance that is studied, examined, and thoroughly analyzed" (*Masking* 102).

3. Schofield (*Masking*), Ross, Green, and Craft-Fairchild argue for this central message of Haywood's early novels in their respective chapters on Haywood. While not wishing to muddy the issue of generic boundaries even more than I already have, I must, however, interject a comment here on the relationship between parody and satire. It may be said that if Haywood's parody promotes the message of men's mistreatment of women, how do we know that it is not, in fact, a satire? This is an important question. Hutcheon's distinction between parody as an intertextual form—that is, targeting other texts—and satire as an extratextual form—targeting something in the "real" world outside of the text—has been widely adopted because it is so useful. As she herself admits, however, the borders between these two genres can become fuzzy at times, and I would argue that nowhere is this fuzziness more apparent than in women's parody. If, for example, to say that Cibber's work is dreadful is to make essentially the same type of statement that a parody does, and to say that writers who believe themselves to be great when they are not are dreadful bores is to make the kind of statement that a satire does, what do we do with a message of the latter sort conveyed via direct use of intertextuality (a specific working from references to other texts or genres)? One might say that this is a case of parody and satire working hand-in-hand, a case Hutcheon identifies as occupying the border territory. At the same time, one might also say that this is one of the instances where twentieth-century parody theory does not adequately account for women's use of parody.

Because investment in the overtly parodied form is one of the most common and most crucial features of women's parody, this overlap of function between the intertextual material and criticism of an extratextual target is characteristic of women's use of the form, illustrating one of the key areas in which conventional parody theory fails to provide adequate paradigms for women's parodic writing.

4. Quoted in Terry, "Semantics" 67. I am greatly indebted to Terry's invaluable work on the semantics of eighteenth-century parody and on the factors contributing to the rise of the genre in this period, as well as to Rose's compendious study of parody, especially his presentation of "parody" and eighteenth-century lexicography.

5. Quoted in Terry, "Semantics" 67. Terry cites Howard Weinbrot's "Parody as Imitation in the Eighteenth Century," *ANQ* 2 (May 1964): 131.

6. Terry notes that Pope uses the word "parody" in connection with *The Dunciad* twice in his correspondence, as well as in the "Advertisement" prefixed to *The Dunciad Varorium,* although he also suggests that Pope elsewhere uses the word in connection with other of his works as though it were more connotive of simple imitation ("Semantics" 71).

7. Terry also argues that Johnson's use of the words "are taken" in the *Dictionary* definition suggests a connotation of theft ("Circumstances" 86).

8. Ross offers by way of evidence specific comments from prefaces by Haywood.

9. Quoted in the *OED,* 2nd ed., 1989, 11:321. *The Art of Painting* of 1744 is a translation from the French work of 1706. Rose also cites this definition from the *OED* (*Parody* 74).

10. This essay references the 1997 Oxford edition of *Betsy Thoughtless.*

11. See, for instance, Backscheider on the connection between the supposed quality of women's writing and assumptions about their writing being motivated by pecuniary needs ("Writing Women" 251).

12. Poovey details the condescending criticism of women's writing with supporting quotations from various reviews (38–40).

13. As Abrams notes, in a comedy "the characters and their discomfitures engage our pleasurable attention rather than our profound concern [because] we are made to feel confident that no great disaster will occur, and usually the action turns out happily" (29). Indeed, we are made to feel comfortable either because we believe that the disasters threatening the characters will not occur, or because we believe that the events which do occur that the characters may consider to be disasters are in reality quite trivial.

14. Farce: ridiculous mockery; absurd pretense; sham (*The World Book Encyclopedia Dictionary,* 1966 ed.).

15. Like Fielding's *Shamela,* Haywood's *Anti-Pamela* equates Richard-

son's heroine with a prostitute; Haywood's burlesque "taking down" of the virtuous Pamela to the level of a prostitute, though, results in a fairly one-dimensional comparison, unlike her thoughtful interrogation of the chaste/fallen pairing in *Betsy Thoughtless*, and comprises a failure to explore the terms she equates or to question the categorizations they imply.

16. Although Backscheider does not refer specifically to the debate between originality and repetition, she implies the association between imitation or repetition and women's fiction in her discussion of booksellers' "stables" of women writers and the "insatiable appetite" for new women's novels ("Women Writers" 255), as well, I think, as implying this association in her analysis of the assumption that women's fiction was hugely autobiographical.

17. For treatment of the association between women, romance, and naive reading, see Backscheider ("Women Writers" 250–51), Schofield (*Masking* 101), and Ballaster (*Seductive* 9–28). Johnson's portrait of Imperia appears in the *Rambler*, no. 115; Ross also points out a thematic relationship between *The Female Quixote* and the portrait of female idleness encouraging an overactive imagination in the *Rambler*, no. 85 (*Excellence of Falsehood* 103).

18. See, for example, Castle's, Ballaster's, and Craft-Fairchild's discussion of masquerade in Haywood's novels; each ground their analyses of masquerade firmly in concepts of mimicry developed by various feminist theorists.

19. Chapter titles implying pastiche include those for 1.7, 2.16, 3.20, and 4.14.

20. Isaac Hawkins Browne's 1736 collection of parodies, *A Pipe of Tobacco;* Terry discusses this volume's introduction of attacks on well-known writers of the day as "politic" ("Semantics" 72).

21. Although Barreca has detailed this phenomenon in several of her books and articles, *Untamed and Unabashed* is the most useful in terms of contextualizing women's humor in the eighteenth century; see particularly her second chapter, on Austen and Lennox.

22. For example, Bette Roberts discusses the problem of Austen's stance toward Radcliffe and suggests that technical difficulties in *Northanger Abbey* derive from Austen's sympathy with the gothic, while Ross discusses sympathy with the romance and critical commentary that the hurried ending is a flaw in *The Female Quixote*.

"Shady bowers! and purling streams!— Heavens, how insipid!"

Eliza Haywood's Artful Pastoral

David Oakleaf

By writing amatory fiction, Eliza Haywood fashioned herself a prominent place in the literary terrain. But when we survey the eighteenth century from the paths that offer the most flattering prospects of Jonathan Swift and Alexander Pope, even Henry Fielding, Haywood barely emerges from the greater obscurity of Grub Street. "Despite great popularity and relevance in their day," Toni Bowers suggests, "amatory fictions are now held in contempt. However interesting these texts may be as part of the Augustan cultural landscape, most critics still feel that they are simply not very good literature; their present value seems to be mainly that of rather embarrassing curiosities" (69). Of course, feminist scholars have recovered angles of vision from which Haywood again shines to advantage,[1] as she did for those contemporaries who nervously registered her accomplishment in poetic conceits yoking Phoebus's poetic light with sexual heat.[2] Yet Bowers implies that many of us still view Haywood with a microscopic eye. We see not a central component of the garden's design but an isolated curiosity, some statue of Venus properly confined to the decent obscurity of a secluded nook.

Nevertheless, scrutiny of Haywood teaches us a lot about the lay of the land. April London demonstrates as much when she exposes the landowner lurking in the lover who possesses sexually a woman swooning in the metonymic garden that is also her body. Given the lingering prejudice that Haywood writes no more consciously than her heroines faint into sexual experience, there may be advantages to locating her gardens themselves with respect to familiar cultural landmarks. They may supply a key to her place, for when she and her contemporaries envision their central values or grapple with cultural contradictions, they imagine gardens. In gardens, they play city against country. In gardens, that is, they balance urban profusion against rural stability, active politics against contemplative retreat, business against domesticity, even female against male. Hence the vitality of eighteenth-century verse pastoral, which Michael McKeon argues "is an unprecedentedly innovative version of the form, a radical instrument of inquiry," partly because it so resourcefully exploits the instabilities of its inherently binary form ("Surveying" 8). Even outside formal verse, pastoral strategies animate writers conscious of their medium and alert to cultural contradictions. Emulating Addison's "Man of a Polite Imagination" in the *Spectator,* many an English landlord devotes himself to the pastoral ideal of "mak[ing] a pretty Landskip of his own Possessions" (3:538, 552). Such landlords ruthlessly displace whole villages to improve, quite literally, their prospects (Sambrook 1361–62).[3] Henry Fielding's benevolent literary exemplar of Addison's ideal, Squire Allworthy in *Tom Jones,* rises at dawn to enjoy the richly varied prospect from his country house despite his late (and interrupted) return from its binary opposite, London (see Oakleaf, "Sliding"). Yet Fielding notoriously places snakes in the pastoral grass of the estate he names Paradise Hall, and these treacherous inmates exploit the landlord's limited vision (Brückmann). Through such paradoxes, pastoral engages rather than evades cultural contradictions.

Since Haywood is Pope's contemporary and Fielding's occasional collaborator, we might suspect that she too commands the ambiguities inherent in the artful rendition of artless nature. A self-reflexive debate on rural life in *The History of Miss Betsy Thoughtless* certainly suggests as much. In what follows, I examine some of the tensions in that late novel and then suggest, necessarily more briefly, that what critics too often disparage as crudity or unconsciousness is in fact craft. Haywood plays more artfully with pastoral oppositions than we commonly recognize.

Written after *Clarissa* and *Tom Jones* (it was published just before

Amelia),[4] *Betsy Thoughtless* (1751) reveals Haywood at her most self-aware. Her literary allusions, Deborah J. Nestor argues, "dramatiz[e] the process by which popular literature acts as the agent of reform" but cannot prevent the heroine's errors. Shrewdly but fruitlessly, that is, Betsy scrutinizes her behavior in the light of Cibber's *Careless Husband* and, when she can finally apply it to herself, appreciates "Young Philander woo'd me long," a pastoral song long familiar to her (Nestor 580–81). Furthermore, this late novel relentlessly foregrounds style. Betsy easily reads Sir Frederick Fineer's triviality in the maladroit "rodomontade strain" (325)[5] of his "heroically learned epistle[s]" (385): "'What a romantic jargon is here?'" she exclaims, "'One would think he had been consulting all the ballads since fair Rosamond, and the children in the wood, for fine phrases to melt me into pity'" (331).[6] Alert to style, Betsy unfortunately fails to recognize that the novel's men readily abandon stylish civility for force; she thus leaves herself open to Sir Frederick Fineer's sexual assault despite her insight.

The novelist also invites us to scrutinize the alleged baronet. *Mynheer* and perhaps even *fine Heer* surely lurk with *veneer* in Fineer's emblematic name, revealing the masquerading foreigner even before Trueworth exposes not the familiar figure of the prosperous Dutch merchant but, appallingly, a penniless servant who is presumably Catholic as well as foreign—a dishonest French valet de chambre (426).[7] Elsewhere, the distraught Miss Flora "fl[ies] about the room, like a princess in a tragedy" before she meanly spills ink on her rival's petticoat (221). Later, she inks this novel's principal examples of "artifice" (194, 210) rather than art, slanderous letters blackening sexual reputations, especially Betsy's. Surely this novelist and former actress is as sardonically alert to conventional female roles as her heroine.

Since the villain in *Betsy Thoughtless* acts like a literary princess, it can come as no surprise that a crucial exchange between heroine and hero turns on rival readings of literary conventions, specifically the conventions of pastoral. After his aunt mercilessly dissects Betsy's reputation to discourage his suit, Trueworth feels even more torn than usual between loving admiration of Betsy and rational disdain for her inveterate frivolity. Desperately testing "how far [Betsy] could relish the retirements of a country life," he provokes a lovers' debate that clarifies his predicament while calling attention to Haywood's own conventions:

Accordingly, the next visit he made to her, [Trueworth] began to represent, in the most pathetic terms he was able, the true felicity that two people, who loved each other, might enjoy when remote from the noise and interruption of a throng of giddy visitors. "The deity of soft desires," said he, "flies the confused glare of pomp and public shews; 'tis in the shady bowers, or on the banks of a sweet purling stream, he spreads his downy wings, and wafts ten thousand nameless pleasures on the fond, the innocent, and the happy pair."

He was going on, but she interrupted him with a loud laugh;— "Hold,—hold," cried she, "was there ever such a romantic description?—I wonder how such silly ideas come into your head?—Shady bowers! and purling streams!—Heavens, how insipid! Well," continued she, "you may be the Strephon of the woods, if you think fit; but I shall never envy the happiness of the Cloe that accompanies you in these fine recesses. What! to be cooped up like a tame dove, only to coo, and bill, and breed? Oh, it would be a delicious life indeed!" (225)

As a nettled Trueworth concludes from "the contempt she had shewn of a country life" (226), this urban Chloe refuses to see herself as a fashionable commodity to be acquired in the city for use and limited display on a gentleman's country estate.

Haywood invokes the ideologically loaded distinction between rural and urban life. Evenhandedly, she distinguishes Trueworth's extreme humor of retirement from Betsy's equally excessive humor of distraction by discriminating their readings (and performances) of pastoral. Betsy's swain might have gathered from her tripled pleasures, the "Plays,—operas,—and masquerades . . . now beginning to come in vogue" (214), that his nymph would refuse to seize the day. Although she evidently prefers shopping to rural seclusion, the issue is not simply that she is urban, he rural. Rather, Trueworth crucially fails to recognize a fellow artist. Posing as a pastoral shepherd, he forgets the pastoral poet and finds himself overmatched rhetorically. In vain he promises "ten thousand nameless pleasures," for Betsy names and dismisses them while capping his triplet ("the fond, the innocent, and the happy pair"): "What! . . . only to coo, and bill, and breed?" His match at "romantic description," the nymph recognizes her swain's nature as art.

Strephon and Chloe. Since mock pastoral had long been a poetic staple—witness Aphra Behn's "The Disappointment" and any number of poems by Rochester—Haywood may even subvert Trueworth's hackneyed art by alluding to the title of Swift's 1731 poem guying lovers' pastoral illusions. Certainly she enjoys even sly self-parody. Consider Miss Forward's seduction as she relates it to Betsy: "'Never was there a finer night:—the moon, and her attendant stars, shone with uncommon brightness, the air was all serene, the boisterous winds were all locked in their caverns, and only gentle zephirs, with their fanning wings, wafted a thousand odours from the neighboring plants, perfuming all around.—'Twas an enchanting scene: nature herself seemed to conspire my ruin, and contributed all in her power to lull my mind into a soft forgetfulness of what I owed myself,—my fame,— my fortune,—and my family'" (109). Forward's zeal to open the gate of her enclosed garden to Mr. Wildly scarcely needs a gloss. With uncharacteristic brevity, Haywood curtly dismisses a coquette who craftily but inartistically stages her own victimization. Even Betsy eventually recognizes that her acquaintance is "one of those unhappy creatures, who make traffic of their beauty" (227).

Yet Trueworth and Forward could well have conned their romantic descriptions, and silly ideas, from "the tender page"[8] of Eliza Haywood. Who pens more romantic descriptions, or descriptions more romantic, than Eliza Haywood? Her novels commonly devote pages at a stretch to romantic description and panting desire. In *Love in Excess,* for example, the callow seducer D'elmont falls in love with the matchless Melliora, a woman who locks her chamber door and later retreats to a convent. Suddenly but inevitably "[he] prefer[s] a solitary walk, a lonely shade, or the bank of some purling stream, where he undisturbed might contemplate on his beloved Melliora, to all the noisy pleasures of the Court" (171). Love consistently lures Haywood's characters to precisely the rustic seclusion Trueworth promises Betsy. It thereby draws them from the Court and the fashionable assemblies that serve the opposite passion, ambition. The desire to visit public places long remains the defining sign of ambition in an eighteenth-century heroine.[9] As long as she is ambitious for notice, Betsy sensibly shuns rural domesticity for town diversions, acting the coquette rather than the heroine. Like the hero of Haywood's first novel, she seems launched on the career from "ambition" to "conjugal affection" (Haywood, *Excess* 41, 273).

But the self-conscious urban nymph's skepticism may serve us better than her swain's literal-mindedness, for the novel's seducers commonly appropriate high style for low purposes. The libertine who crassly offers to take Betsy into keeping, for example, sounds cynical where Alexander Pope's Clarissa blends good humor with good sense, but he gallantly salts his "raillery" with the idiom of *The Rape of the Lock* to suggest that he is not predator but prey: "Why does the jessamine, and the blooming violet play wanton in your hair?—Why is the patch with so much art placed on the corner of this ruby lip,—and here another to mark out the arched symmetry of the jetty brow?— Why does the glittering solitaire hang pendant on the snowy breast, but to attract and allure us poor, admiring men, into a pleasing ruin?" (237). Since her "ready wit" equips her to silence any lover who persists in "the same strain" (237–38), Haywood's heroine may be right to mock Trueworth's "silly ideas" when he, like Miss Forward, (mis)appropriates Haywood's own rhetoric of seduction. However sincere he may feel, Betsy's Strephon of the woods sounds like another wolf who affects the swain only to enter the fold. The "downy wings" with which Trueworth's love god "wafts ten thousand pleasures" recall too precisely for comfort the "fanning wings" with which zephyrs "wafted a thousand odours" in the self-justifying seduction narrative Forward tells Betsy.

Like the novel's other sexual predators, that is, Trueworth apparently regards potential sexual partners as prey to be allured by cunning into gaudy traps. He deploys a romantic jargon more polished than Fineer's, of course, but Betsy quickly recognizes that his amorous bowers and purling streams bait the trap of confinement and solitude: "What! to be cooped up like a tame dove. . . ?" As we might suspect from his strictly instrumental view of the bowers his eloquence contrives, he proves a shady denizen of the town. He urbanely accompanies his future brother-in-law to a courtesan's house, revealing unease only at finding Betsy in Forward's company. After he bluntly rejects Betsy, he consoles himself in the arms of Betsy's former roommate, Miss Flora; that is, with another sexual predator who takes an instrumental view of artifice. Trueworth may be artless, but he is hardly guileless!

Since she represents all this, Haywood evidently does not write for such dull elves as Trueworth. Her readers, like Jane Austen's, should therefore resist the appalling scenario Eve Kosofsky Sedgwick calls "the Girl Being Taught a Lesson" (833–34). The critic who follows this mean-spirited script gloats while the novelist chastises or even humiliates her lively heroine. Because it is one of the earliest female *Bildungsromane,* as Lorna Beth Ellis shows, *Betsy Thoughtless* invites such a response. In keeping with the form (Ellis 288), Betsy grows up only by growing down to social expectation, as the novel's last sentence suggests: "Thus were the virtues of our heroine (those follies that had defaced them being fully corrected) at length rewarded with a happiness, retarded only till she had render'd herself wholly worthy of receiving it" (634). Betsy's undiscriminating pursuit of pleasure leads directly to the abusive marriage that chastens her. After her imprudence lends color to slurs on her reputation and leaves her open to sexual assault, she marries, emblematically, a mean-spirited courtier who commands all the social forms and none of the sociable feelings. Mr. Munden pinches his wife financially and emotionally, but he follows fashionable precedent even when he savagely dashes her pet squirrel against the marble chimney (507): "'[L]et [my husband] not see this,'" writes Margery Pinchwife in William Wycherley's *Country Wife,* "'lest he should come home and pinch me, or kill my squirrel'" (103; 4.3.278–79).[10] In brief, a heroine overly fond of fashionable life marries a man excessively *mondain*—the versatile French adjective for fashionability, high society, and *politesse* that lurks just behind *Munden,* his name.

But Haywood's designedly symmetrical novel starts more hares than Betsy's thoughtlessness. Before he marries a suitably chastened Betsy, Trueworth mirrors her mistakes. His brief affair with Flora provokes her to write a slanderous letter threatening to tarnish his reputation with a deserving partner, just as Betsy's inadvertencies left her vulnerable to an even more damaging letter. Trueworth also enters a short-lived marriage with an emblem of his exaggerated principle of retirement.[11] Miss Harriot, whom he marries, "would always choose to avoid" the court, contenting herself with "the obscurity of a country life" (316). When she dies of smallpox at a site of observation, she calls into question, Harriet Guest argues, the extreme retirement Trueworth so desires. Trueworth, Guest concludes, "is wrong to mistrust Betsy's love for company, and wrong to identify in [Betsy] the cause of the semantic or moral instabilities that play around her sociable person" (496). He was wrong, that is, to trust not Betsy but interested representations of her. As his naive self-representation as a pastoral swain suggests, he proves no better at distinguishing lifelike representations from nature than Partridge does at the performance of *Hamlet* in *Tom Jones*.

In Haywood's deft pastoral, that is, country and city form the poles of a false dichotomy. One pole obviously symbolizes an ambivalent sociability; the other, the equally ambivalent retirement that Guest discusses. They are not even truly distinct. Betsy, for example, fears solitude in Trueworth's rustic seclusion. Yet when Lady Mellasin and Miss Flora decamp, the horror at the opposite pole from sociability invades even the town: "'What a wilderness is this house!' cried [Betsy] to herself.—'What a frightful solitude!'" (275).[12] Similarly, even the fatally retiring Harriot espouses a virtuous retirement less fugitive and cloistered than Trueworth's. Sharing Betsy's pleasure in "Plays,— operas,—and masquerades," she claims that she could enjoy even a sufficiently genteel masquerade, "where only persons of condition are admitted, and none presumes to say that under a vizard, which he either would, or ought to be ashamed of, when it is plucked off" (317). Less hypothetically, she avidly studies London performances so that she can recreate in her country retreat the sociable pleasures of music and theater (317–18). Unlike Trueworth's bower but like Haywood's art, Harriot's retreat exists in active dialogue with both city and country.

So when Haywood finally contrives an actual bower, the "arbour" where Betsy apparently surrenders to the superior wisdom of a mentor-lover, we should not identify it with the panting shepherdess: "— 'How delightful,—how heavenly,' said she to herself, 'is this solitude, how truly preferable to all the noisy giddy pleasures of the tumultuous town, yet how have I despised and ridiculed the soft serenity of a country life.'—Then recollecting some discourse she formerly had with Mr. Trueworth on that subject, 'I wonder,' cried she, 'what Mr. Trueworth would say if he knew the change that a little time has wrought in me!'" (606). This arbor is a liminal place at odds with the stark binary logic of the lovers' earlier exchange, for it embodies the intercourse of town with country. Betsy lies concealed from her husband in a retreat neither rustic nor urban but both, "a very pleasant and commodious house on the bank of the river on the Surrey side." Her hostess is her lawyer's sister-in-law, who occasionally takes lodg-

ers in the suburban house she leases from a neighbor. Her garden
represents not nature but commercial and professional London's appropriation of the country: "[I]ts being so near London, nothing of
moment can happen here, but what you may be apprized of in little
more than an hour" (604).

Simply by being at so many margins, this garden finds itself at the
cultural center. "[P]art of the same estate, and at present rented by a
gentleman of condition, who lives at the next door," even the path
beside the arbor is common to two houses (605). Like Betsy, that is,
the arbor occupies the boundary between the gentle and the commercial or professional. "[T]he only daughter of a gentleman of good
family and fortune in L—e, where he constantly resided, scarce ever
going to London" (27), Betsy spends most of the novel in the house of
one of her guardians, "Mr. Goodman, a wealthy merchant in the city
of London" (33), who conscientiously improves her paternal fortune
before passing it on to her (300). Her "too indolent" (32) father, like
Miss Harriot, embodies excessive retirement: helpless to manage his
legal affairs, he dies when business forces him to London.

Haywood crafts a *locus amoenus* more complex than her hero
guesses. Poised as strategically as the heroine between land and capital, inheritance and suburban rental, this arbor also straddles the
boundary between introspection and prospect. Since she feels that her
marriage has foreclosed her prospects, Betsy appropriately values its
place on the side of the common path that suits her "contemplative
mood" (606). But her landlady plans to move it to "the other side of
the walk." There it will offer a pleasure more appropriate to a woman
of a polite imagination, "the prospect of a very beautiful garden, deco-
rated with plots of flowers, statues, and trees cut in a most elegant
manner" (605). In this bower, which is entered by "a little wicket
gate" and enclosed with myrtle, the plant sacred to Venus, Betsy's
literal minded swain again misreads his Chloe. In a scenario familiar
to all readers of Haywood, he observes unobserved while Betsy contemplates his miniature portrait: "[S]etting his foot upon a pedestal
of a statue, quick as thought, or the flash of elemental fire, [he] sprang
over the myrtle hedge that parted the garden from the walk,—'Ah,
madam,' cried he, catching her in his arms to hinder her from falling,—'what has the unhappy Trueworth done to render his presence
so alarming!—How have I deserved to appear thus dreadful in your

eyes!'" (608). Just as Trueworth naively concludes that Betsy belongs to him, his resolute nymph baffles him again.

Once more, that is, Betsy proves herself the more sophisticated reader of signs. Embracing her because she has embraced his miniature, the ardent swain characteristically confuses the representation with the subject represented. But for Betsy, the distinction between art and life is second nature. As Nancy K. Miller observes of the influential scene in *La Princesse de Clèves* that lies behind this one, solitary enjoyment of a portrait allows the heroine to indulge an impossible sexual desire on her own terms ("Emphasis Added" 42–43). Betsy has stolen the picture precisely because she recognizes that she cannot possess its subject: "'Though I no more must see himself,' said she, 'I may at least be allowed to pay the tribute of my gratitude to this dumb representative of the man to whom I have been so much obliged'" (606). Instead of swooning when Trueworth substitutes himself for his portrait, therefore, Betsy "shew[s] the command she had over herself" (610). She reminds him that marriage has made her "the property of Mr. Munden" (557): "[R]emember, sir, I am a wife, and being such, ought never to see you more" (610). As the quasi-Miltonic language ("quick as . . . the flash of elemental fire") perhaps suggests, heroines should resist the tempters who bound into their gardens.

Like so many novels of mid-century, *Betsy Thoughtless* represents the contested reading of interested representations. Thus Richardson's *Pamela* repeatedly tests its low-born heroine's self-representations against both rival representations and interested misreadings: "Well, Sir," Pamela exclaims at one point, referring not to holy scripture but to her manuscript journal, "that is your Comment; but it does not appear so in the Text" (200). *Tom Jones* also trains its reader to sift rival representations of its hero; according to Susan P. McNamara, it "develops a plot which evolves out of the accumulation of stories orally communicated by . . . persons of limited perspective, and . . . places questions about the interdependence of fiction and reality at its thematic center" (376). Haywood works just as consciously. When Trueworth misreads Betsy's treatment of his portrait, he symbolically recapitulates his prior failure to read correctly her actual character (her worth). He has allowed himself to be swayed by interested *characters* of Betsy; that is, by unflattering representations of her. In addition to Flora's anonymous letter slandering her, these include even his aunt's "thorough enquiry into the character of the young person her nephew was about to marry" (223). Her investigation can amount to no more than sifting carefully what people say about Betsy.

Betsy Thoughtless subsequently rejects the notion that there is an escape from competing urban representations in rural sincerity. Betsy offends Lady Trusty by brusquely spurning the local suitors she urges on her, apparently repeating her earlier "contempt . . . of a country life" (226): "'It is not in L—e,' replied Lady Trusty, a little piqued at these last words, 'but in London you are to expect proposals deserving this contempt;—here are no false glosses to deceive or impose on the understanding;—here are no pretenders to birth, or to estate; every one is known for what he really is, and none will presume to make his addresses to a woman without a consciousness of being qualified to receive the approbation of her friends'" (629). Despite this assurance that signified worth reliably stabilizes social signs in a landed society, Betsy rejects the Trustys' emblematically named neighbor, Mr. Woodland. Likewise, her Strephon of the woods rejects his former humor of retirement: "The first object that presented itself to [Sir Ralph and his lady], was a very neat running footman, who . . . came tripping up towards the house, and was immediately followed by a coach . . . drawn by six prancing horses, and attended by two servants in rich liveries, and well mounted." Inviolable in a bower, Betsy proves more compliant once her reformed lover embellishes his heart with fashionable display. Committing sincerely feeling selves to the public world of contested representations, they can finally embrace: he "sprang into her arms, which of themselves opened to receive him, and while he kissed away the tears that trickled from her eyes, his own bedewed her cheeks" (630).

Haywood invariably plays both ends against a desired middle. Her lovers may linger in gardens poised uncertainly between private desire and public display, later exiling themselves to the country; but even in *Love in Excess,* her first novel, they meet at the court to which D'elmont's ambition takes him and joyfully return to Paris after suitably splendid weddings: "[T]hose who in the Count's absence had taken a liberty of censuring and condemning his actions, awed by his presence, and in time won by his virtues, now swell his praises with an equal vehemence. Both he and Frankville . . . continue, with their fair wives, great and lovely examples of conjugal affection" (273).

Love in Excess ends, that is, when domestic affection garners the public acclaim that gratifies ambition. We should therefore scrutinize carefully the novelist's apparent departures from this balance. When she dedicates *The Fatal Secret* (1723) to William Yonge, "One of the Lords Commissioners of His Majesty's Treasury," for example, Haywood alleges that she is artless: "LOVE is a Topick which I believe few are ignorant of; there requires no Aids of Learning, no general Conversation, no Application; a shady Grove and purling Stream are all Things that's necessary to give us an Idea of the tender Passion. This is a Theme, therefore, which, while I make choice to write of, frees me from the Imputation of vain or self-sufficient:——None can tax me with having too great an Opinion of my Own *Genius,* when I aim at nothing but what the meanest may perform" (1986 ed., 204; italic and roman reversed). Yet this topos of modesty is obligatory in the aspirant to patronage. Since a female writer can hardly assert her self-sufficient discursive power while she is throwing her "enervate Pen" under the protection of a powerful male in public life,[13] we should read her appeal as evidence of a finely tuned craft.

John J. Richetti points out that Haywood here appropriates for her own ends a self-serving male myth. That myth allows men (he instances Henry Fielding) to treat examples of female discursive power as "artless" and hence safely anomalous ("Voice" 264). I am unconvinced only that her "formulation of this strategy" is "crude" (264), characterized by "formulaic crudity" (267). "Haywood's self-depreciation is tinged with irony," Richetti concedes, "and, under all the dedicatory flattery, not a little defiance of the male world of power . . . . And yet it seems all wrong, this hardened Grub Street veteran explaining her work as the dreaming of an innocent, her imaginings real and moving precisely because they come unbidden, unmediated by culture, provoked by nature" (265). What Haywood yearns for, I suspect, is a patron who can savor in this assertion of natural spontaneity a professional writer's deft performance of a compulsory figure. After all, the original readers of her novels consistently if edgily praise her command of language. "*I shade those glories which I can't display,*" laments Richard Savage quite as conventionally as Haywood; her "*descriptions,*" he adds, "*thus at once can prove / The force of language, and the sweets of love*" (Haywood, *Excess* 86). A decade later, James Sterling agrees: "Proportioned to the image, [her] language swells, / Both leave the mind suspended, which excels" (Haywood, *Excess* 279). Clara Reeve credits Haywood with ingenuity rather than artlessness even though she strategically associates her with her heroines in order to celebrate her as a reformed fallen woman, the definitive version of the Girl Taught a Lesson: "Mrs. *Heywood*'s wit and ingenuity were never denied. I would be the last to vindicate her faults, but the first to celebrate her return to virtue, and her atonement for them" (*Betsy Thoughtless* 643).

Since the pastoral writer actually addresses not a nymph (or swain) but a reader alert to the interplay of extremes, Haywood may well calculate the "largely conventional" comments in which she "presents herself as a sufferer on a par with her heroines" (Ballaster 168). The Girl Taught a Lesson, that is, may be a Writer Who Can Teach a Lesson. The woman Haywood guides down a garden path to a shady bower consecrated to love rarely finds fulfillment there. *The British Recluse* (1722), for example, prefigures the patterns and even the idioms of *Betsy Thoughtless*. It offers two versions of country retreat, both of them treacherous. One is the standard bower of bliss: "Never was a Night more delectable, more aiding to a Lover's Wishes! The arching Trees formed a Canopy over our Heads, while through the gently shaking Boughs soft Breezes played in lulling Murmurings and fanned us with delicious Gales; a thousand Nightingales sung amourous Ditties, and the billing Doves cooed out their tender Transports—everything was soothing—everything inspiring! the very Soul of Love seemed to inform the Place and reign throughout the whole" (211; cf. London 105).[14] The canopy suggests the four-poster bed and the intimacies appropriate to it. Although a temperate lover rescues Belinda from the libertine aristocrat who is contriving her ruin, this worthy suitor no longer esteems her. Belinda learns to her sorrow how irrevocably rustic seclusion entraps the woman who chooses it.

The other country retreat in *The British Recluse* is that in which Cleomira's mother quits the court, "entirely throwing off the *fine Lady* . . . to practice the mere *Country Gentlewoman*." Since her daughter has a very small fortune, everything necessitates the mother's caution: "[T]he passionate Fondness I expressed for the Town Diversions and Disdain of a Country Life, confirmed her that it was absolutely necessary at once to . . . repel the Growth of that Ambition which she found had already taken too deep a Root in my youthful Heart."

However, nothing endears this apparently virtuous retreat to the heroine. A consequence of poverty after her father's death, it imposes a stark divide between the public pleasures of youth and the obscure seclusion of adult sexuality: "[I]t was time for me to learn to play the good Housewife and forget that there ever were such Things as Balls, Plays, Masquerades, or Assemblies" (*British Recluse* 162). Worse still, it is utterly ineffective. Cleomira soon finds herself seduced by the libertine who at one point presents himself to her in "the Arbor" while her mother is entertained elsewhere in the same garden (175). Just as Haywood's city offers no security from solitude, her rural seclusion proves powerless to exclude the sexual ambition of the court.

The shady bower's insecurity makes all the more scandalous the price it exacts, which is nothing less than the heroine's identity. Seduced victim or good housewife, the embowered heroine apparently forfeits any claim on public attention. Consider *Fantomina*, which William Beatty Warner brilliantly offers as a novel against which to read *Pamela* ("Elevation" 585–88). Pamela dresses herself in rustic clothes to escape sexuality and preserve her identity; Fantomina disguises herself for love and thereby forfeits her identity as Lady ——. Reshuffling the stages of the harlot's progress, Haywood has Fantomina present herself, in order, as a courtesan, a rude country girl, an obscure widow with little fortune, an "Incognita"—and then the mother of an illegitimate child in her own guise. However successful the heroine's appropriation of roles to attract repeatedly her inconstant lover, a woman once at the center of her society takes refuge in a French convent.

Although it lacks *Fantomina*'s (and *Pamela*'s) resourceful heroine, Haywood's *Lasselia; or, The Self-Abandon'd* (1723) clarifies this pattern, marking all the more clearly Richardson's contested appropriation for virtue of his ladylike heroine's decision to dress in rustic garb for her return home. Haywood conventionally associates sexual desire with rural seclusion and less conventionally figures it as a clownish awkwardness; that is, in terms of country folk as they appear to the court. Abandoning the court because the king wants to make her his mistress, Lasselia virtuously takes refuge on a country estate. There she enjoys a fleeting affair with a neighbor. A much less conspicuous married man than the king, her lover awkwardly discharges his nascent passion in three drops of blood on her handkerchief (see Oakleaf,

"Eloquence") and communicates his passion "in the Habit of a *Rustick*" (ed. Beasley, 118), a "Messenger, who seem'd to be a Country-Fellow" (117). Not to be outdone, his jealous rival dresses as a footman and invades her privacy (137–38). Already buried in rural obscurity, Lasselia herself flees a renewed royal summons in a pilgrim's disguise that thoroughly conceals her identity. She and her lover finally consummate their passion in a remote inn whose owners' greed guarantees her anonymity. She plays the good housewife by living "for some Months" in what the narrator acidly calls "all the Felicity that Love, in the most elevated Degree, can afford to those who devote themselves entirely to that Passion" (131). But public exposure drives her to a convent—as it did her lover's previous mistress. Haywood casts a skeptical eye on the bower of domestic intimacy.

"If we are to open that 'pre-history' of the novel to historical investigation," Warner argues, "we must reread Behn, Manley and Haywood as more than precursors to the texts to follow; we must concede them differences and autonomy as part of another earlier cultural terrain" ("Elevation" 584). As we locate Haywood in that terrain, we can profitably recall how inescapably her contemporaries experiment with traditional forms, notably versions of pastoral that pit town against country, domesticity against public responsibility. Certainly we should resist any attempt, even her own, to characterize her narrative power as artless. Her culture no doubt made sexual intimacy her inevitable subject. But we can surely admire the craft with which she won fame by showing how rarely that subject went unaccompanied by the destructive loss of public identity. Like the late debate in which her lovers test the limits and sincerity of pastoral, Haywood's novels engage naive and knowing readers alike in the interplay of love with ambition.

Notes

1. Hollis remarks that publishers still marginalize Haywood (43), but editions of *Betsy Thoughtless* from Oxford and Broadview have replaced the out-of-print Pandora edition, joining the "few select amatory novellas" (43) edited by Wilputte and others; Beasley's edition of *The Injur'd Husband* and *Lasselia* was recently published by the University Press of Kentucky.

2. See the poems Richard Savage and "an Unknown Hand" prefaced to the second part of *Love in Excess*; in the poem calling Haywood "Great

arbitress of passion," James Stirling also praises "her godlike fires" (Haywood, *Excess* 86–87, 279; cf. 22–23).

3. Sambrook quotes Robert Walpole's neighbor, Thomas Coke, who removed a whole village except the church: "'I am Giant, of Giant's Castle, and have ate up all my neighbours'" (1363).

4. *Betsy Thoughtless* appeared in October, *Amelia* in December 1751 (Whicher 186, 204; Fielding, *Amelia* 543); they share predatory aristocrats and wives tested by trying marriages.

5. I cite Blouch's 1998 edition of *Betsy Thoughtless* throughout.

6. He is called Quaint, Trueworth reports, "'on account of the romantic and affected fashion in which he always spoke:—the rascal has a little smattering of Latin, and I believe has dipped into a good many of the ancient authors'" (433).

7. The *OED* cites no figurative use of *fineer* (the usual spelling) before 1785, so Haywood may deserve pride of place—and anticipate the Veneerings in Charles Dickens's *Our Mutual Friend*; although polite writers avoided technical terms like *veneer*, Haywood perhaps learned them in Betsy's fashionable shops.

8. I take the phrase from *"Verses Wrote in the Blank Leaf of Mrs. Haywood's Novel"* (Haywood, *Excess* 278).

9. Frances Burney's Mr. Villars asks, concerning Evelina, "can your Ladyship be serious in proposing to introduce her to the gaieties of a London life? Permit me to ask, for what end, or what purpose? A youthful mind is seldom totally free from ambition; to curb that, is the first step to contentment. . . . I apprehend nothing more than too much raising her hopes and her views" (18; letter 4); i.e., Evelina might aspire to a marriage her birth and fortune cannot justify.

10. An actress, playwright, and historian of drama, Haywood may allude directly to Wycherley's Pinchwife, an embodiment of country possessiveness, further undercutting Trueworth's idyll.

11. Haywood's original readers were also Fielding's; alert to parallels, they perhaps recognized Betsy as an urban, female version of Tom Jones.

12. Traditionally, solitude is unhealthy in a sociable being, a source of melancholy cured only by society: "[T]oo much solitude might have brought on a gloominess of temper equally uneasy to herself and to those about her; but the society of these worthy friends,—the diversions they prepared for her, and the company to which they introduced her,—kept up her native liveliness of mind, and at the same time convinced her that pleasure was no enemy to virtue, or to reputation, when partook with persons of honour and discretion" (569).

13. In *Oroonoko*, Aphra Behn too regrets that her hero has "only a Female Pen to celebrate his Fame" (*Works* 3:88), but she positions herself as a popular and successful writer known to her audience; as Ballaster notes, fiction and drama were more accessible to women than poetry (73–74).

14. I cite *The British Recluse* from Backscheider and Richetti's Oxford anthology.

"What Ann Lang Read"

Eliza Haywood and Her Readers

Christine Blouch

*No one who has not dabbled among old books knows how
rare have become the strictly popular publications of a non-
literary kind which a generation of the lower middle class has
read and thrown away. Eliza Haywood lives in the minds of
men solely through one very coarse and cruel allusion to her
made by Pope in the Dunciad. She was never recognised among
people of intellectual quality; she ardently desired to belong to
literature, but her wish was never seriously gratified, even by
her friend Aaron Hill. Yet she probably numbered more
readers, for a year or two, than any other person in the British
realm. She poured forth what she called "little Performances"
from a tolerably respectable press; and the wonder is that in
these days her abundant writings are so very seldom to be met
with. The secret doubtless is that her large public consisted
almost wholly of people like Ann Lang. Eliza was read by
servants in the kitchen, by seamstresses, by basket-women, by
'prentices of all sorts, male and female, but mostly the latter.
For girls of this sort there was no other reading of a light kind
in 1724. It was Eliza Haywood or nothing.*

Edmund Gosse, "What Ann Lang Read"

Ann Lang reminds us of a central dilemma within critical discourse
that factors gender into the uneasy equations that balance assump-

tions about texts and their readers. Who was Ann Lang? We have a sole, slim fact from which to speculate: she read Eliza Haywood. This much we know from Edmund Gosse's anecdotal account of stumbling across Ann Lang's library, which consisted entirely of Haywood's novels—"cheap novels" (161)—of the early 1720s. The real, historical Ann Lang, a woman reader who lived and undoubtedly died in the eighteenth century, does not emerge in Gosse's essay; what survives instead is her reincarnation as a seamlessly constructed paradigm of reception. More to the point is the tenacity with which the paradigm endured. The paradigmatic constructed reader—Haywood's reader—certainly antedated Gosse's late nineteenth-century articlation of her, and would prove malleable enough to adapt readily to late twentieth-century critical discourse. There, and expressed only somewhat less explicitly, she framed the terms of Haywood's introduction to the critical audience that reads Haywood today. This essay traces the process of literary history, and literary politics, by which Ann Lang became so particularly problematic a relative in an already complicated reading genealogy. A related question to be explored is the extent to which Ann Lang remains a legacy for the reader of Eliza Haywood today.

Even if Ann Lang collected only Haywood's very early works, her library would have been sizable—more than twenty-five titles, not counting eight volumes of collected works, by the end of 1725. Numerous or not, or rather in part because they *are* so numerous, these early works of Haywood's are the texts most consistently characterized as repeating one another endlessly.[1] As such, the texts that Ann Lang read can accordingly be dispatched *en masse* with facility, and, as our critical history clearly shows, largely were. Inherent in the process loomed an implicit corollary: assumptions about the generic text—with its generic plot, generic protagonist, and generic author—correspond to assumptions about a generic reader.

To redeploy the term "generic" text in this context, is, not surprisingly, a strategy inspired by the irony that while Haywood's works of the 1720s are portrayed by critics as generic, the individual texts still strenuously resist any notion of genre at all. *Love in Excess* is now generally termed a novel, though a qualified (early, amatory, pre-1740) novel, and through many years of creative syntax was termed almost anything but. Like most of Haywood's publications of the 1720s, its history reflects the tortured nomenclature of those subcategories of a category that is itself a diminutive of the "N" word—amatory novella, for example. The difficulty originated with Haywood, of course; according to her, her 1720s works comprise a History, Secret History, Amour(s), Secret Amours, Memoir, Secret Memoir, Intrigue, Secret Intrigue, one Historical Novel, a Discourse, Remarks, several Accounts, and a Conversation, among others. We have generally accepted that the terms were used, as they are read, with relative interchangeability,[2] and thus the works remain simultaneously all genres and none.

However defined, according to Gosse, these texts are "strictly popular," a term that even today lacks the literal or metaphorical apposition of the strictly literary (as it *certainly* did in the eighteenth century); instead the term predictably excludes literature altogether. The retroactive definition of a strictly popular literature has been problematic in any case ever since Ian Watt's argument that, though more accessible to the middle class than other kinds of literature, the novel was not, "strictly speaking," a popular literary form (1957 ed., 42). Even so, popular texts that might to Gosse otherwise be comparable, such as *Roxana* and *Moll Flanders,* are different cases, exempted from Haywoodian categorizations on a flat gender basis: "The footman might read *Roxana,* and the hackney-writer sit up after his toil over *Moll Flanders;* there was much in these romances to interest men. But what had Ann Lang to do with stories so cold and harsh? She read Eliza Haywood" (163).

Thus Haywood's generic, popular texts were assigned a generic, non-literary reader. Accordingly, it is necessary to reconsider Ann Lang, as well as what Ann Lang read, or at least to consider how reading a Haywood text may continue to depend, for us as well as for Gosse, on reading its reader. It was after all Ann Lang, as much as Haywood, who wanted to "belong to literature." The critical attitudes that launched preemptive strikes which so effectively kept Lang and Haywood out thus bear keeping in mind.

We know that assumptions about readers and the act of reading are related, and that the equations are particularly unequivocal for women readers of amatory fiction: "When a lady in Eliza Haywood's novels receives a note from a gentleman, 'all her Limbs forget their Function, and she sinks fainting on the Bank, in much the same posture as she was before she rais'd herself a little to take the Letter.' I am positive that Ann Lang practised this series of attitudes in the solitude of her garret" (Gosse 165). In this formulation, the inability of both the text's author and its reader to discriminate differences among classes of literary function, between bad literature and real life (or real literature), are one and the same; Haywood's literary posturing, so to speak, is reified in Ann Lang's physical postures. The ability to draw literary distinctions, not surprisingly, is a metonym for social and economic class distinctions to Gosse. His answer to his own question—"Who is Ann Lang?"—momentarily makes the question seem rhetorical: "Alas, I am not sure" (161), he replies. His wholly disingenuous disclaimer, however, is the prelude instead to a prompt series of precisely formulated definitions. Ann Lang, he notes, has signed her name in each copy, in letters that are "round and laboriously shaped, while the form is always the same, and never 'Ann Lang, her book,' which is what one would expect" (161). He concludes that it is "not the hand of a person of quality: I venture to concluded that she who wrote it was a milliner's apprentice or a servant-girl" (161). One follows the formula—handwriting, occupation, class—and the addition, which establishes her garret reading habits. That Gosse would have attributed the same reading habits to William Musgrave, whose library included some of the same early Haywood titles, remains unthinkable.[3]

Gosse's gossip about Ann Lang—his book is titled *Gossip in a Library*—is characteristic of a critical discourse that would persist. Even some of his language seems endemic to the discourse of gossip rather than idiosyncratic, which is perhaps why a quaint syntax finds its way into otherwise sophisticated and considerably more contemporary critical works. It is useful in this regard to remember that Patricia Meyer Spacks defines gossip as the unconsidered desire to give an opinion without having to ponder too deeply, as a discourse that protects its participants from engagement with each other, and as one that can "solidify a group's sense of itself by heightening consciousness of 'outside' (inhabited by those talked about) and 'inside' (the temporarily secure territory of the talkers)" (*Gossip* 5). The discourse of gossip marked, perhaps dominated, Haywood's introduction to a general contemporary critical audience, a process that began a few decades ago. Even as they first engaged in the necessary and important task of reintroducing Haywood's work to the inside of general critical discourse, contemporary critics felt compelled to make simultaneous apologia to keep her "outside." This they generally accomplished by gossiping about Ann Lang.

In the influential work *Popular Fiction Before Richardson,* John Richetti paid significant attention to Haywood, and as he reintroduced her texts, also introduced his own version of Ann Lang. He termed this as Haywood's "ideal reader," a "person" (who is a woman) who "could be expected to possess a certain imaginative expertise, a sophistication of a sort which required emotional intensity rather than documentary paraphernalia in order to accept and participate in the narrative" (1969 ed., 168). The notion of inside and outside dominates the coded language of Richetti's formulation, in which the percipient reader, a critic and inside the discourse, understands that a "certain" imaginative expertise constitutes the impercipient reader, who remains outside. Adept as we are at decoding gossip, we perform the simultaneous translation that seems redundant when articulated: Haywood's reader has imagination and emotion, but no expertise and no sophistication—an Ann Lang in her garret. The attitude appeared elsewhere and often, sometimes expressed more implicitly, as when Jerry Beasley wrote that Haywood's works were "widely read among a certain set" (*Novels* 160). Interestingly, such a discourse encourages the percipient critic to reach this conclusion without engaging other critics and without having to ponder too deeply or ask for more salient information ("documentary paraphernalia") about the impercipient reader. In such a context the modern reader (modernity constituting one component of percipience) is privileged almost automatically, a distinction that draws another line between inside and outside; while Ann Lang swoons, modern critics "naturally" find little to admire in her novels (Richetti, *Popular* 180).

That critics as different as Gosse and Richetti link a specific and similarly defined class of reading experience to a specific formulation of social and economic class reminds us of how profoundly class issues manifest themselves in discursive practice. Class was an issue, of course, perhaps *the* issue, to eighteenth-century critics of novels and novel-readers as well; Haywood wrote during a time when, as Henry Fielding would ingenuously complain, the world of letters was in the process of becoming not only a democracy, but an anarchy, and when even criticism had been taken over by a "large body of irregulars." Neither Gosse nor Richetti is an irregular, which bridges many differences; the most striking, in this context, is that while the former intended to effectively exclude Haywood's works from the library, the intention of the latter was quite the opposite. The distinction is not beside the point, and in fact is fundamental to it, since part of my intent is to review the terms of Haywood's introduction to contemporary critical discourse. The unnecessary observation that Richetti's early formulations of Haywood's fiction preceded a substantial body of work that continues to make those fictions available is a given. Here, the focus is rather on the contradictions inherent in the curious agreements of critiques that are differently aimed, historically removed, and nevertheless united by a similarily constituted valuation of readership.

On one level, both Gosse and Richetti might be said to express a retroactive class anxiety by resisting the democratization of Haywood's reading public with a reading theory rooted in the kind of aristocratic ideology defined by Michael McKeon.[4] Ann Lang represents a new class of reader; unfortunately, she consumes literature as indiscriminately as the nouveau riche spend money. Why this "new audience" of women consumed books so voraciously has also been defined. They were "a group eager for the basic pleasures of fiction—identification, projection, vicarious participation, and ideological alignment—and relatively insensitive to the more subtle and specifically 'literary' satisfactions" as well as an audience "unconcerned or unaware of the greater moral and intellectual validity which is the rationale of the novella's moderate realism" (Richetti, *Popular* 176). As do the nouveau riche, these new readers experience pleasure in acquisition and consumption without a corresponding sense of the true end to which the commodity might be used. Ann Lang, Gosse notes, is even somewhat an exception, and kept her books in good condition, while "most of her sisters, of Eliza's great *clientele,* did not know how to treat a book" (163). Still, the Ann Langs who want to belong to literature are only made ridiculous by their attempts to do so—as is Ann Lang when she signs her book in the wrong way, as are the nouveau riche who think that money will entitle them to membership in a class that has erected other, invisible barriers. Ann Lang and her sisters will remain marginal figures to the world of literature, until their social standing improves, or—and not coincidentally, according to Gosse—until they have a real novel to read:

> If Ann Lang lived on until the publication of *Pamela*—especially if during the interval she had bettered her social condition—with what ardor must she have hailed the advent of what, with all its shortcomings, was a book worth gold. Perhaps she went to Vauxhall with it in her muff, and shook it triumphantly at some middle-aged lady of her aquaintance. Perhaps she lived long enough to see one great novel after another break forth to lighten the darkness of life. She must have looked back on the pompous and lascivious pages of Eliza Haywood, with their long-drawn palpitating intrigues, with positive disgust. The English novel began in 1740, and after that date there was always something wholesome for Ann Lang and her sisters to read. (169)

We can only admire the relative consistency of Ann Lang's first encounter with the new species of writing; she gossiped about it at Vauxhall. A more relevant irony in the scenario emerges in the near certainty that not only did the "new" Ann Lang read *Pamela*, she still read Haywood. *Pamela* was, in fact, the cause of Haywood's reemerging with a vengeance from a relative hiatus in novel publication that had lasted through the 1730s. She responded to Richardson with *Anti-Pamela; or Feign'd Innocence Detected*, the successful parody that appeared in 1741. Next, with a prompt and characteristic versatility, Haywood, having succeeded with the satire, published an imitation (*The Virtuous Villager; or, Virgin's Victory*, 1742). Haywood was acknowledged as author of the commercially successful *Virtuous Villager*, but not as author of the pseudonymous *Anti-Pamela.*[5] Thus, depending on her evolving tastes in literature, Ann Lang probably read either the imitation or the parody; more interesting is the distinct possibility that she read and enjoyed both. In any case, she would certainly have continued to encounter Haywood, who published, from 1741 on, every year until her death in 1756.

Still, to return to the fundamental question: Who exactly did read Haywood in the early 1720s? There is evidence that an Ann Lang who was a milliner's assistant could not have afforded a Haywood library, nor would she be likely to have attended Haywood's plays, which Gosse notes she did (162). Haywood's early biographer George Whicher made the point that "no one of scanty means" could have afforded Haywood's early popular sellers, priced at one to three shillings (13); only one of Haywood's early novels, *The City Jilt* (1726), was issued in cheap form, because, according to Whicher, "T. Bailey, the printer, evidently combined his printing business with the selling of patent medicines" (13n). Writing about Haywood in the 1960s, Robert Adam Day agreed that Ann Lang could not have afforded Haywood's books: "In fact, such people as servants would most naturally come by novels like Mrs. Haywood's when they were discarded by the gentry, rather than by purchase, for her books were too expensive to be bought outright by those who worked for a living. On the other hand, many women of the upper classes figure in Mrs. Haywood's dedications, and Lady Betty Germain owned a copy of her *Love-Letters on All Occasions . . .* Doubtless Mrs. Haywood's wares were known to the more frothy minds of the polite world and to the daughters of middle-class trading families" (73). Class anxiety may explain Day's contradictory impulse to expand Haywood's reading public into the upper classes and the polite world at the same time he restricted it to traders' daughters and frothy minds. He also gendered the audience for Haywood's fiction much more absolutely than he did the more general audience for epistolary fiction;[6] the contradiction is especially interesting since the former undoubtedly shared a crossover audience with the latter, of which Haywood was in any case an avid practitioner.

Why was the twentieth-century emergence of Haywood's early reader such a problem of definition? In part because the Ann Lang imagined by Gosse is one of those contradictory constituents of the early novel's public: novel readers who could not afford novels. These readers in reality were more likely held back until roughly 1740 from full participation in the literary scene by the high price of books, as Watt first described it. As Cheryl Turner points out, a number of circulation and publication practices served a bridging role that helps to account for the discrepancy first noted by Watt between income and readership,[7] but these were not likely to have been Ann Lang's source. It appears from the signature with which she unintentionally provided so much information about her life that Ann Lang bought her copies outright, accumulating what she, at least, would have termed a library, one that would carefully preserve her disposable fictions.

Watt's discussion of novel readership remains most germane in this context perhaps in that he foregrounded the tenuous nature of much of the evidence we have for determining that audience and the subsequently conditional nature of many of our conclusions.[8] The theoretical black hole of formal realism—women writers—made those cautions significantly less compelling when gender became the wild card in questions of readership, particularly, as Terry Lovell among others demonstrated, in a Marxist analysis.[9] Subsequent discussions of the composition of novel readership, represented, though certainly not comprehensively, by such critics as Lawrence Stone, Michael McKeon, and J. Paul Hunter, greatly expanded the theoretical boundaries of the discussion, and provided (sometimes conflicting) demographics. It remained for feminist and gender theorists, however, joining the task shared by these other literary critics and historians, to resituate the novel-reading audience in terms of reading and gender. Feminist theorists ranging from Jane Spencer to Catherine Gallagher, a number in fact clearly too varied and numerous to list, addressed the question of the early modern woman reader in particular. Still, Ros Ballaster's *Seductive Forms* was the first significant work about amatory fictions of the early century, or what Ann Lang read, while Turner's *Living by the Pen* was the first significant source of demographic information about readers of the same material. Ballaster's comprehensive readings constitute a compelling argument that the movement from amatory fiction to a post-1740 feminocentric moral idealization eventually limited women authors' "possibilities for negotiation" (210). Her extensive analysis of the construction of a female reader,[10] also invaluable, articulate how the the figure of the bourgeois woman reader as the signifier of a newly constituted cultural order became most clearly articulated by Addison and Steele;[11] the question remains whether the Ann Lang articulated by Gosse approximates this *Spectator* reader. Feminist theorists have necessarily focused, with tremendous effect, on theoretical constructions of the early modern woman reader, but these constructs mediate an uneasy balance with, for example, the decidedly "real" (or so they are defined) constructs of a floating class—women and "upper" servants, for example—who allegedly consumed Haywood's early fiction.

A paucity of uncontested demographic and readership statistics, publication revenue figures gone AWOL, and Haywood's scanty biography have all contributed to the kind of speculation that creates a paradigm of reception as durable as Ann Lang. Identifying the historical person with certainty remains an elusive goal, and one that is negotiated differently in the best recent sources. It should thus not be surprising that none of the accounts to date ultimately identify the real Ann Lang, or even confirm the conventional certainty that she was a she.[12] If she may have been a man, she may also have been an upper servant, a member of the polite world, or a friend of Aaron Hill's or Haywood's. She may or may not have had a frothy mind. We do not know. Nevertheless we retain an inherited attitude problem about her.

The most successful attempts to adjust it begin with the complaints of Haywood's contemporaries about her readers. We know something of the extent to which they had problems of their own with Ann Lang. That Pope thought altogether too many people read Haywood is an implicit assumption of the war he waged in *The Dunciad* to keep Haywood and Ann Lang from belonging to literature. Pope paid a particularly concentrated attention to what Ann Lang read in the *Variorum,* where two Haywood titles appear among the seven carried by the book-laden ass in the text's best-known frontispiece. One of the titles is "Court of Cariman," for *Secret History of . . . the Court of Caramania,* against which Pope had a specific grudge, but it is the pointed addition of the book spine labeled "Haywoods Nov"—covering everything else—that results in Haywood's disproportionate representation on the frontispiece. The matter is complicated further by the speculation that Ann Lang may also have been a *Dunciad* reader. Pope's largely visual caricature is based on the portrait of Haywood by Elisha Kirkall that prefaced her 1724 collected works; the satire thus operates on a notion of shared audience on some level, since its efficacy depends in great measure on the reader's familiarity with the Kirkall print.

Pope is also said to have had a much more specific kind of impact in the conventional wisdom that his satire subsequently drove

Haywood out of print. This notion too makes contradictory assumptions about a shared readership; if Haywood's readers and subscribers constituted a different literary market, as they allegedly did, Pope's impact would sensibly be characterized as oblique, instead of the opposite. One might note that Haywood's fellow *Dunciad* sufferers had a considerably more sanguine view of her appearance,[13] perhaps not surprisingly, but in any case, these other "dunce authors" are rarely considered to have suffered effects so unequivocal. If the majority were paid political writers largely unaffected by Pope because they wrote to order, according to one theory (Feather 104), they were also men, not women authors of popular fiction. More likely reasons for Haywood's relative abandonment of fiction lie elsewhere, and begin with the possibility that Haywood was victim of a transitional period for the novel market as a whole[14]—a phenomenon that Pope had not created, but one on which he could certainly capitalize.

By the middle of the century the debate that centered in very specific ways on women and the act of reading had become a thriving literary discourse in its own right, and significantly, some of its most dedicated participants were women, including Charlotte Lennox in *The Female Quixote; or, The Adventures of Arabella* (1752)—a book that might be said to be about Ann Lang, thirty years and several social classes removed.[15] In *Henrietta* (1753) Lennox satirizes Haywood directly, representing her as the negative valance of social and literary class aspirations in the form of an eager landlady tempting the virtuous protagonist to put aside Fielding as bedtime reading: "[T]here is Mrs. Haywood's Novels, did you ever read them? Oh! they are the finest, love-sick, passionate stories; I assure you, you'll like them vastly; Pray take a volume of Haywood upon my recommendation."[16]
We also encounter Ann Langs in the form of the two Sanson sisters in the anonymous mid-century work *The Sisters; or the History of Lucy and Caroline Sanson* (1754). They too represent a familiar paradigm of the credulous reader: "'Tis no wonder . . . that the young girls grew vain, foolish and affected; *Cassandra, Cleopatra, Heywood's* novels, and above all the works of the inimitable *Fielding,* with a thousand more romantic books of the same kind (wherewith the present age, so happily abounds,) were the constant employment of their days; pleased with the wondrous relations, and magic scenes of

joy, success, and transports, found in these charming entertainers, each began to despise the addresses of rude villagers, and to sigh for enchanted raptures and delightful scenes, with which they had heard the great metropolis so nobly abounded" (4). The relation of reading novels to notions of social mobility remains a conventionally dangerous equation for the Sansons, but one that adds up differently than it does for Richetti and Gosse. Moreover, it is Fielding, more than Haywood, who makes the Sansons sigh for those enchanted raptures. In *The Covent Garden Journal,* Fielding had himself made use of the truism that young women were more susceptible victims of novels than were men, writing that when "the Head of a very sensible Person is entirely subverted by reading Romances, this Concession seems to me more easy to be granted in the Case of a young Lady than of an old Gentleman" (1:281). That he was the culprit in the case of the Sansons, however, might have surprised Fielding.

As Henrietta's and the Sansons' reading reminds us, the mid-century debate about women and reading was being carried out while an equation that Laurie Langbauer termed "men" and "novels"[17] was still in flux, a crucial point in considering Haywood's reader of the early century. In the 1720s Haywood was engaged in a literary practice that, like the Sansons' reading, continues to resist our contemporary sensibilities about both readers and literature. Without a controlling sense of uncertainty, our inherited construct of Ann Lang assumes that readers approached a Haywood novel of the 1720s with the certainty of expectation with which Leslie Rabine describes today's Harlequin reader approaching carefully prearranged publisher's racks—a problematic assumption.[18] Until we reconstruct Haywood's early reader more accurately, our reading of her texts might be better informed on terms that at least foreground the dilemmas these readers presented to their contemporaries, and not to critics of the 1990s.

We also must admit we know less, rather than more, about Ann Lang, because despite Gosse's disclaimer that he knows who she is, it is his very certainty which elicits the interesting proposition that Haywood's works did not last *because* they were read by Ann Lang. We should simultaneously be reminded that, according to Gosse, Ann Lang had *nothing else:* "It was Eliza Haywood or nothing." A natural consequence of the discourse of gossip about Ann Lang and about what she reads has been the historically tenacious conclusion that the former is so eminently readable that we need not bother with the "unreadable"[19] latter at all.

With this lengthy prolegomena in mind, we can turn to one of the works that Ann Lang almost certainly read, one in which Haywood both enacts and annihilates the myth of persecuted virtue. In the compact *Fantomina; or, Love in a Maze* (1725), both the text and the protagonist offer a convenient study of the generic versus the particular. To briefly recount the text's initial situation, a young lady of "Birth, Beauty, Wit, and Spirit," spends an evening at the theater in her box, where: "[S]he perceived several Gentlemen extremely pleased themselves with entertaining a Woman who sat in the corner of the Pit, and, by her Air and Manner of receiving them, might easily be known to be one of those who come there for no other Purpose, than to create Acquaintance with as many as seem desirous of it. . . . This excited a Curiosity in her to know in what Manner these Creatures were address'd" (257–58).[20] The protagonist of *Fantomina*, like Moll Flanders, withholds her true identity; like Moll, she names everything but herself (Beer 75). Fantomina names herself even more often than Moll, four times in separate identities that nevertheless remain generic. The protagonist, introduced in the language of the generic heroine of amatory fiction, soon disappears into the progressive identities of Fantomina, Celia, the Widow Bloomer, and Incognita, and into the fantasy of sexual power that is located in the construct of fluid identity. The fantasy begins the moment she sees the whore in a playhouse pit and decides to indulge her "little Whim" to dress herself like the prostitute. The rest of the text might be said to operate as a play within a play, from the moment "Fantomina" appears in the pit at the following night's performance—of an unnamed play—and begins to stage her own.

Haywood's protagonist initially seems unaware of what her own play's catastrophe will consist of, other than the gratification of what she restates as "innocent Curiosity" (258). The target with whom she decides to "please Herself" (260) is named Beauplaisir (perhaps the nearest eighteenth-century equivalent of "boy toy" imaginable). The moment that the protagonist approaches Beauplaisir as Fantomina, instead of the young lady who knows him in her real identity, marks the beginning of a remarkable transformation in Fantomina and an equally remarkable transformation of a semiotics of desire into co-herent language: "Strange and unaccountable were the Whimsies she was posses'd of,—wild and incoherent her Desires,—unfix'd and undetermin'd her Resolutions . . .—Bent, however, on meeting him, whatever shou'd be the Consequence, she . . . took Lodgings" (261). It is the young lady who is incoherent, experiencing a desire that is literally unarticulated, but Fantomina who engages the room, one of the transitions from passive to active that signals her assumption of authorship. Perhaps most astonishing is the sheer speed with which the new playwright subsequently acquires stage-management skills. These include a facility for quick changes in costume, props, and dia-logue, which support identities that become mutually reinforcing both logistically and sexually:

> And it must be confessed, indeed, that she preserved an Economy in the management of this Intreague, beyond what almost any Woman but herself ever did: . . .—The Business of her Love has engros'd her til Six in the Evening, and before Seven she has been dres'd in a different Habit, and in another Place. Slippers and a Night-Gown loosely flowing, has been the Garb in which he has left the languish-ing *Fantomina*—Lac'd, and adorn'd with all the Blaze of Jewels, has [Beauplaisir] in less than an Hour after seen . . . the Haughty Awe-inspiring Lady.—A thousand Times has he stood amaz'd at the prodigious Likeness between his little Mistress, and this Court Beauty . . . and it is not impossible that it was to the Thoughts of this (as he supposed) unenjoy'd Charmer, she ow'd in great measure the Vigour of his latter Caresses. (266–67)

At this point in the text, the protagonist's ability to manage the ensu-ing series of swiftly and intricately staged progressive identities seems unlimited, and plot complications will mark her increasing command of dialogue. The young lady's increasing control of her sexuality is, from this point on, located squarely in her control of language and a corresponding understanding of Beauplaisir's—especially his body language. As the maid Celia, "who now understood that Language but too well" (269), she anticipates her seduction; by the time she intercepts his town-bound coach as the Widow Bloomer, she controls it. At this point, roughly the second act, the reader is prepared for the forthcoming restaging of the initial seduction scene; it will be the point in the text at which victim and victimizer exchange roles (Schofield *Masking* 191). Fantomina's strategy is to redeploy the incoherence to which in the first seduction she had been "reduc'd." When she subsequently uses tears it will be with a "Parenthesis of Sighs and Groans" (272), the sounds of sex; when next she "flutters with dread" (279), it will be to reinforce Beauplaisir's certainty of his own subjectivity; when next she faints, it will overwhelm Beauplaisir and get her carried to bed. She has become a dramaturge, using a familiar script and the conventional language (and sounds, and breathless silences) of amatory fiction, signaling a series of expectations that would be wholly unexceptional except that their status as artifice remains foregrounded and she has written her own scenes.

One wonders exactly which attitudes Ann Lang would have been inspired to practice in the privacy of her garret after reading *Fantomina,* at least if one grants that the process of destabilizing the protagonist's generic identities may simultaneously destabilize the scenario of the ingenuous reader consuming a predictable script. Nothing about the text is a certainty, but I will suggest how some of the text's ironies might be read, then and now. It is certainly true that even the most ingenuous woman reader can participate in the protagonist's increasing sense of control, which corresponds to the ironic complications of Beauplaisir's spectacular lack of acuity. With two of the four identities in residence, for example, both the Widow and Fantomina write Beauplaisir letters, the former of which is an invitation to visit, the latter a complaint. The irony of Beauplaisir's responses, written and received simultaneously, is grounded literally and deliberately in the language of identity. To his most recent inamorata he writes, "Never was Women form'd to charm like you: Never did any look like you,— write like you,—bless like you" (275). To Fantomina, he apologizes, saying that he "had unluckily forgot the Name of the Woman at whose House you are" (276). One might say that Fantomina has become mistress of her own identity in a literal way, or, in Beauplaisir's words, "Mistress of the soul *and all the faculties of* Beauplaisir" (276; emphasis added). Meanwhile the ironies of these textual encounters mean that the reader remains engaged in a series of self-conscious, at times self-referential, questions about the reception and authorship of texts.

The problem of naming, a process by this point tightly controlled by the protagonist, manifests itself in the play's last act on several levels. The process begins, appropriately enough for an author invested in language control, with a word game, when we learn that the Widow, ready to move on, has "another Project *in embrio*, which she soon ripen'd into Action" (278). The reader may or may not have become perspicacious enough to hazard that she has more *in embryo* than a project. The protagonist's body will signal the imminent collapse of both the protagonist-playwright's authorship and her transgression of sexual identities. The result is a shift in the text's relative positions of power, as novelist ascends and playwright recedes, and as the theatergoer/reader begins to guess at a catastrophe of which the playwright herself is unaware.

Before the fantasy ends, however, it will become more extraordinary. The economy of the theatrical production expands to three separate sets, including, besides the modest lodgings that house Fantomina and the Widow Bloomer, a mansion (hired by the week) from which the young lady writes her last, evocative epistle to Beauplaisir: "There is but one Thing in my Power to refuse you, which is the Knowledge of my Name" (281). To the reader, the understatement represents an additional irony, since the reader knows the young lady's name no more than does the clueless Beauplaisir. His reaction to Incognita, no surprise, is confidence, not imagining that she varies so much from other women "as to be able to refuse the Knowledge of any Thing to the Man she lov'd with that Transcendency of Passion she profess'd, and which his many Successes with the Ladies gave him Encouragment enough to believe" (282). The reader's response to Beauplaisir's response is also confidence—we read at least one of the levels of irony— but clearly a false confidence, and an uncertain consolation for a reader whose position relative to the author corresponds roughly to Beauplaisir's.

The curtain that is dropped in *Fantomina* is as abrupt and anticlimatic as the end of any interrupted fantasy. More bodies intervene; the young lady's absent mother returns, and the protagonist discovers she is pregnant. Even so, it is a very near thing for the talented actress: "By eating little, lacing prodigious strait, and the Advantage of a great Hoop-Petticoat, however, her Bigness was not take notice of, and perhaps, she would not have been suspected till the Time of her going

into the Country . . . if the Time of it had not happen'd much sooner
than she expected" (287). The young lady, attending a ball (we do not
know if it is a masquerade), goes into labor.

Fantomina is what Nancy K. Miller once termed "a heroine's text,"
one that predicates the primacy of female experience with various
thematic and structural mechanisms; and, although the text is ultimately dysphoric, it is not inevitably so, just as Haywood suggests
that not even biology so much as timing dooms her protagonist. Moreover, the young lady is banished primarily because her mother fears a
"Renewing of the Crime" (290); the illegitimate child is a girl (sex
certain, name unknown). A purely dysphoric reading recognizes the
unsatisfactory nature of the text's termination, but elides its ambiguities, forgetting that even Incognita was developing other plans, that
the mansion of her dreams was rented by the week. Such a reading
also fails to account for otherwise oddly polemical nature of the fantasy and for the protagonist's obsessive attention to dramatic logis-
tics. The text relies, for the power of its fantasy, on a recognition of
fantasy's kineticism as well as its danger, and thus euphoric and dysphoric elements coexist, often contradicting one another, in a tension
of texts that begins the moment that protagonist renames herself. That
a birth (perhaps) permanently interrupts the fantasy also identifies
the tension of Fantomina's imaginative experience as exclusively female, reminding us of Susan Winnett's suggestions about reading texts
in light of women's biological morphology.[21]

It is necessary to ask again how Ann Lang might have read
Fantomina's fantasy, and how we might read Haywood's. A case in
point is the single occasion on which Haywood interrupts an otherwise straightforward third-person narration to address a reader she
defines as skeptical, and at least potentially as male:

It may, perhaps, seem strange that Beauplaisir should in such near
Intimacies continue still deceived. I know there are Men who will
swear it is an Impossibility, and that no Disguise could hinder them
from knowing a Woman they had once enjoy'd. I can only say, that
besides the Alteration which the Change of Dress made in her, she
was so admirably skill'd in the Art of feigning, that she had the
Power of putting on almost what Face she pleas'd, and knew so
exactly how to form her Behaviour to the Character she represented,

that all the Comedians at both Playhouses are infinitely short of her Performances. (274)

In this passage, Haywood's deliberately ingenuous invitation to the reader simultaneously raises and forestalls the possibility of his (or her) participation in erotic textuality; in a sleight of hand she introduces those parts of the body most nearly concerned with Near Intimacies, and promptly sidesteps to discuss dress and face. The practice signals one of the text's central ironies, for although Ann Lang is often said to have sought a form of soft pornography, it is not accidental that in a text about sexual aggression, eroticism is notably absent. *Fantomina* lacks even a single warm scene, at least in Haywood's relative terminology. Instead, a series of offstage consummations render the erotic constitution of sexuality as a consideration secondary to the onstage, linguistic process of self-identification. Eroticism, as Incognita *et al.* demonstrate, can be stage-managed. Remaining in the foreground is what Spacks once termed a problem in the imaginative relations between the sexes in which men keep imagining women ("Changelessness" 273).[22] Beauplaisir keeps imagining he knows the text's incognita as object; she remains, however, subject in each identity, "directing the spectacle of courtship that would subject her" (Warner, "Elevation" 587). Even more to the point, the author maintains a similar dialectic with her reader. Whether all of the text's ironies and ambiguities translated, to Haywood's readers, as a series of questions about subjectivity in readership is of course uncertain. At the least, however, if the credulous reader indeed practiced all of Fantomina's postures in her garret, Ann Lang would have become an accomplished actress—and not necessarily, as Haywood suggests in the preceding passage, a tragedian.

A Gentleman, who applies the little Ingenuity he is Master of to no other Study than that of sowing Dissension . . . *pretends* . . . that in the Character of a French Baroness, I have attempted to expose the Reputation of an English Woman of Quality. I shou'd be sorry to think the Actions of any of our Ladies such as cou'd give room for a Conjecture of the Reality of what he wou'd suggest. But suppose there were indeed an Affinity between the Vices I have described, and those of some Woman he knows (for doubtless, if there be, she must be of *his* Acquaintance) I leave the World to judge to whom she is indebted for becoming the Subject of Ridicule, to *me* for drawing a Picture, whose Original is unknown, or to *him* who writes her Name at the bottom of it.

To state what was obvious to many of her readers, Haywood was often disingenuous. It is unlikely that they would have taken the preceding preface to *The Injur'd Husband* (1723) at face value, even without the subsequent and wholly predictable claim to verisimilitude. It should not surprise us that Haywood credited her readers with the ability to discern truths that are often less than literal, and it is one of the contexts in which we might read Ann Lang's responses to Haywood's fiction. The uneasy and unexplicated premise that Haywood thought her readers always took her at her word has marked the literary history of both the author and her readers. In cases in which Haywood's stated purpose is clearly at odds with the fiction, it may be such a critical consensus about Haywood's readers that has muted the kind of analysis one would expect to ensue—an analysis that considers textual contradictions as strategic deliberations, for example. *Fantomina* may be the most irresistible of Haywood's early texts for these purposes, but I would like to briefly suggest other ways that Haywood's early works seem to position questions about readers and textual identification as central.

Another of the works that Ann Lang no doubt read, for example, was *The British Recluse; or, The Secret History of Cleomira, Suppos'd Dead* (1722), Haywood's highly successful second original novel and one on which she apparently spent more time than was her norm.[23] The relationship of the two seduced protagonists makes the text's seduction of its reader a particularly focused experience. Belinda and Cleomira are immediately united by a shared act of readership and authorship, writing their histories to one another: "[T]he Recluse had writ, *Undone by LOVE, and by the Ingratitude of faithless Man,* and the Recluse found in that which the other had writ, these Words, *For ever lost to Peace by LOVE and my own fond Belief.* As I expected! cry'd they out both together" (13). The tale recounts the conversations of the pair, who narrate their seduction (by the same man) in a process that becomes not only erotic but homoerotic. In a characteristic exchange, Cleomira begins: "[H]e had thrown himself down by me while he was speaking, and seizing both my Hands, and gently

forcing them to circle his Waist, join'd his Lips to mine with too strenuous a Pressure to suffer me to reproach the liberties he took" (85).
Her listener responds: "He now began to mingle Kisses and Embraces
with his Vows: My Hands were the first Victims of his fiery Pressures;
then my Lips, my Neck, my Breast, and more!—my Soul dissolved! its
Faculties overpowered!" (97).

Such deliberate placement of erotic discourse in *The British Recluse* provides the text's ongoing, simultaneous commentary on both
erotic and narrative seduction. Erotic discourse here is a story one
woman relates to another as a fiction; it also constitutes a fiction with
which a woman seduces herself. Meanwhile, an independent narrative voice contextualizes not so much the erotic act of seduction as the
erotic act of its relation. The reader, unlike Belinda and Cleomira,
thus has access to the textual discourse as well as to the meaning of
each protagonist's story. The meanings of textual discourse, however,
are ambiguous, and accordingly, so are significant features of the narrative, including a closure that sustains contradictory interpretations.
Cleomira and Belinda, locked in a perfect harmony from the moment
of their first meeting, remain locked in ostensible harmony at its end,
living together ("still," as the narrator promises in a felicitous present
tense) in tranquility. Janet Todd cites this ending as Haywood's version of sentimental friendship, but such a reading is supported only
uneasily by the text. In fact, the sentimental friendship that has been
invoked, perhaps to the point of parody, at the protagonists' first
meeting is just as deliberately parodied at the novel's end. Here, for
the first time, Cleomira interrupts, as Belinda relates that their mutual former lover has come to town: "Has he not seen you since you
came to Town? (interrupted the Recluse somewhat hastily)" (117).
When Belinda replies that she has resolved never to see him again, her
companion "seem'd perfectly pleas'd with this Assurance, and omitted nothing to strengthen her in this Resolution" (117). The strong
suggestion of heterosexual jealousy is wholly warranted; both Cleomira
and the text's reader can guess that Belinda is still in love, and that her
obsessive, eroticized narration has detailed an ongoing emotional involvement, rather than its discharge. The result? "There grew so entire a Friendship between these Ladies, that they were scarce a moment
asunder: Belinda quitted her Chamber, being desir'd by the Recluse to
take part of her Bed. Their common Misfortunes were a Theme not to

be exhausted" (117). Belinda's and Cleomira's final relationship is
something less and more than friendship, sentimental or otherwise; it
also reads as a mutually imprisoning relationship strongly marked
both by heterosexual and homoerotic components as well as by a
paradigm of shared sexual experience, readership, and authorship.
As Haywood's narrator demonstrates, or at least hints, Belinda and
Cleomira have created their own bad fictions. If they fail in their roles
as readers to understand the meaning of each others' stories, Ann
Lang may not.

Texts such as *The British Recluse* and *Fantomina* do not demon-
strably prove that Haywood considered her readers to be engaged in
a constant state of postmodern critical negotiations. Nevertheless it is
easy to see why the texts, as well as their readers, have demanded a
more or less wholesale reconsideration. What also emerges from reading Haywood today is a set of compelling reasons to resist attempts to
impose homogeneity upon both. One must also resist, of course, the
impulse to impose *something,* because there is no doubt that
Haywood's readers at times present an irresistable target. Eliza's readers
loved to excess. Consider, for example:

> Ingenious Haywood writes like one who knew
> The Pangs of Love and all its raptures too;
> O cou'd I boast that more than common Skill,
> Which guides her Fancy and directs her Quill
> When she so lively to her Reader shows,
> A tender Heart oppress'd with Am'rous Woes;
> My Passion I so clearly wou'd display,
> And to your view my Soul so open lay,
> Describe in Words well chose and apt to move,
> The agonizing Torments of my Love;
> The Thousand Wrecking sighs that rend my Breast,
> And Pangs of Jealousy that foe to rest;
> With all the Train of Ills which constant wait,
> On the Distress'd Despairing Lover's Fate
> That you, Unkind and Cruel shou'd confess
> Count *Delmont* never loved to such Excess.
> —"Writ on a blank leaf of a Lady's *Love in Excess*" (anon.)[24]

One can see how critics might consider such a reader and such an author to be engaged in a discourse in which common misfortunes have

become an exhaustible theme. At the same end of the continuum bridging assessments of Haywood's readership, however, is a facile, dangerously tempting, and relentless imposition of retroactive definitions that are as seamless as they are distorting: "[H]eroines of these old stories were all palpitating with sensibility, although that name had not yet been invented to describe their condition" (Gosse 165). The novel—or what Haywood thought she wrote—is a word that had already been invented in Haywood's time; it has been reinvented since.

It seems appropriate, since one of the purposes of this discussion was to review the terms of Haywood's introduction to contemporary critical discourse, to state the obvious, which is that the author, her works, and her readers have by no means negotiated a stable place in literary discourse. One can situate her works in a critical mainstream that may in fact be a tributary. Haywood's early works are particularly illustrative of the difficulties of the process; historically they have proved as complex for feminist theorists to situate as they were easy for traditionalists to dismiss, even as some of the critical negotiations that will determine their fate are being mediated elsewhere. Clearly the early works have found modern readers, the first response to historical neglect. *Fantomina* is certainly a case in point; it has received not only more critical attention than most of Haywood's early works, but has also been relatively widely anthologized, and thus is being consumed by a new (perhaps undiscriminating, perhaps unknowable) audience—university undergraduates. Whether Haywood's works will find readers numerous enough, however, remains a real question, attested to in part by the difficulties of both academic and commercial presses in establishing a threshold profitability for works by Haywood and other women authors of the long century. Ironically, the works so ubiquitous in the 1720s may experience another round of disposability, reprinted with relative fanfare only to be quietly remaindered later.

Still, the fact that Haywood's early works have found readers as good as those we find active in current discussions should mean that Ann Lang as a paradigm of reception is genuinely dead. We know it is not the constructed reader reading Haywood today; it is much harder, however, to articulate the proposition that perhaps it never was. Moreover, like Elvis, Ann Lang remains the subject of continued sightings. Some of the evidence is anecdotal, and some of it is gossip.[25] As readers of Haywood today we might, at a minimum, remind ourselves of the degree to which, historically, a Haywood text has elicited critical attention at the expense of its reader. Ann Lang may also, it seems only fair to add, loom as a proposition that is both more threatening and more relevant for women critics, who remain vulnerable to certain of the charges lodged so consistently against Haywood's historical reader in a way that male readers are not. One leaves, for example, any syntax that signals enthusiasm—the woman reader's first fatal step toward loving an author in excess—in the garret. We are reminded in any case that Ann Lang remains exactly as dead or alive, depending on one's perspective, as she was when first defined.

Notes

1. This was Richetti's argument, first in *Popular Fiction*, where he notes that the "fortuitous" *Love in Excess* served as the basis for her work over the next ten years, which repeated it (205, 207). The proposition that the texts are formulaic has since become more or less formulaic itself, even in such interesting arguments as those made by, for example, Boone (70–71) and Beasley (*Novels* 161). Warner's characterization of these texts as "disposable" is both enlightening and specific; he defines "books written in anticipation of their own obsolescence, and in acceptance of their own transient function as part of a culture of serial entertainments" ("Elevation" 579).

2. McKeon and Schulz, among others, have discussed the relative interchangeability of these terms in text-naming practices of the period, and Haywood's practice was consistent with that of her peers.

3. In the catalog of Musgrave's library (B.M. Add. MS 25,404), seven Haywood titles of the 1720s are included, among them *Idalia; or the Unfortunate Mistress* (1723), one of the titles Gosse mentions in Ann Lang's collection. Among Haywood's later works, Musgrave owned *Betsy Thoughtless* (1751).

4. Specifically, here, as McKeon defines it, one that assumes "the social order is not circumstantial and arbitrary, but corresponds to and expresses an analogous, intrinsic moral order" (*Origins* 131). More of McKeon's discussion of "The Destabilization of Social Categories," particularly his discussion of how the novel mediated the intersection of status and class orientations (171–75), would be relevant in a more extended discussion.

5. Nor is she still, at least consistently; *Anti-Pamela* is often attributed to Haywood only tentatively, for reasons that are not clear. Her authorship is verified by, for example, Alan D. McKillop, who cites the original publisher Cogan's catalogue record of selling the book, "by Mrs. Haywood,"

to Nourse in 1746. See *Samuel Richardson* (Chapel Hill: U of North Carolina P, 1936) 80.

6. This audience "probably excluded the poor, the learned, or the intellectual, the religious, and the commercial 'lower middle class.' . . . It included many members of the nobility and gentry, the bourgeois rich, the young, and the fashionable; and although the tastes of women may have dominated its choices in fiction, it also included many men" (77).

7. See Turner's discussion of circulating libraries, "numbers" books, serial reprint, and other publication practices (146–47).

8. See chapter 1; also especially 35, 47–49.

9. See especially chapter 2 of *Consuming Fiction*, although Lovell also uses Watt's thesis to demarcate her general argument.

10. See chapter 2.

11. Earlier important accounts of the construction of the female reader by Addison and Steele obviously include Shevelow's.

12. The sex of Haywood's reader is a case in point. McKeon both raises and questions the common perception that "women and servants of both sexes" were reading what Ann Lang read; see *Origins* 51–52. Hunter's chapter in *Before Novels* on "Readers Reading" (61–89), which provides among other information excellent notes on sources for literacy figures, is primarily concerned with revising upward Lawrence Stone's estimates of literacy during the century; he focuses much less on the question of the constitution of Haywood's and other women authors' reading public, noting that they were "evidently writing primarily for women readers" (71) in the early century. In "The Novel and Social/Cultural History," Hunter amplifies the issue considerably, but also retains the argument that Haywood's early works "seem to have had fairly distinct audiences defined by gender"; on this basis he registers a demur with Ballaster, arguing that cross-reading increased as the century progressed (37, 14n). Turner represents a compromise position: "Although female readers were probably the largest general source of demand for women's novels, these works were read and enjoyed by men, who did not necessarily restrict themselves to authors of repute" (138).

13. Theobald gave Haywood a copy of *Dunciad* "as a testimony of his esteem" and "acquaints her that Mr. Pope, by the profits of its publication, saved his library, wherein unpawned much learned lumber lay" (quoted in Whicher 126). William Chetwood wrote that Pope "has taken her for his Goddess of Dulness in his *Dunciad*, but she need not blush in such good Company" (57).

14. A point made by, among others, Turner (52), and previously by Day (222).

15. That Arabella's passage into enlightened readership is problematic is

evident, as a number of critics have discussed; for example, Langbauer analyzes the "price for renouncing romance and the acceding to male order" (83) as Arabella's loss of her identity as a woman. More recent excellent accounts of Lennox's and Arabella's negotiation of the form of fiction include those works listed in the related bibliography by Gallagher, Ross, and Levin.

16. Quoted in Ballaster (206).

17. See the introduction to Langbauer's *Women and Romance*, especially 2.

18. Rabine describes how Harlequin publishers' packaging, distribution, and display practices provide "guarantees" for readers (see 179–85). And although I draw on the analogy of the Harlequin romance to make a point about critics reading Haywood's readers, my use of the analogy is also problematic. Nevertheless work begun in the 1980s by critics such as Rabine and Janice Radway, focusing on the contemporary romance reader, would be relevant in a longer discussion to theoretical constructs of the woman reader of the 1720s.

19. The most spectacular definition of the unreadability of Haywood's early works is a series of observations by Richetti, who wrote that Haywood's language in *Love in Excess* is "virtually unreadable," a technique, "(perhaps instinct is a better word) is to evoke a female ethos to which her readers' response is a moral-emotional sympathetic vibration rather than a self-conscious and deliberate assent" (*Popular* 182). Nearly twenty years later, he redefined her unreadability as deliberate, as language that is "entirely and deliberately formulaic, a breathless rush of erotic/pathetic cliches that is in a real sense unreadable," meant to be "scanned hastily" for its evocative power, like Italian arias, "more like expressive noise than language" ("Voice" 266).

20. I cite the original edition of *Fantomina*, in *Secret Histories, Novels and Poems*, vol. 3 (London: D. Browne and S. Chapman, issued 1724, dated 1725), and cite original editions elsewhere unless noted. Most are recently issued or in forthcoming collections; *Fantomina* is particularly accessible, available for example in the excellent anthology *Popular Fiction by Women 1660–1730*, eds. Backscheider and Richetti.

21. Winnett argues in part that it is a gender bias of narrative theory which permits critics to conceptualize narrative dynamics in terms of an experience so effectively generalized that we forget that it has its source in an experience of the male body. Winnett reformulates narrative experience in terms of women's physical experience of sexual pleasure and of breastfeeding and childbirth, experiences based on a female morphology that manifest dynamic patterns unlike those of male body-centered narratologies. Specifically female experiences of arousal and discharge, Winnett argues, do not

result in a quiescence that can "conceptualized as a simulacrum of death" (509); the result is a narratological experience that is "*prospective*, full of the incipience that the male model will see resolved" (509) retrospectively.

22. Spacks argues that it is the imagined stability of women that makes them potentially comprehensible as male-imagined paradigms of the woman-as-sinner or woman-as-saint, while "the imagined volatility of women makes them hardly worth trying to understand" (282).

23. *The British Recluse* went through at least three editions in two years before its inclusion in the collected works of 1724. More than a year had passed between Chetwood's announcement of the book and its advertisement for publication; four Haywood titles would follow in 1723, and seven in 1724.

24. *The Ladies Journal* 5 (16 February 1726–27).

25. One may or may not, for example, read a mild backlash into the context of recent discussions of Haywood's work, particularly at conferences, but as I have noted, such speculation would constitute gossip.

Works Cited

Abrams, M.H. *A Glossary of Literary Terms.* 6th ed. Fort Worth, Texas: Harcourt Brace Jovanovich, 1993.

Addison, Joseph. *The Late Tryal and Conviction of Count Tariff.* London, 1713.

Addison, Joseph, et al. *The Spectator.* Edited by Donald F. Bond. 5 vols. Oxford: Clarendon, 1965.

Amman, Jean Coenrad. *The Talking Deaf Man: or, A Method Proposed Whereby he who is Born Deaf, may learn to Speak* (1694), No. 357, English Linguistics 1500–1800 series. Menston, England: Scholar P Limited, 1972.

Arabian Nights Entertainments: Consisting of One Thousand and One STORIES, told by the Sultaness of the Indies to divert the Sultan from the Execution of a Bloody Vow he had made to marry a Lady every Day, and have her cut off the next Morning, to avenge himself for the Disloyalty of his first Sultaness, &c. Containing a better Account of the Customs, Manners, and Religion of the Eastern Nations, viz Tartars, Persians, and Indians, than is to be met with in any Author hitherto published. Translated into French from the Arabian MSS, by M. Galland, of the Royal Academy; and now done into English from the last Paris Edition. 10th ed. Vol. 1. London: Printed for T. and T. Longman, at the Ship in Pater-noster Row, 1753.

Armstrong, Nancy, and Leonard Tennenhouse. *The Imaginary Puritan: Literature, Intellectual Labor, and the Origins of Personal Life.* Berkeley: U of California P, 1992.

————. *Desire and Domestic Fiction.* New York: Oxford UP, 1987.

Aubin, Penelope. *A Collection of Entertaining Histories and Novels.* London, 1739.

Austen, Jane. *Emma.* London, 1816.

————. *Persuasion.* London, 1818.

Azim, Firdous. *The Colonial Rise of the Novel.* New York: Routledge, 1993.

Backscheider, Paula. *Daniel Defoe: Ambition and Innovation.* Lexington: UP of Kentucky, 1986.

————. "'Endless Aversion Rooted in the Soul': Divorce in the 1690–1730 Theater." *The Eighteenth Century: Theory and Interpretation* 37 (1996): 99–135.

————. "The Shadow of an Author." *Eighteenth-Century Fiction* 11 (1998): 79–102.

————. *Spectacular Politics.* Baltimore: Johns Hopkins UP, 1993.

————. "Woman's Influence." *Studies in the Novel* 11 (1979): 3–22.

————. "Women Writers and the Chains of Identification." *Studies in the Novel* 19 (1987): 245–59.

Backscheider, Paula, and John Richetti, eds. *Popular Fiction by Women, 1660–1730.* Oxford: Clarendon, 1996.

Backscheider, Paula, and Timothy Dykstal, eds. *The Intersections of the Public and Private Spheres in Early Modern England.* London: Frank Cass, 1996. First published in *Prose Studies* 18 (1995).

Baine, Rodney Baine. *Daniel Defoe and the Supernatural.* Athens: U of Georgia P, 1968.

Bakhtin, Mikhail. *The Dialogic Imagination.* Translated by Caryl Emerson and Michael Holquist. Austin: U of Texas P, 1981.

Ballaster, Ros. *Seductive Forms: Women's Amatory Fiction from 1684 to 1740.* Oxford: Clarendon, 1992.

Bannett, Eve Taylor. "The Marriage Act of 1753: 'A most cruel law for the Fair Sex.'" *Eighteenth-Century Studies* 30, no. 3 (1997): 233–54.

Barbauld, Anna Letitia. "On the Origin and Progress of Novel-Writing." In *The British Novelists.* London, 1810.

Barker, Jane. *Love Intrigues: Or, the History of the Amours of Bosvil and Galesia.* In *Popular Fiction by Women, 1660–1730,* edited by Paula Backscheider and John Richetti, 80–111. Oxford: Clarendon, 1996.

Barker-Benfield, C.J. *The Culture of Sensibility: Sex and Society in Eighteenth-Century Britain.* Chicago: U of Chicago P, 1992.

Barreca, Regina. *Untamed and Unabashed: Essays on Women and Humor in British Literature.* Detroit: Wayne State UP, 1994.

Bartolomeo, Joseph. *A New Species of Criticism: Eighteenth-Century Discourse on the Novel.* Newark: U of Delaware P, 1994.

Battestin, Martin. *Henry Fielding: A Life.* London and New York: Routledge, 1989.

———, ed. *The Dictionary of Literary Biography.* Vol. 39. Detroit: Gale Research Company, 1985.

Beasley, Jerry C. *Novels of the 1740s.* Athens: U of Georgia P, 1982.

———. "Politics and Moral Idealism: The Achievement of Some Early Women Novelists." In *Fetter'd or Free? British Women Novelists, 1670–1815,* edited by Mary Anne Schofield and Cecilia Macheski, 216-36. Athens, Ohio: Ohio UP, 1986.

———. "Portraits of a Monster: Robert Walpole and Early English Prose Fiction." *Eighteenth-Century Studies* 14 (1981): 406–31.

Beckett, J.V. "Introduction: Stability in Politics and Society, 1680–1750." In *Britain in the First Age of Party 1680–1750: Essays Presented to Geoffrey Holmes,* edited by Clyve Jones, 1-18. London: Hambledon P, 1987.

Beer, Gillian. "Representing Women: Re-presenting the Past." In *The Feminist Reader: Essays in Gender and the Politics of Literary Criticism,* edited by Catherine Belsey and Jane Moore, 63–80. London: Macmillan, 1989.

Behn, Aphra. *The Works of Aphra Behn.* Edited by Janet Todd. 7 vols. London: Pickering and Chatto; Columbus: Ohio State UP, 1992–1996.

Bender, John. *Imagining the Penitentiary: Fiction and the Architecture of the Mind in Eighteenth-Century England.* Chicago: U of Chicago P, 1987.

Bennett, G.V. *The Tory Crisis in Church and State 1688–1730: The Career of Francis Atterbury, Bishop of Rochester.* Oxford: Clarendon, 1975.

Bhattacharya, Nandini. *Reading the Splendid Body: Gender and Consumerism in Eighteenth-Century British Writing on India.* Newark: U of Delaware P, 1997.

Blouch, Christine. "Eliza Haywood and the Romance of Obscurity." *Studies in English Literature* 31 (1991): 535–52.

———. "Eliza Haywood: Questions in the Life and Works." Ph.D. diss., U of Michigan, 1991.

———. "Haywood, Eliza (1693?-1756)." In *Eighteenth-Century Anglo-American Women Novelists: A Critical Reference Guide,* edited by Doreen Alvarez Saar and Mary Anne Schofield, 263–300. New York: Macmillan, 1996.

Bohls, Elizabeth. *Women Travel Writers and the Language of Aesthetics, 1716–1818.* Cambridge: Cambridge UP, 1995.

Boone, Joseph Allen. *Tradition Counter Tradition: Love and the Form of Fiction.* Chicago: U of Chicago P, 1987.

Bourdieu, Pierre. *Distinction: A Social Critique of the Judgment of Taste.* Translation. Cambridge: Harvard UP, 1984.

Bowers, Toni. *The Politics of Motherhood: British Writing and Culture 1680–1760.* New York: Cambridge UP, 1996.
———. "Seduction Narratives and Tory Experience in Augustan England." *The Eighteenth Century: Theory and Interpretation* 40, no. 2 (summer 1999): 128–54.
———. "Sex, Lies, and Invisibility: Amatory Fiction from the Restoration to Mid-Century." In *Columbia History of the British Novel,* edited by John Richetti et al. New York: Columbia UP, 1994.
———. "Tories and Jacobites: Making a Difference." *English Literary History (ELH)* 64, no. 4 (winter 1997): 857–70.
Brant, Clare and Diane Purkiss, eds. *Women, Texts and Histories 1575–1760.* London: Routledge, 1992.
Brown, Laura. *Ends of Empire: Women and Ideology in Early Eighteenth-Century English Literature.* Ithaca: Cornell UP, 1993.
Brückmann, Patricia. "An Early Hint of Miss Bridget's Affairs, with a Parallel Note on Mr. Allworthy." *Man and Nature/L'Homme et la nature* [now *Lumen*] 6 (1987): 73–79.
Burnet, James [Lord Monboddo]. *Of the Origin and Progress of Language.* 2nd ed. 6 vols. Edinburgh, 1774–1796.
Burney, Frances. *Camilla; or, A Picture of Youth.* London, 1797.
———. *Evelina; or, The History of a Young Lady's Entrance into the World.* World's Classics, edited by Edward A. Bloom and Lillian D. Bloom. Oxford: Oxford UP, 1968.
———. *The Wanderer; or, Female Difficulties.* London, 1814.
Canguilhem, Georges. *The Normal and the Pathological.* 1966. Translated by Carolyn R. Fawcett. New York: Zone Books, 1989.
Castle, Terry. *Masquerade and Civilization: The Carnivalesque in Eighteenth-Century Culture and Fiction.* Stanford: Stanford UP, 1986.
Chartier, Roger. *Cultural Origins of the French Revolution.* Durham, NC: Duke UP, 1991.
Chetwood, William Rufus. *A General History of the Stage.* London: W. Owen, 1749.
[Cicero]. *Ad C. Herennium de Ratione Dicendi.* Translated by Harry Caplan. London and Cambridge, Massachusetts: Heinemann and Harvard UP, 1954.
Cixous, Hélène and Catherine Clément. *The Newly Born Woman.* Translated by Betsy Wing. Minneapolis: U of Minneapolis P, 1978.
Clark, J.C.D. *English Society 1688–1832: Ideology, Social Structure and Political Practice During the Ancien Regime.* Cambridge: Cambridge UP, 1985.

————. *Samuel Johnson: Literature, Religion and English Cultural Politics from the Restoration to Romanticism*. Cambridge: Cambridge UP, 1994.

Cleary, Thomas R. *Henry Fielding: Political Writer*. Waterloo, Ontario: Wilfrid Laurier UP, 1984.

Colley, Linda. *Britons: Forging the Nation 1707–1837*. New Haven: Yale UP, 1992.

————. *In Defiance of Oligarchy: The Tory Party 1714–60*. Cambridge: Cambridge UP, 1982.

Coventry, Francis. *An Essay on the New Species of Writing founded by Mr. Fielding*. London: W. Owen, 1751.

Craft-Fairchild, Catherine. *Masquerade and Gender: Disguise and Female Identity in Eighteenth-Century Fictions by Women*. University Park, Penn.: Pennsylvania State UP, 1993.

Cruickshanks, Eveline. *Political Untouchables: The Tories and the '45*. New York: Holmes and Meier, 1979.

————. "Religion and Royal Succession." In *Britain in the First Age of Party, 1680–1750*, edited by Clyve Jones, 19–44. London: Hambledon P, 1987.

Davis, Lennard J. *Factual Fictions: The Origins of the English Novel*. New York: Columbia UP, 1983.

Davys, Mary. *The Works of Mrs. Davys*. London, 1725.

Day, Robert Adam. *Told in Letters: Epistolary Fiction Before Richardson*. Ann Arbor: U of Michigan P, 1966.

Defoe, Daniel. *Conjugal Lewdness; or, Matrimonial Whoredom. A Treatise concerning the Use and Abuse of the Marriage Bed*. 1727. Facsimile Edition, with an introduction by Maximillian Novak. Gainesville, Fla.: Scholars' Facsimiles & Reprints, 1967.

————. *An Essay upon Publick Credit*. London, 1710.

————. *The Life and Strange Surprizing Adventures of Robinson Crusoe of York, Mariner*. Edited by J. Donald Crowley. Oxford: Oxford UP, 1972.

————. *Memoirs of Count Tariff*. London, 1713.

————. *Moll Flanders*. London, 1722.

————. *Review*. Edited by A.W. Secord. 9 vols. 19 Feb. 1704—11 June 1713. New York: Columbia UP, 1938.

————. *Robinson Crusoe*. London, 1719.

————. *Roxana: The Fortunate Mistress*. Edited by Jane Jack. London: Oxford UP, 1964.

DeJean, Joan. *Tender Geographies: Women and the Origins of the Novel in France*. New York: Columbia UP, 1991.

Diverting Works of the famous Miguel de Cervantes, Author of the History of Don Quixote . . . With an Introduction by the Author of the London Spy. London, 1709.

Doane, Mary Ann. "Film and the Masquerade: Theorizing the Female Spectator." *Screen* 3–4 (1982): 74–87.

Donaldson, Laura. *Decolonizing Feminisms: Race, Gender, and Empire-building.* Chapel Hill: U of North Carolina P, 1992.

Doody, Margaret. *A Natural Passion: A Study of the Novels of Samuel Richardson.* Oxford: Clarendon, 1974.

———. *The True Story of the Novel.* New Brunswick: Rutgers UP, 1996.

Downie, J.A. "1688: Pope and the Rhetoric of Jacobitism." In *Pope: New Contexts,* edited by David Fairer, 9–24. New York and London: Harvester Wheatsheaf, 1990.

———. "The Development of the Political Press." In *Britain in the First Age of Party 1680–1750: Essays Presented to Geoffrey Holmes,* edited by Clyve Jones, 111–27. London: Hambledon P, 1987.

Dryden, John. *Of Dramatic Poetry and Other Critical Essays.* Edited by G. Watson. London: J.M. Dent, 1962.

———. *Ovid's Epistles, Translated by Several Hands.* London, 1680.

Eagleton, Terry. *The Rape of Clarissa.* Minneapolis: U of Minnesota P, 1982.

Eco, Umberto. *The Open Work.* Translated by Anna Cancogni. Cambridge: Harvard UP, 1989.

Ellis, Lorna Beth. "Engendering the *Bildungsroman:* The *Bildung* of Betsy Thoughtless." *Genre* 28 (fall 1995): 279–301.

Elshtain, Jean Bethke. *Public Man, Private Woman.* Princeton: Princeton UP, 1981.

Elwood, John R. "Henry Fielding and Eliza Haywood: A Twenty Year War." *Albion* 5 (fall 1973): 184–92.

———. "The Stage Career of Eliza Haywood." *Theatre Survey* 5 (November 1963): 107–16.

Epstein, Julia. *The Iron Pen: Frances Burney and the Politics of Women's Writing.* Madison: U of Wisconsin P, 1989.

Etherege, George. *The Man of Mode.* Edited by W.B. Carnochan. Regents Restoration Drama Series. Lincoln: U of Nebraska P, 1966.

Evans, Martha Noel. *Fits and Starts: A Genealogy of Hysteria in Modern France.* Ithaca: Cornell UP, 1991.

Fairer, David, ed. *Pope: New Contexts.* New York and London: Harvester Wheatsheaf, 1990.

Faller, Lincoln. *Crime and Defoe: A New Kind of Writing.* Cambridge: Cambridge UP, 1993.

———. *Turned to Account: The Forms and Functions of Criminal Biography in Late Seventeenth- and Early Eighteenth-Century England.* Cambridge: Cambridge UP, 1987.

Feather, John. *A History of British Publishing*. London: Routledge, 1988.

Ferguson, Margaret W. "Juggling the Categories of Race, Class, and Gender: Aphra Behn's *Oroonoko*." In *Women, "Race," and Writing in the Early Modern Period*, edited by Margo Hendricks and Patricia Parker, 209–24. New York: Routledge, 1994.

Fielding, Henry. *Amelia*. Edited by Martin C. Battestin. Oxford: Oxford UP, 1983.

———. *The Author's Farce (Original Version)*. Edited by Charles B. Woods. Lincoln: U of Nebraska P, 1966.

———. *The Covent Garden Journal*. Edited by Gerard Edward Jensen. 2 vols. New York: Russell and Russell, 1964.

———. *The Covent-Garden Tragedy*. London, 1732.

———. *The Historical Register for the Year 1736*. London, 1737.

———. *The History of Tom Jones*. Edited by Fredson Bowers. 2 vols. Middletown, Conn.: Wesleyan UP, 1975.

———. *Tom Thumb*. London, 1730.

———. *The Tragedy of Tragedies*. London, 1731.

Fields, Polly S. "Manly Vigor and Woman's Wit." In *Compendious Conversations*, edited by Kevin Cope. New York: Peter Lang, 1992.

Feiling, Keith. *A History of the Tory Party, 1640–1714*. Oxford: Clarendon P, 1924.

Finch, Anne. "The Introduction." In *The Norton Anthology of Literature by Women: The Tradition in English,* edited by Sandra Gilbert and Susan Gubar, 100-102. New York: W.W. Norton, 1985.

Firmager, Gabrielle. Introduction to *The Female Spectator*. London: Bristol Classical Press, 1993.

Flynn, Carol Houlihan. *The Body in Swift and Defoe*. Cambridge: Cambridge UP, 1990.

Foucault, Michel. Introduction to *The History of Sexuality*. Vol. 1, translated by Robert Hurley. New York: Vintage Books, 1980.

———. *Madness and Civilization*. Translated by Richard Howard. New York: Vintage Books, 1973.

———. "What Is an Author?" In *Aesthetics, Method, and Epistemology,* edited by James D. Faubion and ranslated by Robert Hurley and others, 205-22. New York: Free P, 1998.

Fox-Genovese, Elizabeth. *Feminism without Illusions: A Critique of Individualism*. Chapel Hill: U of North Carolina P, 1991.

The Friendly Daemon; or the Generous Apparition. London, 1726.

Fritz, Paul S. *The English Ministers and Jacobitism between the Rebellions of 1715 and 1745*. Toronto: U of Toronto P, 1975.

Gallagher, Catherine. *Nobody's Story: The Vanishing Acts of Women Writers in the Marketplace, 1670–1820.* Berkeley: U of California P, 1994.

Gardiner, Judith Kegan. "The First English Novel: Aphra Behn's *Love Letters,* the Canon, and Women's Tastes." *Tulsa Studies in Women's Literature* 8 (1989): 201–22.

Gerrard, Christine. *The Patriot Opposition to Walpole: Politics, Poetry, and National Myth, 1725–1742.* Oxford: Clarendon P, 1994.

———. "Pope and the Patriots." In *Pope: New Contexts,* edited by David Fairer, 25–44. New York and London: Harvester Wheatsheaf, 1990.

Gildon, Charles. "An Epistle to Daniel Defoe." In *Robinson Crusoe Examined and Criticized,* edited by Paul Dottin. London: Dent, 1923.

———. *The Golden Spy.* London, 1709.

Glass, Bentley, Owsei Temkin, and William Straus Jr., eds. *Forerunners of Darwin: 1745–1859.* Baltimore: Johns Hopkins UP, 1959.

Goldgar, Bertrand. *Walpole and the Wits: The Relation of Politics to Literature, 1722–1742.* Lincoln: U of Nebraska P, 1976.

Goldsmith, Oliver. *An History of the Earth, and Animate Nature.* 8 vols. London, 1774.

Gosse, Edmund. "What Ann Lang Read." In *Gossip in a Library.* London: William Heinemann, 1891.

Green, Katherine Sobba. *The Courtship Novel, 1740–1820.* Lexington: UP of Kentucky, 1991.

Guerinot, J. V. *Pamphlet Attacks on Alexander Pope, 1711–1744: A Descriptive Bibliography.* New York: New York UP, 1969.

Guest, Harriet. "A Double Lustre: Femininity and Sociable Commerce, 1730–60." *Eighteenth-Century Studies* 23, no. 4 (summer 1990): 479–501. Spec. iss. *The Politics of Difference,* edited by Felicity Nussbaum.

Guskin, Phyllis J. Introduction to *Clio: The Autobiography of Martha Fowke Sansom, 1689–1736,* edited by Phyllis J. Guskin, 15–50. Newark: U of Delaware P, 1997.

Habermas, Jürgen. *The Structural Transformation of the Public Sphere.* Translated by Thomas Burger. Cambridge: MIT P, 1991.

Hackett, Helen. "'Yet Tell Me Some Such Fiction': Lady Mary Wroth's *Urania* and the 'Femininity' of Romance." In *Women, Texts and Histories 1575–1760,* edited by Clare Brant and Diane Purkiss, 39–68. London: Routledge, 1992.

Hall, Kim F. *Things of Darkness: Economies of Race and Gender in Early Modern England.* Ithaca: Cornell UP, 1995.

Hammond, Brean. "Mid-Century English Quixotism and the Defence of the Novel." *Eighteenth-Century Fiction* 10, no. 3 (1998): 247–68.

———. *Professional Imaginative Writing in England, 1670–1740: "Hackney for Bread."* Oxford: Clarendon P, 1997.

Haywood, Eliza. *The Adventures of Eovaai. A Pre-Adamical History.* 1736. Edited by Earla A. Wilputte. Peterborough, Ont.: Broadview, 1999.

———. *Anti-Pamela; or, Feign'd Innocence Detected, in a Series of Syrena's Adventures.* 1742. New York: Garland, 1975.

———. *The British Recluse; or, The Secret History of Cleomira, Supposed Dead.* 1722. In *Popular Fiction by Women 1660–1730: An Anthology,* edited by Paula R. Backscheider and John J. Richetti, 154–224. Oxford: Clarendon, 1996.

———. *The British Recluse.* London: D. Brown, 1722.

———. *The City Jilt.* London, 1724.

———. *The City Jilt.* 1724. In *Selected Fiction and Drama of Eliza Haywood,* edited by Paula R. Backscheider. Oxford: Oxford UP, 1999.

———. *The City Jilt, or the Alderman turn'd Beau.* 1726. In *Three Novellas,* edited by Earla A. Wilputte, 65–103. East Lansing, Mich.: Colleagues, 1995.

———. *The Dumb Projector.* London, 1725.

———. *The Fair Captive.* London, 1721.

———. *The Fair Hebrew.* London, 1729.

———. "Fantomina; or Love in a Maze." In *Secret Histories, Novels and Poems.* Vol. 3. London, 1725.

———. *Fantomina; or, Love in a Maze.* In *Popular Fiction by Women 1660–1730: An Anthology,* edited by Paula R. Backscheider and John J. Richetti, 227–48. Oxford: Clarendon P, 1996.

———. *The Fatal Secret.* London, 1724.

———. *The Fatal Secret; or, Constancy in Distress.* 1723. 3rd ed. 1725. In *Masquerade Novels of Eliza Haywood: Facsimile Reproductions.* New York: Scholars' Facsimiles & Reprints, 1986.

———. *The Female Spectator.* Vols. 1 and 2. London, 1744–46.

———. *The Female Spectator.* Edited by Gabrielle M. Firmager. Melksham, Great Britain: Bristol Classical P, 1993.

———. "The Force of Nature; or, The Lucky Disappointment." In *Secret Histories, Novels and Poems.* Vol. 4. London, 1725.

———. *The Fortunate Foundlings.* 1744. New York: Garland, 1974.

———. *Frederick, Duke of Brunswick-Lunenburgh.* Rpt. in *The Plays of Eliza Haywood,* edited by Valerie C. Rudolph. Eighteenth-Century English Drama Series. New York and London: Garland, 1983.

———. *The Fruitless Enquiry. Being a Collection of several Entertaining Histories and Occurrences, which Fell under the Observation of a Lady in her Search after Happiness.* London: Printed for J. Stephens, 1727.

———. *The History of Jenny and Jemmy Jessamy*. New York: Garland, 1974.

———. *The History of Miss Betsy Thoughtless*. 1751. Edited by Christine Blouch. Peterborough, Ont., and Orchard Park, New York: Broadview, 1998.

———. *The History of Miss Betsy Thoughtless*. 1751. Edited by Beth Fowkes Tobin. Oxford: Oxford UP, 1997.

———. *The History of Miss Betsy Thoughtless*. London and New York: Pandora, 1986.

———. *Idalia, or the Unfortunate Mistress*. London: Printed for D. Browne Junr., W. Chetwood, and S. Chapman, 1723.

———. *The Injur'd Husband*. London: Printed for D. Browne, W. Chetwood, F. Woodman, and S. Chapman, 1723.

———. *The Injur'd Husband* and *Lasselia*. Edited by Jerry C. Beasley. Lexington: UP of Kentucky, 1999.

———. *The Invisible Spy*. London: Gardner, 1755.

———. *Lasselia; or, The Self-Abandon'd*. 1723. In *Four Novels of Eliza Haywood: Photoreprints*. Int. Mary Anne Schofield. Delmar, New York: Scholars' Facsimiles & Reprints, 1983.

———. *A Letter from H— G—*. London, 1749.

———. *Letters from the Palace of Fame. Written by a First Minister in the Regions of the Air, to an Inhabitant of this World, Translated from an Arabian Manuscript*. 3d ed. London: Printed for J. Roberts, 1727.

———. *Life's Progress Through the Passions: Or, The Adventures of Natura. By the Author of The Fortunate Foundlings*. London: Printed by T. Gardner, 1748.

———. *Love in Excess; or, The Fatal Enquiry*. 1719–20. Edited by David Oakleaf. Peterborough, Ont., and Orchard Park, New York: Broadview, 1997.

———. *Memoirs of a Certain Island Adjacent to the Kingdom of Utopia. Written by a Celebrated Author of that Country. Now translated into English*. 2nd ed. 2 vols. London, 1726.

———. *Memoirs of the Baron de Brosse*. London, 1724.

———. *Mercenary Lover*. London, 1724.

———. *Mercenary Lover*. 1724. In *Selected Fiction and Drama of Eliza Haywood*, edited by Paula R. Backscheider, 121-62. Oxford: Oxford UP, 1999.

———. *The Mercenary Lover: Or, the Unfortunate Heiresses*. London: N. Dobb, 1726.

———. *The Parrot. With a Compendium of the Times. By the Authoress of The Female Spectator*. London, 1746.

———. *Persecuted Virtue; or The Cruel Lover*. London, 1729.

―――. *Philidore and Placentia, or L'Amour trop Delicat*. 1727. In *Four Before Richardson: Selected English Novels, 1720–1727*, edited by William H. McBurney. Lincoln: U of Nebraska P, 1963.

―――. *The Rash Resolve; or the Untimely Discovery*. New York: Garland, 1973.

―――. *Secret Histories, Novels and Poems. In Four Volumes. Written by Mrs. Eliza Haywood*. 2nd ed. London, 1725.

―――. *The Secret History of the Present Intrigues of the Court of Caramania*. 2nd ed. London: Printed and Sold by the booksellers of London and Westminster, 1727.

―――. *Selected Fiction and Drama of Eliza Haywood*. Edited by Paula Backscheider. Oxford: Oxford UP, 1999.

―――. *The Spy Upon the Conjuror: Or, A Collection of Surprising and Diverting Stories, with Merry and Ingenious Letters. By way of Memoirs of the Famous Mr. Duncan Campbell, demonstrating the astonishing Foresight of that Wonderful Deaf and Dumb Man. The Whole being Moral and Instructive. Written to my Lord―――― by a Lady . . . Revised by Mrs. Eliza Haywood*. London: J. Peele, 1724.

―――. *The Tea Table*. London, 1724.

―――. *Three Novellas: The Distress'd Orphan, The Double Marriage, The City Jilt*. 1726. Edited by Earla A. Wilputte. East Lansing, Mich.: Colleagues, 1995.

―――. *The Unfortunate Princess: or the Life and surprizing Adventures of the Princess of Ijaveo*. 2nd ed. London: Printed for James Hodges, 1741.

―――. *The Wife*. London: Printed for T. Gardner, 1756.

―――. *A Wife to be Lett*. In *Selected Fiction and Drama of Eliza Haywood*, edited by Paula Backscheider, 1-82. Oxford: Oxford UP, 1999.

―――, trans. *La Belle Assemblée: Or, the Adventures of Six Days. Being a Curious Collection of Remarkable Incidents which happen'd to some of the First Quality in France. Written in French for the Entertainment of the KING, and dedicated to him, by Madam de Gomez. translated into English. Compleat, in Three Parts*. 2d ed. London: Printed for D. Browne, Jr., 1725.

―――, and William Hatchett. *The Opera of Operas*. London, 1733.

Heath, Stephen. "Joan Rivière and the Masquerade." In *Formations of Fantasy*, edited by Victor Burgin, James Donald, and Cora Kaplan, 45-61 London: Methuen, 1986.

Heinemann, Marcia. "Eliza Haywood's Career in the Theatre." *Notes and Queries*, n.s., 20 (1973): 9–13.

Hendricks, Margo. "Civility, Barbarism, and *The Widow Ranter*." In *Women, "Race," and Writing in the Early Modern Period*, edited by Margo Hendricks and Patricia Parker, 225–39. New York: Routledge, 1994.

Hill, Aaron. *The Plain Dealer* 53 (21 September 1724) and 62 (23 October 1724).

Hill, Brian W. *The Early Parties and Politics in Britain, 1688–1832*. New York: St. Martin's P, 1996.

——. *The Growth of Parliamentary Parties 1689–1742*. Hamden, Conn.: Archon Books, 1976.

The History of the Life and Adventures of Mr. Duncan, A Gentleman, who, tho' Deaf and Dumb, writes down any Stranger's Name at first Sight; with their future Contingencies of Fortune. Now Living in Exeter Court over-against the Savoy in the Strand. London, 1720.

Hollis, Karen. "Eliza Haywood and the Gender of Print." *The Eighteenth Century* 38 (1997): 43–62.

Holmes, Geoffrey S., ed. *Britain After the Glorious Revolution 1689–1714*. London: Macmillan; New York: St. Martin's, 1969.

——. *British Politics in the Age of Anne*. Rev. ed. Edited by Ronceverte, W. Va.: Hambledon P, 1987.

Home, Henry. *Elements of Criticism*. Reprint, with an introduction by R. Voitle. Hildesheim: Olms, 1970.

Hudson, Nicholas. "From 'Nation' to 'Race': The Origin of Racial Classification in Eighteenth-Century Thought." *Eighteenth-Century Studies* 29, no. 3 (1996): 247–64.

Hume, David. *A Treatise of Human Nature*. Edited by L.A. Selby-Bigge and rev. by P.H. Nidditch. Oxford: Clarendon, 1978.

Hunter, J. Paul. *Before Novels: The Cultural Contexts of Eighteenth-Century English Fiction*. New York: W.W. Norton, 1990.

——. "The Novel and Social/Cultural History." In *The Cambridge Companion to the Eighteenth-Century Novel*, edited by John Richetti, 9–40. Cambridge UP, 1996.

Hunter, Richard and Ida Macalpine. *Three Hundred Years of Psychiatry 1535–1860; A History Presented in Selected English Texts*. London: Oxford UP, 1963.

Hutcheon, Linda. *A Theory of Parody. The Teachings of Twentieth-Century Art Forms*. New York: Methuen, 1985.

Ingrassia, Catherine. "Additional Information on Eliza Haywood's 1749 Arrest for Seditious Libel." *Notes and Queries* 44 (June 1997): 202–4.

——. *Authorship, Commerce, and Gender in Early Eighteenth-Century England: A Culture of Paper Credit*. New York: Cambridge UP, 1998.

Irigaray, Luce. *This Sex Which Is Not One*. Translated by Catherine Porter, with Carolyn Burke. Ithaca: Cornell UP, 1985.

Jameson, Fredric. "Postmodernism, or the Cultural Logic of Late Capitalism." *New Left Review* 146 (1984): 53–92.

———. "Metacommentary." *PMLA* 86 (1971): 9–18.

———. *The Political Unconscious: Narrative as a Socially Symbolic Act.* Ithaca: Cornell UP, 1981.

———. "Reification and Utopia in Mass Culture." *Social Text* 1 (1979): 130–48.

Johnson, Samuel. *A Journey to the Western Islands of Scotland.* Edited by Mary Lascelles. Yale Edition of the Works of Samuel Johnson. Vol. 9. New Haven: Yale UP, 1971.

———. *Lives of the English Poets.* Edited by A.B. Hill. Oxford: Oxford UP, 1905.

———. *Life of Savage.* Edited by Clarence Tracy. Oxford: Clarendon P, 1971.

Jones, Clyve. "The House of Lords and the Growth of Parliamentary Stability, 1701–42." In *Britain in the First Age of Party, 1680–1750,* edited by Clyve Jones, 85–110. London: Hambledon P, 1987.

Juneja, Renu. "The Native and the Nabob: Representations of the Indian Experience in 18th-century English Literature." *Journal of Commonwealth Literature* 27, no. 1 (1992): 183–98.

Kaplan, Cora. "Pandora's Box: Subjectivity, Class and Sexuality in Socialist Feminist Criticism." In *Feminisms,* edited by Robyn Warhol and Diane Herndl, 857–77. New Brunswick, N.J.: Rutgers UP, 1991.

Katz, Jonathan Ned. *The Invention of Heterosexuality.* New York: Dutton, 1995.

King, Helen. "Once Upon a Text: Hysteria from Hippocrates." In *Hysteria Beyond Freud,* edited by Sander L. Gilman, Helen King, Roy Porter, George Rousseau, and Elaine Showalter, 3-90. Berkeley: U of California P, 1993.

Lacan, Jacques. "The Mirror Stage as Formative of the Function of the I." In *Écrits, A Selection,* translated by Alan Sheridan, 1–7. New York: W.W. Norton, 1977.

———. *On Feminine Sexuality: The Limits of Love and Knowledge.* Book 20 of *The Seminar of Jacques Lacan.* Translated by Bruce Fink. New York: W.W. Norton, 1998.

Langbauer, Laurie. *Women and Romance: The Consolations of Gender in the English Novel.* Ithaca: Cornell UP, 1990.

Laqueur, Thomas. *Making Sex: Body and Gender from the Greeks to Freud.* Cambridge: Harvard UP, 1990.

Levin, Kate. "'The Cure of Arabella's Mind': Charlotte Lennox and the Disciplining of the Female Reader." *Women's Writing* 2, no.3 (1995): 271–90.

Lewis, Reina. *Gendering Orientalism: Race, Femininity, and Representation.* New York: Routledge, 1996.

Linnaeus. [Charles Linné]. *A General System of Nature, through the Three Grand Kingdoms of Animals, Vegetables, and Minerals, Systematically Divided.* Translated by William Turon, M.D. 7 vols. London: Lackington, Allen, and Company, 1802.

Lockwood, Thomas. "Eliza Haywood in 1749: *Dalinda* and her Pamphlet on the Pretender." *Notes and Queries*, n.s., 234 (4 December 1989): 465–77.

———. "William Hatchett, *A Rehearsal of Kings* (1737), and the Panton Street Puppet Show (1748)." *PQ* 68 (1989): 315–23.

London, April. "Placing the Female: The Metonymic Garden in Amatory and Pious Narrative, 1700–1740." In *Fetter'd or Free? British Women Novelists 1760–1815*, edited by Mary Anne Schofield and Cecilia Macheski, 101–23. Athens, Ohio: Ohio UP, 1986.

Lovell, Terry. *Consuming Fiction.* New York: Verso, 1987.

MacKinnon, Catherine. *Toward a Feminist Theory of the State.* Cambridge: Harvard UP, 1989.

Mandeville, Bernard. *The Fable of the Bees.* Edited by Philip Harth. London: Penguin, Penguin Classics, 1989.

Manley, Delariver. *The New Atalantis.* Edited by Ros Ballaster. London: Pickering and Chatto, 1991.

———. *The Novels of Mary Delariviere Manley 1705–1714.* Edited by Patricia Köster. 2 vols. Gainesville, Florida: Scholars' Facsimiles and Reprints, 1971.

Marana, Giovanni Paolo. *Letters Writ by a Turkish Spy.* Translated by various hands. 8 vols. London, 1687–1734.

Marshall, P.J. and Glyndwr Williams. *The Great Map of Mankind: Perceptions of New Worlds in the Age of Enlightenment.* Harvard UP, 1982.

Maupertuis, [Pierre Louis Moreau de]. *Vénus Physique, contenant deux dissertations, l'une sur l'origine des hommes et des animaux; et l'autre sur l'origine des noirs.* 1745. In *Forerunners of Darwin: 1745–1859*, edited by Bentley Glass, Owsei Temkin, and William Straus Jr., 51–83. Baltimore: Johns Hopkins UP, 1959.

Mayer, Robert. *History and the Early English Novel: Matters of Fact from Bacon to Defoe.* Cambridge: Cambridge UP, 1997.

McBurney, William. *A Check List of English Prose Fiction 1700–1739.* Cambridge: Harvard UP, 1960.

———, ed. *Four Before Richardson: Selected English Novels, 1720–1727.* Lincoln: U of Nebraska P, 1978.

McClure, Ruth K. *Coram's Children: The London Foundling Hospital in the Eighteenth Century.* New Haven: Yale UP, 1981.

McKeon, Michael. "Historicizing Patriarchy: The Emergence of Gender Difference in England, 1660–1760." *Eighteenth-Century Studies* 28, no. 3 (1995): 295–322.

———. *The Origins of the English Novel 1600–1740*. Baltimore: Johns Hopkins UP, 1987.

———. "Surveying the Frontier of Culture: Pastoralism in Eighteenth-Century England." *Studies in Eighteenth-Century Culture* 26 (1998): 7–28.

McLaren, Angus. *Reproductive Rituals: The Perception of Fertility in England from the Sixteenth Century to the Nineteenth Century*. New York: Methuen, 1984.

McNamara, Susan P. "Mirrors of Fiction within *Tom Jones:* The Paradox of Self-Reference." *Eighteenth-Century Studies* 12 (1979): 372–90.

Mengel, Elias F., Jr. "The *Dunciad* Illustrations." *Eighteenth-Century Studies* 7 (1973–74): 161–78.

Micale, Mark S. *Approaching Hysteria: Disease and Its Interpretations*. Princeton: Princeton UP, 1995.

Miller, Jane. *Seductions: Studies in Reading and Culture*. Cambridge: Harvard UP, 1991.

Miller, Nancy K. "Emphasis Added: Plots and Plausibilities in Women's Fiction." *PMLA* 96 (1981): 36–48.

———. *The Heroine's Text: Readings in the French and English Novel, 1722–1782*. New York: Columbia UP, 1980.

Mills, Charles W. *The Racial Contract*. Ithaca: Cornell UP, 1997.

Mirzoeff, Nicholas. "Paper, Picture, Sign: Conversations between the Deaf, Hard of Hearing, and Others." In *"Defects": Engendering the Modern Body*, edited by Helen Deutsch and Felicity Nussbaum, 75-92. Ann Arbor: U of Michigan P, 2000.

———. *Silent Poetry: Deafness, Sign, and Visual Culture in Modern France* Princeton: Princeton UP, 1995.

Mish, Charles C. *English Prose Fiction, 1600–1700*. Charlottesville, Va: Bibliographical Society of the U of Virginia, 1967.

Modleski, Tania. *Loving With a Vengeance: Mass-Produced Fantasies for Women*. New York: Methuen, 1984.

Montesquieu, Charles. *Persian Letters*. Translated by John Ozell. London, 1722.

Mr. Campbell's Packet, for the Entertainment of Gentlemen and Ladies. London, 1720.

Mudimbe, V.Y. *The Invention of Africa: Gnosis, Philosophy, and the Order of Knowledge*. Bloomington: Indiana UP, 1988.

Nestor, Deborah J. "Virtue Rarely Rewarded: Ideological Subversion and Narrative Form in Haywood's Later Fiction." *Studies in English Literature, 1500–1900* 34 (1994): 579–98.

Nicholson, Colin. *Writing and the Rise of Finance: Capital Satires of the Early Eighteenth Century.* Cambridge: Cambridge UP, 1994.

Nussbaum, Felicity. "Women and Race: 'A Difference of Complexion.'" In *Women and Literature in Britain, 1700–1800,* edited by Vivien Jones. Cambridge: Cambridge UP, 2000.

———. "Dumb Virgins, Blind Ladies, and Eunuchs: Fictions of Defect." In *"Defects": Engendering the Modern Body,* edited by Helen Deutsch and Felicity Nussbaum, 31-53. Ann Arbor: U of Michigan P, 1999.

———. *Torrid Zones: Maternity, Sexuality, and Empire in Eighteenth-Century English Narratives.* Baltimore: Johns Hopkins UP, 1994.

Oakleaf, David. "The Eloquence of Blood in Eliza Haywood's *Lasselia.*" *Studies in English Literature* 39 (1999): 483–98.

———. "Sliding Down Together: Fielding, Addison, and the Pleasures of the Imagination in *Tom Jones.*" *English Studies in Canada* 9 (1983): 402–17.

Pearson, Jacqueline "The History of *The History of the Nun.*" In *Rereading Aphra Behn: History, Theory, and Criticism,* edited by Heidi Hutner, 234-52. Charlottesville, Va.: UP of Virginia, 1993.

Plumb, J.H. *The Growth of Political Stability in England, 1675–1725.* London: Macmillan; Baltimore: Penguin Books, 1967.

———. *The King's Minister.* Vol. 2 of *Sir Robert Walpole.* London: Penguin, 1972.

Pocock, J. G. A. *Virtue, Commerce, and History.* Cambridge UP, 1985.

Poovey, Mary. *The Proper Lady and the Woman Writer: Ideology as Style in the Works of Mary Wollstonecraft, Mary Shelley, and Jane Austen.* Chicago: U of Chicago P, 1984.

Pope, Alexander. *The Correspondence of Alexander Pope.* Edited by George Sherburn. Vol. 3. Oxford: Clarendon, 1956.

———. *The Dunciad.* 1729. In *The Twickenham Edition of the Poems of Alexander Pope,* edited by James Sutherland. 3rd ed. rev., vol. 5. London: Methuen, 1963.

———. *The Dunciad, Variorum. With the Prolegomena of Scriblerus.* London, 1729.

———. *The Dunciad. An Heroic Poem. In Three Books.* Dublin [i.e., London], 1728.

———. *The Poems of Alexander Pope.* Edited by John Butt et al. 11 vols. London: Methuen, 1939–1969.

———. *The Poems of Alexander Pope: A Reduced Version of the Twickenham Text.* Edited by John Butt. New Haven: Yale UP, 1963.

———. *The Rape of the Lock.* 1714. In *The Poems of Alexander Pope,* edited by John Butt, 217–42. London: Methuen, 1963.

———. *The Rape of the Lock.* In *The Twickenham Edition of the Poems of Alexander Pope,* edited by Geoffrey Tillotson. 3rd ed. rev., vol. 2. London: Methuen, 1962.

Rabine, Leslie W. *Reading the Romantic Heroine: Text, History, Ideology.* Ann Arbor: U of Michigan P, 1985.

Radway, Janice. *Reading the Romance: Women, Patriarchy, and Popular Culture.* Chapel Hill: North Carolina UP, 1984.

Reeve, Clara. *The Progress of Romance.* London, 1785.

Richardson, Samuel. *Clarissa; or, the History of a Young Lady.* Edited by Angus Ross. London: Penguin Books, 1985.

———. *Pamela; or, Virtue Rewarded.* Edited by T. C. Duncan Eaves and Ben D. Kimpel. Boston: Houghton Mifflin, 1971.

Richetti, John J. *The English Novel in History, 1700–1780.* London: Routledge, 1999.

———. *Popular Fiction Before Richardson: Narrative Patterns 1700–1739.* Oxford: Clarendon, 1969.

———. *Popular Fiction Before Richardson: Narrative Patterns 1700–1739.* 1969. Reprint, with a new introduction by the author, Oxford: Clarendon, 1989.

———. "Voice and Gender in Eighteenth-Century Fiction: Haywood to Burney." *Studies in the Novel* 19 (1987): 263–72.

Riviere, Joan. "Womanliness as a Masquerade." In *Formations of Fantasy,* edited by Victor Burgin, James Donald, and Cora Kaplan, 35-44. London: Methuen, 1986.

Roberts, Bette. "The Horrid Novels." In *Gothic Fictions: Prohibition/Transgression,* edited by K. Graham, 89–110. New York: AMS, 1989.

Rogers, Pat. *Grub Street: Studies in a Subculture.* London: Methuen, 1972.

Rose, Margaret. *Parody: Ancient, Modern and Post-Modern.* Cambridge: Cambridge UP, 1993.

———. *Political Satire and Reforming Vision in Eliza Haywood's Works.* Milano: Europrint Publications, 1996.

Ross, Deborah. *The Excellence of Falsehood: Romance, Realism, and Women's Contribution to the Novel.* Lexington: UP of Kentucky, 1991.

Rousseau, George S. "'A Strange Pathology': Hysteria in the Early Modern World, 1500–1800." In *Hysteria Beyond Freud,* edited by Sander L. Gilman, Helen King, Roy Porter, George Rousseau, and Elaine Showalter, 91-221. Berkeley: U of California P, 1993.

Rousseau, Jean-Jacques. *Discourse on the Origins of Inequality (Second Discourse), Polemics, and Political Economy. The Collected Writings of Rousseau.* Vol. 3. Edited by Roger D. Masters and Christopher Kelly and translated by Judith R. Bush et al. Hanover: UP of New England, 1992.

Rowe, Elizabeth Singer. *Friendship in Death*. In *Popular Fiction by Women, 1660–1730*, edited by Paula R. Backscheider and John J. Richetti, 323-34. Oxford: Clarendon, 1996.

Rumbold, Valerie. *Women's Place in Pope's World*. Cambridge: Cambridge UP, 1989.

Said, Edward W. *Orientalism*. New York: Vintage, 1979.

Sansom, Martha Fowke. *Clio: The Autobiography of Martha Fowke Sansom, 1689–1736*. Edited by Phyllis J. Guskin. London: Associated UP, 1997.

Savage, Richard. *The Poetical Works of Richard Savage*. Edited by Clarence Tracy. Cambridge: Cambridge UP, 1962.

Sambrook, A.J. "The English Lord and the Happy Husbandsman." *Studies on Voltaire and the Eighteenth Century* 57 (1967): 1357–75.

Scheffer, Johannes. *History of Lapland containing a Geographical Description and a Natural History of that Country*. London, 1704.

Schofield, Mary Anne. "Descending Angels": Salubrious Sluts and Pretty Prostitutes in Haywood's Fiction." In *Fetter'd or Free? British Women Novelist, 1670–1815*, edited by Mary Anne Schofield and Cecilia Macheski, 186–200. Athens: Ohio UP, 1986.

———. *Eliza Haywood*. Boston: Twayne, 1985.

———. *Masking and Unmasking the Female Mind: Disguising Romances in Feminine Fiction, 1713–1799*. Newark: U of Delaware P, 1990.

Schulz, Dieter. "'Novel,' 'Romance,' and Popular Fiction in the First Half of the Eighteenth Century." *Studies in Philology* 70, no. 1 (Jan. 1973): 77–91.

Scott, Joan. "Gender: A Useful Category of Historical Analysis." *American Historical Review* 91 (1986): 1053–75.

Scott, Sarah. *A Description of Millenium Hall*. Edited by Gary Kelly. Peterborough, Ont.: Broadview, 1995.

Scudéry, Madeline de. *Artamenes; or, The Grand Cyrus, That Excellent Romance in Ten Parts*. Englished by F.G., Esq. London, 1691.

The Secret Memoirs of the late Mr. Duncan Campbel[l], the Famous Deaf and Dumb Gentleman. Written by Himself, who ordered they should be publish'd after his Decease. To which is added, An Appendix, by Way of Vindication of Mr. Duncan Campbe[l]l, against that groundless Aspersion cast upon him, That he but pretended to be Deaf and Dumb. London, 1732.

Sedgwick, Eve Kosofsky. *Between Men: English Literature and Homosocial Desire*. New York: Columbia UP, 1985.

Shaftesbury, Earl of (Anthony Ashley Cooper). *Characteristics of Men, Man-ners, Opinions, Times, etc.* Edited by J. Robertson. New York: Dutton, 1900.

Sherman, Stuart. *Telling Time: Clocks, Diaries, and English Diurnal Form, 1660–1785* Chicago: U of Chicago P, 1996.

Shevelow, Kathryn. *Women and Print Culture.* London: Routledge, 1989.

Sibscota, George. *The Deaf and Dumb Man's Discourse. Or A Treatise con-cerning those that are Born Deaf and Dumb, containing a Discovery of their knowledge or understanding; as also the Method they use, to mani-fest the sentiments of their Mind.* London, 1670.

Sill, Geoffrey M. *Defoe and the Idea of Fiction, 1713–1719.* Newark: U of Delaware P, 1983.

The Sisters; or the History of Lucy and Caroline Sanson, Entrusted to a false Friend. London: T. Waller, 1754.

Snader, Joe. "The Oriental Captivity Narrative and Early English Fiction." *Eighteenth-Century Fiction* 9, no. 2 (1997): 267–98.

Spacks, Patricia M. *Desire and Truth: Functions of Plot in Eighteenth-Cen-tury English Novels.* Chicago: U of Chicago P, 1980.

———. "Ev'ry Woman is at Heart a Rake." *Eighteenth-Century Studies* 1 (1974): 27–46.

———. "Ev'ry Woman is at Heart a Rake." In *The Past as Prologue, Essays to Celebrate the Twenty-fifth Anniversary of ASECS,* edited by Carla H. Hay and Syndy M. Conger, 45-62. New York: AMS, 1995.

———. "Female Changelessness: Or, What Do Women Want?" *Studies in the Novel* 19 (fall 1987): 273–83.

———. *Gossip.* Chicago: U of Chicago P, 1985.

Speck, W.A. *The Birth of Britain: A New Nation 1700–1710.* Cambridge, Mass.: Blackwell, 1994.

———. *Stability and Strife: England 1714–1760.* Cambridge: Harvard UP, 1977.

Spencer, Jane. *The Rise of the Woman Novelist: From Aphra Behn to Jane Austen.* Oxford: Basil Blackwell, 1986.

Spender, Dale. Introduction to *The History of Miss Betsy Thoughtless,* by Eliza Haywood. New York and London: Pandora, 1986.

Staves, Susan. "British Seduced Maidens." In *The Past as Prologue: Essays to Celebrate the Twenty-fifth Anniversary of ASECS,* edited by Carla H. Hay and Syndy M. Conger, 91-114. New York: AMS, 1995.

Stebbing, Henry. *An Inquiry into the Force and Operation of the annulling Clauses of a late Act for the better Preventing of Clandestine Marriages.* London, 1754

Steegmuller, Francis, ed. and trans. *The Letters of Gustave Flaubert.* Vol. 1. Cambridge: Harvard UP, 1980.

Stoler, Ann Laura. *Race and the Education of Desire: Foucault's* History of Sexuality *and the Colonial Order of Things.* Durham: Duke UP, 1995.

Stone, Lawrence. "Literacy and Education in England 1640–1900." *Past and Present* 42 (1969): 69–139.

Straub, Kristina. *Sexual Suspects. Eighteenth-Century Players and Sexual Ideology,* Princeton: Princeton UP, 1992.

The Supernatural Philosopher: or, the Mysteries of Magick, In all its Branches clearly Unfolded. London, 1728.

Sutherland, James. Introduction to *An Author To be Lett,* by Richard Savage. 1729. Los Angeles: William Andrews Clark Memorial Library, 1960.

———. Introduction to *The Dunciad,* by Alexander Pope. 2nd ed. London: Methuen, 1953.

Swift, Jonathan. *The Correspondence of Jonathan Swift.* Edited by Harold Williams. Vol 3. Oxford: Clarendon, 1963.

———. *Gulliver's Travels.* Edited by Paul Turner. Oxford: Oxford UP, 1971.

———. *Gulliver's Travels.* Oxford: Basil Blackwell, 1941.

———. *Jonathan Swift: The Complete Poems.* Edited by Pat Rogers. London: Penguin, 1983.

[———]. *Memoirs of the Court of Lilliput. Written by Captain Gulliver. Containing an Account of the Intrigues, and some other particular Transactions of that Nation, omitted in the two Volumes of his Travels. Published by Lucas Bennet, with a Preface, shewing how these Papers fell into his hands.* London, 1727.

———. "A Tale of a Tub." *Jonathan Swift: Selected Prose and Poetry.* Edited by E. Rosenheim Jr. New York and Toronto: Rinehart, 1959.

Sydenham, Thomas. *Selected Works of Thomas Sydenham, M.D.* New York: William Wood & Co., 1922.

Szechi, David. *Jacobitism and Tory Politics, 1710–14.* Edinburgh: John Donald Publishers, 1984.

Tavernier, Jean Baptiste. *A New Relation of the Inner-Part of the Grand Seignor's Seraglio.* London, 1677.

Terry, Richard. "The Circumstances of Eighteenth-Century Parody." *Eighteenth-Century Life* 15 (1991): 76–91.

———. "The Semantics of 'Parody' in the Eighteenth Century." *Durham University Journal* 54, no.1 (1993): 67–74.

Thompson, E.P. *Whigs and Hunters: The Origins of the Black Act.* New York: Pantheon Books, 1975

Thomson, Rosemarie Garland. *Extraordinary Bodies: Figuring Physical Dis-*

ability in American Culture and Literature. New York: Columbia UP, 1997.

Thorn, Jennifer. "'Althea Must Be Open'd': Eliza Haywood, Reproductivity, and Individualism." *Eighteenth-Century Women,* forthcoming.

Tobin, Beth Fowkes. Introduction to *The History of Miss Betsy Thoughtless,* by Eliza Haywood. Oxford: Oxford UP, 1997.

Todd, Dennis. *Imagining Monsters: Miscreations of the Self in Eighteenth-Century England.* Chicago: U of Chicago P, 1995.

Todd, Janet. *The Sign of Angellica: Women, Writing, and Fiction, 1660–1800.* New York: Columbia UP, 1989.

Tracy, Clarence. *The Artificial Bastard: A Biography of Richard Savage.* Cambridge: Harvard UP, 1953.

Turner, Cheryl. *Living by the Pen: Women Writers in the Eighteenth Century.* London: Routledge, 1992.

Varey, Simon. "Exemplary History and the Political Satire of Gulliver's Travels." In *The Genres of Gulliver's Travels,* edited by Frederik N. Smith, 39–55. Newark: U of Delaware P, 1990.

Veith, Ilza. *Hysteria: The History of a Disease.* Chicago: U of Chicago P, 1965.

Waller, Edmund. "To A Friend, of the Different Successes of their Loves." In *The Poems of Edmund Waller,* edited by George Thorn Drury, v. 2, 73. London: George Routledge & Sons, 1900.

Ward, Edward. *The London Spy.* 4th ed. London, 1709.

Warner, William B. "The Elevation of the Novel in England: Hegemony and Literary History." *ELH* 59 (1992): 577–96.

———. "Formulating Fiction: Romancing the General Reader in Early Modern Britain." In *Cultural Institutions of the Novel,* edited by Deidre Lynch and William B. Warner, 279–305. Durham: Duke UP, 1996.

———. *Licensing Entertainment: The Elevation of Novel Reading in Britain, 1684–1750.* Berkeley: U of California P, 1998.

Watt, Ian. *The Rise of the Novel: Studies in Defoe, Richardson, and Fielding.* Berkeley: U of California P, 1957.

Wechselblatt, Martin. "Finding Mr. Boswell: Rhetorical Authority and National Identity in Johnson's *A Journey to the Western Islands of Scotland.*" *ELH* 60 (1993): 117–48.

Welcher, Jeanne K. *Gulliveriana VIII: An Annotated List of Gulliveriana, 1721–1800.* Delmar, New York: Scholar's Facsimiles & Reprints, 1988.

Welch, Jeanne K. and George E. Bush Jr. Introduction to *Gulliveriana III: Travels into Several Remote Nations of the World, Vol. III (1727) and Memoirs of the Court of Lilliput (1727),* v-xiii. Delmar, New York: Scholar's Facsimiles & Reprints, 1972.

Whicher, George Frisbie. *The Life and Romances of Mrs. Eliza Haywood.* New York: Columbia UP, 1915.

Williams, Sir Harold. *The Text of Gulliver's Travels.* Cambridge: Cambridge UP, 1952.

Wilputte, Earla. "The Textual Architecture of Eliza Haywood's *Adventures of Eovaai.*" *Essays in Literature* 22 (1995): 31–44.

Winnett, Susan. "Women, Men, Narrative, and Principles of Pleasure." *PMLA* 105, no. 3 (1990): 505–18.

Winzer, Margaret A. *The History of Special Education: From Isolation to Integration.* Washington, D.C.: Gallaudet UP, 1993.

Wycherley, William. *The Country Wife.* Edited by Thomas H. Fujimura. Lincoln: U of Nebraska P, 1965.

Young, Robert J. C. *Colonial Desire: Hybridity in Theory, Culture and Race.* New York: Routledge, 1995.

Zimmerman, Everett. *Defoe and the Novel.* Berkeley: U of California P, 1975.

Contributors

ANDREA AUSTIN is a doctoral candidate in English at Queen's University, Ontario, and has published articles on Frances Burney, on Mary Leslie, and on parody and hypertext.

PAULA R. BACKSCHEIDER is Pepperell Eminent Scholar, at Auburn University. Her books include, *Daniel Defoe: His Life; Spectacular Politics; Reflections on Biography;* and a collection of essays, *Revising Women: Eighteenth-Century "Women's Fiction" and Social Engagement.* She has edited *Selected Fiction and Drama of Eliza Haywood* and is, with John Richetti, editor of *Popular Fiction by Women, 1660–1730: An Anthology.*

ROS BALLASTER is Fellow in English Literature at Mansfield College, Oxford University. She is the author of *Seductive Forms: Women's Amatory Fiction from 1684–1740* (Clarendon Press, 1992), and editor of Delarivier Manley's *The New Atalantis* (Penguin Classics, 1991) and Jane Austen's *Sense and Sensibility* (Penguin Classics, 1995).

CHRISTINE BLOUCH is Associate Professor of English at Bradley University. She has published in *SEL* and edited the Broadview edition of *The History of Miss Betsy Thoughtless.* She is currently working with editor Alex Pettit on a collection of Haywood's nonfiction for Pickering & Chatto.

REBECCA BOCCHICCHIO is Assistant Professor of English at Sierra

College. She is currently revising her manuscript, *Literary Treatments: Hysteria in Fiction by Women in Eighteenth- and Nineteenth-Century England.*

TONI BOWERS is Associate Professor of English at the University of Pennsylvania. Her book *The Politics of Motherhood: British Writing and Culture, 1680–1760* was published by Cambridge U.P. in 1996. She is working on a new book, *"Force or Fraud": Gendered Agency and Party Politics in British Seduction Stories, 1680–1750*, that includes an expanded version of her Haywood essay in this volume. Professor Bowers has published essays on women's place in eighteenth-century culture in a number of scholarly collections.

DAVID A. BREWER is Assistant Professor of English at Ohio State University and is currently completing a book manuscript entitled *Imaginative Expansion and the Afterlives of Texts in Eighteenth-Century Britain.* His other publications include "Making Hogarth Heritage" (forthcoming in *Representations*). The present essay serves as the beginning of a book-length second project on attribution and authorship in the age of anonymous publication.

MARGARET CROSKERY is Assistant Professor of English at Ohio Northern University. Her other publications include an essay on narrative strategies in Elizabeth Gaskell's *Cranford* in *Nineteenth-Century Literature* and a book-length project on the role played by eighteenth-century popular fiction in shaping both eighteenth-century and modern perceptions of the "literary" novel.

FELICITY NUSSBAUM, Professor of English at the University of California Los Angeles, is the author most recently of *Torrid Zones: Maternity, Sexuality, and Empire in Eighteenth-Century English Narrative* (Johns Hopkins UP) and co-editor of *Defects: Engendering the Modern Body* (U of Michigan P). Her current work is on femininity and race.

DAVID OAKLEAF is Associate Professor of English at the University of Calgary. He has edited Haywood's *Love in Excess* and published multiple articles on eighteenth-century fiction.

JOHN RICHETTI is A.M. Rosenthal Professor of English at the University of Pennsylvania. He has published extensively on eighteenth-century British literature. His most recent book is *The English Novel in History, 1700–1780* (1999).

KIRSTEN T. SAXTON is Assistant Professor of English and Women's

Studies at Mills College. She has published elsewhere on Haywood and is currently revising a book manuscript entitled *Deadly Plots: Narratives of Women and Murder in England, 1680–1760.*

JENNIFER THORN is Assistant Professor of English at Duke University and is completing a book, the working title of which is *Exoticism and Authorship: Eighteenth-Century British Writing and the Division of Knowledge.* She has published articles on Haywood and reproductivity and on race and translations of the *Arabian Nights Entertainments,* and she is the editor of *Writing British Infanticide: Gender, Narrative, and the Professions, 1722–1859.*

Index

from amatory fiction, 231–32;
*Memoirs of the Court of
Lilliput* and, 220–23, 231

Hall, Kim F., 199
Hammond, Brean, 144–45, 238n.
23
Harlequin romances, 311, 324n. 18
Harley, Robert (Earl of Oxford), 52
Harvey, William, 99–100
Hatchett, William, 6, 146, 166n.
15, 227, 235n. 4
Haywood, Eliza: acting career of,
6–7, 224, 240; admirers of, 2,
223, 224–26, 294–95; anti-
Walpole works, 146, 151–53,
154–56, 157; attacks on, 4, 5,
7–8; biographies of, 5–6; on
Duncan Campbell, 194, 196–
97, 202, 207–12, 214–15;
categorization of works, 301–2;
critical works by, 7; depicted in
Pope's *Dunciad,* 7, 146, 149,
197, 219–20, 227–30, 232–34,
268; domestic realism and, 5,
243–58; early life of, 6; English
social values and, 4–5; feminism and, 3; Henry Fielding
and, 6, 7, 146, 147, 236n. 13,
240–41; grave of, 11; as the
"Great Arbitress of Passion," 3,
93n. 4, 219–20, 223, 225;
Hillarians and, 146; illegitimate
children of, 6, 166n. 15;
literary career of, 2, 4–9;
*Memoirs of the Court of
Lilliput* attributed to, 217–18,
219–20, 234; patronage and,
294; personal success and, 138;
political works, 6–7, 37; on the
press, 30–31; primacy of
passion and, 70, 71–72;

Richetti's criticism of, 116;
Richard Savage and, 6, 7,
166n. 15, 224–27, 233, 294;
Scriblerians and, 149, 219–20,
223, 226, 227, 230–32, 233;
self-depreciation, 10, 262, 294;
self-presentation, 9–10, 11;
Jonathan Swift and, 238–39n.
25; Tory politics and, 3;
women's writing and, 8
Heath, Stephen, 101
Hill, Aaron, 146, 147, 165n. 8, 194
Hillarians, 146
*Hind and the Panther Transvers'd,
The* (Prior and Montagu), 261
*Historical Register for the Year
1736, The* (Fielding), 146, 240
"History of Clara and Ferdinand,
The" (Haywood), 179
*History of Jenny and Jemmy
Jessamy, The* (Haywood), 71,
243, 248
*History of Miss Betsy Thoughtless,
The* (Haywood), 9; amatory
plots in, 249–53, 287–88; *The
British Recluse* and, 295–96;
experimentation with fictional
forms in, 23–24; feminist
revisions and, 254–55; Fielding
and, 41, 240–41, 248–49;
narrative qualities, 255–58;
novelistic language in, 26–27;
as parody, 259–60, 263–80;
pastiche and, 263, 267, 275;
pastoral themes in, 284, 285–
92, 293; portrayal of marriage
in, 34; power relationships in,
38; psychological themes in,
32; public sphere in, 39;
representations in, 292–93;
satire of Fielding in, 7; self-
parody in, 287; self-reflexive